*Vision
and
Conflict
in the
Holy Land*

Vision
and
Conflict
in the
Holy Land

Edited by RICHARD I. COHEN

Yad Izhak Ben-Zvi
Jerusalem

St. Martin's Press
New York

Associate Editor: PRISCILLA FISHMAN

Published by the Yad Izhak Ben-Zvi Center for the Study of Eretz Israel, P.O.Box 7660,
Jerusalem 91076, Israel.

First published in the United States of America, 1985, by
St. Martin's Press, Inc., 175 Fifth Avenue, New York, N.Y. 10010

Library of Congress Cataloging in Publication Data
Main entry under title:

Vision and Conflict in the Holy Land.

  Includes bibliographical references.
  1. Palestine in Judaism—addresses, essays, lectures. 2. Jews—restoration—addresses,
essays, lectures. 3. Messianic era (Judaism)—addresses, essays, lectures. 4. Palestine—
history—1917-1948—addresses, essays, lectures. 5. Jews—Palestine—history—20th
century—addresses, essays, lectures. I. Cohen, Richard I.
BM729.P3V57 1985   296.3   85-1972
ISBN 0-312-84967-2 (St. Martin's)

Designed by Pini, Jerusalem
Printed in Israel

Contents

Symposium: Messianic Concepts and Settlement in the Land of Israel

JEWISH DIASPORA — PALESTINE RELATIONSHIPS (1917-1948)

FOREWORD

The interest of Israeli scholars in the history of Palestine has grown considerably over the past decade, and the parameters of their research have been extended. In this volume, which focuses on major themes from the early Middle Ages to contemporary history, we have limited ourselves to several topics that seem to reflect areas of preoccupation in recent scholarship. Notwithstanding the diversity of subjects discussed, a common theme appears to emerge and unite the various articles — Palestine as a continued source of vision for and conflict between the monotheistic religions.

The volume opens with a series of articles treating the meaning and importance of Jerusalem and Palestine for the Christian world, from the conquest by Constantine through Ottoman rule. In the following section, the relationship of medieval Jewry to Palestine is analyzed from the vantage point of Ashkenaz and Spanish Jewry, and through the prism of Kabbala.

A unique symposium follows, devoted to the issue of messianism among a group of Jewish immigrants to Palestine in the nineteenth century. The discussants, each a recognized specialist in a particular field of research, have presented a wide range of arguments in support of and in objection to the "messianic thesis," exemplifying a fine scholarly discussion of a recurrent problem in historical research — the scientific appraisal of spiritual movements.

The last section of the volume deals with contemporary history, beginning with the period of the British Mandate over Palestine. It opens with an in-depth study of a seminal document of that rule, and closes with three essays on Palestine as the visionary haven for the Jewish homeless during World War II. Throughout these articles, Palestine Jewry's attempts to respond to the hopes of the refugees in the face of political exigencies is elaborated upon. It is hoped that the reader will find that these pages open up fresh avenues for an evaluation of Palestine's history.

THE HEBREW UNIVERSITY
JERUSALEM

RICHARD I. COHEN

JERUSALEM AS A FOCUS OF CONFRONTATION BETWEEN JUDAISM AND CHRISTIANITY

AMNON LINDER

*C*onstantine the Great's conquest of Palestine in 334 opened a new historical era characterized by anti-pagan and anti-Jewish dimensions. In Jerusalem this was epitomized by the construction of churches on former pagan sites and by prohibitions on Jewish residence in the city. Jerusalem's churches developed a ritual and liturgy of their own and, as the city became the center for Christian pilgrimages, that liturgy spread through the Christian world. A. Linder analyses in depth aspects of seventh century Christian literature that evolved around rituals and figures sanctified in Jerusalem's churches, to show how the Church saw the confrontation between Judaism and Christianity. The article provides a seminal background to the evolution of the history of Jewish-Christian relations in the Middle Ages.

*C*onstantine's victory over Licinius at Chrysopolis in 324 initiated a new period in the history of Jerusalem. Aelia Capitolina—a small garrison town in a remote province since it was rebuilt by Hadrian in 135 on the ruins of Jewish Jerusalem—suddenly became one of the main centers of the new Christian empire and its spiritual capital.[1] Following his victory, Constantine initiated an ambitious project of building churches in and around Jerusalem, utilizing the unlimited resources of the Roman Empire for this purpose. In 335 the participants in the Church Council at Tyre attended the consecration of the Constantinian structures in the Holy Sepulchre complex in Jerusalem. By the middle of the fourth century the Constantinian churches in Jerusalem, Bethlehem and Hebron were highly important centers of pilgrimage and worship.[2]

The ideological basis for the new imperial policy towards Palestine, and particularly towards Jerusalem, emerges clearly from a number of official documents that were designed to publicize Constantine's intentions.[3] It is even more strikingly expressed in the rich literary heritage left behind by Eusebius

Pamphilii.[4] Eusebius's testimony is of special importance because as one of Constantine's close advisors he took an active part in shaping the emperor's attitudes on religious matters. He was particularly interested in the 'Christian revival' of the Holy Land, as a bishop of Caesarea and as a prominent scholar of the Bible and Jewish history.

Constantine's policy in Palestine was marked essentially by an aggressive approach towards the Jewish and pagan population of that province. His hostile attitude towards the pagans is clearly reflected in the contemptuous and humiliating phrasing of the "Edict for the Population of the Province" (324 C.E.),[5] which in theory granted them religious tolerance. It was this hostile attitude that determined the government's church-building program in Palestine. At this period Christianity was not as yet in the habit of erecting churches on the sites of pagan holy places; however the complex of the Holy Sepulchre in Jerusalem was built on the site of Hadrian's Temples of Venus and Jupiter, thus necessitating their complete destruction. The Church of the Nativity was erected on the site of a grove consecrated to Adonis, and the Church of the Theophany in Mamre was built on ground considered holy by the pagans. This practice was to demonstrate the change brought about by Constantine, namely that the Constantinian church was taking the place of the pagan temple—and not merely in a metaphorical sense.

The building of the Holy Sepulchre complex in Jerusalem, in particular, emphasizes this way of thinking. There is no significant evidence of a local tradition regarding the site of the hill of Golgotha and the place of Jesus's tomb. Eusebius actually hints at the scepticism and disbelief which followed Constantine's identification of these sites.[6] The rationale of this identification becomes clear from the comparison between the Constantinian churches in Jerusalem and in Contantinople. Both were erected as churches containing the tomb of the Founder (κτίστης), similar to the classical hero shrines (ἡρῶον), i.e., each was a burial shrine built in the center of the capital, from which the state and the political system derive their legitimacy.[7] The Hadrianic Temples of Venus and Jupiter, the titular gods of the pagan Roman Empire, manifested the pagan nature of the former imperial legitimacy, while the new imperial churches demonstrated the Christian legitimacy of that empire. Two of the most important Christian churches were thus designed as sepulchral churches of the founders in the two capitals—the tomb of Jesus in Jerusalem, and that of Constantine himself in Constantinople. This religio-political concept demanded that the tomb complex be built on the ruins of the pagan temples.

2

In Eusebius's description of the Invention of the Cross, this fundamental confrontation between Christianity and paganism is transferred back to the erection of the Temple of Venus. According to his account, the construction of that temple was from the beginning an act of *theomachia* (war against God), an intentional sacrilege on the part of the pagans who sought in this way to hide the remnants of the crucifixion and blot out its memory forever. Jerome's letter to Paulinus of Nola contains a similar explanation.

The animosity towards the pagans was also fed by clearly biblical sources, since the Christian attitude towards the New Jerusalem was formed mainly from biblical concepts and images. The gradual abandoning of the pagan name Aelia Capitolina and the restoration of the biblical name Jerusalem is characteristic of this process, as is the description of Constantine in the Greek and Eastern liturgy which is patterned on the figures of David and Solomon, the biblical builders of Jerusalem.

The anti-pagan dimension of the Roman government in Palestine at that time was supplemented by an acute anti-Jewish dimension, and here too Jerusalem is the focus of the government's concern. While the government endeavored to change its pagan character, which dated from Hadrian's time, into a Christian one, it tried equally hard to preserve the 'Gentile', non-Jewish stamp that had been impressed upon the city by that same emperor. It even adopted measures to strengthen this character. Jerusalem was meant to develop as a 'Christian-Gentile' city.

Within the framework of Hadrian's plan to turn the city into a pagan Roman colony, the Jews had been forbidden to take up permanent residence in Jerusalem or even to visit it.[8] In fact, however, the latter prohibition was never completely nor efficiently carried out, for it was impossible to enforce a total cessation of pilgrimage to Jerusalem, and evidence exists of the presence of pilgrims already in the second half of the second century. The prohibition of permanent residence in the city was easier to enforce, and it appears that no Jewish community existed openly in Jerusalem until the Arab conquest. The official prohibitions remained in effect and to some extent appear to have been enforced at the end of the third and the beginning of the fourth centuries, since Eusebius specifically stressed these prohibitions in works he had written before 324, that is, prior to the conquest of Palestine by the Christian regime. Hadrian's prohibitions were renewed during Constantine's rule, apparently at the consecration of the Holy Sepulchre complex in 335. Several fourth century sources bear evidence to the strictness with which the authorities enforced the prohibitions, with the exception of Jewish pilgrimage on the Ninth of Av which was permitted in return for payment, and entailed the degradation and humiliation of the pilgrims.

The renewal of the Hadrianic prohibitions by the Christian authorities was not out of character. On the contrary, it typified the propensity common to Christians and pagans alike, namely the idealization of the second century regime, and in particular the image of the 'good and enlightened ruler', which the fourth century saw exemplified by figures such as Trajan, Hadrian, Antoninus Pius and Marcus Aurelius. This basic image of an enlightened philosopher-emperor is frequently employed in the official propaganda as well as in intellectual and artistic compositions which return to second century sources as examples to be imitated. The Christian contribution to this trend was expressed mainly in the tendency to remove the stigma of persecutors of the Church with

3

which some of the earlier emperors had been, rightly or wrongly, labelled. Thus, Eusebius tends to present Hadrian's image in a positive light claiming that his attitude to the Church was guided by principles of humanity, moderation and justice; while by his attitude to the Jews — his harsh suppression of Bar-Kokhba's revolt (a leader whom Eusebius describes as having persecuted the Church), the destruction of Jewish Jerusalem and its transformation into a Gentile city — Hadrian, even if unknowingly, fulfilled a divine mission.

'Israel of the Spirit' and 'Israel of the Flesh'

The generally positive approach towards the second century heritage doubtlessly facilitated the formulation of a positive attitude towards Hadrian and his prohibitions. It is clear, however, that this attitude derived mainly from another source, i.e. from deeper layers of Christian consciousness, from Christianity's awareness of the special and complicated ties which link it to its origin and its sources in Judaism. These ties blended into an extremely complex body of emotional and intellectual attitudes which grew and developed from the second century onwards as the rift between the two religions grew wider. As a religion bearing a 'historical' mission based on unique events which happened within historical time, Christianity was obliged to find a suitable solution to the elements linking it to the Jewish past from which it had detached itself. This ongoing necessity gained urgency from time to time as Christianity continued to bear the Old Testament within its sacred canon, and was thus increasingly made aware of the rich complex of the Jewish past and of the aspirations for a glorious Jewish future.

The ambivalent nature of this attachment which, in the third and fourth century Christian view, linked the two religions—a connection both unifying and dividing—is easily recognized by the definitions that were based on the distinction between 'Israel of the Spirit' and 'Israel of the Flesh'. It was against this background that Hadrian's hostility to the Jews was accepted, for it fit in with the view regarding the historical fate of the Jews during the period that began with the crucifixion. According to this view, Jerusalem appears as the most complete expression of Old Covenant Judaism. As a royal capital Jerusalem expresses the political existence of the Jewish people in the Promised Land; in the Temple, in the sacred service and in the priesthood Jerusalem preserves the religious distinctiveness of the Chosen People. These elements— the Temple, priesthood, law, political-national distinctiveness—were considered as the components of the Old Covenant. However, upon the establishment of the New Covenant between God and mankind, as a result of the historical events connected with Jesus and the founding of the Christian Church, those elements became obsolete; the Old Covenant lost its validity. Various quotations from the Scriptures were presented as proof for the abrogation of the

4

principles of the Old Covenant; the verse "Until Shiloh comes" (Gen. 49:10), for example, was allegorically interpreted as prophesying the end of Jewish political sovereignty after the coming of Shiloh, who was identified with Jesus. This became a common argument in medieval anti-Jewish polemic writings.[9] The destruction of the Old Jerusalem along with its characteristic elements by Titus and then by Hadrian, was thus conceived as an indispensable stage in the realization of history as the process of mankind's salvation.

All Christian writers who dealt with the subject of the transition from the Old Covenant to the New Covenant subscribed to the view that this change was inevitably bound to inflict terrible calamities upon the Jews. This view was undoubtedly influenced by Jewish apocalyptic literature, and those who subscribed to this concept had no difficulty in marshalling corroboration from biblical prophecies of doom (e.g. Isaiah chapters 3 and 64, Jeremiah 4, Ezekiel 11:5-16, and Zephaniah 1), which they interpreted as prophesying the destruction of Jerusalem and the Temple by Vespasian and Hadrian. Similarly, Jesus's explicit prophecy of the destruction of the Temple, originally a prophecy of the redemption of Jerusalem, was transmitted in the Synoptic Gospels as a virulently anti-Jewish prophecy which foretells the destruction of the city and the Temple.[10] The profound significance of these calamities accompanying the change of Covenant is rooted in the understanding of the calamity as a punishment justly meted out to the Jews for their wicked refusal to recognize Jesus and for their crucifixion of him. The religious and political destruction of Jerusalem and the exchange of its Jewish inhabitants for Gentiles was interpreted as one of the expressions of a fundamental historical process, namely God's rejection of the rebellious Jews and His call to the Gentiles to be His new 'Chosen People'. It was this aspect of Jerusalem's destruction as a punishment which stimulated people's imagination and attracted the attention of the theologians who expounded on the subject. Thus, Eusebius specified "[...] the calamities which befell the entire Jewish race immediately after it had conspired against our Lord," as one of the five themes of his History of the Church.[11] That same notion reappears in several cycles of popular legends, such as those connected with Veronica and with the destruction of Jerusalem.[12]

Numerous sources, and Eusebius's books in particular, testify to the profound influence which these anti-Jewish views had on the people actively involved in carrying out Constantine's building project in Jerusalem. Eusebius considered it important that the Anastasis Church was outside the area of the Terrestrial Jerusalem that had been destroyed by God, since Jesus's tomb was located outside the city that was sentenced to be destroyed, but was located within Aelia Capitolina, the cornerstone for the New Celestial Jerusalem. He similarly emphasized that the Divine revelation on the Mount of Olives took place outside the city confines, the Church of Eleona on the Mount of Olives being a kind of New Jerusalem as opposed to the Old Jerusalem. His argumentation changed in the year 335 when he asserted that the Church of the Martyrium (the Basilica in

5

the Holy Sepulchre complex) was built "in the heart of the Hebrew royal capital." Elsewhere he again stressed the contrast between New Jerusalem, that is to say the Holy Sepulchre complex, the fulfillment of the prophetic promises, and Old Jerusalem, destroyed as a punishment for the deicide perpetrated by its inhabitants. The same confrontation recurs in the sources dating from the second half of the fourth century which tend to locate the final encounter between the Church and Judaism in Jerusalem. Thus, Cyril, Bishop of Jerusalem, presents a literal interpretation of II Thessalonians 4:3, prophesying the rebuilding of the Temple in Jerusalem and the martyrdom of the Jerusalem Church as the last stages before the Second Coming. The Christian commentators generally explained this passage allegorically; nevertheless, the figure of the Anti-Christ who establishes his seat in the Temple which he had rebuilt in Jerusalem that is once again inhabited by Jews, became widely accepted in medieval apocalyptic literature.

The plan of Julian the Apostate to rebuild the Temple, reinstitute its ritual, and resettle Jews in Jerusalem, was one component in the emperor's fight against Christianity. In this context, its true significance was the attempt to nullify Constantine's 'Jerusalem Plan' by abolishing the Christian exclusivity in the city vis-à-vis the Jews. Julian's plan and, even more, the furious reactions against it within Christianity, demonstrate the importance attributed to Constantine's program for a Christian Jerusalem as early as the sixties of the fourth century. According to this viewpoint, the truth of Christianity—and of Judaism—appears to be conditioned by exclusive possession of Jerusalem and the Temple.

One hears echoes of that confrontation reverberating in the virulent preaching of John Chrysostom against the Jews in Antioch in 386-387. In his view, the efforts of the Jews to rebuild the Temple were clear acts of *Theomachia* because the destruction of the Temple, the exile of the Jews, and their servitude had come upon them by God's will and would therefore last forever. We know from Jerome's writings that towards the end of the fourth century Eusebius's ideas on this subject were in circulation in and around Jerusalem. He describes the Jewish

Plan of the Constantinian Church of Eleona

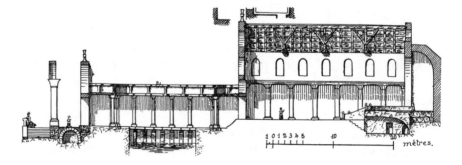

6

pilgrims to Jerusalem on the Ninth of Av and the profound significance this spectacle had for him, because it symbolized the terrible punishment that had been meted out to the Jews who had come to bewail the destruction of their Temple — with the Holy Sepulchre gleaming on one side and the cross of the Church of Eleona glittering on the other. We find a similar attitude in his commentary to Ezekiel 11:23 — the glory of the Lord forsook the Temple and stands upon the Mount of Olives, and in the radiance of the Cross He looks down upon the ruins of the former Temple of the Jews.

Pilgrimage and Propagation

The development of Jerusalem as the most important center of pilgrimage for the Christian world of the fourth to sixth centuries naturally reinforced these concepts among churchmen in Jerusalem, and due to the large flow of pilgrims from the entire Christian world they were spread throughout the Universal Church. One can appreciate the extent of this propagation by the importance given to the dissemination of the Jerusalem liturgy. Egeria took great pains to record the Jerusalem liturgy she witnessed during her pilgrimage, with the aim of transmitting it to the nuns in her Spanish convent.[13] Rabbula, Bishop of Edessa (411-435), who made a pilgrimage to Jerusalem, instituted the commemoration of the Vision of the Cross on the seventh of May, after his return.[14] Furthermore, the entire calendar of Jerusalem was transmitted to Ḥiva, perhaps via Antioch-North Syria, and was in force there at least until the eleventh century, when it was recorded by al-Beyrunni.[15] Finally, one of the troparia (the seventh) sung in Jerusalem on the Great Friday of the crucifixion was transferred to Europe via Benevent, and remains in liturgical use to this day.[16]

In contrast to other holy places and centers of pilgrimage in the Christian world, whose sanctity was to a large extent due to the commemoration of local martyrs and saints, Jerusalem's special status was mainly due to its having been

Drawing of a Christian pilgrim ship, found on a wall in the Church of the Holy Sepulchre. The Latin inscription reads DOMINE IVIMUS (allusion to Psalm 122:1)

7

the scene of events during the last week of Jesus's life, which terminated in the crucifixion, and of the activities of his disciples soon thereafter. The prime importance of these events is, of course, rooted in the universal significance which the Church attributes to them, though on the actual historical and ritual level—and it is on this level that one needs to examine and evaluate the phenomenon of pilgrimage to Jerusalem—they symbolize to a very great extent the antagonism between Judaism and Christianity in Jerusalem.

This element clearly emerges from the Jerusalem liturgy which crystallized in the second half of the fourth and the first half of the fifth centuries and was to undergo no significant change until the conquest of the Holy Land by the Crusaders. The *Typicon* of the Anastasis Church, a Greek manuscript copied in Jerusalem in 1122, which reflects the liturgical customs of the 'Great Week' in fifth century Jerusalem, corresponds to the ancient Armenian *Lectionarium* which is a translation of a Greek text from the beginning of the fifth century.[17] The principal churches of Jerusalem and its immediate environs naturally served as the main centers of pilgrimage and for that reason were the focal points for the creation and dissemination of the concepts which bear on the confrontation between Christianity and Judaism. The Holy Sepulchre complex (Golgotha, the Anastasis, and the Martyrium) mark the crucifixion, the burial, the resurrection, the Invention of the Cross, as well as a number of additional important events and personalities (as, for example, the Centurion Longinus, the Believing Thief, and Helena) of obvious significance for the confrontation between Judaism and Christianity.

The Church of Eleona on the Mount of Olives marked the confrontation between the Old Jerusalem of the Temple, and the New Jerusalem where Jesus taught the prayer "Our Father who art in Heaven" and about the Last Things. Gradually, more churches and chapels were added, such as the *Embomon* (the Church of the Ascension) on the top of the Mount of Olives, and the places marking the treachery and suicide of Judas Iscariot. The Church of Zion that was built with much splendor shortly after 381 symbolized the New Chosen People that inherited the prophecies and the fulfillment of Zion's resurrection, as against the prophecies of Jewish Jerusalem's destruction which were considered to have been realized by the ruins of the Temple Mount. Identical attitudes were fostered in other pilgrim sites such as the Church of Jacob, the brother of Jesus, who had been killed by the Jews; the Church of Stephen the Proto-Martyr, also a victim of the Jews, whose bones were "discovered" in 415, taken to the Church of Zion, and then transferred to the magnificent church founded by the Empress Eudocia in 439; and the Church of St. Peter, built on the ruins of the 'palace of the High Priest Caiphas'.

We have merely mentioned a few of Jerusalem's main churches. The complete list of churches and days of remembrance that molded the concept of the confrontation between Old and New Jerusalem is a lengthy one, particularly if one adds to the sites marking obvious Christian personalities and events other

Inscription attesting to Emperor Justinian's construction of the Nea Church. It reads: "And this is the work which our most pious Emperor Flavius Justinianus carried out with munificence, under the care and devotion of the most holy Constantinus, Priest and Hegumen, in the thirteenth [year of the] indiction"

locations and ceremonies which marked biblical events in a Christian interpretation. The growing trend of the cult of Mary, which found particular expression in Jerusalem during the fifth and sixth centuries with the erection of the Church of the Tomb of Mary in the Valley of Jehoshaphat by Emperor Maurice and the New Church of St. Mary (Nea) by Justinian,[18] did not result in any significant reduction in this basic confrontation. Indeed, the opposite is true. Thus, depositing the Temple vessels, that had been discovered in Africa, inside the Nea Church fits perfectly with the concept of the confrontation between the New-Christian-Jerusalem and the Old-Jewish-Jerusalem.

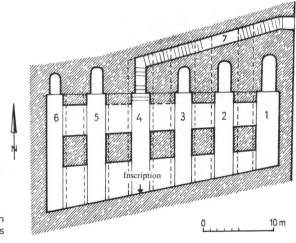

Plan of the Nea Church vaults

9

10

Underground vaults in the recently excavated Nea Church.

Preservation of the Constantine Prohibition

It is against this background that one can understand the stubborn zeal with which the Jerusalem Church preserved Constantine's prohibition of Jews living in Jerusalem. It appears that in 438/9 the Jews of Tiberias succeeded in prevailing upon Empress Eudocia to have the Constantinian prohibitions abolished; however, she was obliged to revoke her decision in the face of the determined, violent pressure exercised by Church circles in Jerusalem that were headed by zealous monks.[19]

During the restoration of the Byzantine empire in the reign of Heraclius we come across a similar conceptual approach involving the Constantinian prohibitions. Heraclius, who succeeded in liberating Jerusalem from the Persians and in redeeming the Cross that had fallen into their hands during the conquest of the city in 614, initiated an extensive propaganda campaign which was to present him as the 'New Constantine', re-founder of the Christian Roman Empire. Great importance was therefore attributed to the liberation of Jerusalem and to the redemption of the Cross which Heraclius, in person, restored to the Church of the Holy Sepulchre in 630 or 631,[20] at which time he renewed the Constantinian prohibitions. Not only were the Jews forbidden to live in Jerusalem, but they were even prohibited from coming within three miles of the city. It appears that at that same time Heraclius forced religious conversion upon all the Jews and Samaritans within his domain, and persuaded the Frankish King Dagobert to issue a similar law in his kingdom.[21]

The association of the renewal of the Constantinian prohibitions in Jerusalem with the conversion enforced by the state demonstrates the influence exercised by the Jerusalem Church.

The forced conversion of 630/631 constituted an act of revenge and punishment for the active participation of the Jews on the side of the Persians during their conquest of Jerusalem in 614, and for acts of forced proselytization and the desecration of Christian holy places in the city (given wide publicity by members of the Jerusalem Church). It also faithfully echoes the legends of the Invention of the Cross that were composed mainly in Jerusalem and from there spread all over the Christian world. (We shall deal with this subject in greater detail further on).

Eight years later (in 638) Jerusalem fell into the hands of the Muslims and again the Jerusalem Church, under the leadership of Patriarch Sophronius, exerted pressure to maintain the prohibitions forbidding Jews to live in Jerusalem. Even though the Muslim conquerors permitted the Jews to return to the city—in the initial phases this even included a return to the Temple Mount—medieval tradition tells of a limitation on the number of families permitted to move to Jerusalem.[22] The renewal of Christian rule in Jerusalem in 1099 was immediately accompanied by the reinstitution of the Constantinian prohibitions; Jews were forbidden to settle in Jerusalem and apparently also to

11

visit there. Only gradually, from the third decade of the twelfth century onwards, was the severity of this prohibition eased and a small number of Jews were permitted to live in the city upon a large payment to the royal treasury.[23] The connection between these and the Constantinian prohibitions was clearly stated by Rabbi Abraham Bar Ḥiyya between 1120 and 1129:

> [...] The Romans who destroyed the Temple in the days of the wicked Titus, even though they desecrated its sanctity, did not claim regarding the holy Temple that they had a share in it and that it was fit to be a place of prayer for them. But when the wicked Constantine was converted they made these claims. In the beginning, after the Romans had destroyed it, they did not prevent the Jews from coming to it and praying inside it. Likewise, the kings of Ishmael used to deal kindly with them [...] until at this time the wicked kingdom of Edom invaded the Temple [...] and since that time they have desecrated the Temple by making it into their house of prayer and placing the images of their religion inside it. They did away with the daily offerings by preventing the Jews from praying in the Temple and conducting in it the obligatory prayer which takes the place of the daily offerings; for from the day that these wicked ones conquered the Temple they did not let the Jews come inside it. Not one single Jew is in Jerusalem these days.[24]

These prohibitions were re-introduced in 1229, with the renewal of Christian rule over Jerusalem, though they were mitigated by 1236 and abolished upon the cessation of Christian rule over the city in 1244.[25]

This attachment of the Jerusalem Church to the Constantinian prohibitions and its theological reasons were well known in the West since the fifth century at least. Augustine's interpretation of Genesis 13:15 is based on his knowledge that the Jews were forbidden to live in Jerusalem, and he connected these prohibitions — as well as the dispersal of the Jews to their places of exile — with Constantine. Similarly, Isidore of Seville recounts the terrible punishments meted out to the Jews in the wake of the crucifixion, and places special emphasis on their loss of Jerusalem and the Temple. According to him, "not a single Jew is now permitted to come there."[26] Obviously, the theological significance of these restrictions helped spread the view that no Jews lived in Jerusalem during the period of Christian rule over the city—this claim was widely accepted in Christian polemic writings—and the claim was not even abandoned in the face of renewed Jewish settlement in Jerusalem following the Muslim conquest of 638 and again in the years 1187 and 1244. Thus, Julian of Toledo claimed (686) that Jerusalem and Bethlehem "are free of Jews at present."[27] Fulbert of Chartres similarly wrote, at the beginning of the eleventh century, that "the Jew is not permitted to bring sacrifices outside of Jerusalem and he cannot do so in Jerusalem itself."[28] In 1455 Gennadius, the exiled Patriarch of Constantinople, wrote that the Jews are unable to return to Jerusalem not only as a result of Christian regulations, but because their exile is eternal, as proved by the failure of their attempts to rebuild Jerusalem and the Temple in the days of Hadrian, Constantine and Julian.[29]

Legends and their Impact

An examination of the rich Christian literature created around the rituals and the figures sanctified in Jerusalem's churches, supplies an additional dimension of how the Jerusalem Church viewed the nature of the confrontation between Judaism and Christianity in Jerusalem. The importance of this literature stems from its rapid and widespread distribution throughout the Christian world, resulting in the transmission of these ideas in their entirety. We can gain an understanding of this literature from a Jerusalem collection apparently compiled in the first third of the seventh century against the background of the fierce controversy raging between Jews and Christians in Jerusalem, and preserved in an eighth century Greek manuscript (Codex Sinaiticus 493).[30] This collection comprised, originally, sixteen works, five of which deal with the ritual of the Cross, its Invention in Jerusalem by Judas-Cyriacos and Helena, and with the vision of the Cross in the skies of Jerusalem in 351 (Cyril's letter to Constantius); five deal with the Believing Thief who symbolizes the Church of the Gentiles, in contrast to the second thief who symbolizes Judaism; five works deal with Stephen, and one with the martyrdom of Jacob, the brother of Jesus. Even a superficial examination of this collection reveals its clearly anti-Jewish character, and a detailed analysis of each of the works makes this bias even more obvious. Let us look more closely at just three of the works that constitute one unit dealing with the Invention of the Cross in Jerusalem, upon Constantine's initiative, by his mother Helena and by Judas-Cyriacos: no. 1 (pp. 3-5: Constantine's Vision of the Cross), no. 2 (pp. 5-24: The Invention of the Holy Cross), and no. 15 (pp. 185-207: The Martyrdom of Judas-Cyriacos). We are mainly interested in the way the last reinforces the image of Judas-Cyriacos as a martyr, already outlined in no. 2.[31]

The earliest descriptions of the Invention of the Cross and the other relics[32] of the crucifixion were quite modest. They generally linked the discovery to Constantine, Helena, and Macarius, Bishop of Jerusalem, and lacked any miraculous or supernatural phenomena. This kind of description is still found in the funeral oration for Theodosius by St. Ambrose, Bishop of Milan, in 395. Rufinus already introduced a miracle into his portrayal of the Invention (in 403), and at this time Jews appear in the description of the Invention as transmitted by Paulinus, Bishop of Nola. The end of the fourth century witnessed the creation of numerous legends surrounding the Invention of the Cross; these may be classified in two main types. The cycle of legends connected with Empress Protonike was composed in Syria around 400 C.E., or at the latest during the first three decades of the fifth century. It circulated primarily in Syria and

13

Armenia, although its influence is also visible in the Greek and Latin versions of the second, Helena — Judas-Cyriacos, cycle of legends.

The Helena — Judas-Cyriacos legend was created in the Greek East during the first half of the fifth century, was soon translated into Latin, and spread to the West. This was the only version of the Invention of the Cross to gain acceptance in the West, and the large number of vernaculars into which it was translated demonstrates its tremendous popularity. In the Jerusalem version — as known through the Codex Sinaiticus 493 — the legend begins with a description of Constantine's vision of the Cross on the eve of his battle with the barbarians on the banks of the Danube, and continues with his victory after he adopted the symbol of the Cross and with his baptism. He sends Helena, his mother, to Judaea to search for the Cross. Helena arrives in Jerusalem at the head of a large army and orders that all the Jews from the vicinity of Jerusalem assemble "since Jerusalem was completely empty of them."[33] Some three thousand Jews were collected, ostensibly in order to discuss matters of religion. After Helena had selected the most learned among them, Judas — one of those selected — realizing that she was looking for the Cross on which "our fathers" had crucified the Messiah, warns the others not to agree to this lest "the customs of our fathers be lost and the law lapse."[34] If the Christians were to find the Cross "the Hebrew people will no longer rule; instead the kingdom and the glory will be turned over to the worshippers of the crucified, and he will reign for ever and ever."[35] When the Jews are sentenced to be burnt on the scaffold by Helena, they hand Judas over to her. Even then he tries to keep the secret, but upon being sentenced to death by starvation, he gives in, prays to God, and in answer to his supplication the hiding-place of the Cross is miraculously revealed. Judas finds three crosses and advises Helena how to identify Jesus's cross (by placing a corpse on each one of the crosses; when the corpse is placed on the "true" cross, the dead woman is restored to life); he goes on to find the other relics from the crucifixion. The description ends with an argument between Judas, who has been baptized and is now called Cyriacos, and Satan who bewails having lost through this Judas what he had won thanks to Judas-Iscariot. Judas-Cyriacos was made Bishop of Jerusalem, and Helena strengthened the Jerusalem Church and "instigated the persecution of those Jews who did not believe in the cross, exiled them from Judaea [and dispersed them over the whole land]."[36] This unit ends with the description of Judas-Cyriacos's martyrdom during the reign of Julian the Apostate, in accordance with Satan's promise.

This legend, which apparently originated in Jerusalem (the Jerusalem Church celebrates the Feast Day of Cyriacos on March 31) or, at any event, in Palestine — Syria, and spread mainly to the Latin West, deserves our attention for a number of reasons, first and foremost for its allegorical expression of several of the Church's basic attitudes towards Judaism. It clearly shows the transfer of animosity — as regards the Invention of the Cross — from the pagans to the Jews. Eusebius and Jerome still blamed the pagans for intentionally

14

having hidden the Cross in order to suppress the memory and any remnants of the crucifixion. However, this legend places the burden of the guilt squarely on the Jews, implying in this way that Christianity no longer considers the pagans, but Judaism, to be its main enemy. The legend, moreover, assumes that the Jews' opposition to Christianity was not due to an unintentional error since, after all, their attempts to mislead Helena were designed to enable the Jewish people to preserve its existence as a separate political and religious entity even though the Jews were fully aware of Jesus's divinity and of the sin of deicide committed by their forefathers. The refusal of the Jews 'to see the light' was deliberate and wicked, and that is why they cannot be forgiven nor, indeed, be tolerated. The image of Judas is most instructive because it expresses allegorically a number of characteristics which Christianity is wont to assign to Judaism. His very name points to a 'Jewish type', a device frequently employed in literature and art for the sake of easy and immediate identification of the 'Jewish type'. Of course, the phonetic similarity between *Judas* and *Jew* facilitates this identification. However, it derives mainly from the commonly held belief in the collective guilt of the whole Jewish people for the crucifixion. This accounts for the identification of all Jews with Judas-Iscariot, and the certainty that "God's curse upon Judas" rests upon the Jews.

At the same time we see how Judas—as the 'type' of Judaism—plays the principal part in the search for the Cross, its Invention and identification; in the end there is even his confrontation with Satan, which simultaneously emphasized the symmetric continuation and contrast between Judas-Iscariot and Judas-Cyriacos. This aspect of the legend gives general expression to the widespread belief—which was also held by many theologians—that the first and primary sources of Christianity are found in Judaism. From this derives the Christian tendency to detect Christian truths concealed not only in the prophecies of the Old Testament, but also in late talmudic and midrashic literature. It also accounts for the motif, widespread in medieval legends, of the Jews who are able to see the corporeal reality of the Eucharist as a baby or a lamb.[37] For the 'blindness' of the Jews who refuse to recognize the truth is, after all, nothing but a willful blindness, a demonic and wicked refusal to accept the truths which they recognize in their secret hearts and even disseminate in public—though against their will.

Against this background the description of Helena's exploits in Jerusalem assumes a consistent and logical dimension with a clearly visible threat to Jewish existence running through it. The Empress's personality and actions, which the author of the legend raised to the rank of sanctity and piety, clearly manifest the hostile attitude adopted by the Imperial authorities towards the Jews from the end of the fourth century, and the rapid deterioration of their legal standing during that period. Helena of the legend gives expression to the active intervention of the authorities in the confrontation between Christianity and Judaism, by placing the coercive apparatus of the state at the disposal of the

15

Church. The means of persuasion which she adopts towards the Jews include torture, death by burning, starvation, and threats. The author of the legend praises Helena for her persecution of Judaea's Jewish population; this praise clearly echoes the prohibitions from the days of Hadrian and Constantine.

In the final analysis, the most crucial aspect of this description is the legitimization it grants to the idea of enforced conversion by the state. Judas-Cyriacos was converted to Christianity after having witnessed the miracle of the Invention of the Cross, but this miracle was preceded by acts of violence and coercion. The author also depicts the expulsion of the Jews from Judaea as a punishment for their refusal to be converted to Christianity. The great importance which the author ascribes to the conversion of the Jews — represented here by the figure of Judas-Cyriacos — is expressed in the final confrontation between Judas and Satan. The final conversion of the Jews will atone for their rebellion against Jesus, signify their rejection of Satan and a return to the former Covenant with God within the framework of the New Covenant. This concept clearly rests on the eschatological significance of the conversion of the Jews at the End of Days, as authoritatively formulated in Paul's Epistle to the Romans (chs. 9 and 11), and is one of the important elements in the cult of the Cross. Most Christian eschatological descriptions place the last stages before the *Parousia* (the Second Coming of Jesus) in Jerusalem, and this includes the final conversion of the Jews. The legend of Judas-Cyriacos faithfully portrays these ideas, and it emphasizes their 'Constantinian dimension', one of the main characteristics of the specific Jerusalem tradition which had taken shape in the city since the time of Constantine and Bishop Cyril.

The acute anti-Jewish dimension of the cult of the Cross, which was formulated in Jerusalem by the seventh century, is clearly visible in the sermons of Andrew, a Jerusalem monk, the representative of the Jerusalem Patriarch at the Sixth Ecumenical Council in Constantinople (680), who later became Archbishop in Crete. In the Invention of the Cross Andrew saw a victory for Christianity and a defeat for the Jews who wanted the Cross and the remnants from the crucifixion hidden, out of hatred and fear that the Cross symbolized the ruin of Judaism. Thus, towards the end of the seventh century the concept took the shape of Judaism being in confrontation with Christianity; it may be schematically defined as combining a recognition of conscious and willful *theomachia* on the part of the Jews, an appeal for state intervention, and the use of coercive means for inducing the Jews to change their religion. This pattern recurs in many medieval hagiographic and historiographic sources in both the West and the East, and clearly influenced the formation of the attitude adopted towards the Jews in the Middle Ages.

The element of *theomachia* stands out in the Christian descriptions of the conquest of Jerusalem by the Persians in 614 and by the Muslims in 638. The Jews are portrayed as inciting the conquerers to desecrate the Christian holy places, to raze their churches and destroy their symbols, such as the large golden cross atop the Mount of Olives. In the early 560s, an Armenian Monophysite source from Jerusalem (a letter by Gregory Erzeruni) attributed Justinian's coercive actions against the Jerusalem Church, which had been accustomed to celebrate Christmas on Epiphany (January 6, and not December 25), to the incitement of "a certain heretical Jew". This incitement led to the use of violence against the Monophysites in Jerusalem, to a number of "divine revelations" on Mount Zion, and finally to the acceptance of the December 25 date for Christmas in Jerusalem.[38]

Since the eighth century an extremely common motif in Christian legend is that of the Jew who advises the rulers—Muslims as well as Christians—to destroy the symbols holy to Christianity. During the vicissitudes of the struggle in the Byzantine empire between the Iconoduls (icon worshippers) and the Iconoclasts (icon destroyers) this belief harbored a real threat for the Jewish communities.[39] In general we find this basic pattern having a direct bearing on Jerusalem, on the Jewish-Christian confrontation involving the right to live in Jerusalem, and on the Constantinian complex of the Holy Sepulchre. Authentic historical events—clashes between Jews and Christians in Jerusalem during the period of Muslim rule—strongly reinforced the influence of such legends and rumors, which spread both East and West, and led to several forced conversions and persecutions of diaspora communities.

Sebaeus relates that the Jews tried to cause the expulsion of the Christians from Jerusalem by defiling a Muslim place of prayer with slaughtered pigs; however, their attempted libel of the Christians was exposed.[40] In 688 Adamnanus wrote down the story told by Arculf—a French pilgrim who passed through Iona—of the head-cloth which according to tradition had been placed on Jesus's head in his grave and which, in the seventh century, was kept in the Church of the Holy Sepulchre in Jerusalem.[41] This description, which in several aspects resembles the story of St. Veronica and the head-cloth preserved by her, reverts to the confrontation between Jews and Christians; the head-cloth was kept by Jews until a quarrel broke out between them and the Christians, whereupon the Muslim ruler decided the issue by placing the head-cloth on a pyre. The head-cloth then flew up, hovered over the two camps that had been quarrelling over it until it finally descended on the Christian camp; since then it had been kept in the Church of the Holy Sepulchre. This story is repeated in Beda's popular book on the holy places, written in 702-703.[42] The Karaite Salmon ben Jeruham who lived in Jerusalem in the tenth century testifies: "The uncircumcised have now reached such a position that they beat us in order to get us out of Jerusalem and to sever us from it."[43] Towards the end of the third decade of the tenth century, Emperor Romanus Lecapenus ordered forced conversion of his Jewish subjects in the wake of rumors that had reached him from Jerusalem of damage having been done to the Church of the Holy Sepulchre, of a religious disputation having taken place there from which the Jews emerged victorious as a result of bribing the Muslim rulers, and of a

17

heavenly miracle that led to a mass conversion to Christianity. We know from our sources with what severity the conversion was enforced throughout the Empire, including Italy.[44]

From Italy the rumors spread westward. In 932 the Venetian Doge Pietro Candiano II called on the Church Council in Erfurt to follow in the footsteps of Byzantium and forcibly convert or exile the Jews in the West (following Helena's example!).[45] Even though his suggestion was not accepted by the Council, it found followers in a number of places. In Mainz, for example, Archbishop Friedrich urged Gerhard the Presbyter to collect the texts of the Church's legislation against the Jews. He received permission from Pope Leo VII to banish from his province those Jews who refused to convert to Christianity (though the Pope reasserted his opposition to forced conversion).[46] In 966 the Muslims and Jews in Jerusalem attacked, looted and burnt the Church of the Holy Sepulchre as well as other churches, and in the turmoil killed the Patriarch of Jerusalem.[47]

A fresh wave of forced conversions and expulsions took place in the West following the news that the Church of the Holy Sepulchre had been destroyed by Caliph El-Ḥakem (1009). Rumors had it that this destruction was caused by the Jews of the diaspora, who had convinced the Caliph that he would lose his rule and his domains unless he destroyed that particular church which attracted so many pilgrims from the West. The focus of this activity is found in the French Royal Domain; the rumors concerning the plot came from Orleans,[48] and the orders for forced conversion were published by King Robert the Pious.[49] These orders were also carried out in other places; such evidence exists regarding Limoge,[50] Normandy,[51] and outside France regarding Mainz and other parts of Germany.[52] The wave of conversions and expulsions subsided in about 1014/15, but it foreshadowed the persecutions of 1096, another expression of that same basic pattern which is intimately linked to Jerusalem and to the Constantinian Church of the Holy Sepulchre.

A work which describes the life of the Welsh Saint David (written before the conquest of Jerusalem by the Crusaders) gives us some idea of the extent of the belief in Jerusalem as a focus for Jewish-Christian confrontation.[53] The author of the legend relates that during the saint's pilgrimage to Jerusalem he was asked by the local archbishop to help the Christians against the Jews who were gaining the upper hand by force and violence. The saint agreed to the request; by means of frequent sermons he influenced many people to convert to Christianity, and reinforced the faith of others. This story, which originated in the Celtic fringe of Europe, reveals how widespread the basic idea inherent in it had become in Europe.

Summary

From the fourth century and until the Muslim conquest of the city in 638, Jerusalem developed as a Christian pilgrimage center of great importance in shaping Christian liturgy and spreading it throughout the Christian world. Jerusalem was also the focus for the crystallization of various concepts which found expression in the ritual followed by the city's churches as well as in the literature dealing with personalities and events connected with the city.

The idea of Jerusalem as a focus of confrontation between Judaism and Christianity occupies a central position in this complex of concepts and in their expression in ritual and literature. According to the tradition which developed in the Jerusalem Church, the Jewish people—with Jewish Jerusalem as its most complete expression—was seen as an entity whose positive function in the history of mankind had come to an end with the crucifixion and rejection of Jesus. From then on, this people, intentionally and with satanic malice, acted against God. It is for this reason that its disintegration as a political, national and religious entity was decreed. The complete destruction of Jewish Jerusalem and its transformation into a Christian city, with the resultant expulsion, dispersion and subjugation of the Jews, was seen as Divine punishment and as an essential stage on mankind's road to complete salvation. The expulsion and subjugation were effected by the State, which thus fulfilled a sacred mission. The conversion of the Jews was viewed as a logical conclusion of the abrogation of the Old Covenant upon the coming of the Messiah, and as a decisive element in the eschatological development which will reach its climax with the latter-day revelation of God. Here too, a central function was accorded to the State which put its means of coercion at the disposal of the missionary Church.

This Jerusalem tradition, whose principal features are clearly visible as early as the fourth-fifth century, spread rapidly over the entire Christian world and was easily absorbed. Its practical implementation during the early Middle Ages was only partial and fragmentary, except for several waves of enforced conversion in the Byzantine empire. However, it turned into an ideological trend with considerable practical implementation towards the middle and the late Middle Ages as the idea of the Crusade took root in Europe, and as the major political forces realized their political-cultural distinctiveness and grew in strength. During those centuries, the history of the Jewish diaspora in Western Europe was largely conditioned by the influence of this tradition.

19

Translated by Batya B. Rabin.

The author wishes to thank the Memorial Foundation for Jewish Culture for its assistance which made the preparation of this article possible.

1   The anti-Jewish aspects of this development have not yet been sufficiently investigated. On the subject of the influence exercised by the basic distinction between Terrestrial Jerusalem and Celestial Jerusalem, cf. J. Prawer, "Christianity between Terrestrial Jerusalem and Celestial Jerusalem," *Jerusalem through the Ages* (Jerusalem, 1969), pp. 179-192; R.J.Z. Werblowsky, "Jerusalem: Holy City of Three Religions," *Ex Oriente Lux* 23 (Leiden, 1975): 429-436. For a more extensive treatment of several important developments in the hagiography of Christian Jerusalem (including references to sources and relevant literature), cf. A. Linder, "The Myth of Constantine the Great in the West; Sources and Hagiographic Commemoration," *Studi Medievali* (3rd. ser.) 16 (1975):43-95; idem, "Ecclesia and Synagoga in the Medieval Myth of Constantine the Great," *Revue belge de philologie et d'histoire* 54 (1976):1019-1060.

2   L. Voelkl, "Die konstantinischen Kirchenbauten nach den literarischen Quellen des Okzidents," *Rivista di archeologia cristiana* 30 (1954):99-136; idem, *Die Kirchenstiftungen des Kaisers Konstantin im Lichte des römischen Sakralrechts* (Köln, 1964); A. Baumstark, *Palästinapilger des ersten Jahrtausends und ihre Berichte* (Köln, 1906), pp. 30-34, 41-43. Christian pilgrims from the West came to the site of Golgotha immediately after the conquest of the city, even before the completion of the Church of the Holy Sepulchre, as is depicted in a drawing of a pilgrim ship, lately discovered in archaeological excavations in the Church of the Holy Sepulchre. Cf. M. Broshi, "New Excavations in the Church of the Holy Sepulchre" (Hebrew), *Qadmoniot* 10 (1977):32.

3   These were mainly preserved in Eusebius's writings. See C. Dupont, "De quelques problèmes découlant de la conquête de l'Orient par Constantin: leur solution par ce prince," *Revue internationale des droits de l'Antiquité* 18 (1971):479-500; idem, "Décisions et textes constantiniens dans les oeuvres d'Eusèbe de Césarée," *Viator* 2 (1971):1-32.

4   Constantine's biography is of particular importance. The authenticity of this work has been queried, though scholars have lately tended to accept it. See F. Winkelmann, "Zur Geschichte des Authentizitätsproblems der Vita Constantini," *Klio* 40 (1962):187-243; idem, *Die Textbezeugung der Vita Constantini des Eusebius von Caesarea* (*TUGAL* 84) (Leipzig, 1962).

5   This edict was published in all the eastern provinces, and Eusebius copied it from the text published in Palestine. The authenticity of this source has been similarly questioned, but it was verified when a fragment was discovered in Papyrus London 878. See A.H.M. Jones, "Notes on the Genuineness of the Constantinian Documents in Eusebius' Life of Constantine," *Journal of Ecclesiastical History* 5 (1954):196-200.

6   The view that the discovery of the site was based on a local tradition is not proved by the sources. See, however, R.W. Hamilton, "Jerusalem in the Fourth Century," *PEQ* 84 (1952):83-90; J. Lassus, "L'Empereur Constantin, Eusèbe et les lieux saints," *Revue de l'histoire des religions* 171 (1967):135-144.

7   A. Grabar, *Martyrium; Recherches sur le culte des reliques et l'art chrétien antique, 1: Architecture* (Paris, 1946), esp. pp. 234-244.

8   Not all scholars agree that there were such prohibitions, and much has been written on this subject. See the bibliography in the article by A. Linder, "Roman Rule and the Jews at the Time of Constantine" (Hebrew), *Tarbiz* 44 (1975):136-139.

9   A. Posnanski, *Schiloh: Ein Beitrag zur Geschichte der Messiaslehre*, 1 (Leipzig, 1904).

10   D. Flusser, "The Prophecy of the Liberation of Jerusalem in the New Testament" (Hebrew), *Erez-Yisrael* 10 (1971):226-236.

11   *Historica Ecclesiastica*, 1, ed. E. Schwartz *(Die griechischen christlichen Schriftsteller, 9) (Breslau, 1903).*

12   E. von Dobschuetz, *Christusbilder: Untersuchungen zur christlichen Legende* (*TUGAL* 18) (Leipzig, 1899), pp. 197-262.

13   "Ut autem sciret affectio vestra, quae operatio singulis diebus cotidie in locis sanctis habeatur, certas vos facere debui sciens..." *Itinerarium Egeriae, Patrologiae Latinae Supplementum,* 1 (Paris, 1958), p. 1071.

14   F.C. Burkitt, "The Early Syriac Lectionary System," *Proceedings of the British Academy,* 1921-1923, pp. 301-338.

15 A. Baumstark, "Ausstrahlungen des vorbyzantinischen Heiligenkalenders von Jerusalem," *Orientalia Christiana Periodica* 2 (1936):129-144.

16 W. Schütz, "Was habe ich dir getan, mein Volk?" *Jahrbuch für Liturgik und Hymnologie* 13 (1968):1-38.

17 Fifth century Jerusalem liturgy is fairly well known mainly from the Armenian *Lectionarium* (the order of the readings during the service) which reflects the practice of the first half of the fifth century; the Georgian *Lectionarium* which bears traces of the Jerusalem liturgy from the second half of the fifth to the ninth century; and the Greek *Typikon* (the order of the service) which originated in the tenth century. For publications on the Armenian source, cf. F.C. Conybeare, *Rituale Armenorum* (Oxford, 1905); A. Renoux, "Un manuscrit du lectionnaire arménien de Jérusalem (Cod. Jérus. arm. 121)," *Muséon* 74 (1961):361-385. For the Georgian sources see M. Tarchnischvili, *Le grand lectionnaire de l'église de Jérusalem (Ve-VIIIe siècle)* (Louvain, 1959); also G. Garitte, *Le calendrier palestino-géorgien du Sinaiticus 34 (Xe siècle)* (Brussels, 1958). For the Greek source see A. Papadopoulos-Kerameus, *Analekta hierosolymitikes stachologias,* 2 (Brussels, 1894; repr. 1963), and J.B. Thibaut, *Ordre des offices de la Semaine Sainte à Jérusalem* (Paris, 1926).

18 As a result of N. Avigad's recent excavations, the location of this church in the Jewish Quarter is no longer in doubt. See N. Avigad, "A Building Inscription of Emperor Justinian and the Nea Church in Jerusalem" (Hebrew), *Qadmoniot* 10 (1977):80-83.

19 F. Nau, "Résumé des monographies syriaques: Barṣauma (et alii)," *Revue de l'Orient chrétien* 9 (1914):118-125.

20 V. Grumel, "La reposition de la vraie croix à Jérusalem par Héraclius: Le jour et l'année," *Byzantinische Forschungen* 1 (Amsterdam, 1966):139-149.

21 For the different views on this subject cf. A. Sharf, "Byzantine Jewry in the Seventh Century," *BZ* 48 (1955):106-115; K. Burdach, *Der Gral: Forschungen über seinen Ursprung und seinen Zusammenhang mit der Longinuslegende* (Stuttgart, 1938), pp. 119-122.

22 Cf. S. Assaf, "The Beginnings of Jewish Settlement in Jerusalem after the Arab Conquest" (Hebrew), *Yediot* 7 (1940):22-29. Goitein saw this limitation as a late forgery, expressing anti-Jewish sentiments on the part of Muslim and Christian circles. Cf. S.D. Goitein, "Did Omar Prohibit the Stay of Jews in Jerusalem?" *Palestinian Jewry in Early Islamic and Crusader Times* (Hebrew), ed. J. Hacker (Jerusalem, 1980), pp. 36-41.

23 J. Prawer, "The Jews in the Crusader Kingdom of Jerusalem" (Hebrew) *Zion* 11 (1946): 41-52; idem.," Jerusalem, Capital of the Crusader Kingdom," *Judah and Jerusalem* (Hebrew) (Jerusalem, 1957), pp. 90-104.

24 See Abraham Bar-Ḥiyya, *Sefer Megillat haMegalleh* (Hebrew), Poznanski edition (Berlin, 1924), pp. 99-100. Cf. also the testimony of Judah Al-Ḥarizi, *Taḥkemoni* (Hebrew), Y. Toporowski edition (Tel Aviv, 1952), pp. 247-248.

25 See B.Z. Kedar, "The Jews of Jerusalem 1187-1267, and the Role of Naḥmanides in the Re-establishment of their Community," *Jerusalem in the Middle Ages* (Hebrew), ed. B.Z. Kedar (Jerusalem, 1979), pp. 122-136.

26 *De fide catholica contra Judaeos,* written in 614/5; cf. *PL* 83, col. 516.

27 *De comprobatione aetatis sextae, PL* 96, cols. 558-559.

28 *Tractatus contra Judaeos,* written between the years 1007-1029, see *PL* 141, col. 312.

29 Quoted by A.L. Williams, *Adversus Judaeos: A Bird's Eye View of Christian Apologiae until the Renaissance* (Cambridge, 1935), p. 191.

30 R. Devreesse, "Une collection hiérosolymitaine au Sinaï," *RB* 47 (1938):555-558; E. Ehrhardt, *Uberlieferung und Bestand der hagiographischen und homiletischen Literatur der griechischen Kirche von den Anfängen bis zum Ende des 16. Jahrhundert,* 1 (*TUGAL*) (Leipzig, 1937), pp. 146-148.

31 Works no. 1-2, which are attributed to Menander the Protector, were published in the version of Codex Sinaiticus 493 (=*BHG*[3] 396) by E. Nestle, "Die Kreuzauffindungslegende," *BZ* 4 (1895):319-345. Variants of this version were published by A. Olivieri, "De inventione Crucis libellus," *AB* 17 (1898):414-420 (=*BHG*[3] 401, 407); A. Delatte (ed.), *Anecdota Atheniensia,* 1 (Liège, 1927), pp. 289-298 (=*BHG*[3] 397c, 409g). Latin versions of this legend were published by A. Holder, *Inventio sanctae Crucis* (Leipzig, 1889); K. Wotke, *Wiener Studien* 13 (1891):300-311. For the Judas-Cyriacos legend in the East, see N. Pigoulewsky, "Le martyre de saint

21

Cyriaque de Jérusalem," *Revue de l'Orient chrétien* 26 (1927):305-356.

32 See J. Straubinger, *Die Kreuzauffindungslegende* (Paderborn, 1912).

33 Nestle (above, n. 31), p. 325.

34 *Ibid.*, p. 326.

35 *Ibid.*, p. 327.

36 *Ibid.*, p. 331. The part of the sentence in brackets appears in other versions, e.g. Delatte (above, n. 31), p. 298.

37 B. Blumenkranz, "Juden und Jüdisches in christlichen Wundererzählungen," *TZ* 10 (1954):437-439.

38 M. van Esbroeck, "La lettre de l'empereur Justinien sur l'Annonciation et le Noël en 561," *AB* 86 (1968):351-371; idem, "Encore la lettre de Justinien: Sa date—560 et non 561," *AB* 87 (1969):442-444.

39 A. Starr, "An Iconodulic Legend and its Historical Basis," *Speculum* 8 (1933):500-503.

40 *Sefer haYishuv* 2 (Hebrew), ed. S. Assaf and L.A. Mayer (Jerusalem, 1944), p. 20, no. 18.

41 Adamnanus, *De locis sanctis,* ed. P. Geyer, *Itinera hierosolymitana saeculi IV-VIII* (Leipzig, 1898), pp. 236-238.

42 Beda, *De locis sanctis, PL* 94, col. 1182-1183.

43 In his commentary on Psalms 30:10. On this subject, cf. see J. Mann, *Texts and Studies in Jewish History and Literature,* 2 (repr. New York, 1972), pp. 18-20.

44 A. Sharf, "The Jews in Byzantium," B. Roth, "Italy," both in *A World History of the Jewish People* (Hebrew), ed. B. Roth and Z. Baras, *The Dark Ages* (Tel Aviv, 1973), pp. 37-38, 64-65.

45 *MGH, Leges* IV, *Const.* I, ed. L. Weiland (1893), pp. 6-7.

46 B. Blumenkranz, *Les auteurs chrétiens latins du moyen âge sur les juifs et le judaïsme (Etudes juives* 4) (Paris, 1963), p. 220; idem, *Juifs et chrétiens dans le monde occidental (Etudes juives* 2) (Paris, 1960), pp. 180, 206-207. For the papal encyclical see *PL* 132, col. 1084-1085.

47 S.D. Goitein, "Jerusalem in the Arab Period 638-1099," *The Jerusalem Cathedra,* 2 (Jerusalem, 1982), p. 184.

48 Radulfus Glaber, *Historia,* III, 7, *PL* 142, col. 657-658.

49 M. Haberman, *The Persecutions of Germany and France* (Hebrew), (Jerusalem, 1945), pp. 19-21.

50 Ademar de Chabannes, *Historiae,* III, ed. G. Waitz; *MGH, Scriptores* IV (1841), p. 137.

51 Haberman (above, n. 49), *loc. cit.*

52 B. Blumenkranz, "Germany, 843-1096," *The Dark Ages* (Hebrew) (above, n. 44), pp. 102-103.

53 *Vita S. Davidi ex Ms. Ultrajectino, Acta Sanctorum* 1, Martii I, pp. 41-45.

THE STRUGGLE OVER THE
CHRISTIAN HOLY PLACES
DURING THE OTTOMAN PERIOD

RACHEL SIMON

*D*uring the more than three hundred years of Ottoman rule, a variety of Christian interest groups waged a continuous struggle for authority over the Christian holy places in Palestine. R. Simon delineates the attitudes of these forces, often backed by European powers, while pointing out the changing policy of the Ottoman Empire with regard to these Christian interventions. Simon further shows how these powers, on the eve of the Crimean War, utilized the religious struggle to further their own political interests.

Most of the literature dealing with the question of the rights to the holy places in Palestine has been written by interested parties arguing the legal and historical rights of their respective religious communities. The array of documents adduced by the various advocates is intended primarily to substantiate the claims of their religious communities, and the resolution of the particular claim is assumed to be the result of its persuasiveness or legal merit.

While the legal approach is important, a number of other factors, essentially political in nature, must also be taken into consideration; the outcome of a specific claim is often a function of the political influence or power of the various religious communities and of the European states that support them. Thus the question of rights to the holy places must be viewed within the framework of two power struggles: between the various European states, and between Europe and the Ottoman Empire. The political and economic status of the local Christian communities in Palestine is an additional factor that enters into this struggle.

These several elements played a role in the struggle over the rights to the holy places in Palestine, in particular to the Holy Sepulchre in Jerusalem and the Church of the Nativity in Bethlehem, from the time of the Ottoman conquest of Palestine up to the Crimean War. International conflicts, foreign ambassadors in Istanbul, Christian minorities in the Ottoman Empire and in Palestine in particular, the relations of the Christian communities with the central government in Istanbul and local government in Jerusalem — all contributed their influence to the struggle over the holy places.

The local Christians in the Ottoman Empire were among the "Protected Peoples" whose lives, beliefs, properties and liberties were protected by the Muslim state, as long as they fulfilled certain obligations to it. Theoretically foreign Christians were considered enemies of the Muslim state, but temporary agreements were reached permitting foreigners to remain in the Ottoman Empire, under the protection of the representatives of their own state. The extent of these arrangements, the "Capitulations Agreements", were usually limited to the Sultan's lifetime, though they were often renewed.[1] Sultanic orders, such as *firmāns*, became valid only after lengthy procedures, were in force only during the ruler's lifetime, and could also be revoked by him at will.[2] These factors made the implementation and observance of agreements with the Sublime Porte far from automatic.

The major rivals for control over the holy places were the Roman Catholics and the Greek Orthodox; to a lesser extent claims were put forward by Armenians, Copts, Ethiopians, Syrians and others. The pressures exercised on behalf of these communities were not equal, for the power of these groups was based on their numbers in Palestine — especially in the vicinity of the holy places — and in the Empire, as well as on their economic and political status. To this was added direct foreign support to the communities, and pressures exerted on their behalf in Istanbul.

The largest community was the Greek Orthodox,[3] whose members in Palestine were mostly farmers. The administration and upkeep of the holy places was in the hands of the "Fraternity of the Holy Sepulchre" which was formalized in 1662. Thereafter, its members were almost solely of Greek descent, and they alone could rise to higher positions in the Church. The lower priesthood was a separate body constituted of local Palestinian Christians who received the most elementary religious training. As a result, contact between the official Church and its members was minimal, and it is hard to say to what extent the Church dignitaries represented the masses, whose popular religion inclined to heterodoxy, veneration of holy places, and religious practices containing many pre-Christian elements. In this respect the Greek Orthodox masses were similar to other local Christians, whose emotional attachment to the holy places often seemed to Westerners to be close to idolatry.

The Greek Orthodox community was influential in Istanbul, the center of the Empire's political power, where many leading members of the Church, including the Patriarch of Jerusalem and the Ecumenical Patriarch, had their residences.[4] The Greeks of Istanbul were active in political circles, mostly as translators, and thus were familiar with the channels for pressing demands relating to the holy places.

Greek Orthodox Patriarch in Jerusalem, 1631

The economic power of the Greek Orthodox Church in Palestine was not based primarily on the local population, which was poor. Some revenue derived from pilgrims but most of the income came from abroad, in the form of grants and religious endowments. This enabled the Church to buy extensive properties in Palestine. However, economic problems arose, especially after the 1820s when the areas from which most of the money came (i.e., Greece and the Balkans) were cut off from and at times even at war with the Empire. At such periods of financial stress Russian penetration into Palestine increased and Russia tried to control the financial affairs of the Greek Orthodox Church to which the Russian Pravoslav Church was subordinate.[5]

The Armenians were the second largest Christian group in Palestine. Their political influence, derived from their wealth, was proportionately greater than the size of their community. They were responsible for all other local Christians in the Empire, except for the Greek Orthodox, and thus it was difficult for the smaller groups to have a say concerning their rights in the holy places. The Armenian Patriarch of Jerusalem stayed in Istanbul for long periods of time and, from 1741 onwards, the Armenians had a permanent representative in the capital who lobbied to advance his community's claims.[6] Many of the members of the Armenian community in the Ottoman Empire were merchants and bankers, and as such were in a position to help individual co-religionists to advance politically, which in turn gave them additional political leverage. They also made generous contributions to the Patriarchate of Jerusalem, which were by and large invested in real estate.[7]

Head of the Armenian Church in Jerusalem, 1631

During most of the Ottoman period, the Roman Catholics in Palestine were foreigners, living mainly near the important holy places. After 1342, the Catholic custodian of the holy places was the Franciscan Order, numbering between 20 to 60 in Jerusalem. Often mistreated by the Ottoman government, in 1552 the Franciscans were expelled by the Ottomans from their center near David's Tomb on Mt. Zion, and moved to their new location near the Holy Sepulchre.

It seems that the Catholic Church did not attach much importance to the actual presence of its leading members in Jerusalem, and Catholic Patriarchs ceased to reside in Jerusalem after 1291, when the Crusaders were driven out of the city. A Patriarch returned only in 1847, both because of the return of his Greek Orthodox counterpart four years earlier, and also in order to supervise the Franciscans.[8] The fact that the financial resources of the Roman Catholics came from abroad created considerable difficulties, especially in those times when the Ottomans and the Catholic states were at war. Nonetheless, due to Catholic missionary activity the community increased, becoming the second largest Christian sect in Palestine in the second half of the nineteenth century.[9]

Political pressure, mainly on behalf of the Latins (the term commonly used for European Roman Catholics) and the Greek Orthodox, was exercised through the foreign ambassadors in Istanbul. As a result of the Capitulations Agreements which both the European countries and the Ottoman Empire initially regarded as favorable, the Western powers were permitted to act for the benefit of their

25

subjects and their property in the Empire. However, as the Christian sects did not have full ownership in the holy places, but merely enjoyed "protection" rights, the foreign powers could only help them to preserve and extend these rights.

Relations between the Greek Orthodox, who were Ottoman subjects, and the Russian state were on a different footing from the relations between the Latins, who were European subjects, and the European states. The former relations developed steadily with the consolidation of the Russian Empire and the gradual strengthening of its position vis-à-vis the Ottoman Empire; the Russians tried to increase their intervention in favor of the Greek Orthodox in order to enhance their penetration into the Ottoman Empire. Thus the actual position of the various Christian communities in the holy places was a result of the balance created between internal and external pressures.

The struggle over the holy places will be examined by case studies of the churches of the Holy Sepulchre and of the Nativity, the most important holy sites in Palestine.

Changes of Status in the Church of the Holy Sepulchre

At the end of the Mameluk period Greeks, Armenians, Latins, as well as Jacobines, Ethiopians, Nubians and Georgians unwillingly had to share their rights in the Church of the Holy Sepulchre.[10] In order to restrain the quarrelling Christians, the keys to the church entrance were deposited with the Muslim family of Nuseiba as early as 1289,[11] for any Christian key-holder would have been able to enter the church at the expense of all other religious sects.

The situation began to change when Palestine was conquered by Selim I at the end of 1516 and became part of the Ottoman Empire. At that point the laws and orders of previous rulers ceased to be binding, unless incorporated in Ottoman ordinances. In Jerusalem Selim had found both Greek Orthodox and Armenians holding some positions in the Church of the Holy Sepulchre and on March 19, 1517 he gave them *firmāns* ratifying their possessions.[12] There is no mention of *firmāns* on behalf of the Latins from that date. However, since then, many contradictory *firmāns* were issued[13] and the position of the various sects in the church changed several times, in accordance with political, economic and demographic changes.

The Capitulations Agreement with France of 1535/6 improved the position of the Franciscans in Jerusalem, due to the prominent position given to France in the Ottoman Empire.[14] Thereafter, similar agreements favoring the Catholics appeared frequently, indicating not only that the Catholic ambassadors were working hard in Istanbul but, as mentioned often in the Sultanic orders to the Latins, that the earlier *firmāns* were not carried out; the local Christians were reluctant to let the few foreigners strengthen their position in the church. Eventually, however, the Latins achieved their aim. In 1555, following their expulsion from David's Tomb, they were allowed to repair two important areas in

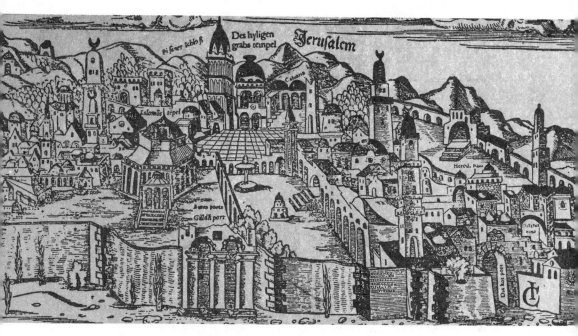

Jerusalem in 1544. The central building is the Church of the Holy Sepulchre

the church (the sepulchre and the big cupola) and thus exercise and display their rights. This achievement was accomplished with the help of Carl V, the German Emperor, and his son Philip II, King of Spain, at a time when the Ottomans were at war with an enemy common to them and to the French — the Austrians.[15] Due to the joint military-political aim, the Ottomans had to appease their allies and strengthen the position of the Latins in Palestine.

During the second half of the sixteenth century the Eastern Christian communities managed to oust the Latins from some of the sites under their control. During that period the Ottoman Empire was at war with Catholic Europe;[16] this had an effect on the diplomatic and financial help to the Franciscans who were custodians of the holy places, and weakened their position as a foreign minority in the Empire. However, the position of the Latins was improved again when, in 1604, France became the protector of all those Westerners whose countries did not have diplomatic relations with the Empire.[17] The same year a *firmān* decreed the return to the Latins of all that was taken from them by force;[18] they were the only ones allowed to celebrate Mass at the sepulchre. At that point the Druse Emir of Mt. Lebanon, Fakhr al-Din II who collaborated with Tuscany, was threatening Ottoman authority in Lebanon and the Galilee. The Ottoman army was busy on the European front, the Empire needed good diplomatic relations with France,[19] and therefore had to improve the status of the Latins.

The naval and economic power of Venice in the eastern Mediterranean increased her political influence in the Ottoman Empire. Thus Venice was of great help to the Latins up to 1645, when the Ottoman–Venetian war over Crete

27

started. In 1615, Venice had helped the Latins gain the right to repair the church,[20] and in 1632 they regained the rights that had been given two years earlier to the Greek Orthodox. In 1660 the Latins still held the exclusive right to say Mass in the sepulchre, which means that the *firmān* of 1636, returning this right to the Franciscans (after it was given to the Greek Orthodox in 1631 and 1634), was being observed.[21] But from the late 1660s onwards, travellers described the Greeks as having the best positions in the church, reflecting a temporal decrease in European influence over Istanbul.[22]

In 1674 the French Ambassador visited the church and, according to Greek sources, after he and his entourage had injured Greek priests and damaged objects, Ottoman authorities induced him to leave town. In Istanbul he renewed his efforts against the Greek Orthodox. The King of France wrote to the Grand Vezir in Istanbul, and pointed out that, according to the Capitulations Agreement of 1673, the church should be exclusively in Latin hands. This argument was presented to the Sublime Porte, many documents were cited, and *'ulemā* were called as witnesses. Finally, in 1690, the case was decided in favor of the Latins.[23] Undoubtedly, the French were instrumental in this achievement. The French Ambassador at the Porte, Marquis de Castagnères, was ordered by Louis XIV to return the custody over the holy places to the Latins. This was achieved through the cordial relations that the French Ambassador developed with the Grand Vezir Muṣṭafa Köprülü at a period when the dominant power in the empire was in his hands.[24] According to British sources of that time, the strong position of the French Ambassador was a result of military aid and misleading reports given by France to the Ottoman Empire. The British Ambassador Trumbull commented in July 1690: "Tis certain this Empire at present is more govern'd by the French than the Turkish interest."[25] Nevertheless, it seems that the Franciscans sought diplomatic help in Istanbul as well as straight financial support, but rejected foreign political intervention in Palestine. This is demonstrated in what they told Maundrell in 1697, namely, that they felt much safer without the direct French protection.[26] In 1698 when the peace treaty was drafted they asked the Austrian Emperor not to send any more Latin consuls to Jerusalem, since this only made things more difficult for them.[27]

The peace treaty of Carlowitz in 1699, which initiated foreign dictation over the Ottoman Empire, enabled the Austrian Ambassador in Istanbul to bring before the Sultan demands from religious dignitaries connected to the Holy See, relating to religious matters and places of pilgrimage in Jerusalem.[28] Peter the Great, in turn, approached the Sultan on behalf of the Greek Orthodox subjects under Ottoman rule and sought to discuss religious matters during the peace conference, especially the return of the holy places to the Greek Orthodox. In this he failed, but a separate agreement in 1700 gave free access to Russian pilgrims to Palestine.[29] This marks the beginning of Russian attempts to penetrate the Ottoman Empire through religious means, with Russia itself then on the way to becoming an international power.

At the end of the seventeenth century the Catholics no longer participated in the ceremony of the Holy Fire on Easter Saturday, when a holy fire is alleged to descend from heaven to the Holy Sepulchre. By then they regarded the ceremony as disgraceful and indecent. Since it is hard to believe that a change in religious views would have caused them to renounce rights in the sepulchre, it may be assumed that they were forced by the Eastern communities to leave. The Greeks tried, but failed to expel the Armenians as well from that ceremony.[30] Indeed, during the Easter ceremonies, that were at times very stormy, Janissaries had to be stationed in the church to keep order between the various contesting communities.[31]

At the beginning of the eighteenth century the Latins received several permits to repair the Church of the Holy Sepulchre, but were unable to make use of them until the Peace of Passarovitz of 1718. During the peace negotiations, the French Ambassador at the Porte, de Bonnac, promised the release of 150 Turkish prisoners-of-war in exchange for such permits, while the King of France contributed to the repair of the main cupola and other parts of the church.[32]

The 1740 Capitulations Agreement with France was to a great extent a result of the efforts made by the French Ambassador in Istanbul, Marquis de Villeneuve, in achieving the Belgrade Peace Treaty of 1739.[33] One of the outcomes of this cooperation was the *firmān* of 1740 which is the most comprehensive one issued to the Latins, and recognizes their ancient rights in and around Jerusalem.[34] On this *firmān* the Latins based their later demands.

Violent fighting occurred in the Church of the Holy Sepulchre in September 1756 when, on St. Lazare's eve, armed Latins and local Arab Catholics broke in, injuring Greek Orthodox pilgrims and smashing ritual objects.[35] Their success was, however, short-lived and on April 2, 1757, a large number of Greek pilgrims who came annually on Easter took over the church. Their occupation of the site was confirmed in writing by a local *qāḍi* [Muslim judge], and was later ratified in a *firmān* which is the basis of the status quo at the church to this day. The Greek Orthodox Patriarch was very active in Istanbul and spent large sums of money persuading influential circles in order to obtain this *firmān*.[36] In this case, the combination of local Greek Orthodox power in Jerusalem and influence in Istanbul culminated in a *firmān* in their favor in the Church of the Holy Sepulchre. The Armenian Patriarchs were also busy taking care of the interests of their community, but because their center was in Jerusalem it took them longer to present documents and evidence in Istanbul and many important papers were lost in transit.[37]

During this period the influence of the Ottoman government in the events in Palestine was relatively weak due to the political power of a local sheikh, Dahir al-'Umar, whose authority spread from the Galilee southwards, extending at times to southern Palestine. The attempts of the Governors of the Province of Damascus, of which southern Palestine (the districts of Nablus, Jerusalem and Gaza) was a part, to restrain him were not successful. His rule over the Galilee made it difficult for these governors to fulfill their duties in their Palestinian districts, and this situation is reflected in the affairs connected with the Church of the Holy Sepulchre.[38]

Europe was then involved in the Seven Years' War, making it harder for the European states to interfere in Istanbul in favor of the Latins. At the same time, Russia had become sufficiently powerful to negotiate treaties on terms that were quite favorable to her and her protegées. For example, in 1774 the treaty of Küçük Kaynarca was signed with the Ottomans, ending a six-year war during which a Russian navy sailed from the Baltic Sea to the eastern Mediterranean and collaborated with rebellious elements, including Dahir al-'Umar. The oft-quoted paragraphs 7 and 14 of the treaty of Küçük Kaynarca provided that the Ottoman Empire "will protect the Christian religion and its churches" and that it "allows Russian ministers to make representations in regard to the new church at Constantinople." There is no mention of an all-embracing Russian protection of the Greek Orthodox community. However, by political pressure and repeated false "quotations" Russia created the impression that she was the Protector of Orthodoxy in the Ottoman Empire.[39] This line was taken in order to facilitate Russian penetration into the Ottoman Empire.

Towards the end of the eighteenth century Russia's policy with regard to the Ottoman Empire increasingly emphasized religious interests. To a great extent this stemmed from the deep piety and mystic feelings in the Russian people, including the ruling class. Russian interest in Palestine had also been intensified considerably by the thousands of Russian and Armenian pilgrims to the Holy Land since the beginning of the century. In their naiveté and simple piety they were most emotional and unrestrained, pressing their case by dint of their numbers. The pilgrims also contributed significantly to the financial coffers of the Eastern Patriarchate of Jerusalem. In addition, money was collected in churches in Russia, and men in the Russian army and navy contributed one day's salary a year for the holy places.[40] The pilgrimage and the financial contributions made the Russian people feel closely connected with events concerning the holy places, and gave them a say in church affairs.

While Russian intervention in Istanbul on behalf of the Orthodox community living near the holy places increased, the interest of the Western camp in religious issues declined, due to the French Revolution and the subsequent secularization of the Republic. The period was also marked by French territorial gains at the expense of the Ottoman Empire.[41] Napoleon's motives in invading Palestine in 1799 were political and military; he intended to weaken the Ottoman Empire, and advance towards India and thus weaken Britain. He did not try to strengthen the Catholic position in the holy places, which he did not visit at all. It was only later, when he was back in France, that he took greater interest in religious affairs in order to harness them to political purposes. After concluding a peace treaty between France and the Empire (June 25, 1802), Bonaparte instructed Brune, his

Ambassador to the Porte, on October 18, 1802 to restore France to her former stature and influence in Istanbul. Following this, the Embassy sought to place under its protection not only French Catholics but also Christians from Syria and Armenia, as well as pilgrims going to the holy places. The French gains in this respect were slight, and local inhabitants who did not feel themselves closely related to the French criticized their activities.[42]

The Greek Orthodox community was able to expand its rights in the Holy Sepulchre when the Catholic states failed to take part in the repairs necessitated by the great fire that devastated a substantial part of the church in October 1808. The *firmāns* stated specifically that the Greeks were only acting as agents of the Sultan, and that this did not imply any change in their rights. The entire Greek Orthodox world participated in the restoration whereas the Catholic world was not in a political or economic condition to do so. Although the Catholics did not participate by their own fault, they were annoyed that the Greeks got the job, and accused them of placing large inscriptions in the church commemorating their part in the repairs and their rights in this connection. The Greeks were also blamed for changes in the church building, the most egregious being the hiding of the graves of the Crusader Kings.[43] The Franciscans wrote to the Catholic states of Europe for help in this affair, but the help that they received was so negligible[44] that in 1814 they turned to the Russian Tsar in desperation.[45] Nothing came of this appeal, and the situation of the Franciscans was not improved. Meanwhile the hostility between the communities increased because of the Greek repairs in the church. As a result, the rules concerning ritual grew more stringent, and objects belonging to one sect that were left at a shared place of worship were immediately removed by the other groups.[46] Nevertheless, the Latins succeeded in installing a larger organ than the one they had before the fire, to the great annoyance of the Eastern communities and the Muslims alike.[47]

In 1818 the Catholic Ambassadors to the Porte agreed to cooperate over the protection of the holy places. Evidently this kind of intervention was no longer considered to be reactionary and improper. Even if their religious ardor was not all that strong, the European governments were fully aware of the political value of involvement through religious means. France, Spain, Naples (and even Britain, though not Catholic) protested to the Sublime Porte regarding a *firmān* ratifying the rights of the Greek Orthodox community in 1817. As a countermove, the Russian government discussed with the Greek Orthodox Patriarch of Jerusalem steps to be taken against the Catholics. The result was that the 1817 *firmān* was not cancelled and the stronger position of the Eastern Churches remained unchanged,[48] reflecting the stronger influence of Russia and the Greek Orthodox community on the Ottoman Empire. These negotiations show Russian eagerness to use the religious conflict for political purposes and the readiness of the Greek Church to accept the support of external political pressure in its internal struggles.

In 1819 France dispatched an envoy by the name of Marcellus to gather

31

The Church of the Holy Sepulchre, 1819, and, outside the walls, the site of the "Last Supper"

information in the Holy Land, and to try to improve the status of the Latins there. He came to Palestine in June 1820, and introduced himself as an official representative acting in the name of the French king. He offered the Greek clerics a real peace between the communities in exchange for what he called "trivial concessions" (i.e. giving to the Latins full rights in the Holy Sepulchre, half of the Katholikon in the Church of the Nativity, Gethsemane, etc.), but the Greeks were reluctant to surrender their historic rights. When Marcellus said that all these places were Catholic property bought in 1305, the Greeks replied that according to state laws no foreigner could own real estate in the Empire and that the Latins merely retained certain rights to the use of the holy places because of the rulers' benevolence. Marcellus could not convince them even when he explained that his real motive was to fight the Armenians, whose position vis-à-vis the Greeks in the Empire was strengthened on the eve of the Greek Revolution. A report on the matter was sent to the Porte by the Greek Orthodox Patriarch of Jerusalem, the Russian Ambassador, and the Governor of Damascus, following which the Greeks received another *firmān* "... de donner une forte leçon à la legation de France."[49] Nevertheless, France was able to gain ground in the Ottoman Empire at the expense of Russia as a result of the Greek Revolution, when the status of the Greek Orthodox community in the Empire deteriorated and with it, momentarily, the influence of its self-proclaimed protector: Russia.

The French, however, did not manage to alter basically the order of things in the holy places,[50] due to the stronger position of the local Christians in Palestine. Following the Peace of Adrianople (1829) when Russia's new policy towards the Ottoman Empire hinged upon her preference of a weak and passive neighbor over a strong and active one,[51] the struggle over the holy places remained an important tool to advance her policy. Russia was in no hurry to conquer the Ottoman Empire, but tried every possible means, including religion, to penetrate it and increase her influence on the Porte.

During the period of Egyptian rule in Palestine (1831–1840), Alexandria became a center of diplomatic activities, and the status of the "Protected Peoples" and foreigners improved due to Muhammad Ali's friendly attitude toward these groups. This attitude was expressed concerning the holy places as well. The difficulties concerning entry into the Church of the Holy Sepulchre were removed by giving duplicate keys to the three main Christian communities in addition to those traditionally held by the Muslims.[52] Restoration and building of places of worship became easier, local Christians were permitted to enter the State Administration, and consulates were opened in Jerusalem, although the local population was not in favor of these moves. Due to these changes both the European powers and the local Christians could exert more direct pressure on the local authorities in Jerusalem concerning the holy places and other issues to interest to them. After the peace of Kütahya (1833) between the Ottomans and the Egyptians, the Sublime Porte reserved the right to issue *firmāns* relating to areas under Egyptian rule on such important matters as commerce, diplomatic relations, and the status of foreigners.[53] The Egyptians were ready to allow minor repairs in the churches, but one had to get a *firmān* from the Porte for more serious repair work.[54]

The position of the Russians in the Ottoman Empire strengthened after Sultan Mahmud II appealed to Russia for help against the Egyptian forces, and the Russian navy was deployed near Istanbul to serve as a deterrent force. As a result, the Ottoman–Russian mutual defense treaty of Hünkâr Iskelesi (1833) was signed, making Russia much more of a force to contend with in the area.[55] Thereafter Russian diplomats and occasional visitors tried to intervene in Alexandria and Istanbul on behalf of the Greek Orthodox Patriarchate of Jerusalem and, to the dismay of the local authorities in Palestine and rival foreign agents, they were quite successful.[56] The French, who were considered to be the Protectors of the Catholic Church in the eastern part of the Mediterranean basin, tried to benefit from their good relations with Muhammad Ali in order to improve the position of the Catholics in the holy places, but with little effect.[57]

Many groups had their means of influence over the government. The European consulates and foreign visitors in Jerusalem increased, and this strengthened the self-confidence of the Latins. On the other hand, the local Christians who served in the state administration (Egyptian or Ottoman), tried to advance the interests of their communities and they were supported by Russian pressure in Istanbul. As a result, the conflicting pressures neutralized each other and the situation in the Church of the Holy Sepulchre remained basically constant.

Changes in the Status of the Communities in the Church of the Nativity

The conflict over the Church of the Nativity developed along similar lines to that of the Church of the Holy Sepulchre, and as a result of similar pressures. In the mid-sixteenth century the church was in ruins, except for the underground sections where destruction was also considerable. Even the star that marked the place of the Nativity had been removed.[58]

At the beginning of the seventeenth century, with the church still in ruins, the underground areas were under Catholic control, but ancient Greek pictures could still be found in the nativity cave.[59] In 1627, due to the intervention of the Greek Orthodox Patriarch of Jerusalem, that community regained supervision over the places of pilgrimage in Bethlehem, but the Latins were permitted to keep their monastery adjacent to the church.[60]

A series of *firmāns* issued to the Latins, which declared the Greek Orthodox documents to be forgeries, did not succeed in ousting the latter group from its strongholds in Bethlehem, due to its overwhelming majority among the local population. In 1671 the Greeks repaired the Church of the Nativity, but in 1688 the Latins seized control over it and damaged many Greek relics.[61] As mentioned above,[62] there was a strong French influence on the Empire at this point, reflecting the military and political help provided to the Ottomans and the existence of competent ambassadors in Istanbul. The peak of Catholic dominance was in 1717 (on the eve of the treaty of Passarovitz) when the Latins managed to place a star with a Latin inscription over the site of the Nativity. They remained dominant until 1757, when a *firmān* restored to the Greek Orthodox community most of the holy places in Bethlehem and elsewhere, though from a later description it is apparent that the Latins retained some of their rights, including the Nativity Star.[63]

Indeed, the infringement upon this particular right, i.e., the removal of the Nativity Star in 1847, presumably by the Greeks, triggered the Crimean War. The fact that another star was put in its place on Christmas eve 1852 could no longer prevent the forthcoming war.[64]

34

The Church of the Nativity, Bethlehem, 1700

The Struggle over the Holy Places, and the Crimean War

One result of the role the European powers played in driving the Egyptians out of Syria and Palestine in 1840, was their search for significant footholds in the Ottoman Empire. Palestine was among the areas chosen, the pretext being the powers' deep concern for the holy places. They realized the weakness of the Porte but for the time being, for reasons concerned with the European balance of power, preferred the Empire to exist independently, intact but weak, so that a new local element or a European power would not develop on its ruins. Foreign activity in Palestine increased from this period on, and the struggle for mastery in Europe was played out in the Holy Land as well.

France started clamoring for the enforcement of the agreements of 1740.[65] Prussia, in turn, drew up a program in 1841 for the internationalization of Palestine, including a major role for herself. The program was based on the responsibilities of the powers towards the holy places and the Ottoman Christians (similar to the Russian demands), but the other powers refused to participate in the Prussian program.[66] They could not agree on a joint policy that was motivated by religion. Another foreign suggestion, to create a separate political entity in Palestine, was partly accepted by the Porte; the districts of Jerusalem, Nablus and Gaza were placed directly under the administration of Istanbul, and Jerusalem

35

later became an independent province due to its special importance.[67] Even while the Ottoman Empire was in a weak military and political position, and was ready to reform parts of its institutions according to Western patterns, the Porte was reluctant to let external forces dictate internal affairs.

In 1843 the Greek Orthodox Patriarch resumed residence in Jerusalem, apparently because it was thought necessary to have an important religious dignitary there to look after the interests of the community and the implementation of *firmāns* concerning Greek Orthodox affairs. The Russian Embassy in Istanbul took care of the diplomatic side of the struggle. As a counter-measure, a French Consulate was opened in Jerusalem that same year,[68] partially neutralizing the Greek Orthodox move. This reflected the fact that, in the period after Bonaparte, French foreign policy once again took up the banner of religion. This policy was further developed by Louis Napoleon in his bid for power following the Revolution of 1848. He took an active interest in the holy places in order to gain the support of the politically powerful Ultramontanists.[69]

Despite the declared religious interests of Paris, relations were strained between the French Consul in Jerusalem and the Latins in the region who did not receive any financial help from France after 1843. The Consul did not take any interest in the removal of the Star in the Church of the Nativity (1847) until the Franciscans threatened to place themselves under the protection of the Sultan. The French Consul stepped in only after the Catholic Consul of Sardinia had intervened;[70] then, in the name of France, the self-proclaimed Protector of the Holy Land, he took extreme steps that were beyond his authority. He demanded to sit in judgment of a case that involved Ottoman subjects as well as French citizens. This was opposed by the Governor of Jerusalem who complained angrily to Istanbul. But the Sublime Porte failed to react vigorously to this protest and, as it were, encouraged French designs in the area.[71] Apparently the Catholic Patriarchate did not appreciate the Consul's activity, and the Latin Patriarch Valerga, who resumed his residence in Jerusalem in 1847, went to Europe to seek help from the Pope and the Catholic kings.[72]

Meanwhile France increased its involvement. On May 28, 1850, General Aupick, the French Ambassador in Istanbul, presented to the Porte demands based on France's interpretation of the Capitulations Agreement of 1740 and on a report prepared by a special French envoy, Boré, in 1848.[73] The basic claim put forward by France was that an international treaty can only be abrogated if both parties so agree, and therefore the 1740 agreement was still in force. After being pressed, 'Ali, the Ottoman Minister of Foreign Affairs, replied that the Porte abided by his agreements, but that the matter under discussion demanded further investigation. Meanwhile an international committee rejected the Greek version of Omar's covenant of 638 with Sophronius, Bishop of Jerusalem, on which the Greeks based their claims in the holy places.[74]

At the same time counter-pressures increased. In September 1851 the Russian Ambassador to the Porte, Titov, demanded that no changes be made in the protection of any of the holy places in Palestine and warned that he would leave his post in Istanbul immediately if such a change occurred.[75] The new French Ambassador, de Lavalette, suggested that all the holy places be placed under joint protection and ownership, but in October 1851 the Sultan rejected this proposal because he opposed any cooperation which meant increased foreign intervention in Ottoman affairs.[76] Besides, no community was ready to relinquish rights in a specific place, and most of them already had some rights of worship in places shared by the others. The Sultan did not want to be pressed in this investigation, and in November 1851 the international committee was suspended in spite of French protests[77] and even military threats.[78]

Meanwhile an Ottoman committee investigated all the documents concerning the holy places and gave its report on January 25, 1852.[79] The report surveyed the *firmāns* issued over hundreds of years, many of which were contradictory. Following this report, the Ottoman authorities came to some decisions. On February 8, 1852, the Sublime Porte sent notes to the French Ambassador ("French Note") and to the Greek Orthodox community in Jerusalem ("Greek *Firmān*") which were sufficiently ambiguous as to satisfy neither party.[80] The procedural obstacles that faced the implementation of the Greek *firmān* increased the Russians' doubts about the value and sincerity of Ottoman promises. In addition it seemed that the Sultan's orders could be changed at will, and that their enforcement was far from automatic. Thus, it was deemed necessary by the powers to force the Ottoman state to honor its word.

December 1852 was a turning point in this struggle.[81] By this time the Catholic states and their co-religionists in Palestine had achieved their immediate aims, and objections from Russia and the Greek Orthodox community were beginning to mount. With the restoration of the Star to the Church of Nativity on Christmas eve 1852, one of the main sources of tension between the two sides was resolved. Louis Napoleon was crowned Emperor Napoleon III and no longer needed the religious issue as a means of forwarding his political aims at home. The basic conceptual change in the struggle was that Russia demanded categorically a right that in the past it had only hinted at, namely full protection rights over the twelve million Greek Orthodox in the Ottoman Empire (who were Ottoman and not Russian citizens), according to her interpretation of the Treaty of Küçük Kaynarca. At the end of December 1852 Russia backed this demand by moving armed forces towards the Ottoman border and putting her navy in the Black Sea on the alert.[82]

At the end of February 1853, Lord Stratford de Redcliffe returned to Istanbul as the British Ambassador. He was very much involved in Ottoman affairs, and was respected and trusted by the Ottomans. One of his instructions was to press for a compromise between France and Russia concerning the question of the holy places, because of the dangers involved not only to the Ottoman Empire but to the whole balance of power in Europe. Menshikov, who was a special envoy of the Tsar, came to Istanbul on February 28, 1853. His instructions were to: 1) establish renewed regulations in the holy places on the basis of the situation prior to the "French Note"; 2) obtain a *firmān* that would recognize the rights of the Greek Orthodox community and Russia's right to protect that community, and that would be incorporated in a binding convention; 3) enter into a defense treaty with the Ottoman Empire, in the event that France raised any difficulties.

These Russian demands were much more exigent and broad than in the past, and included claims that would have put the Ottoman Empire in a subordinate position to the Russian Empire. The Ottoman refusal to accept these claims was also due to the personalities of the two foreign envoys. Whereas the British Ambassador was trusted and familiar with the Ottoman ruling class, the Russian envoy was arrogant, unaccustomed to Ottoman manners and habits, and not acquainted with the Ottoman statesmen. This difference influenced their abilities to push forward the interests of their respective governments.

Redcliffe succeeded in solving the immediate problems relating to the holy places on April 20, 1853, and this was ratified in a *firmān* of May 3, 1853; but the matter was already out of hand. Menshikov had managed to quarrel with everyone and arouse general suspicion. The leading Ottoman circles let it be known, thanks to the confidence that Redcliffe inspired in them, that they were fed up with Russian dictates. Menshikov felt he could achieve no more and left Istanbul on May 21, 1853. Six days later the Tsar ordered his troops to cross the Pruth River into the Ottoman Empire. At the beginning of June the British and French navies were directed to the Bay of Besika, at the entrance of the Dardanelles.[83] These steps marked the beginning of the Crimean War.

The dispute over the holy places was solved before the Crimean War broke out, and served only as a smoke-screen which hid the real purposes of the Great Powers — i.e., increasing each ruler's power at home, and finding a way to infiltrate and seize territorial and human strongholds in the Ottoman Empire and thereby strengthen their position in Europe.

Summary

During most of the Ottoman period the struggle over the holy places occurred between local groups in Palestine and a small foreign community, each backed by its country of origin. Up to the end of the seventeenth century, European Catholic states compelled the Ottomans to issue *firmāns* affirming the Latins' rights in the holy places, but, "les Latins ont les Firmans, et les Grecs les Sanctuaires."[84] Although legally the Latins had their rights (and well-organized archives to back their claims), very often they could not execute them, due to local conditions. The power of the Palestinian Christian population, relations with local authorities, and economic conditions were more important factors in determining religious rights in the holy places than the existence of legal documents and international agreements.

In the eighteenth century, the European Catholic states were in a favorable military position vis-à-vis the Ottoman Empire, and thus gained political benefits, including a say in the holy places. But in spite of the extensive rights acquired in 1740 by France, such political achievements could be nullified by local factors. The situation in the holy places was eventually ratified in 1757 by a *firmān* confirming Greek Orthodox hold over most of the shrines. By 1774, as a result of her combined political-military strength, Russia obtained a treaty that gave her an opening to penetrate the Ottoman Empire. Russia exploited this treaty following the increase of her power vis-à-vis the Ottoman Empire and the decrease in importance of the European powers due to the French Revolution and the decline of the importance of religion in Europe. Russia thought that due to her military preponderance she could enforce her far-fetched interpretation of the Küçük Kaynarca treaty of 1774. Thus, at the end of the century the line-up of powers contesting the holy places changed, with the largest local community (the Greek Orthodox) having the political support, sometimes backed by military threats, of a foreign power (i.e., Russia) that had annexed parts of the Ottoman Empire. On the other hand, members of the small foreign community (the Latins) were almost neglected by their own governments in Europe.

By the nineteenth century, the combination of the struggling elements had placed the Sublime Porte in a difficult position. The Greek Orthodox, the largest minority group in the Empire, was backed by the Empire's most dangerous external foe, and its spiritual leadership came from Greece, which had separated itself from the Empire. On the other hand, the Latins in the Empire remained a small foreign element, though the number of indigenous Catholics was on the increase. They were backed by a dangerous neighbor and opponent, Austro-Hungary, and by France, whose relations with the Ottoman state were generally amiable. France was one of the centers of culture from which the Ottomans tried to learn, but at times she also posed a military-ideological threat. The third element in this struggle, the Armenians, did not have any foreign support to speak of, but they continued to be an important financial-commercial factor throughout the Empire.

Thus it was hard for the Porte to decide to whom to show favor. The Porte vacillated, trying to avoid taking a stand in a dispute for which, as a Muslim, it had only contempt. The Sultan was amenable until it was clear that more concessions would mean the end of his sovereignty over the "Protected Countries". Even the "Sick Man of Europe" was not ready to commit political suicide. The Crimean War was the result of inability to bridge two extremes: the Sultan's unwillingness to give up more of his sovereignty, and the Tsar's reticence to renounce his protection over Eastern Orthodoxy, which was an integral part of his policy to guard autocracy and fight revolution and liberalism.

Until the mid-nineteenth century the foreign powers exerted pressure on the Porte in order to improve the position of their brethren in the holy places. Due to the changes in the political situation both in Europe and Ottoman Empire, the powers used the 1847 incident in Bethlehem as a pretext to achieve their own national and imperialist aims. However, in contrast to previous incidents which had been of equal gravity, this time an internal Ottoman affair was exploited in order to achieve political gains *outside* the Empire, at the expense of the Ottomans. The Sublime Porte had always regarded the struggle over the holy places as a political question and did not care which Church protected what, as long as the Ottoman state retained the ultimate authority. But the Ottomans were not ready to relinquish to foreign states any extraterritorial powers based on religious rights. They recognized the danger of slow political intervention and infiltration through protection over sites and rights of Ottoman subjects, and were not ready to give in on such crucial matters. The political wisdom of the Ottoman Empire lay in locating the "red line" in this matter, and taking care not to cross it. Although the Ottoman Empire despised the Christians and their religious struggles, it tried to achieve the utmost political (and financial) benefits from these sectarian conflicts.

The development of the struggle over the Christian holy places in Palestine depended on international factors and local elements. During most of the period under review the foreign governments interfered in order to support their correligionists; only on the eve of the Crimean War did the powers use this struggle in order to achieve political gains at home.

1 See M. Khadduri, *War and Peace in the Law of Islam* (Baltimore, 1955).

2 U. Heyd, "Farmān", *EI*² 2, pp. 804–805.

3 A. Bertram and J.W.A. Young, *The Orthodox Patriarchate of Jerusalem* (Oxford, 1926), pp. 85–86, 284–290, App. 9; A. Bertram and H.L. Luke, *Report of the Commission Appointed by the Government of Palestine to Inquire into the Affairs of the Orthodox Patriarchate of Jerusalem* (Oxford, 1921), pp. 17–18; A. Metaxakis, *Les exigences des orthodoxes arabophones de Palestine* (Constantinople, 1909); A. Popoff, *La question des lieux saints de Jérusalem dans la diplomatique Russe du XIXème siècle. 1ère partie (1800–1850)* (St. Petersbourg, 1910), p. 243; E.J. Bliss, *The Religions of Modern Syria and Palestine* (Edinburgh, 1912), pp. 44–74, 340–342.

4 In 1843 the new Patriarch Cyril returned to Jerusalem. Bertram and Young, *op. cit.*, pp. 26–27, 79–80, 171–172; Bliss, *op. cit.* p. 53; G. Williams, *The Holy City*, 2nd ed. (London, 1849), vol. 2, pp. 540–6.

5 Popoff, pp. 10, 113, 147–149, 159–161, 166–168, 248; Bertram and Young, pp. 64–66; Metaxakis, p. 44 (all, above, n. 3); Neophytos, monk of Cyprus, "Extracts from Annals of Palestine 1821–1841," trans. by S.N. Spyridon, *JPOS* 18 (1938):69–71, 83, 127 (hereafter, Neophytos).

6 A.K. Sanjian, *The Armenian Communities in Syria under Ottoman Domination* (Cambridge, Mass., 1965), pp. 104–115; A. Kalaydjian, "The Correspondence (1725–1740) of the Armenian Patriarch Gregory the Chain-Bearer" (hereafter, Kalaydjian) in M. Ma'oz (ed.), *Studies on Palestine during the Ottoman Period* (Jerusalem, 1975), pp. 563–566; S. Ajamian, "Sultan 'Abdülhamid and the Armenian Patriarchate of Jerusalem" (hereafter, Ajamian), in Ma'oz (*ibid.*), pp. 341–343.

7 Kalaydjian, pp. 562–567; Sanjian, pp. 104, 116, 178, 193, 204–206.

8 Sanjian, p. 170; Williams, p. 569; B. Collin, *Le Problème juridique des lieux saints* (Paris, n.d.), pp. 23, 60; L.G.A. Cust, *The Status Quo in the Holy Places* (London, 1930), p. 7; J. Finn, *Stirring Times* (London, 1878), vol. 1, pp. 38, 44–51, vol. 2, pp. 224–225, 466–467; H. Temperley, *England and the Near East: The Crimea* (London, 1936), pp. 284–285; Msgr. Mislin, *Les Saints Lieux* (Paris, 1851), vol. 2, pp. 89–90; M. Assaf, *The Arabs under the Crusaders, the Mameluks and the Turks* (Hebrew), (Tel Aviv, 1941), pp. 194, 382. On the expulsion of the Franciscans in 1552 from their center in David's Tomb, and the massacre inflicted on them in 1558, see Cust, *op. cit.*, p. 7; Finn, 1, p. 38; U. Heyd, *Ottoman Documents on Palestine, 1552–1615* (Oxford, 1960), pp. 177–179; G. Sandys, *Sandys Travells*, 6th ed. (London, 1670), p. 123; C. Biggs, *Six Months in Jerusalem* (London, 1895), pp. 236–237; A. Cohen, "The Expulsion of the Franciscans from Mount Zion in the Early Ottoman Period — A Reassessment" (Hebrew), *Cathedra* 22 (1982):61–74.

9 The Patriarchate was also very active in procuring large tracts of land, especially around Beit Jala. Mislin, 2, pp. 84–87; Finn, 1, pp. 359–362, 464–465; 2, pp. 11, 84–87, 102; Assaf, p. 382 (all, above, n. 8); Popoff (above, n. 3), p. 247; A. Goodrich-Freer, *Inner Jerusalem* (London, 1904), p. 158ff.

10 *The Wanderings of Felix Fabri*, vol. VII, part 1 (New York, 1971), pp. 427–439 (Palestine Pilgrims' Text Society).

11 Cust (above, n. 8), p. 18.

12 Sanjian, pp. 174–175; Bertram and Young, pp. 57–58 (above, n. 3); St. H. Stephan and L.A. Mayer (tr.), "Evliya Tashelebi's Travels in Palestine", *QDAP* 8 (1939):147. Evilya Çelebi's story about the ratification of Omar's covenant with the Franks must be anachronistic, due to their position in the seventeenth century, and his ignorance about their non-existence as a community in Omar's time and their weakness in Selim's time. There is no mention of a *firmān* from the time of the Ottoman conquest in Custodia di Terra Sancta, *Catalogo dei firmani ed altri documenti legali emmanati in lingua araba e turca concernenti i santuari le proprietá i diritti della custodia di terra sancta conservati nell'archivio della stessa custodia in Gerusalemme* (Tipografia dei P.P. Francescanni, 1922). Contemporary descriptions of the conquest (Ibn Iyās, Haydar Çelebi, etc.) do not mention the ratification of documents to either church.

13 Only published sources were used for this paper. Most of the documentary material was published by the Roman Catholics, and it is quite probable that the other communities have many more permits than appeared in print.

14 Goodrich-Freer (above, n. 9), p. 156. In 1537 they were released from the prison in David's Tower, thanks to the intervention of François I, King of France.

15 E. Pierotti, *Visit to the Holy Land* (London, 1852), p. 109; C.R. Conder, *The City of Jerusalem* (London, 1909), p. 213; L. Dressaire, *Jérusalem à travers les siècles* (Paris, 1931), p. 320; H.B. Ridgaway, *The Lord's Land* (New York, 1876), p. 247; E. Sullivan (ed.), *Buck Whaley's Memoirs* (London, 1909), pp. 205–206.

16 Among the important events are the wars over northern Africa, the Ottoman failure at the siege of Malta (1565), Suleyman's death at the siege of Szigeth (1566), the conquest of Cyprus from Venice (1570–71), the Ottoman defeat at Lepanto (1571), the victory against Austro-Hungary at Cerestes (1596); there were no wars with Europe in 1574–1593. E.S. Creasy, *History of the Ottoman Turks*, 1 (London, 1877), pp. 281–314, 347–357; S.J. Shaw, *History of the Ottoman Empire and Modern Turkey*, 1 (Cambridge, 1976), pp. 102–111, 175–185.

17 I. de Testa, *Recueil des traités de la Porte Ottomane avec les puissances étrangères*, 1 (Paris, 1864), p. 143.

18 *Ibid.*, 3, pp. 313–315.

19 Sandys, pp. 130–132. On the Treaty of Sitvatorok (1606) where for the first time the Ottomans had to treat the Austrian Emperor as an equal and to act according to international law, see Shaw, 1, pp. 187–188 (above, n. 16).

20 The Ottoman-Venetian war in Crete lasted from 1645–1668. Shaw (above, n. 16), 1, pp. 201–203, 212–213; Collin (above, n. 8), p. 36; C. Wardi, "The Question of the Holy Places in Ottoman Times," in Ma'oz (above, n. 6), p. 389.

21 F. E. Roger, *La Terre Sainte* (Paris, 1664), pp. 128–132; Archbishop of Jordan Vassilios, *The Controversy over the Holy Places during the Ottoman Period. A Greek Orthodox View*

41

(Jerusalem, 1970), p. 2; Custodia Terrae Sanctae, *Les lieux saints de la Palestine* (Jerusalem, 1922) (hereafter, Custodia), pp. 17–18.

22   O. Lébédew (tr.), *Récits de voyages d'un arabe* (St. Petersbourg, 1902), pp. 10–11, 16; E. Robinson and E. Smith, *Biblical Researches in Palestine, Mount Sinai and Arabia Petraea,* 1 (London, 1841), pp. 51–52; W.R. Wilson, *Travels in Egypt and the Holy Land, 1819* (London, 1824), p. 179. The Ottomans were at war in the west and suffered a defeat at St. Gothard (1664), see Shaw (above, n. 16), 1, p. 212.

23   Popoff (above, n. 3), p. 129; Collin (above, n. 8), pp. 134–136 (documents); C. Thompson, *The Travels of C. Thompson,* 3 (London, 1744), p. 129. The important military events of the period were: wars against Poland and Russia (1672–76), failure of the siege of Vienna (1683), the defeat at Mohacz (1687), Janissary disturbances (1687), the fall of Belgrad (1688, recaptured in 1690), Venetian expansion in the Morea; see Shaw (above, n. 16), 1, pp. 213–225.

24   Creasy (above, n. 16), p. 84.

25   Collin, p. 135 (documents); A. Wood, "The English Embassy at Constantinople 1660–1762," *EHR* 40 (1925):545.

26   H. Maundrell, *A Journey from Aleppo to Jerusalem at Easter, A.D. 1697* (London, 1810), p. 46, relates that the French Consul in Sidon also held the title "Consul of Jerusalem". By the order of his king, he had to visit Jerusalem every year at Easter "under the pretence of preserving the Sanctuary from the viclations, and the Fryars who have the custody of it, from the exactions of the Turks. But the Fryars think themselves much safer without this protection."

27   T. Tobler, *Denkblätter aus Jerusalem* (Constanz, 1856), p. 394; J. von Hammer, *Geschichte des osmanischen Reiches,* 6 (Pest, 1830), p. 761.

28   G. Young, *Corps de droit Ottoman,* 2 (Oxford, 1905–6), pp. 134–135 (paragraph 13); Shaw (above, n. 16), 1, pp. 223–225.

29   Creasy (above, n. 16), 2, pp. 107–108; D. Hopwood, *The Russian Presence in Syria and Palestine 1843–1914* (London, 1969), pp. 4–5.

30   In 1601 "popish monks" participated in the ceremony; see W. Foster (ed.), *The Travels of John Sanderson in the Levant 1584–1602* (London, 1935), p. 108. For a description of the ceremony and the Catholic change of heart, see Maundrell (above, n. 26), pp. 94–97.

31   Maundrell, *loc. cit.*; T.H. Papadopoullos, *Studies and Documents relating to the History of the Greek Church and People under Turkish Domination* (Brussels, 1952), p. 370.

32   Popoff, pp. 49, 86; Dressaire, p. 321; H. Vincent and F.M. Abel, *Jérusalem – Recherches de topographie, d'archéologie et d'histoire,* 2 (Paris, 1914), pp. 297–298. Paragraph 4 of the Treaty of the Pruth forbade the Russian Ambassador to reside in Istanbul; for background and text of this treaty and the Treaty of Passarovitz, see Shaw (above, n. 16), 1, pp. 229–233.

33   Collin (above, n. 8), p. 33; Shaw, 1, pp. 243–245; J.C. Hurewitz, *Diplomacy in the Near and Middle East,* 1 (Princeton, 1956), p. 1.

34   De Testa (above, n. 17), 1, pp. 195–196; Young (above, n. 28), 2, pp. 129–130.

35   Popoff (above, n. 3), p. 130.

36   *Ibid.,* pp. 88–90, 130; Collin (above, n. 8), p. 138 (documents); P. Masson, *Histoire du commerce français dans le Levant au XVIIIe siècle* (New York, 1967), p. 267.

37   Sanjian, pp. 178–185; Kalaydjian, pp. 565–566.

38   U. Heyd, *Dahir al-'Umar, the Ruler of the Galilee in the 18th Century* (Hebrew), (Jerusalem, 1942); A. Cohen, *Palestine in the 18th Century* (Jerusalem, 1973).

39   In 1768–74 the Ottoman Empire and Russia were involved in a war that terminated with the treaty of Küçük Kaynarca; for the relevant paragraphs see Hurewitz (above, n. 33), 1, pp. 156–157; for background and text see also Shaw, 1, pp. 247–250. During the long negotiations, the Russians demanded on February 15, 1773, among other things, "that the Porte should allow to the sovereign of Russia . . . the right of . . . protecting those inhabitants of the Ottoman Empire who profess the religion of the Greek Church." Temperley, pp. 304, 324–325, 330, 466–467, 471–472. A.J.P. Taylor, *The Struggle for the Mastery in Europe 1848–1918* (Oxford, 1954), p. 52, points out that the idea to use article 7 in its broader aspects was suggested to the Russians in 1853 by Muṣṭafa Reṣid Paṣa, the former Grand Vizier, and that Nesselrode accepted it. Taylor thinks that the Russian policy-makers did not consult

carefully the treaty they based their claims upon, but it seems that Russia was well aware of the limited meaning of these paragraphs, as Nesselrode acknowledged to the British Ambassador on June 6, 1853; de Testa, 3, p. 287.

40 Finn (above, n. 8), 1, pp. 33, 81–82; Hopwood (above, n. 29), p. 3; M.J. Woodcock, *Scripture Lands* (London, 1849), p. 119; J. Dupuis, *The Holy Land* (London, 1856), p. 60.

41 France acquired the Venetian-held Greek Islands following the Treaty of Campo Formio (October 17, 1797) and invaded Egypt in 1798. On the Ottoman-French relations, see B. Lewis, *The Emergence of Modern Turkey* (Oxford, 1961), pp. 64–72; E.Z. Karal, *Fransa-Mısır ve Osmanlı İmparatorluğu (1797–1802)* (İstanbul, 1938); I. Soysal, *Fransız İhtilâli ve Türk Fransız Diplomas Munasebetleri (1789–1802)* (Ankara, 1964).

42 For the text of the peace agreement of October 18, 1802, see de Testa (above, n. 17), 2, pp. 252–253. On the negotiations following it, see Mislin (above, n. 8), 2, p. 45. For a later and opposite opinion, see A.W. Kinglake, *Eöthen* (Philadelphia, n.d.), p. 176. During the invasion of Palestine, Bonaparte said that Jerusalem did not lie on his line of march; see Temperley, p. 284. It was only later that he took more political interest in religious affairs. However, Napoleon did have some plans to make political use of Christian and Jewish motivations during the Palestinian campaign; see J.M. Thompson, *Napoleon's Letters* (London, 1954), pp. 94–96, 134–135, 150–153.

43 Popoff, pp. 1, 9–11, 16–17, 123, 342–343; Bertram and Luke, p. 194; Williams, pp. 282–285 (both above, n. 3); M.L. Bunel, *Jérusalem, la cote de Syrie et Constantinople en 1853* (Paris, 1854), pp. 81, 109; M.J. de Géramb, *A Pilgrimage to Palestine, Egypt and Syria* (London, 1840), pp. 76–82; Count Forbin, *Travels in Greece, Turkey and the Holy Land in 1817–18* (London, n.d.), pp. 43, 50. On a controversy with the Muslims over the restoration, see Popoff, pp. 130–131; 'Abd al-Raḥmān al-Jabartī, *'Ajā'ib al-āthār fī al-tarājim wal-akhbār* (Cairo, 1227 H.), 4, p. 110.

44 Popoff, p. 131; L'Abbé Beqk, *Impressions d'un pèlerin de Terre Sainte au printemps de 1855* (Tours, 1859), p. 82; Collin, p. 46; H. Light, *Travels in Egypt, Nubia, Holy Land, Mount Lebanon and Cyprus in the year 1814* (London, 1818), pp. 180–182. At this time the Ottomans and Russia were involved in a war that terminated in the Treaty of Bucharest (1812); Shaw, 2, pp. 12–14.

45 Popoff, pp. 3–4. For instructions to the French Ambassadors in 1792, see Collin, p. 45.

46 *Ibid.*, pp. 131–133.

47 *Ibid.*, pp. 16–17; Malta Protestant College, *Journal of a Deputation sent to the East in 1849* (London, 1854), p. 326.

48 Popoff, pp. 17–20, 30–33, 50–52, 56–57, 90–93.

49 *Ibid.*, pp. 73–76, 106–111, 119.

50 *Ibid.*, pp. 113, 149, 164–165.

51 *Ibid.*, pp. 78–79, 114–125; R.J. Kerner, "Russia's New Policy in the Near East after the Peace of Adrianople," *CHJ* 5 (1937):280–290.

52 Popoff, p. 246; E. Hogg, *Visit to Alexandria, Damascus and Jerusalem during the Successful Campaign of Ibrahim Pasha*, 2 (London, 1835), pp. 213–216.

53 Y. Hofman, "The Administration of Syria and Palestine under Egyptian Rule (1831–1840)," in Ma'oz (above, n. 6), pp. 311–333; M. Abir, "Local Leadership and Early Reforms in Palestine, 1800–1834," in Ma'oz (*ibid.*), pp. 284–310.

54 Popoff, pp. 170–174; Neophytos (above, n. 5), pp. 86–89; Olin, *Travels in Egypt, Arabia Petraea and the Holy Land (1840)*, 2 (New York, 1844), pp. 299–301; J.D. Paxton, *Letters from Palestine (1835–38)* (London, 1839), pp. 119–120, 148; Kinglake (above, n. 42), pp. 177–179.

55 Popoff, p. 170; Hurewitz (above, n. 33), 1, pp. 105–106.

56 Popoff, pp. 172–173, 191–193, 202, 206; Neophytos, p. 86.

57 Paxton, p. 148; Olin, pp. 113–114 (both above, n. 54).

58 J. Roy, *A Collection of Curious Travels and Voyages* (London, 1693), pp. 375–377; A.C. Luke (tr.), *A Spanish Franciscan's Narrative of a Journey to the Holy Land (about 1555)* (London, 1927), pp. 34–35; J. Lotfie (ed.), *Torkington's Pilgrimage* (London, n.d.), pp. 47–50; A Greek indictment dated 1821 (a moment of weakness for that community in the Empire, due to the

43

Greek war of independence) claimed that in 1520 the Franciscans bought a small cell in the church and in 1566 managed to acquire certain sections inside the church, whereas previously they were allowed to enter only in order to recite their prayers. In 1570 they were able to acquire yet another section. Popoff, p. 128.

59   Sandys (above, n. 8), pp. 139–141.

60   Popoff, p. 128.

61   *Ibid.*, p. 129; Metaxakis, p. 40; R.W. Hamilton, *A Guide to Bethlehem* (Jerusalem, 1939), p. 29.

62   See above, notes 23–25.

63   Popoff, pp. 117–118; Thompson (above, n. 23), 3, pp. 157–159; F.R. Chateaubriand, *Journal de Jérusalem* (Paris, 1854), pp. 67–68; F. Hasselquist, *Voyages and Travels in the Levant in the Years 1749, 50, 51, 52* (London, 1766), pp. 144–145.

64   Finn, 1, pp. 11, 31–32; 2, p. 36; Mislin, 2, pp. 229–230; Temperley, pp. 285, 296–297 (all, above, n. 8).

65   Temperley, pp. 284–286; M.T. Florinsky, *Russia. A History and an Interpretation*, 2 (New York, 1958), p. 861. See also note 61 above.

66   Popoff, pp. 223–239.

67   *Ibid.*, pp. 283–284; M. Ma'oz, *Ottoman Reform in Syria and Palestine 1840–1861* (Oxford, 1968), pp. 32–33.

68   Finn, 2, p. 21; Temperley, p. 284; T. Parfitt, "The French Consulate and the Jewish Yishuv in Eretz-Israel in the 19th Century" (Hebrew), *Cathedra* 5 (1977):144–161.

69   Temperley, pp. 280, 284–285, 290, 293, 508; Florinsky (above, n. 65), p. 861; A. Ramm, "The Crimean War," in *The New Cambridge Modern History*, 10 (Cambridge, 1960), p. 469; J.M. Thompson, *Louis Napoleon and the Second Empire* (Oxford, 1954), pp. 82–157.

70   Finn, 1, p. 13; Tobler (above, n. 27), pp. 391–393.

71   Popoff, pp. 326–330.

72   Sanjian, p. 196.

73   Finn, 1, pp. 72ff; de Teste, 3, pp. 229–230, 240, 297–298; Collin, pp. 47, 121–156 (documents); T.G. Stavrou, "Russian Interest in the Levant 1843–1848," *MEJ* 17 (1963):101–102.

74   Popoff, pp. 335–337, 343–344; Temperley, p. 288.

75   Temperley, *loc. cit.*; de Testa, 3, pp. 275, 301–302.

76   Temperley, p. 288.

77   De Testa, 3, pp. 251–252.

78   Temperley, pp. 288–289. The closure of the Dardanelles could not be carried out because in December 1852 Louis Napoleon seized power and needed all his forces at home.

79   De Testa, 3, pp. 256, 303–305.

80   *Ibid.*, pp. 230–232 ("French Note"), 274–281, 294–312; Collin, pp. 157–159 (documents) ("Greek *Firmān*"); Temperley, pp. 290–291, 294–296.

81   Temperley, p. 297.

82   *Ibid.*, pp. 295–300; de Testa, 3, pp. 260–261. See above, note 39.

83   De Testa, 3, pp. 236–237 *(firmān)*, 271–312; Temperley, pp. 304–332; H. Temperley and L.M. Penson, *Foundations of British Foreign Policy. From Pitt (1793) to Salisbury (1902)* (Cambridge, 1938), pp. 139–144.

84   Mislin, pp. 229–230.

RUSSIAN ACTIVITY IN PALESTINE
IN THE NINETEENTH CENTURY

ALEX CARMEL

T *he revitalized interest of European powers in Palestine in the nineteenth century has attracted the attention of historians of various nationalities and persuasions. A. Carmel presents a comprehensive description of Russian activity in Palestine during that period, both complementing and expanding on problems raised in R. Simon's article in this volume. The author also takes issue with some of the commonly accepted notions of the Russian involvement in Palestine in the last century.*

From an international viewpoint, Napoleon's invasion of Palestine in 1799 was the most dramatic event in the history of the country since the Ottoman conquest in the early sixteenth century. For three hundred years, Europe had shown no particular interest in Palestine. The discovery of the New World and the rise of the Protestant Church, to which the notion of "holy places" was foreign, both took place simultaneously with the Turkish conquest of Palestine. It was these two events that were largely responsible for drawing Europe's attention elsewhere.

France, which extended protection to most of the foreigners and Catholic institutions in Palestine as part of the capitulations agreements, had been only slightly active in the country for hundreds of years prior to Napoleon's invasion; the scope of its activities during this period was determined by the relationship between the local authorities and the central government in Constantinople. Russia, in turn, had established a legal basis for its activities on behalf of the Greek Orthodox minority and its institutions in Palestine only in 1774 (through the Treaty of Küçük Kaynarca).

Due to the chaos that reigned during that period, very few pilgrims and Christian travellers were willing to risk the dangers involved in a journey to the Holy Land. Still, the history of Palestine in the Ottoman period emerges from the travel literature of the times, and the decline of the Ottoman Empire is still visible in the country's ruins.

45

Palestine became the focus of international attention in the spring of 1799, when Napoleon reached the country via Egypt in the midst of the war between revolutionary France and England. The siege on Acre was doomed to failure, but as the British historian Fisher pointed out long ago:

> Much as they might mock at the pope and the priest, [they] read with a thrill the bulletins of the young French general who had taken Palestine, had set up his quarters in the monastery of Nazareth, and had read the Bible to his officers under the Syrian sky . . .. The recovery of Palestine from the Turks, which appealed even to the Baptist chief of a British cabinet at the end of the great war [1914–1918], was an idea which exercised a yet more powerful attraction for the countrymen of St. Louis . . .[1]

In Palestine, Napoleon's short-lived conquest made no immediate change. The French retraced their steps and the infamous "rule of the pashas", which banned foreign activity, was reinstated. For Palestine, the importance of Napoleon's campaign was to show up only later. France had had a taste of wresting the Holy Land from the hands of the infidels and found it to its liking. It now became clear that only a shadow remained of the powerful Turkish conqueror of the sixteenth century. A few years earlier, the Russians had also defeated the Ottomans and had, *inter alia*, gained the right to protect the Greek Orthodox community in the Ottoman Empire, including most of the Christian Arabs in Palestine. Now, only a miracle had saved the Turks in Acre, when besieged by ten thousand ailing, homesick French soldiers. The Christian world realized that Turkish rule over Palestine was not what it had been; nor did this escape the eye of England and Prussia.

At the same time, the Holy Land began to gain importance in the eyes of the Protestant Church, and it was assigned a greater role in the vision of the Latter Days.[2] On January 3, 1826, John Nicolayson entered the gates of Jerusalem with determination in his heart and money in his pocket, to establish a permanent home for the Church of England in the Holy City.[3]

The 1830s marked an important turning point for foreign activity in Palestine. In 1831, Muhammad Ali, the governor of the Egyptian province, turned against the Ottoman Sultan, sent his army into Palestine, moved northward and, supported by France, penetrated Asia Minor. At this point, in order to prevent the collapse of the Ottoman Empire (which in its weakened state was a desirable neighbor), the Tsar hurriedly signed a defense treaty with the Sultan and saw to it that powerful Egypt did not replace the weakened Ottomans.

46

The Egyptians substituted a centralized administrative government for the shoddy Turkish administration in Palestine and, to calm the international storm that the conquerors had aroused by changing the status quo, adopted a liberal policy toward the non-Muslims and foreigners in Palestine. Thus, for the first time, the Egyptians opened Palestine's doors to Europeans, to prove to the Christian powers that their tolerant regime was infinitely superior to the Turkish administration that preceded it. Even John Nicolayson, the subject of a nation as powerful and friendly to the Ottomans as Britain, wrote:

> Only when the Egyptian army under the command of Ibrahim Pasha entered Palestine could I really settle in Jerusalem for the first time. Thus the establishment of the permanent (Protestant) mission in J e r u s a l e m itself took place only in 1833.[4]

Nicolayson's tireless activity quickly led the Catholic and Greek Orthodox churches to reorganize themselves in Palestine. Similarly, the increasing involvement of France and Russia in the region prompted England to establish its first permanent foreign consulate in Jerusalem. Thus, during the period of Egyptian rule, the basis was laid for widespread European activity in Palestine, with Russia playing a leading role.

Russian Activity in Palestine before World War I: An Overview

Despite the vast literature on this subject, the motivations for Russia's policies in Palestine have remained largely unfathomed.[5] Apparently, these policies were not well thought out, and the sources at our disposal are not conducive to a methodical investigation of these motivations. What follows, then, will constitute an attempt to describe the special relationship between Russia and Palestine, and a review of the major steps by which Russia sought to protect, and if possible to further, its interests in the country.

Russian pilgrims camp in Galilee

Baptism in the Sea of Galilee

Russian activity in Palestine should be viewed in light of two factors that made its involvement different from that of other powers. Most inhabitants of 'Holy Russia' bore deep religious ties to the 'Holy Land'. Palestine was truly part of their lives, even if the holy places were then ruled by non-believers. This relationship was expressed in massive pilgrimages to Palestine, a phenomenon that overshadowed both in numbers and in fervor such activity in the rest of the Christian world. In the first half of the nineteenth century when the powers began to set foot in Palestine, France and England found that their major rival, Russia, held a natural and unchallenged advantage in the area of pilgrimages. A report by the British vice-consul, W.T. Young, for Easter 1840, clearly shows his distress at the sight of the group of enthusiastic, zealous pilgrims from Russia arriving in Jerusalem, "many of them old soldiers in their regimentals." Russia had not yet formulated a policy toward Palestine, but it was already suspected by its rival, England, of planning a conspiracy: "The pilgrims from Russia have been heard to speak openly of the period being at hand when this country will be under the Russian government."[6] This is probably one of the first manifestations of open hostility to Russia by other powers in the country — even before Russia had conspired anything, good or bad, or had a permanent representative in Jerusalem.

Cakes of olive-oil soap prepared for pilgrims; designs show Church of the Holy Sepulchre, and St. George

Most of the pilgrims who had aroused Young's anger were poor villagers. Kopek after kopek had been set aside until a village could afford to send one of its men (or even better, one of its women) to Jerusalem to bring back the "holy fire" from the Church of the Holy Sepulchre in a lamp carried by the pilgrim. Over the years, thousands of churches in Russia, some of them in remote places, were lit by lamps that burned the "holy fire" from Jerusalem, thereby sustaining Russia's ties to the holy city. In the eyes of Western Christianity, particularly the Protestants, the ceremony associated with the "holy fire" was an act of paganism. However, the thousands of Russians who annually crowded into the Church of the Holy Sepulchre on the day before Easter firmly believed that the miracle of the kindling of the "holy fire" was wrought by their cries of "Oh Lord, give us our fire."[7] The story of these pilgrims, many of whom perished during the arduous journey, is told by Stephen Graham, an English author who accompanied them.[8] By water or land, by train or by foot (and even crawling on their knees), masses of Russians in black cloaks and sheepskins converged on the "holy places" and proved by means of their fervent devotion and impressive presence, the depth of Russian feeling for Palestine.

Nineteenth century woodcut showing Temple Mount. It was used to imprint design on skin prior to tatooing pilgrims, to commemorate the pilgrimage. Note the Hebrew word ירושלים in mirror writing

The second factor that characterized Russian activity and lent it an advantage over the other powers competing in Palestine, was the existence of a large Greek Orthodox community to which the great majority of Christian Arabs belonged. In terms of religion, most Russians and most of the Christian inhabitants of Palestine drew upon the same Eastern Christian source once centered in Constantinople. When the powers began a frantic search for possible protegés in Palestine during the first half of the nineteenth century — in 1840 France extended patronage to 3,000 Catholic Arabs; the Protestant powers were beginning their missionary activities — the country already contained 20,000 Greek Orthodox Christians who were politically oriented toward Russia, their declared protector since 1774. They constituted an absolute majority of the Christians in Palestine.[9]

Ostensibly, Russia's place in Palestine was secure. In retrospect, however, it seems that it was this sense of security that shaped Russia's hesitant, unimaginative policy in the Holy Land. The Russians were aware of their advantages and, unlike the other powers, had no need to justify their activity in the country. Anyone entering the arena in the 1840s as well equipped as Russia could afford a little moderation — and this was just what the Russians sought. Russia was feared in those days by all the powers (and not only on the "Eastern Question"); it had no need or desire to provoke them further in Palestine. Maintaining the status quo, in which it obviously enjoyed the upper hand, seemed to be in Russia's best interest. At no time, then or later, did any official Russian body call for Russian dominion over Palestine. However, neither did any official Russian body make concessions in Palestine to another power, even after the outbreak of World War I, when France and England could also boast of considerable achievements upon which to base their claims in Palestine.[10]

In fact, during the seventy to eighty years of rivalry between the powers, Russia's initial advantage dwindled to a considerable extent. It is true that when World War I began, most pilgrims in the Holy Land were still Russian. The impressive buildings in the Russian Compound, and the new hospices in Jaffa, Haifa, Nazareth, Jericho and elsewhere, made life more bearable for these

Feeding the masses of pilgrims

pilgrims than for those who arrived in mid-century. The hospital in Jerusalem and half a dozen clinics run by the Russians saved the lives of hundreds of pilgrims who, under the previous conditions, would surely have died. But even then, according to Grigori Rasputin who visited the country at this time, the thousands of Russian pilgrims who crowded onto Russia's outmoded ships (at five times above capacity) and could not be properly accommodated in Palestine, were treated like a herd of cattle.[11] However, compared with the medical institutions established by the Western powers, and the new hospices and modern hotels erected by Jews, Catholics, Protestants and Templars, the Russian accommodations were insignificant both in number and in quality.

Moreover, Catholic and Protestant pilgrimages were now increasing rapidly and, in addition, a stream of wealthy tourists from the West began to reach Palestine. Western pilgrims and travellers may have been less colorful than the devout Russians, but they left more money in the pockets of local merchants, and were thus more desirable. In 1882, the first large organized group arrived, composed of over 1,000 French Catholics — a large group even by Russian standards. In contrast to the Russians, these wealthy Frenchmen impressed the inhabitants of Palestine with the orderliness of their visit. Of particular interest is the comment of a Protestant writer, probably J. Schumacher, the American vice-consul in Haifa: "The (French) pilgrims do not conceal the fact that they are modelling themselves after the Crusades, and intend to repeat them (and conquer Palestine)."[12] This is reminiscent of the earlier suspicions of vice-consul Young with regard to the Russian pilgrims!

Indeed, mass pilgrimages were still considered a clear indication of vested interests in Palestine. The more extensive they were, the more they were suspect. For this reason, the Turkish authorities began to encourage the Nabi Musa celebrations that, from the 1870s onwards, annually attracted over 10,000 Muslims to Jerusalem. These celebrations, which were held during the Easter season and whose participants were permitted to carry arms, were undoubtedly intended to accentuate Muslim interest in the holy places and provide a counterbalance to the growing Christian pilgrimage.[13] By World War I, Russia no longer held an unchallenged card in the game over possession of Palestine.

Alongside the decline in Russia's status as a leader in the sphere of pilgrimages, there was another, even greater, loss — a steady drop in the number of Greek Orthodox Christians in Palestine. In 1840, nine out of ten Christian Arabs belonged to this denomination; in 1880 they numbered, at the most, only seven out of ten. During those four decades the number of Catholic Arabs quadrupled to nearly 12,000, and the Protestant mission was also making headway at the expense of the Greek Orthodox community. The first reliable census in Palestine, carried out in 1922, showed that the Greek Orthodox had lost their absolute majority. Only 45 percent of the Christian Arabs (33,369) were Greek Orthodox, while the two large Catholic sects (the Roman and Greek Catholics) were closing the gap at 35 percent (25,436).[14]

Loss of numerical superiority was only one problem facing the Greek Orthodox community. Its finest young people now began to attend Western schools, and many became Catholics and Protestants, and sought the protection of France, England, and especially Germany. The some twenty schools established by the Russians in the span of seventy years — some having only one class and existent thanks to the "baksheesh" paid to parents — could not compare in numbers or in quality with the programs run by the Western churches.[15] The extremely wealthy Greek Orthodox Patriarchate in Jerusalem not only scorned its Arab flock and refused to spend money on educating the young, but also did its best to prevent the Russians from intervening in the educational system, which was under the sole authority of the Greek Patriarch. The bitter disputes that ensued had a negative effect upon Russian activity. This was compounded by the reluctance of community members to learn the Russian language. Young Christian Arabs seeking to enter the world of commerce were of the opinion that learning French, English or even German at the more modern Western schools in Palestine was infinitely more useful.

However, education, medicine and religion (the Greek Orthodox Patriarchate zealously kept the Russians from repairing dilapidated village churches) were not the only spheres in which Russia was unable to maintain its status in the eyes of the community it protected. In the course of time, Russia's political standing in Palestine also deteriorated. In the 1850s, Russia made one forceful attempt to protect Greek Orthodox rights in the holy places, but the West retaliated in the Crimea, inflicting a military defeat the likes of which the Russians had not known since the days of Napoleon Bonaparte. In 1872, Russia exerted all its influence to keep in office a Greek Patriarch of Jerusalem to whom it wished to honor for his faithful friendship to Russia and the Greek Orthodox Arab community. It failed.

Beyond the borders of Palestine, Russian power was also challenged. In the late 1870s, for the first time in fifty years, Russia managed to defeat the Turks; however, the Western powers convening in Berlin turned the military victory into a political downfall. In 1904, Japan wreaked havoc on Russia, where the ravages of revolution had already begun to take their toll. Three years later, an impoverished Austria also outwitted Russia, annexing the province of Bosnia. Hence the Arabs under Russian patronage, who decorated their homes with portraits of the Tsar and wept if any ill befell him,[16] had much cause for concern during the second half of the nineteenth and early twentieth century.

However, the fact that on the eve of World War I most of the Christian Arabs in Palestine were still Greek Orthodox, masked the deterioration in Russia's status. Reality was also distorted by the tendency of Western institutions to exaggerate the scope of Russian influence in Palestine (an exaggeration that has found its way into research studies largely based on Western sources), in the hope of making their own countries more active. Russia's decline did not culminate in a sudden collapse that might have motivated the adoption of a new, more consistent policy, or led the Western powers to ease their pressure on Russia, which would

Greeting card prepared for Russian pilgrims to Palestine, mid-nineteenth century

have been beneficial.

As time went on, the Russians began to sense the weakening of their two advantages, but the "patchwork" policy they employed to counteract this was hardly helpful. Many new laws enacted to improve the situation were ineffective, and some were so ridiculous that they made Russia's rivals even more concerned and suspicious. Other steps taken were ostentatious and caused great alarm. A case in point was the Russian Compound affair. While the West was slowly expanding its presence in the Old City of Jerusalem and Russia's religious delegation in Jerusalem was experiencing financial hardship, a representative of the Russian Company of Steam Navigation and Trade began at the end of the 1850s to build 'New Jerusalem' (as the Russian Compound was first called) outside the city walls. Without doubt, this was the most impressive building project in Palestine in modern times. It is no wonder that inferiority in pilgrim traffic and in number of protegés made the Western powers all the more sensitive to the noisy lumbering of the Russian bear.

Why didn't Russia exploit the meager presence of Western powers in nearby Syria to establish schools there? Didn't it realize that an Arab with Russian sympathies should be appointed Greek Orthodox Patriarch of Antioch (whose see was in Damascus), rather than leaving the post in the hands of the legitimate Greek hierarchy? The Western powers believed it was only their constant alertness and tireless activity that kept Russia from realizing its true aim of taking over Palestine. From the outset, the Russians were aware of the oversensitivity of the other powers (so clearly expressed in the Crimean War), and tried their best to avoid provocation in Palestine. Only twice — after the Crimean War and following the Berlin Congress — was Russia sufficiently humiliated to deviate from its cautious, hesitant policy and breathe some spirit into its activity in Palestine — again only for a short time. As will be shown below, Russia's inconsistent policy in Palestine rarely enabled its representatives in the country to return the hail of blows inflicted by the other powers in Palestine and by Turkey. It is, thus, not surprising that the Russian bear began to stumble and, by the time World War I erupted, Russia no longer had any real claims upon which to base its right to Palestine. It was England and France, Russia's constant opponents and now its allies, who were called upon to decide the future of that country.

Russian Activity in Palestine before the Crimean War

D. Hopwood claims that Russia's first official representative in Palestine was a consul sent to Jaffa in 1820 to assist pilgrims passing through the town on their way to Jerusalem.[17] This is difficult to verify since the documents of the Tsarist Foreign Office are not available for examination. Hebrew sources relate that in 1819 the Russian consul in Acre warned the Jews that Abdullah Pasha, the district governor, intended to execute the local rabbi for ignoring his specific orders regarding the burial of a Jew condemned to death. The Greek monk Neophytos of Cyprus, a member of the Brotherhood of the Holy Selpulchre, even mentions in his *Annals* a Russian consul at Jaffa (George Mostras) as early as February 1812.[18]

Although it is difficult to establish precisely when the first Russian official in Palestine was appointed, it is clear that high level representation was existent only toward the late 1830s. After, or perhaps simultaneous with, the opening of the first British consulate in Jerusalem early in 1839,[19] Russian consular activity was heightened. In December 1838, K.M. Basili of the Russian Foreign Office was appointed consul in Jaffa. In August 1839, the Russian consulate was moved from Jaffa to Beirut, and thereafter served both Syria and Palestine. Four years later, Basili was raised to the post of consul-general. From time to time, Basili also travelled to Jerusalem, particularly during the Easter season. He was ordered by his government to assist the pilgrims, to be as friendly as possible with the Patriarch and the institutions of the Orthodox Church, to maintain good relations with the heads of the other denominations, and "to pay attention to the interests of religion and the Eastern Church which never cease to engage the attention of the Imperial Court."[20] In view of the transportation difficulties in those days, Basili was able to fulfill very few of those guidelines.

In contrast, the consuls of England, Prussia and France, who had meanwhile settled in Jerusalem itself, undoubtedly were very effective in representing the various affairs and religious interests of their countries. However, it should be remembered that at this early stage of foreign activity in Palestine, the consuls' duties were as yet extremely limited.[21] From the start, however, they lost no opportunity to attack the "long arm" of Russia. Thus, for example, the British consul-general in Beirut, Hugh Rose, was convinced that Russia was behind the difficulties posed by the Turks when the Anglican Church was built in Jerusalem in the early 1840s.[22] This accusation cannot be proven.

Rose, who battled fiercely to prevent a Russian political victory in Palestine at Britain's expense, was astonished when, a few years later, the Russian representative proposed that Britain assume responsibility for Palestine's Russian Jewish community. Basili even said he was certain the Russian government would be happy to move the whole Jewish population of Russia to Palestine and grant them British protection, just to be rid of them. In the eyes of the British, then anxious for as many protegés as possible, the generosity of the Russians was astonishing. In a detailed report to Foreign Minister Palmerston on his talks with Basili — one of the most enlightening contemporary documents on the state of the Jews in Palestine[23] — Rose comments that Russia would never have shown such good will to the French, its primary rival, and to their Catholic protegés. He assumes that Basili's willingness had its basis in the Christian hatred of Jews in the Near East. It was hatred that kept the Russians from extending protection to the Jews while seeking Russia's major objective — to establish itself as the uncontested guardian of the Greek Orthodox community. Rose was probably right in this assumption, which explains the long-standing indifference of the Russian representatives in Palestine toward their Jewish subjects. "The Jews who were Russian subjects loved their consul from afar, and came to him only when there was no choice" — this is how Judge Frumkin summed up the relationship at the end of the Ottoman period.[24] It should also be noted that it was the Jews of Jerusalem who rejected Basili's generous offer to transfer them under British protection. Fear of the missionary intentions of the British consul, James Finn, led many Jews to prefer the questionable guardianship of the Russians, and very few took up Basili's suggestion.[25] In any case, this episode proves that Russia was making no effort, obvious or otherwise, to gain control of Palestine, at least in the 1840s. A country willing to place the largest Jewish community in the world under British patronage in Palestine could not have been aspiring to be the region's chief decision-maker. In the 1850s and thereafter, Russia became less willing to donate its Jewish subjects to other powers, but this resulted more from the blow the powers had dealt to Russia's status in Palestine than from a change of objectives.

Throughout the history of Russian activity in Palestine during the last century of Ottoman rule, the consul who left the greatest mark was Basili. The main reason is that during his term of office, a Russian religious delegation was sent to

Jerusalem and remained active in one form or another until World War I. The undefined authority and semi-secular duties of this delegation led them to compete with the Russian consuls in Jerusalem in the years that followed, severely affecting consular activity.

The idea of sending a permanent religious delegation to Jerusalem was first proposed by the Procurator of the Holy Synod. Tsar Nikolai I turned the proposal over to the Foreign Minister, K.R. Nesselrode, who wrote a detailed memorandum on the miserable state of the Greek Orthodox community in Palestine, downtrodden by the Muslims and in danger of succumbing to Catholic and Protestant missionaries with whom the backward Greek clergy could not compete. According to Nesselrode, Russia had not sent a senior church representative to Palestine until then in order to avoid rousing Turkish suspicions and jealousy on the part of the other powers. However, now that an Anglican Bishop to Jerusalem had been appointed (in 1841), a delegate of the Russian clergy could be sent to the Holy City without fear. Still, Nesselrode suggested that the delegate carry out his mission disguised as a pilgrim. The fact that he was an emissary of the Russian government had to be kept secret. In 1843, Porfiri Uspenski was sent to Palestine. He donned the pilgrim's mantle, but had clear orders to collect information that would enable Russia to better deal with its affairs in the Holy Land. This was hardly what the Procurator of the Synod had imagined when he raised the idea of a religious delegation two years earlier.

After nearly a year in Palestine, visiting remote villages where a Russian had never yet set foot, Porfiri returned home with grim descriptions of the plight of Russia's protegés, who were easy prey for the Catholics and Protestants. Porfiri told his superiors that the large sums of money collected in Russian churches every year for Palestine were subverted into the pockets of the corrupt Greek Orthodox clergy. The dilapidated churches in the villages housed the sheep of these Arab priests, who could not even read or write. The emissary lamented the fact that while the Greek hierarchy and Arab clergy exchanged insults and fought incessantly, the well-oiled Catholic and Protestant missionary machine was making inroads with the children of the Orthodox community, whose elementary education was neglected by everyone else. His conclusion was that the other powers in Palestine were slowly but surely pulling the rug from under Russia's feet. Steps had to be taken at once to protect the status of the Eastern Church in the Holy Land.

The Church and the Foreign Office in St. Petersburg deliberated for five years before they sent Porfiri back to Jerusalem. In 1848, the first religious delegation set forth to rehabilitate the Orthodox Church and to help it defend itself against Western influences which had become even stronger since the appointment in 1847 of a Roman Catholic ("Latin") Patriarch, whose seat was moved from Rome to Jerusalem for the first time since the Crusades. The delegation was allotted a paltry annual budget of 10,000 rubles and was headed by Porfiri, whose rank was lower than that of the Latin Patriarch Joseph Valerga and the Protestant

57

Bishop Samuel Gobat. Upon departure, Porfiri was granted the inferior title of an Archimandrite and instructed to continue his disguise as a pilgrim. Hence there was no chance that he and his four colleagues could succeed in their mission. Deprived in advance of any official standing, Porfiri, committed as he was, could not secure for Russia any lasting achievement in Palestine. The Turks did not recognize him, the Greek Orthodox clergy were extremely hostile because he tried to intervene in their affairs, and the Orthodox Arabs, who appreciated his efforts, were nonetheless disappointed that their great protector could not work out in the open.

Russia's interest in its delegation in Jerusalem was not long-lasting. When the Crimean War erupted five years later, St. Petersburg hastened to evacuate Basili and the consulate staff from the country, but Porfiri was forgotten. It was only with great difficulty that the Russian pilgrim was extricated from Jerusalem by the Austrian consul.[26]

While Russia failed to provide the community it protected in Palestine with its most elementary needs, Tsar Nikolai took a stubborn and even an aggressive stand on the rights of the Eastern Church in the holy places — a stand both unfortunate and ill-timed. When Napoleon III sought to enhance France's status in this area too, and to alter the status quo to the detriment of the Greek Orthodox, Russia felt things had gone too far. The never-ending stream of Greek Orthodox Arabs joining the Catholic Church which Porfiri was always warning about was, indeed, a source of anger, but the Arabs of Palestine had never been of central importance to the Russian Tsar. However, as the Tsar told the British Ambassador to the Ottoman Empire:

> There are several millions of Christians whose interests I am called upon to watch over, while the right of doing so is secured to me by Treaty. I must truly say that I make a moderate and sparing use of my right, and I will freely confess that it is one which is attended with obligations occasionally very inconvenient; but I cannot recede from the discharge of a distinct duty . . . .[27]

Pressured by France, the Turks now threatened to keep the Tsar from fulfilling this commitment, which he saw as infinitely more important than the preference for devout Catholic nuns over ignorant Arab priests in some school in the Galilee or Judea. England and France were oblivious to Russia's restrained policy in Palestine and doubted the sincerity of the Tsar's promise that he was not seeking to expand Russia's borders at the expense of the Turks. They interpreted his rigid stand toward the Ottomans on the question of the Holy Places as further proof of Russia's aggressive intentions. Thus they joined forces to wipe out the Russian powerhouse in the East.[28]

From the Crimean War until 1870

The devastating Russian defeat in the Crimean War motivated it to adopt a forceful, more consistent policy in Palestine, at least in theory. A decision was reached to create a new religious mission, as explained in a memorandum drawn up by the Foreign Minister for the use of the Tsar:

> Our political relationship with Turkey and her own position vis-à-vis the other Powers have completely changed ... At the present time every half-measure will not only bring no benefit, but may even harm our mission in Jerusalem ... We must establish our "presence" in the East not politically but through the church.[29]

Now that real Russian influence had dwindled, it was important to put on a show of strength. Thus this new religious delegation was headed by a bishop rather than an archimandrite.

The new religious delegation did make a strong impression, but not exactly the kind that was desired. Early in 1858, the streets of Jerusalem rang with cheers in honor of the first Russian bishop in Jerusalem. Only six years later, the head of the delegation, Cyril Naumov, a theology professor summoned from the podium to represent Russia in Palestine, was called home in shame. A ridiculously small annual budget of 11,000 rubles for Naumov and his twelve associates, ill-defined authority which led to a serious dispute with the Russian consul (also sent to Jerusalem in 1858, for the first time), and various grandiose plans thought up behind his back and implemented by the Russians in Jerusalem — all these doomed Naumov's delegation to failure even before beginning its work. Under the existing circumstances Naumov could neither care for the pilgrims, aid the local Arabs and Greek Orthodox along the lines of the Western churches, nor improve relations with the Jewish community which Russia now also hoped to rely on in its hour of need. As we shall see below, the Tsar's brother had other ideas that contrasted greatly with the instructions issued by the Foreign Minister regarding the type of activity desired in Jerusalem. Bishop Naumov, who continued to insist that he be allowed to fulfill the duties imposed upon him, was presented by the new consul as licentious and a good-for-nothing. He was sent home in 1864 in the wake of the biggest scandal experienced by Russia in Palestine before World War I.[30]

Just at this moment, when Russia's powerlessness was most visible to all, Grand Duke Constantine, the second son of Tsar Nikolai I and brother of Alexander II, who became Tsar in 1855, sent Boris Pavlovich Mansurov to Jerusalem on a mission of his own. The Grand Duke wanted to investigate whether the steamship company he was setting up could benefit from transporting Russian pilgrims to Palestine.[31] At that time, maritime transportation was nearly monopolized by Austrian and French steamships.

Mansurov, a bustling man of action, came to Jerusalem and saw more than he was asked to see. He immediately discovered that the country was overflowing with European institutions whose growing influence was far surpassing that of the local authorities and the Orthodox religious frameworks. Mansurov asserted, and rightly so, that Russia was hardly taking part in the competition between the powers. He said that Eastern populations were mainly impressed by the visual — and that Russia's activities were not noticeable at all. There were no monasteries, hospitals or hospices — in other words, none of the institutions that the other powers had been concentrating on with such intensity. A Russian steamship company would thus be useful not only in itself, but as a show of Russian power in Palestine and a means of supporting Russia's protegés. The company would bring pilgrims to the country, plan their trips, and tend to their needs. It would establish a consulate that would also serve as a branch office of the company — a combination of functions then common in the coastal cities. It would build hospices to accommodate pilgrims, a proper hospital, a church, and quarters for the religious delegation, all in one compound. Mansurov believed this ambitious project could be largely financed by the collections in Russian churches "on behalf of the Holy Land."[32] The fact that the religious delegation was to play only a modest role in the project, and that funds that had formerly gone to the Greek Orthodox Church would now be channelled elsewhere, posed formidable problems indeed. Nevertheless, Constantine, for whom the Palestine issue was close to heart, swiftly adopted Mansurov's recommendations.

Shortly after Mansurov's return, the Tsar established a Palestine Commission under royal patronage. Headed by Grand Duke Constantine, and with Mansurov serving as the acting director, the Commission collected a fortune of over one million rubles within five years from the Tsar, the Russian Treasury, and public and private donors — including the churches. In 1859, the Grand Duke came to Palestine to affix his signature to the huge real-estate transactions carried out at the recommendation of Mansurov. Among the purchases were the Turkish parade grounds (the Maidan) to the west of the city, eventually known as the Russian Compound; a large plot at the top of Mt. of Olives; and a valuable piece of land near the Church of the Holy Sepulchre where the Russians later built the Church of Aleksandr Nevski. Five years later, the Russians could proudly point to their 'New Jerusalem'. For 25 years, the other powers had been building all over the country; busy as they had been, however, Russia could point to the most concentrated and impressive construction project of all![33]

The envy of the other powers and the Russians' pride were short-lived. When construction activities were at their peak, the Grand Duke was appointed Viceroy to the King of Poland. The Palestine Commission disbanded and its money ran out. For the time being, the buildings designed to house the consulate and the religious delegation remained on paper. The opulent church and the enormous hospices stood unused because there was no more money to complete the interiors. All the wind had blown out of the Grand Duke's sails. The Russian Compound, surrounded by a high wall, was for the time being an impressive complex of buildings without purpose. Russian pilgrims continued to be robbed by the Greek clergy in whose monasteries they sought shelter, as in the past. The large religious delegation, which according to the original plan of the Foreign

Nineteenth century picture postcard

Office was to cure Russia's ills in the Holy Land, was replaced with a low-ranking priest named Leonid Kavelin, charged with care of the pilgrims.[34]

It seems that Russian activity in Palestine in the mid-1860s was saved from a total standstill only by chance. The Tsar appointed a new committee to deal with affairs in Palestine. Its members included the Procurator of the Holy Synod, the director of the Asian Department of the Foreign Office, and Mansurov. However, Mansurov, desiring to complete the abandoned Russian Compound buildings and accustomed to working independently, did not get along with his colleagues, and the old disputes flared up once more in Jerusalem between the Greek Orthodox Patriarch, the Russian consul, and Leonid Kavelin who headed the diminished religious delegation. To avoid a new scandal, Count Nikolai Pavlovich Ignatev, Russia's forceful Ambassador to Constantinople, sent Antonin Kapustin, who was in charge of the Embassy church, to relieve Leonid temporarily and find out, once and for all, the source of the constant bickering in the Holy City.

Contrary to the original intentions, Antonin remained in Palestine for nearly thirty years.[35] With piety, resourcefulness and boundless energy, Antonin searched the land for sites of historical-religious significance. Before long, he had purchased tracts of land throughout the country that eventually became Russia's major footholds in Palestine. In 1866, for example, he bought a large plot in Beit

61

Jalla, which had a sizeable Greek Orthodox population and was an important center of Catholic missionary activity. This became the site of the first Russian school in Palestine and a teacher's seminary for women. In 1868, in the face of numerous obstacles, Antonin succeeded in purchasing 'Abraham's Oak' in Alonei Mamrei. Nearby, he founded a hospice for Russian pilgrims, and in the early twentieth century, a church was added on. In Ein Karem, also a focal point of Catholic activity, Antonin battled for possession of a large tract of land that became a Russian colony in the fullest sense of the word. It had extensive orchards, hospices, a school, and quarters for Russians desiring to live out their lives in the Holy Land. In the region of Abu Kabir, near Jaffa, Antonin acquired the hill where, according to tradition, Jesus brought Tabitha back to life. The church and monastery built there served Russian pilgrims arriving and departing from Jaffa. Antonin also bought property on the Mount of Olives and elsewhere.

In 1871, even his benefactor, Ambassador Ignatev, asked Antonin to control his penchant for buying property, saying that it made Russia's rivals in the Holy Land envious and suspicious, and caused them to double their own efforts; and a year later, the Holy Synod explicitly forbade Antonin to continue the "undesirable" acquisition of land.[36]

Pilgrims visiting a Russian Orthodox church in Ein Karem

Thus, another chapter in the history of Russian activity in Palestine came to an end. Most of the land upon which Russia's institutions were built was purchased not only against the will of the Russian government, but actually also in opposition to Turkish law. Only in 1873 did Russia sign a pact that permitted its subjects to acquire real-estate in the Ottoman Empire, with the proviso that within the purchased territory, Russian subjects would not be protected by the Capitulations.

The Orthodox Palestine Society

The final chapter in the history of Russian involvement in Palestine, during which most of the activity was organized and coordinated by a single body, is bound up with the person of Vasili Nikolaevich Khitrovo. Khitrovo first visited Palestine in 1871; from then on, it was part of his life. In cooperation with Antonin, who had almost no backing from home, Khitrovo began to drum up renewed interest in the Holy Land. During his first trip to the country, he discovered that thirty years after Porfiri Uspenski's outcry over the miserable plight of Russia's proteges in Palestine, the lot of the Greek Orthodox Arabs in the Holy Land had hardly improved. The exception were those — and their numbers were growing — who had become Catholics or Protestants, or whose children benefited from the services of the Western churches. Khitrovo's sermonizing and appeals to set up a Holy Land Society in Russia to manage its affairs in Palestine, as was done in the West, fell at first on deaf ears. However, just as the Crimean War had motivated Russia to reorganize its activities in Palestine in the late 1850s, at least in theory, the Berlin Congress provided further impetus for Russia to take itself in hand. Clause 22 of the Treaty of San Stefano which had compelled Turkey to recognize and extend Russian rights in the Holy Land was now replaced by Clause 62 of the treaty signed at the Berlin Congress which, instead, stressed the rights of France in the holy places.[37] Although it is difficult to find evidence in the sources that the setbacks of the late 1870s led Russia to reassess its policies in Palestine, this would seem a reasonable enough assumption.

Thus, Russia's official representation in Jerusalem was raised to a consulate-general and Antonin who refused to submit to the jurisdiction of anyone but his forceful patron Ignatev — now out of favor and no longer serving in Constantinople — was jailed. The consul-general Ilarionov now sought to assume control of Russian activities in Palestine, hoping to put an end, once and for all, to the religious delegation he considered the source of all Russia's misfortune.

Vasili Khitrovo saved Antonin from the ruin with which he was threatened. Exploiting the political changes, he was able to find supporters for his ideas, which contrasted sharply with the secular manner in which the consul-general and the Foreign Office sought to run Russian affairs in the Holy Land. An official of the highest rank won over by Khitrovo was Count E.V. Putyatin, the former Minister of Education, who had royal connections. Putyatin spoke to Maria Alexandrovna,

63

the wife of the Tsar, who was well-known for her deep attachment to the Holy Land. It was upon her express wish that the religious delegation remained in Jerusalem. Another influential friend of Putyatin was Konstantin Petrovich Pobedonostsev, tutor to the Tsarevich Alexander III and, from 1880, the Procurator of the Holy Synod. After the assassination of Alexander II in 1881, the Tsarevich assumed the throne and appointed his former tutor to be his close advisor.

That year, the new Tsar's brother, Grand Duke Sergei, visited Palestine where the people of Jerusalem were greatly impressed with the devotion of this pilgrim, who spent most of his time at prayer.[38] Upon his return home, the memory of the Holy Land remained firmly entrenched in his heart. This encourged Khitrovo to put into effect a plan he had been thinking of for years. With the aid of his influential friends, the Orthodox Palestine Society was founded in St. Petersburg in 1882, with Grand Duke Sergei as president. The aims of the society, as stated in its constitution, were to collect, study, and distribute in Russia information on the Holy Places of the East,[39] assist Orthodox pilgrims, found schools, hospitals and hostels, and grant material aid to the local Greek Orthodox communities, its churches, monasteries and clergy.

As a private body, the Orthodox Palestine Society was not subject to the Holy Synod and the Foreign Office — and thus, at first, it did not enjoy government funding. However, the presidency of the Grand Duke and the patronage of the Tsar awarded the society considerable status and prestige from the start. In the early years, the Russian consuls, and Mansurov — who represented the old Palestine Commission mainly concerned with the Russian Compound — tried to harass the new society, which was an ally of the religious delegation. For this reason, the Tsar ordered the dissolution of the Commission in 1889, transferring its authority to the society. He also began to appoint delegates of the Holy Synod and Foreign Office to sit on its executive committee, thus transforming it into a semi-official body. To signify this change, the title "imperial" was added to the society's name. In 1896, two years after the death of Antonin, the society also assumed responsibility for the religious delegation. Hence, other than purely consular services, all Russian activity in Palestine at the end of the century was concentrated in the hands of the Imperial Orthodox Palestine Society. Finally, even the consuls gave in and cooperated with it.

The financial standing of the society improved rapidly. At first it was wholly dependent on *ad hoc* collections and gifts, and could not plan its activities in advance. In 1886, Pobedonostsev, as head of the Holy Synod, agreed that throughout Russia the church offerings on Palm Sunday would be set aside for the society's use. The annual income from this collection — a quarter of a million rubles — supplied the society with most of its income. In the early twentieth century, when the flow of money slowed down, the Russian Treasury granted it 30,000 rubles a year. In 1912, the Treasury increased its funding in order to prevent the collapse of the Russian educational system in Syria, Lebanon and

Palestine. The society spent part of its income in Russia itself, where it maintained over forty branches with 5,000 members. However, most of its resources were channelled to Jerusalem, with the intention of finally strengthening Russia's position in Palestine.[40]

However, by the time the Imperial Orthodox Palestine Society was firmly entrenched in 1889, forty-five years had passed since Porfiri's return from Palestine with the tidings of Russia's decline in the Holy Land. Now, as the ninteenth century drew to an end the gap between Russia and the West was already too wide to close. While the Russians had disputed endlessly among themselves and with the Greek Orthodox hierarchy, the West had acquired status, protegés, and valuable experience. When Russia tried to regain its lost standing in the 1880s, it was already so weak, and its rivals so strong, that the foundations upon which it sought to build crumbled away beneath it. An attempt was made — half of Hopwood's book is devoted to the educational system founded by the Russians during these years — but in Palestine, as opposed to Syria and Lebanon, the yields were few. For example, a single Protestant school founded and run by J.L. Schneller during this period, seems to have left a deeper imprint on Palestine than the whole of the Imperial Russian endeavor.[41] Hopwood also clings to the awe-inspiring image of the Russian society harbored by the other powers, and since he does not compare its real educational achievements with those of parallel Western institutions, he too attributes to the society far greater importance than it actually had.[42]

Khitrovo and the new society saw their chief mission as the betterment of the Greek Orthodox Arab community, Russia's natural ally in Palestine. However, it was here that the society met with fierce opposition. The Greek Patriarch viewed the Russian program as harmful interference in his internal affairs and an attempt to turn Greek Orthodox Arabs into Russian Orthodox Arabs. The Greek Orthodox were particularly sensitive and suspicious that Russian involvement would lead the Arabs to seek independence from the Greek hierarchy, because the Russians had already aided the Bulgarians in this regard. The Jerusalem Patriarch had played a major role in the Bulgarian affair — one of the stormiest episodes in the history of the Greek Orthodox Church in the nineteenth century.

It had been the custom that the Bulgarian Patriarch was, in effect, appointed by the Greek Orthodox Patriarch in Constantinople. However, the Russian Ambassador Ignatev, a true Pan–Slavist, strongly upheld the right of the Bulgarians to break away from the Greek hierarchy and fight for religious independence. When the Bulgarians expelled the Greek Orthodox clergy from their country and founded an independent national church, Russia awarded it instant recognition. Whereupon the Patriarch in Constantinople called a meeting of Greek church leaders in the East that denounced the Bulgarian church and expelled it from the Orthodox Church (1872). The only one who refused to sign the Constantinople declaration was Cyril, the Jerusalem Patriarch. As a result, the assembly in Constantinople demanded that the Brotherhood of the Holy

Sepulchre (an institution nearly identical to the Jerusalem Patriarchate) remove Cyril from his post. Cyril had been a faithful friend of Porfiri Uspenski since his first stay in Palestine in the 1840s (when Cyril was Bishop of Lydda), and he was a firm supporter of Russia. When he was later elected Patriarch of Jerusalem, he deviated from long-standing custom and moved his seat from Constantinople to Jerusalem. This decision, supported by Porfiri, who believed it would renew the relationship between the Greek Patriarch and his forsaken Arab flock in Palestine, weakened Cyril's ties with the Greek Patriarchate in Constantinople.

The events of the 1870s bore out the Greek suspicions, and when Cyril openly rebelled against the authority of the Patriarch in Constantinople, in support of the Bulgarians, the Greek Orthodox Church in the Ottoman capital used all its influence to bring about the rebel's downfall. On the other hand, Russia, forcefully represented by Ambassador Ignatev, did its utmost to keep Cyril, whom the Greeks believed to be a Russian agent, in Jerusalem. A key figure in this affair, which caused an uproar in Palestine and was covered widely by the press,[43] was Nazif Pasha, the Governor of Jerusalem. Through the Russian consul, Ignatev tried first by enticement and then by intimidation to bring the Governor and the Brotherhood of the Holy Sepulchre over to Cyril's side. The consul offered Nazif Pasha a substantial bribe, but also threatened to have him fired if he did not support Cyril. He tried to frighten the Brotherhood by threatening to establish a separate Arab church for the local Orthodox population if it dared to dismiss the Patriarch.

The Orthodox Arab community, which was not well-organized, withheld support of Cyril because it feared taking a stance that might worsen relations with the Governor. The Brotherhood, on the other hand, was encouraged by the Governor's vacillation and openly opposed Cyril.

The person who tipped the scales in Russia's battle for prestige in Jerusalem was the consul-general of Germany — Baron von-Alten — who persuaded the Governor to ignore Russia's threats and enticements. When the Russian consul cabled Ignatev that Nazif Pasha was not succumbing to pressure and had recommended to the Turkish government, upon the advice of the German and British consuls, that Cyril should be dismissed for the good of Turkey,[44] Cyril's fate was sealed. The Brotherhood removed him from his post, and Bismarck, to whom the Russian government officially complained regarding the German consul's interference in its affairs, dismissed von-Alten.[45] This episode, for which Hopwood found documented evidence in the files of the Russian Foreign Office,[46] illustrated the unique problematics of Russian activity in Palestine. Documents from the Foreign Office in Berlin, which was also involved in the incident, present the viewpoint of another power. Thus we see the severe difficulties Russia encountered at the hands of its protegés, the Greek Orthodox hierarchy, which culminated in an alliance with Russia's sworn enemies. It seems that no other power suffered such troubles from those who were, or were assumed to be, its protegés. This episode also points to the impotence of the Orthodox Arab hierarchy and its large flock in Palestine, who could not support Russia wholeheartedly while financially dependent upon the Greek hierarchy (which paid the rent for most of the Orthodox community, as was then customary among Christians) and were in fear of a showdown with the local Turkish government.

The aggressive tone Russia used in its dealings with the Governor of Jerusalem during this incident was not only unusual for the Russians, but for all the powers in Palestine. Unfortunately, this outburst only made things worse, reinforcing the threatening image of Russia that its rivals had fostered all along. The best evidence of this is the German consul-general's alignment with the intimidated Governor. Here we also see that in the competition between the powers, the local consuls were even hungrier for prestige than their governments; they undermined their colleagues every step of the way. When Alexander II and Foreign Minister Gorchakov summoned the German Ambassador in St. Petersburg (on Christmas Day according to the Western calender!), to protest against the hostile attitude of the German consul-general in Jerusalem,[47] Bismarck conducted a personal investigation to find out whether von-Alten had deviated from his explicit orders not to interfere in the affairs of other powers in Palestine. Bismarck did not have to look too far: von-Alten's own report contained sufficient proof that Germany's policy of disinterest on the Eastern question had been ignored. The activities of the consul in Jerusalem "were indeed interference".[48] Thus, Russia, desiring to keep a sympathetic Patriarch in power, brought down a hostile consul. But this was small comfort to Cyril; as old as he was, he was seated on a horse and driven from Jerusalem. Russia's allies in the Holy Land were put to shame for all to see.[49]

Now the only means Russia had left to teach its Greek protegés a lesson was to make good its threat to freeze the income from Bessarabian assets in Russian banks. (Bessarabia had been annexed by Russia in 1812.) These funds were the main source of income for the Greek Patriarchate in Jerusalem. Now, most of the money was frozen, and only a small portion was transferred directly to the Arab hierarchy in Palestine, in order to release it from dependence on the Greek Patriarchate. Since the Greek clergy was infinitely more concerned with the material than the spiritual realm, the economic pressure of the Russians soon began to hurt.[50] In 1877, when the Greeks became desperate, Ignatev forced them to readmit Cyril, ostracized and dying, to the Greek Orthodox Church. Only then (and again in 1882) did the Tsar start to release the annual income from Bessarabia to be sent to the Holy Land.

After this painful episode and ten years of open enmity, it is easy to comprehend the sensitivity of the Greeks when they discovered in the early 1880s that the new Russian society had decided to devote itself primarily to the Arab Orthodox community. At first the society tried to ignore the traditional problematic relations with the Patriarchate, and directly tackled two areas in which the miserable state of the Orthodox population was particularly obvious: the shabby village churches and the almost non-existent educational system. Only in Mujaidil (Migdal Ha'emek), a village with a large concentration of Orthodox

Arabs, some of whom had joined the Protestant Church, were the Russians able to renovate the local church. In all the other villages, the Jerusalem Patriarch, with the support of the Turkish government, halted the work on "his" churches in mid-air. The Patriarch declared that if the Imperial Orthodox Palestine Society desired to assist in the repair of churches, the money had to be handed over to him for distribution.

In 1885, the society decided to test this in the village of Rame in the Galilee. The Patriarch was paid for renovating the church, but nothing was ever done; neither was the money returned to the donors, on the grounds that the Greeks had not yet received the remaining portion of the Bessarabian funds. Several years later, when the society sought to carry out the repairs in Rame by itself, the governor refused to grant it a permit. This ended Russian endeavors to restore the run-down churches of the Orthodox community. In the surge of building that commenced in Palestine at this time, as a result of competition between the powers, and of Jewish immigration, the contribution of Greek Orthodoxy was very small indeed.

Russian Orthodox dignitaries

The obstacles that the Patriarch placed in the path of the Imperial Orthodox Palestine Society did not prevent it from erecting an impressive monument to Russian Orthodoxy. On a plot purchased in the Old City in 1859, it built the Russki Dom (the Russian House) to serve as its headquarters, and the Church of Aleksandr Nevski. Archaeological excavations on this site, which was near the Church of the Holy Sepulchre, later unearthed some of the most important finds in Jerusalem. These finds and others, from all over the country, were studied by Russian scientists and publicized in the society's journals. The foremost churches

The women's hospice in the Russian Compound

established by the society were the Church of Ascension (A-Tur), with the highest tower on the Mount of Olives; the Church of St. Peter and St. Paul in Abu Kabir, at the entrance to Jaffa; and the Church of Mary Magdalene (the "Onion Church") in Gethsemane — one of the most beautiful churches in the whole country.[51]

The Imperial Orthodox Palestine Society also devoted special attention to pilgrim accommodations. In 1891, it completed the hostels in the Russian Compound that had begun to deteriorate even before being put to use, because Mansurov had lacked the necessary funds for their completion. However, the special rates offered to pilgrims making the trip to Palestine via Russian trains and steamships increased the number of visitors so sharply that the huge Russian Compound buildings could hardly contain them. To meet these demands at the beginning of the twentieth century, the Society built the Nikolai Hospice — the largest of them all. Roomy hospices were also built in Haifa, Nazareth and Jericho to ease the pressure on Jerusalem. Still, the problem was never fully solved, for at the turn of the century over 10,000 pilgrims were arriving each year.[52]

The medical services provided for pilgrims at the large hospital in the Russian Compound and at pilgrim centers all over the country were also improved. Although the local clinics were open to the Arab population too, they could not compete with the excellent service provided by the Western missions. It should also be noted that in contrast to the Catholic and Protestant hospitals, the

69

hospitals and clinics of the Russians were closed to Jews.[53] This shows how uninterested Russia was in winning the favor of the Jewish community.

It soon became clear that the society was paying very little attention to the religious delegation. After the death of Antonin in 1894, no one of stature had been found to take his place thereon and, aside from the school opened in the Russian Compound, it accomplished very little.

The last and, in the long run, the most important sphere in which the Imperial Society hoped to assist the Orthodox Arab population was that of education. According to Ottoman law, the education of the Greek Orthodox millet (community) was the responsibility of the Greek Patriarch. However, throughout the period, the Patriarchs did very little in this respect. Most of the community members were illiterate, and the Greeks saw illiteracy as the best guarantee of their continued ruling status. Even if the Greeks had desired to do something, they were no match for the Western missions, which were particularly active and effective in the area of education. Contributions from Russia toward the building of an educational system disappeared with other funds, into the pockets of the Greek clergy in Jerusalem. Porfiri Uspenski, Cyril Naumov and Antonin Kapustin all tried to open schools, but most of them closed down within a short while. The three schools founded by the Russian society in the Jerusalem area in the early 1880s suffered a similar fate. The Greek Patriarch, who feared that the Russians were plotting to educate a new generation of Orthodox Arabs to undermine the authority of the Greeks, revealed the most stubborn resistance when it came to education.

However unyielding the Greeks were in their opposition, the Russians were just as determined not to give in on a subject that was undoubtedly the major source of the Orthodox Arab community's weakness. To avoid confrontation as much as possible, Khitrovo decided to open "twenty to thirty" schools in the north of the country, far from the Patriarch's seat of power.[54] These were Khitrovo's words to Antonin in 1882; he little imagined the difficulties involved or realized that even this initial achievement was beyond the society's abilities. By way of comparison, the English Church Missionary Society succeeded in establishing 48 schools in Palestine by World War I.[55]

Contrary to common belief, however, the real problems in this area arose less from the opposition of the Greek Orthodox than from the inferiority of Russian endeavors. This was obvious from the moment the society opened its first school in Mujaidil at the end of 1882. The small, dark room where four children were taught reading and writing by an Arab priest, lacked a certified teacher; the pupils themselves were the two sons and two nephews of the "teacher", who justified the fact that the other parents sent their children to the Protestant school in the village.[56] The condition of the three other schools, founded one after another in Rame, Kafar Yasif and Sejera, was similar and so depressed the Russian visitors who came to see the society's first educational attempts, that Khitrovo travelled to Palestine to see them for himself in 1884. Only then did he realize that lacking certified teachers, proper buildings, and elementary equipment (including textbooks), it was not only impossible to compete with the Western missions, but impossible to run a school at all. It was of no use to Khitrovo that the Patriarch, who was now in conflict with certain members of the Brotherhood of the Holy Sepulchre, was willing, in exchange for Russian support, to allow the society to be responsible for educational programs as long as he remained the supervisor. Without proper teachers, all the goodwill of the Russians was to no avail.

Hiring or training instructors proved to be a major obstacle which the society was never able to overcome. With great difficulty, and with the promise of high wages that taxed its budget, the society did attract Russian teachers to the Holy Land. However, these were usually young graduates of teachers' colleges who lacked experience. Most returned to Russia after a short time, discouraged by the low standards of living, the alien surroundings, lack of familiarity with the language, their unruly pupils' lack of study habits, etc. The teachers, who came and went, formed almost no ties with their place of work or their Arab colleagues; all they felt toward the locals was scorn. Indeed, the Russians had no Catholic nuns or Protestant deaconesses prepared to work anywhere without pay. The educational system they wished to develop lacked the infrastructure upon which the Western system in Palestine was based: the large nucleus of missionaries of various denominations whose lives were devoted to teaching the people of the East, regardless of material possessions, personal comfort, pension rights, etc.

Alongside attempts to bring teachers from Russia, the society invested considerable efforts in training local Arabs to teach. In 1886, eleven boys with teaching potential were chosen from different parts of the country, assembled in a rented building in Nazareth, and instructed by Aleksandr Quzma, a Russian-trained Arab from Damascus who had been appointed supervisor of the society's educational system in Palestine.[57] This school eventually became a teachers' seminary (later named after Khitrovo). By the end of the nineteenth century, the teaching staff included five Russian and four Arab teachers. An elementary school established by the society in Nazareth was affiliated with the seminary, and last-year students spent most of their time there acquiring practical experience. However, the parents of the children at this "model" school were unhappy that their offspring were being experimented upon by student teachers scarcely older than the pupils themselves. The outstanding graduates of the seminary received their final training in Russia, but these were few, and some never returned to Palestine. In the early twentieth century, the seminary moved to the new Russian Hospice.[58] Admission to this institution, which also had a dormitory, was the dream of many Greek Orthodox youngsters, because studies there were free. However, few were found qualified, and of these only a small number completed their training and worked as teachers, as intended by the society.

A girls' school founded by the society in Beit Jalla experienced a similar fate. The institution was initially opened in Jerusalem in 1858 with the assistance of a Russian benefactress, and was actually the first Russian school in Palestine. Due to the opposition of the Jerusalem Patriarchate, however, it was moved to rented quarters in Beit Jalla. In 1866, Antonin bought a large plot of land there with money provided by the Tsarina Marya Aleksandrovna, and built a new school for girls. Unable to find teachers, he turned the school over to the society, which considerably enlarged the premises and, in 1890, turned it into a boarding school. It contained a clinic, chapel, comfortable quarters for teachers and students, and other services that were of high standard, even when compared with Western schools in Palestine. The Achilles' heel of the Beit Jalla seminary which, like the seminary in Nazareth, was affiliated with a model primary school, was the small number of graduates who went on to teach in the Russian educational system in Palestine.

Thus, in two prominent Russian educational institutions in the Holy Land an effort was made to accentuate quality. As a result, however, the number of graduates was low and these institutions were able to provide only a partial answer to the need for qualified local teachers.

Less attention was devoted by the society to the country's elementary schools. Of the dozen and a half or two dozen it maintained at the end of the nineteenth century, only a few were under its direct supervision. The others, especially those in the smaller villages, usually were pre-existing Greek Orthodox institutions adopted by the society. In conjunction with the Russian Foreign Office and Russia's diplomatic corps in the East, the society sought to monitor the school curriculum and adapt it to local needs and the interests of Russia.

In view of the basically hostile attitude of the Jerusalem Patriarchate, the society, from its earliest days, established schools in Syria and Lebanon where the competition of Western missions was less intense. As time went by, a paradoxical situation evolved in which four-fifths of the Imperial Orthodox Palestine Society's schools were outside that country. While the conditions in Syria and in Lebanon frequently dictated different approaches, the desire to unify the school system was a constant concern.

The teaching of the Russian language also required attention. All the society's schools taught Russian, and in some schools it was the language of instruction. Whereas the Foreign Office, the Embassy in Constantinople, and the local consuls preferred the Russian language to be kept to a minimum because it deterred students from enrolling and had little value outside the classroom, the Imperial Society insisted that the schools of 'Holy Russia' teach in the 'holy' language as much as possible. The society also rejected the idea of allowing students to study French or English — languages which, from an objective point of view, were more useful, and thus more in demand by the educated population. The society found these languages contemptible because they represented Russia's religious adversaries.

As the Russian educational system in Palestine (and particularly in Syria and Lebanon) expanded, its problems and its expenses increased. In 1912, the Russian treasury stepped in to prevent the system's collapse — on condition that the society halt its expansion of educational services. Two years later, the Tsar ordered the inclusion of English and French in the syllabus. World War I, which broke out soon afterward, kept the new program from being implemented and led to the closing of the Russian schools.

The beginning of the twentieth century was marked by a slowdown in the society's activities, and by a deterioration in their quality. Khitrovo died in 1903 and, two years later, Grand Duke Sergei was assassinated. Within a brief span, the society had lost the two figures upon whose shoulders most of the burden had rested from the very start. The Revolution of 1905 and the Russian intelligentsia's decreasing interest in religious matters, took their toll on the society's membership. By 1914, it had only 3,000 members. The drop in income caused by the war in Japan and the Revolution turned the slowdown into a standstill and eventual regression.

The society's one hundred schools in Syria and Lebanon swallowed up most of its budget and moved the focal point of activity outside Palestine. Even as thorough a researcher as Eli Kedourie seems to have overlooked the fact that most of the 11,000 pupils attending the schools of the Imperial Orthodox Palestine Society in 1912, neither lived nor studied in Palestine at all. The handful of schools established in Palestine itself could not tip the scales in Russia's favor. This is the reason that the educational activity of the society left no great mark on the Holy Land.[59] "For the sake of Zion I will not be silent, for the sake of Jerusalem I will not be still" — proclaimed the society's banner. However, when Tsar Nikolai II enumerated its achievements at the festivities marking its 25th anniversary (1882–1907), Zion and Jerusalem were no longer the society's chief interests. The society maintained eight hostels accommodating 10,000 pilgrims, a hospital and six clinics; it had published 347 volumes on Palestine; it had two million rubles in assets; and it supported 101 schools with a student population of 10,400.[60] R.M. Haddad is certainly right in saying that "Russian influence and Russian schools came too late and died too quickly to leave the indelible mark left by the Latin and Protestant institutions." Yet on the other hand, he too believes that "Russia succeeded in establishing a network of primary and secondary schools which, while achieving most in Palestine, were not without importance for the rest of Syria..."[61]

Thus Tsarist Russia missed its last opportunity to reinforce its standing in the Holy Land. The Orthodox Arab communities in Syria and Lebanon promised to be an easier arena for the Imperial Orthodox Palestine Society's educational pursuits, and its abdication of the Palestinian framework left France and Britain with the best chances of succession to Turkish rule over the Holy Land.

In conclusion, two factors contributed significantly toward the decline of Russian influence in Palestine. First, the Protestants, especially those of German origin — who formed the majority of the foreign Christians in the Holy Land — succeeded in cutting into the communities under Russian protection. Second, the outstanding institutions established by those Protestants, as well as by the English, French, Austrians and others, after the Egyptians opened up the Holy Land to the West, soon overshadowed the activities of the Russians.

When attention is focused solely on Russian activities in Palestine, they certainly seem impressive. Yet it would seem that a correct evaluation of Russia's achievements is possible only within an overall view that takes into consideration the activities of all the great powers in the country during the period under discussion. Within this broader view, Russia did well — but without a doubt her three main competitors did better.

Translated by Gila Brand.

1   H.A.L. Fisher, *A History of Europe* (London, 1938), pp. 827–828.
2   M. Vereté, "The Restoration of the Jews in English Protestant Thought, 1790–1840," *MES* 8/1 (1972):3–50.
3   J. Nicolayson, "Mitteilungen für eine Skizze der Geschichte der englischen Mission und des evangelischen Bisthums zu Jerusalem," *Zions-Bote* 1 (1852):7.
4   *Ibid.*, pp. 7–9, emphasis in original.
5   The most serious attempts to cover the subject were made by the Greek historian Stavrou, and the English historian Hopwood. See Th. G. Stavrou, *Russian Interests in Palestine, 1882–1914* (Thessaloniki, 1963); D. Hopwood, *The Russian Presence in Syria and Palestine, 1843–1914* (Oxford, 1969). Stavrou tried to restrict his work to the history of the Orthodox Palestine Society and its activity in the Holy Land, whereas Hopwood broadened his canvas in terms of time and place, probably in an attempt to balance Stavrou's pro-Greek bias. While Stavrou relies upon a plethora of Russian and Greek publications, some of them rare and unavailable in the West, which lend depth and credibility to his work, Hopwood makes extensive use, albeit fragmented and sporadic, of Russian Foreign Office archival material. The difference in source material probably accounts for the pro-Greek stance in Stavrou's case and the rather pro-Russian stance of Hopwood. Both researchers show an unfamiliarity with the geography of Palestine that makes it difficult for readers to place the various Russian institutions in Jerusalem and particularly in less well-known areas (such as Beit Jalla — a "20-mile walk from Bethlehem" — Stavrou, p. 113). In addition, certain episodes of importance in the history of Russian activity in Palestine are only hinted at or not mentioned at all. For example, Hopwood notes that in 1857 Cyril Naumov was instructed to extend goodwill towards Russian and Polish Jews, "one of the elements of the population whom we recently let slip out of our hands against all reason" (p. 53). In the same way that the Jews slipped out of the hands of the Russian government, they also slipped out of Hopwood's hands. In vain the reader will seek mention of a Jewish community which, after all, was the largest body of Russian subjects then in Palestine. Nevertheless, the historian can find much material in the abundance of quotes from Russian archival sources. This, it seems, is the major value of the book. See also M. Maoz's detailed criticism of this work, in *Asian and African Studies* 8 (1972):215–218. This article has made considerable use of Stavrou and Hopwood's quotations from Greek and Russian sources, though the conclusions drawn are sometimes different.
6   Young to Foreign Minister Palmerston on 28.4.1840. See A.M. Hyamson, *The British Consulate in Jerusalem in Relation to the Jews of Palestine*, 1 (London, 1939), p. 29.
7   For a detailed description of this ceremony, see A. Carmel, *Palästina-Chronik 1853 bis 1882* (Ulm, 1978), pp. 147–151.

8 S. Graham, *With the Russian Pilgrims to Jerusalem* (London, 1914).

9 Lacking reliable censi, the population statistics for Palestine prior to 1922 can only be roughly estimated. Both figures, with slight changes, are acceptable to the Greek Orthodox, Catholics and Protestants and thus may be considered more or less accurate. For comparison, see *Handbook of the Anglican Bishopric in Jerusalem and the East* (Jerusalem, 1941), p. 6; P. Medebielle, *The Diocese of the Latin Patriarchate of Jerusalem* (Jerusalem, 1963), p. 31, n. 10; H. Guthe, "Die griechisch-orthodoxe Kirche im Heiligen Lande," *ZDPV* 12 (1889):87. For other attempts to estimate the Christian population of Palestine in the nineteenth century, see R. Bachi, *The Population of Israel* (Jerusalem, 1974?), pp. 31–37, 362–375; S.P. Colbi, *Christianity in the Holy Land* (Tel Aviv, 1969), pp. 77–108.

10 For an analysis of Russia's position on Palestine during the secret talks between the Allied countries during World War I, see L. Stein, *The Balfour Declaration* (London, 1961), pp. 236–239, 339–349. The former Russian Foreign Minister Sazonov also deals with this topic: S. Sazonov, *Fateful Years, 1909–1916* (New York, 1928), pp. 257–258.

11 According to Hopwood, pp. 130–131.

12 Carmel (above, n. 7), p. 357. On the family of Jacob Schumacher, who sometimes wrote articles for the press about events in Palestine and particularly in Haifa, see the memoirs of his granddaughter N. Marcinkowski-Schumacher, *Wenn's aus blauen Himmel regnet* (Wuppertal, 1978).

13 Carmel (above, n. 7), pp. 198–201.

14 *Palestine, Report and General Abstracts of the Census of 1922*, compiled by J.B. Barron (Jerusalem, n.d.), table XII, p. 43.

15 The Anglican Church Missionary Society alone had 48 schools in Palestine in 1914; also see *Anglican Bishopric* (above, n. 9), p. 23.

16 Hopwood (above, n. 5), p. 212.

17 *Ibid.*, p. 15.

18 M. Salmon, *Three Generations in the Yishuv, 1812–1913* (Hebrew) (Jerusalem, 1951), pp. 33–35; Neophytos of Cyprus, *Extracts from Annals of Palestine, 1921–1841*, translated by S.N. Spyridon (Jerusalem, 1979, reprint), pp. 11–12.

19 M. Vereté, "Why was a British Consulate Established in Jerusalem?" *English Historical Review* 75 (1970):316–345; Young's letter to Foreign Minister Palmerston, 4.2.1839, in which he announces his arrival in Jaffa, Hyamson (above, n. 6), p. 2.

20 Hopwood (above, n. 5), p. 15.

21 According to Warder Cresson, the American consul in Jerusalem in the 1840s, "... and thus in *Jerusalem* — which is, in a commercial point of view, but a paltry inland Eastern town, without trade or importance of any kind — sit the five consuls of the Great European powers (as well as one appointed by the United States of America), looking at one another, and it is difficult to say why and wherefore." See N. Sokolow, *History of Zionism 1600–1918*, 1 (London, 1919), p. 137.

22 A.L. Tibawi, *British Interests in Palestine 1800–1901* (Oxford, 1961), p. 63; cf. Hyamson (above, n. 6), pp. 61 ff.

23 Rose to Palmerston, 27.3.1847, quoted by Hyamson (above, n. 6), pp. 97–100; and cf. *ibid.*, preface, pp. xxxviii ff.

24 G. Frumkin, *A Judge in Jerusalem* (Hebrew) (Tel Aviv, 1954), p. 106.

25 Hyamson (above, n. 6), preface, p. xxxix. A large part of the British consulate documents published by Hyamson deal with the British protection extended to Jews who were formerly Russian subjects.

26 On the mission of Porfiri, see particularly, Hopwood, pp. 33 ff.; Stavrou, pp. 25 ff. (both, above, n. 5); also see the clearly Greek (and anti-Russian) version of N. Moschopoulos, *La Terre Sainte — Essai sur l'histoire politique et diplomatique des Lieux Saints de la chrétienté* (Athens, 1956), pp. 243–248.

27 J.C. Hurewitz, *Diplomacy in the Near and Middle East — A Documentary Record, 1535–1914* (Princeton, 1956), p. 136.

28 On the Crimean War and its background, see particularly, H.W.V. Temperley, *England and the Near East — The Crimea* (London, 1936). The importance of the Palestine factor in this case has been stressed by Stavrou (p. 30, no. 15); also see V. Rachelson, "The Holy Places as a

Cause of the Crimean War" (Hebrew) (unpublished M.A. thesis, Bar Ilan University, Ramat Gan, 1972).

29 Cited by Hopwood (above, no. 5), pp. 50–51.

30 On Naumov's delegation, see *Das Heilige Land — Organ des Vereins vom h. Grabe* 2 (1858):59–64 (hereafter, *DHL*); Moschopoulos (above, n. 26), pp. 243 ff.; Hopwood, pp. 46 ff.; Stavrou, pp. 40 ff. (both above, n. 5).

31 W.E. Mosse, "Russia and the Levant, 1856–1862 – Grand Duke Constantine Nikolaevich and the Russian Steam Navigation Company," *JMH* 26 (1954):39–48.

32 A copy of Mansurov's report fell into the hands of the British envoy in St. Petersburg, who reported on it to London. Also cf. Hopwood, pp. 56–61; Stavrou, pp. 40 ff.

33 On Constantine's purchases, see Guthe (above, n. 9), p. 89; Hopwood, p. 71; Carmel (above, n. 7), p. 71; Stavrou, p. 93.

34 Stavrou, pp. 46–47; Hopwood, pp. 82–87.

35 There are various accounts of Antonin's appointment as head of the Russian mission in Jerusalem. We rely upon that of Hopwood (p. 86 ff.), which is based on the most reliable sources as far as Ignatev's activity in Palestine is concerned. (Cf., for example, Stavrou, pp. 46–47.)

36 On the purchases of Antonin and the difficulties involved, see *DHL* 15 (1871):110–111; and the book by A. d'Alonzo, of the French Consulate in Jerusalem, *Russie en Palestine* (Paris, 1901).

37 On the 100th anniversary of the Berlin Congress, the State Archives of the Federal Republic of Germany published the protocols which explain why French rights in Palestine were endorsed. Compare I. Geiss, *Der Berliner Kongress 1878 — Protokolle und Materialien* (Boppard am Rhein, 1979), p. 301.

38 On the Grand Duke's visit, see, for example, Carmel (above, n. 7), pp. 333–334; on the arrival of the new consul, see *ibid.*, pp. 285–286.

39 For information on the society's research activities and publications, see Stavrou, pp. 136–147, 194–199.

40 On the establishment of the society, see Stavrou, chapter 3; Hopwood, pp. 99–113.

41 S. Akel, *Der Pädagoge und Missionar Johann Ludwig Schneller und seine Erziehungsanstalten* (Bielefeld, 1978).

42 In particular, see Section 3 of Hopwood's book, pp. 96–153. This rather exaggerated assessment is found in many essays on the subject. The reasons will be discussed later on.

43 See, for example, Carmel (above, n. 7), pp. 153 ff., and n. 111.

44 Hopwood quotes the cable (on p. 184) without giving the exact date.

45 See "File on the Complaint of the Imperial Government of Russia against Consul-General von Alten in Jerusalem", political archives of the German Foreign Office in Bonn, Türkei file 105.

46 Hopwood, pp. 180–194.

47 Prince Heinrich von Reuss VII to Bismarck, 24.12.1872, on the meeting of that date; Türkei file 105 (see n. 45, above).

48 Von-Alten to the German envoy, von Keudell, in Constantinople, 8.12.1872, *ibid.* The emphasis in the margins of von-Alten's report is Bismarck's. Kaiser Wilhelm I, apparently suprised by the Chancellor's forceful response, tacked on the following note to the report: "Was hat denn v(on) Alten begangen?"

49 On the activity and deposition of Cyril, see also *DHL* 33 (1889):90–91.

50 This was the conclusion reached by the commission appointed during the British Mandate to investigate the matter, though the Greeks claimed otherwise. Also see Mouschopoulos (above, n. 26), pp. 315 ff.

51 On Russia's building plans near the Church of the Holy Sepulchre and the archaeological excavations at this site, see Stavrou, pp. 94–99.

52 On the building progress of the Russian Compound, see *DHL* 24 (1880):96–97; 57 (1913):48–50 (including photograph).

53 Hopwood, p. 117, n. 5.

54 *Ibid.*, p. 141.

55 See *Handbook of the Anglican Bishopric* (above, n. 9).

56 Compare Tibawi (above, n. 22), p. 162.

57 He served in this post until the dissolution of the society during World War I. Many thanks to Dr. Butrus Abu-Manneh for directing me to Quzma's diaries, which are in the possession of his granddaughter in Haifa.

58 P. Sauer, *Beilharz-Chronik* (Ulm, 1975), p. 96. The building currently serves several capacities, including that of the local police headquarters.

59 Kedourie does not actually state that all the society's educational activities were in Palestine, but that seems to be implied. In any case, his statements can be misunderstood. Most of the educational activity took place outside Palestine — a fact that should be emphasized to put an end to what is a very common error, probably arising also from the society's name. See E. Kedourie, *The Chatham House Version and Other Middle–Eastern Studies* (London, 1970), p. 328.

60 Hopwood, p. 131; also cf. Colbi (above, n. 9), p. 84, who cites a maximum figure of 1,074 pupils within the borders of Palestine. Both estimates are probably close to the truth.

61 R.M. Haddad, *Syrian Christians in Muslim Society* (Princeton, 1970), pp. 84–85. The author relies on Tibawi (above, n. 22), pp. 173–177, whose work is full of errors. For example, he predates the establishment of the Imperial Society by over fifty years (p. 173, at the foot, 174 at the top). Comprehensive, detailed information about the Russian educational system in Palestine is available in the work of d'Alonzo (above, n. 36), Hopwood and Stavrou. Also see C. Exepi, "Les écoles russes de Palestine et de Syrie," *Echos d'Orient* 3 (1900):177–181.

THE TIES OF THE JEWS OF ASHKENAZ TO THE LAND OF ISRAEL

ABRAHAM GROSSMAN

A *commonly accepted hypothesis describes early Ashkenazi Jewry, from its beginnings in the ninth century until the First Crusade (1096), as being under the hegemony of Erez Israel, and attributes this to the influence of Italian Jewry. A. Grossman systematically analyzes the areas of contact between Ashkenazi Jewry and Erez Israel, and concludes that this assumption is exaggerated. He presents an alternative hypothesis: Palestinian influence existed until the middle of the eleventh century, when halakhic teachings of the Babylonian geonim penetrated en masse, and their authority grew. Grossman shows that this development occurred in spite of the fact that toward the end of the tenth and during the eleventh century Christian Europe was more open to a strengthening of ties with Palestine.*

The ties of early German Jewry to the Land of Israel from its first settlement on the banks of the Rhine in the ninth century C.E. up to the First Crusade (1096) have yet to be subjected to serious analysis.[1] Research into this question has been based mainly on the examination of fragmentary issues and does not present a complete picture. Some of the conclusions reached are based on a general impression and occasionally are nothing more than supposition. This stems from the paucity in contemporary sources of explicit data concerning the ties of the Jews of Ashkenaz (as German Jewry was then called) with the Jewish community in Palestine. Even the Cairo Geniza, which shed new light on the ties of Palestinian Jewry with the countries of the Mediterranean basin,[2] has made but a small contribution to the study of the relations between Palestine and the Jewish centers of Christian Europe.

Solomon Judah Leib Rapoport was the first to inquire into these ties, more than one hundred years ago, raising the matter of the special affinity of the Jews of Ashkenaz for literary works composed in Palestine. He believed that this relationship had developed through the intermediation of the Jews of Italy, to whom he devoted the bulk of his discussion. Even though Rapoport did not enter into specifics — producing, rather, a general evaluation of the literary works of those countries—he dealt with the matter carefully.

Rapoport did not argue, or even imply, that the ties of Italian Jewry to Palestine were stronger than their ties to Babylonia, but he did claim that the ties to Palestine on the part of Italian Jewry and the communities it influenced were greater than those of other contemporary Jewish centers.

> ...For in truth, our brethren in the other lands were solely attentive to the teachings of Babylonia, home of the geonim who provided responsa to all their queries; not so with our brethren in Italy... their connection with Erez Yisrael was long-lasting, and it is doubtless for this reason that the Palestinian Talmud is also of great importance to them.[3]

Detailed examination of the origins of various customs, mainly in the area of liturgy, sufficed to lend credence to Rapoport's conclusion and it was accepted, on the whole, by numerous researchers.

During the past two generations this view has again come under scrutiny, possibly motivated to some extent by wishful thinking. Indeed, the influence of Palestine on the Jews of Ashkenaz (and, of course, Italy) has been described by a number of scholars as seminal and as greater than that of Babylonia. This assumption was even proposed as a solution to various questions concerning the development of the philosophic works of early German Jewry and the existence of various customs that are not entirely clear to us. Some have even pointed to this influence in the development of various institutions in the Jewish communities of Germany and northern France in the ninth through eleventh centuries. Some of the finest scholars in Jewish studies have contributed to the formulation of this theory. Thus, for example, B. Klar concluded:

> Jewish historiography of recent generations, when seeking to introduce order into this political and cultural phenomenon called "Jewish history" whose theatre of operations is the entire world, has divided it according to the geographical units of modern times... but this division is not suitable to the first millennium following the destruction of the Temple... For that period, the appropriate division should be between Babylonia and its sister communities on the one hand, and Palestine and its satellites on the other... These two centers of power divided Jewry between them... This dualism determined not only Jewry's political fate but its spiritual lineaments for a thousand years... the dichotomy was more decisive and deeper still, however, and embraces the entire image and coloration of Jewry everywhere in terms of its spiritual development and *Weltanschauung*.[4]

S. Assaf wrote similarly:

> The scope of the influence and power of the two centers—Babylonia and Palestine—were very great, and it seems that that they divided the world between them. This division occurred long before the Arab conquest of both Babylon and Palestine... Indeed, for long afterwards, the Jews of Byzantine and Italy thrived in the main on the spiritual nourishment

derived from Palestine. Through Italy, the communities of France and
Germany also drew sustenance.[5]

Other historians followed suit, and some discerned competition between
Babylonia and Italy for spiritual hegemony over Jewry during the tenth and
eleventh centuries.[6] In fact, however, the theory that the early Jewry of
Ashkenaz was subject to the influence of Palestine has not been examined
thoroughly and systematically and should be viewed as a hypothesis which still
awaits verification.

Four arguments have been proposed to support this hypothesis.

1. The early Jewish community in Ashkenaz was composed of numerous
immigrants from Italy. It may be reasonably supposed that they introduced the
strong ties of Italian Jewry with Palestine to their new home.

2. We know of two questions posed by Ashkenazi Jews to the rabbis in
Palestine. The first, dated 960, concerned "a rumor we have heard concerning
the coming of the Messiah." The second was posed by R. Meshullam ben Moses
to the Gaon R. Elijah ha-Cohen in Palestine, c. 1070.[7]

3. Early Ashkenazi liturgy was greatly influenced by prayers and blessings
formulated in Palestine.[8]

4. The linguistic tradition of Ashkenaz is closely related to that of
Palestine.[9]

We may respond to the first point by noting that a large part of the community in
Ashkenaz originated in southern Europe, and arrived from northern (that is,
north of the Loire) and southern France and, by all accounts, the influence of
Babylonia on Spain and Provence was greater. These immigrants, therefore,
brought Babylonian traditions with them.[10] In fact, the entire theory of Italian
Jewry's preference for Palestine over Babylonia in the period under discussion
is, in general, a dubious one, and is somewhat exaggerated. Indeed, while some
sources testify to its ties to Palestine, such ties also existed—and very
strongly—with Babylonia as well.

As for the two questions put to the rabbis in Palestine, we have also found
close literary connections between the rabbis of Italy and Ashkenaz, and those of
Babylonia. R. Meshullam b. Kalonymos of Lucca, who had great influence on
the earliest rabbis of Ashkenaz, turned to R. Sherira Gaon for counsel.[11] Agus
has tried to account for the oddity of a scholar of Ashkenaz turning to Babylonia
and not to Palestine in his own way. He proposes a division: in matters of
halakha, they turned exclusively to the rabbis of Palestine, while in matters of
talmudic exegesis—of the sort which R. Meshullam posed—they turned to
Babylonia as well. But this is a dubious distinction, for matters of exegesis
frequently have halakhic ramifications. Such is certainly the case in the
essentially halakhic question (No. 11) posed by R. Meshullam concerning the
manner of eating the paschal sacrifice.[12] Furthermore, the phrasing "Thus they
sent from *metiva*" (the Babylonian academies) often occurs in R. Meshullam's
responsa, as well as in those of his father, R. Kalonymos. It is clear from the

context that R. Meshullam's reference is to a responsa issued by Babylonian geonim in matters of practical halakha.[13] These questions may have been posed by R. Kalonymos and R. Meshullam themselves, though it is also possible that they possessed and relied upon responsa to questions submitted by others.

The last two arguments are weightier and possess real value. The influence of the prayers and *piyyutim* (religious poetry) of Palestine on the liturgy of Ashkenaz certainly argues for strong ties between the two communities. One cannot infer, however, that Ashkenaz Jewry preferred the heritage of Palestine over that of Babylonia, for the essence of that influence was limited precisely to matters of *piyyut* in prayer. The fixed body of prayer remains rooted in Babylonian tradition.

> It is customary to say that the practice of Ashkenaz is rooted in that of ancient Erez Yisrael... while the source of Spanish (Sephardi) and Yemenite practice is in ancient Babylonia. It must be emphasized that this dichotomy does not apply to fixed prayer. Everything involving fixed prayer in the Ashkenazi rite... is rooted in decisions of the Babylonian geonim and derives indirectly from the Babylonian Talmud: the *Siddur* of R. Amram Gaon (ninth century) set guidelines for fixed prayer everywhere, and established uniformity of practice; the rabbis of Ashkenaz and France knew this well.[14]

Nor does linguistic tradition suffice to prove preference for Palestine, as will be dealt with below. A fundamental fact of great importance in this entire discussion refutes it: the halakhic-literary output of the rabbis of Ashkenaz before 1096 is replete with the teachings of the scholars of Babylonia — both halakhic works and, especially, responsa literature. These sources exerted supreme influence on the halakhic rulings of the early German rabbis, including questions on which opinions in Babylonia and Palestine were divided. The little it contains of Palestinian thought during the geonic period — the basic argument for determining the strong ties of the community of Ashkenaz to Palestine — is minimal in comparison to that originating in Babylonia. This remains true even if we take into account the difference in the scope of the literary creation in the respective centers. This is apparent in the responsa of R. Meshullam ben Kalonymos, R. Gershom b. Judah Me'or ha-Gola, R. Joseph Tov Elem (Bonfils) of France, R. Judah ha-Cohen, the rabbis of the second half of the eleventh century, and especially in *Ma'aseh ha-Makhiri*. The latter work was cited by Assaf as support for his interpretation, for it preserves the teachings of Palestine. In fact, however, this work clearly refutes Assaf's claim. The contribution of Palestine is quantitatively minuscule in comparison with the teachings of the Babylonian rabbis that are cited on a full range of topics. This book provides clear evidence of the great influence of Babylonian doctrine in Ashkenaz in the latter half of the eleventh century, and not the opposite.

The same holds true concerning the use of the Palestinian Talmud, a most significant factor in Rapoport's thesis concerning the strong ties of early

Ashkenazi Jewry to Palestine. That source was cited infrequently by the early rabbis of Ashkenaz.[15] Their quotations testify to the fact that the work was indeed available to them (or at least to some of them); therefore their infrequent use of it cannot be ascribed to ignorance. Although Ashkenaz Jewry had not yet adopted the principle of following Babylonian teachings exclusively,[16] such was the case *in practice* in most of the halakhic issues discussed by its rabbis. Their preference for Palestinian tradition in a number of cases is no doubt of great importance, but does not change the essential picture; rather, this reflects family traditions and not a general heritage of any sort.

Community Development and Family Traditions

Two major questions yet to be discussed pertain to the development of the community and to attempts to distinguish between orientation and tradition. The Jewish community in medieval Ashkenaz apparently originated in the early ninth century; its cultural flowering had already begun by the tenth. We are therefore dealing with a period of more than two hundred years.

1. We must determine whether, over this interval, it is possible to discern development of the ties to the Palestinian and Babylonian heritages. If no such development can be discerned, the period at hand may—in this matter—be regarded as a constant.

2. We must investigate the possible existence of a number of traditions or schools of thought regarding the associations of Ashkenazi Jewry with both heritages prior to 1096; the community may, on the other hand, have been uniform in this respect.

Family tradition in Ashkenaz was extremely powerful. Examination of the practices and spiritual heritage of that community's rabbis prior to 1096 (during the five generations or so during which such traditions may be traced) reveals that sons held to fathers' traditions with great devotion, even when unaware of their rationale or source.[17] Thus a variety of family traditions sprouted, flourished, and were strictly preserved. As a result, we can hardly speak of any general Ashkenazi practice before 1096; we must rather speak of the traditions of certain families.

An inquiry into the ties of early Ashkenazi Jewry to Palestine through examination of these two central questions, is closely related to the investigation of other topics:

1. The actual relations that existed between Ashkenazi Jewry, and Palestine and Babylonia respectively;

2. The role of Palestine in the consciousness of the Christian environment in which the Jews lived and functioned;

3. The methodology of the Ashkenazi rabbis in study and in halakhic judgments;

4. The source and development of customs prevalent in early Ashkenazi Jewry;

5. The source and development of early Ashkenazi halakhic traditions;

6. The source and development of the early Ashkenazi rabbis' literary and linguistic traditions;

7. Ancient traditions in the prayers and practices of the Ashkenazi communities.

We shall not deal with all these questions. The last three deserve separate analysis and lie beyond the framework of this discussion.[18] This is also the case concerning the origins and development of customs, and the links between Ashkenazi Jewry and Babylonia, which will be discussed only partially. Nor do the sources at our disposal—especially those relating to the tenth and early eleventh centuries—enable us to provide full and well-grounded answers to the remaining topics; they are, however, capable of indicating directions of development or of suggesting reasonable hypotheses. They certainly refute a number of conclusions which have previously been proposed.

Commercial Contacts with the East

Both Jewish and other sources make note of frequent journeys of Jewish merchants from Germany and northern France to the lands of the Muslim Caliphate, including Palestine. Charlemagne is said to have been aided in his plans to attack Bishop Richulf of Mainz by "a Jewish merchant who was wont to travel to the Holy Land and to bring many expensive and exotic things from there to the lands beyond the seas."[19] Even if one questions the reliability of the story's details, the very attempt in the ninth century to describe a Jewish merchant as one accustomed to travelling to Palestine demonstrates that such a situation existed and was generally known. We may suppose that similar merchants transmitted the question posed in the year 960 by "the men of the Rhine," as well as the questions put by R. Meshullam ben Moses to the Gaon R. Elijah a century later.[20] It may even have been pilgrims whose assistance was sought to transmit questions and responsa. Rashi mentions the practices of "readers who have come from Erez Yisrael" while intoning the biblical chant.[21] The oath taken by Reuven bar Isaac of northern France, and his subsequent settling in Palestine, were almost certainly fueled by tales he had heard from merchants or Crusaders.[22]

Since all these accounts have been preserved by mere chance, and since they speak of merchants accustomed to travelling to Palestine and about "readers" (in the plural), it may be surmised that these were not deviant cases, and that various direct channels of communication existed by which the traditions of Palestine became known in Ashkenaz, in addition to the intermediation of Italian Jewry.[23] Indeed, one of the trade routes of the Rādhānite merchants

83

passed through Palestine—according to the ninth century testimony of Ibn Khurradadhbah. Whether these merchants set out from Europe or from the Orient, they could certainly have served as an important conduit for transmission of cultural traditions, from Palestine, Babylonia and elsewhere.[24]

More numerous are the comments (scores, in fact) concerning the ties of the Jewish community in Germany and northern France with Jewish centers in the Muslim Caliphate, especially Babylonia.[25] There is no doubt that these ties lasted into the eleventh century, after cities began to flourish and the numbers of non-Jewish merchants who ventured into the Muslim realm increased. Much testimony has been preserved in the questions posed to R. Gershom ben Judah and to R. Judah ha-Cohen, in the first half of the eleventh century, concerning the journeys of merchants to "the overseas country." Given the length of their absence (at times more than a year), the nature of the goods they brought back, and the Arabic expressions which penetrated their speech, it is apparent that they had journeyed to lands of the Muslim Caliphate. These merchants are the ones who brought the teachings of the Babylonian Geonim to the rabbis of western Europe, including those of Ashkenaz.

It is not by chance that all the contemporary rabbis of Italy, Germany and France made steady use of this knowledge, and that at times they were aware of it but a short while after it had been made public. Portions of the teachings of R. Hai Gaon (d. 1038) were known to the rabbis of Ashkenaz as early as the first half of the eleventh century; an interrelationship existed between the teachings of R. Kalonymos and his son, R. Meshullam of Lucca (in northern Italy), and those of R. Moses ben Ḥanoch and his son, R. Ḥanoch, who were active at the same time in Spain. These cultural ties—made possible mainly by travelling merchants—have not been sufficiently appreciated and have not been accorded the necessary attention. Moreover, there is no validity to the nearly universal theory that there was no cultural contact between Ashkenaz and Spain at the time.

Thus we must view the closer ties of the early rabbis of Ashkenaz with any particular cultural heritage—and especially those of Palestine, Babylonia and Italy—as products of conscious and voluntary decisions; it is hard to ascribe them to ignorance of other traditions. This applies in particular to the late tenth and early eleventh centuries.

84   Palestine in Christian Awareness

The general atmosphere of western Europe of the tenth century—and *a fortiori* the eleventh—was fertile ground for intensifying ties to Palestine. The first steps towards the renewal of the Jewish community of medieval Germany began at the time that the Christian ties to Palestine began to develop and become a subject of public awareness. Christian religious orders began to compete for the acquisition of holy places in Palestine—especially in Jerusalem—that were under Muslim control. Charlemagne—who received the keys to the Church of the Holy Sepulchre from Harun al-Rashid—encouraged a constant flow of pilgrims to Jerusalem, and was most generous to the various Christian institutions located there. The belief that Jesus had founded a thousand-year kingdom (preceding the establishment of the absolute Kingdom of Heaven on Earth) that would end with the general. Day of Judgment, brought many Christian pilgrims to Jerusalem in anticipation of the year 1000. Another factor which heightened interest in Jerusalem at the time was the rise of the Cluny movement and its great influence on the religious and cultural life of Europe's Christians.

The important role occupied by Palestine and Jerusalem in the public consciousness is clearly expressed in the great excitement which engulfed western Europe at the outset of the eleventh century, following the rumor that the Holy Sepulchre had been desecrated by Caliph al-Ḥakham. The Jews were accused of having encouraged him, a charge which led to grievous pogroms in the cities of Germany and northern France. Indeed, the expulsion of the Jews from Mainz in 1012 may have been linked to this accusation.[26] The number of Christian pilgrims from western Europe during the eleventh century, generally led by bishops and noblemen, was also very great. The enthusiam reached its peak at the end of the eleventh century during the First Crusade and the Crusader conquest of Jerusalem in 1099.[27] One must assume that these events increased the Jews' interest in Palestine and Jerusalem. The theologically-rooted struggle for Palestine between Islam and Christianity—between "the sons of Ishmael" and "the sons of Esau"—and the Christian association of Jerusalem with messianic expectations, certainly strengthened these ties and raised expectations of salvation linked to the Holy Land.[28] The question posed in 960 C.E. concerning the coming of the Messiah on the one hand, and the role of "Zion" as a prominent motif in the poetry of R. Simeon ben Isaac (greatest of the early Ashkenazi religious poets) on the other, hint at and strengthen this supposition.[29] Logic suggests that this atmosphere also heightened interest in the spiritual heritage of Palestine.

Literary and Halakhic Traditions

Evidence of the halakhic and literary traditions of the early rabbis of Ashkenaz, their practices, methodology, and halakhic legislation, exists from the eleventh century onwards, with some information dating back to the late tenth century. Examination of these sources reveals that the depiction of Ashkenazi Jewry as a community operating under the hegemony of Palestine lacks any basis. One can, however, state that the influence of the Palestinian tradition was greater in the early generations, with Babylonian influence increasing gradually. This process was greatly accelerated by the mid-eleventh century, at which time a clear turning-point was reached, with Babylonian tradition recognized as primary. This process is evident in the close and strong ties to the Babylonian tradition starting in the mid-eleventh century, and apparently also in the change in halakhic legislation (the nature of the sources quoted in judgments, and the methodology used) which dates from this time. This finds expression in the multiplicity of Babylonian rabbinic sources cited from this time onwards by Ashkenazi rabbis, and in the unwillingness to disagree with them or with the Babylonian Talmud, even when this tradition differs from that of the Palestinian Talmud. The increase in use of Babylonian sources far exceeds that of the preceding era. It is true that R. Meshullam ben Kalonymos, R. Gershom ben Judah, and R. Judah ha-Cohen had availed themselves of Babylonian teachings, at times citing them without attribution.[30] But such use was relatively rare and is not found in most of their deliberations.

Ma'aseh ha-Makhiri provides clear testimony of the change which took place in the latter half of the eleventh century. This work, which is replete with the thought of Babylonian rabbis on many subjects, dates from the 1070s.[31] Evidently a comprehensive compilation of Babylonian responsa called *Sefer Basar 'al-Gabei Geḥalim* (lit. "Meat upon Hot Coals") was published in Mainz a short time before. Its author/compiler may have been R. Jacob ben Yakar, head of the Mainz yeshiva in the mid-eleventh century and Rashi's most prominent mentor.[32] This anthology further testifies to the strong ties to the teachings of the Babylonian rabbis in the mid-eleventh century. It is a fact that the surviving fragments of a book of halakhic rulings,[33] compiled by R. Judah ha-Cohen in the preceding generation, include no responsa of Babylonian authorities; only occasional references were made to them during the course of discussion. Though this does not constitute decisive proof, it does serve as an indication of the shift in loyalty at that time.

The matter is not merely quantitative. The Ashkenazi rabbis of the late tenth and early eleventh centuries were prepared to enter into clear dispute with the scholars of Babylonia and even with the Babylonian Talmud. R. Judah ben Meir ha-Cohen Leontin did so, and his disciple, R. Gershom ben Judah, followed suit — explicitly stating that he preferred the view of his mentor to that found in the *Halakhot Pesukot* and responsa of the Geonim (in the case of reversal of an oath), "because R. Leon is the rabbi from whom I acquired most of my knowledge, may his sacred memory be blessed — a splendid scholar — and it did not seem to him..."[34] The authority of the Babylonian rabbis was no more important to him than it was to his mentor, a matter worthy of further examination.

To a certain extent, R. Judah ha-Cohen, a disciple of R. Gershom ben Judah, followed the same route.[35] R. Gershom ben Judah took open issue with the Babylonian Talmud and favored the Palestinian tradition. R. Judah commented: "And in the name of Rabbenu Gershom of blessed memory, I heard that aromatic spices must be used when a festival begins at the end of the

Sabbath, and although our Gemara does not require spices, the Palestinian Talmud states..."[36] We have not yet analyzed exhaustively a single case of such explicit dispute with the Talmud or with the sages of Babylonia in the second half of the eleventh century.[37] Their authority was by then recognized as preeminent. Moreover, when the sons of Makhir found that their forefathers' and their own tradition contradicted the ruling of the Babylonian Talmud, they expressed open amazement, without raising the possibility of its being an alternative tradition (see below). It is apparent that they did not imagine that their forebears had deliberately not acted according to the Babylonian Talmud, but rather according to Palestinian tradition.

Reliance on the Bible

This shift in the eleventh century found further expression in methods of study and in halakhic ruling. The earlier rabbis had had very close associations with tannaitic literature and with the Bible, even in matters of practical halakha. The number of supporting references to tannaitic literature cited by R. Meshullam and R. Judah ha-Cohen in their responsa is substantially greater than those cited in contemporary Spanish responsa or by rabbis in any other post-talmudic period. This approach is most evident in the writings of R. Judah ha-Cohen, who referred to tannaitic writings and particularly to the Mishna, far more frequently than he did to the Babylonian Talmud. This was further expressed in the phrasing of halakhic disputation: "As this Mishna states, so we learn"; "...as is found in the anonymous Mishna which I have cited"; "All these were explained in the Mishna, and we may not interpret differently"; "...as the Sages did not relate in the Mishna..." and so on.[38] There is no doubt that such phrasing was deliberate and bears testimony to a preference for tannaitic sources when they can elucidate the matter at hand. This holds true even when this elucidation is occasionally strained, and when better and cleared evidence is available in amoraic sources.[39]

From the mid-eleventh century onwards, this special relationship to tannaitic sources disappeared. R. Isaac ben Judah, R. Isaac ha-Levi, R. Solomon ben Samson, Rashi, the sons of Makhir and others — leaders of the centers of Jewish learning in Mainz, Worms and Troyes — called far less upon those sources and far more frequently upon the Babylonian Talmud. This trend was apparent in other Jewish centers as well.

It is also possible to attribute the strong ties of the early Ashkenazi rabbis to tannaitic sources to a preference for the early sages as such, without linking this affinity directly to the scholarship of Palestine.[40] Support for this hypothesis emerges in the German rabbis' sparse use of the Palestinian Talmud. But even if this is indeed the case, their ties with Palestinian scholarship stem, in reality, from their methods of study. In any event, the Babylonian Talmud was not perceived as the primary source for halakhic rulings, as it was in all other Jewish centers in the post-talmudic era.[41]

The reliance on biblical references (in fact, on homiletic commentary on biblical verses) in matters of practical halakha, on the part of R. Meshullam ben Kalonymos,[42] R. Gershom ben Judah, R. Judah ha-Cohen, and R. Joseph Tov Elem is most interesting—with R. Gershom ben Judah particularly noteworthy for this technique. These rabbis made use of three types of homiletic commentary. The first was built on verses interpreted in the Talmud; their further exegesis was meant only to hint at the talmudic commentary though it was not explicitly cited.[43] Scores of biblical passages were invoked and interpreted in this manner, mainly by R. Gershom ben Judah; in certain cases, he even placed the interpretation in the mouth of an imaginary disputant.[44] This practice is unusual among halakhic arbiters, and bears testimony to links with the biblical text.

At present, however, we will not deal with this type of commentary, but with two other types: the use of existing exegesis while expanding its scope and applications, and the creation of totally new exegesis. In practice, it appears that most of this exegesis is meant as mere support, with the respondent basing his halakhic decision on his own judgment. But the fact is that this method, too, is not customary in the post-talmudic era.[45] Thus, for example, R. Gershom ben Judah decided that a man faced with the choice of participating either in a funeral or in a wedding should choose the latter; he learned this from Isaiah 45:18 ("He did not create it a waste, but formed it for habitation") which, in the Talmud, was applied to a different matter.[46] R. Gershom ben Judah likewise legislated a new interpretation concerning inheritance: "And it is further written, 'When he wills his property to his sons...' (Deut. 21:16)—the father bequeathes and not the surrogate parents."[47] He even noted explicitly that this interpretation was his own and was not of talmudic origin.

Such interpretations led R. Joseph Tov Elem to conclude that a community has no right to levy taxes on land, and R. Judah ha-Cohen determined the extent of a community's rights in exercising authority over its members.[48] This approach was seemingly acceptable at the time. When many of the students in the Mainz yeshiva challenged a ruling of R. Gershom ben Judah and his colleagues to the effect that a ritual circumcision scheduled for Rosh Hashana must precede the blowing of the *shofar*, R. Gershom convinced them to accept his ruling by providing an interpretation of a biblical verse.[49]

88

The number of such interpretations in these rabbis' writings is great. R. Gershom ben Judah made explicit reference to the method of relying on the Bible and Mishna as prime sources in his ruling: "Therefore we have proof neither from the Bible nor from Mishna..., but rather we should avail ourselves of the Bible and Mishna..." Elsewhere, he wrote, "And even though this judgment is not explicitly written, nor is it explicit in the Mishna, we should say that from careful reading of the Bible and of Mishna, such is the judgment."[50]

We are unable to determine whether R. Judah ben Meir ha-Cohen Leontin followed the same pattern, but it is an illuminating fact that the only two words which have survived in the original in his writings are *halakha kamikra*—"Halakha is as the biblical verse renders." [51] Such fine-tuning of biblical passages is not required for the plain meaning of the passage, and often it does not fit the approach of halakhic midrash. As noted, most such cases— those of R. Gershom ben Judah in particular—are meant to provide nothing more than incidental support. This is indicated by R. Gershom himself: "...We should say that from careful reading of the Bible and of Mishna, such is the judgment."

This method is extremely rare in other Jewish centers. We do not encounter it among the Babylonian Geonim (apart from R. Sa'adia Gaon, as we shall note), nor among the early Sephardi rabbis of the tenth and eleventh centuries (R. Moses ben Ḥanokh, his son R. Ḥanokh, and R. Joseph ibn Avitur). [52] The technique disappears altogether in Ashkenaz itself in the latter half of the eleventh century. In the hundreds of surviving responsa of this period, there are neither innovative exegeses nor traditional interpretations applied to new situations. It is true that R. Samuel ben Judah ha-Cohen relied in theory on biblical exegesis, but he was merely quoting his father. Indeed, his colleagues expressed surprise about his use of this method. [53] On the other hand, hundreds of biblical exegeses have been preserved in *Sefer Ḥasidim* (for the specific purpose of pointing to the moral content of biblical passages). The ties between the Ḥasidim of Ashkenaz and the early rabbis of that region (prior to 1096) were very close, both in methodology and in literary creativity, and it is possible that this book preserves a remnant of the early rabbis' technique. [54]

We have no clear evidence that this reliance on the Bible should be ascribed to the tradition of Palestine, but we believe such a connection may be proposed, due to three factors:

1. Strong ties to the Bible are found in the religious poetry of Palestine and the apocalyptic literature written in the early Middle Ages. [55]

2. Hints at such a tie are preserved in the few extant responsa of Palestinian Geonim. However, most of these responsa are extremely concise, and the rabbis occasionally noted their ruling without providing support for it. Thus it is hard to discern their methodology. Two pieces of biblical exegesis have been preserved in Palestinian responsa in a work named *Hagahot Mordekhai ha-Gadol*. One of them notes this link explicitly:

Why do we recite *kedusha* on the Sabbath and not during the week? *Kedusha* is not written concerning the six days of creation, and it is written concerning the Sabbath, for it reads "And God blessed the seventh day, and hallowed (*va-y'kadesh*) it..." and elsewhere it is written "to make a difference between the holy (*ha-kadosh*) and the profane." And why do we say it on the Day of the New Moon and on festivals? It is written: "...a perpetual burnt-offering for the month..." Thus from the Bible. Where is it in the Mishna? "R. Ḥiyya teaches..."[56]

3. Such exegesis appears in the responsa of R. Saʻadia Gaon. Only he among the Babylonian geonim put this method to real use, and it may reasonably be supposed that he acquired it during his years of study in Palestine prior to settling in Babylonia. On one occasion, he hinted at this.[57]

Our contention, however, could seemingly be contradicted by Pirkoi ben Baboi in his letter to North Africa:

> And accordingly, the Lord established two centers for the people of Israel, who deal in Torah by day and by night, ... and wage the wars of Torah until they ferret out the truth and discern the true halakha, and provide proof from biblical verses and Mishna and Talmud, so that the people of Israel may not err in matters of Torah.[58]

It appears, however, that this is but a figure of speech—found elsewhere as well—and we must not read too much into it. One can judge only the evidence of one's own eyes, and in the thousands of surviving responsa of the Babylonian geonim, biblical verses are invoked for halakha in extremely few cases, much fewer than in the several dozen found in R. Gershom ben Judah's responsa alone. Pirkoi may have simply used common figures of speech; but it may also be that he sought to describe the yeshivas of Babylon in an ideal fashion, in a tendentious letter which attempted to divert the Jews of North Africa and perhaps of other centers from the tradition of Palestine.[59]

Factors Strengthening the Babylonian Tradition

Even if the final two points of evidence (ties to tannaitic sources and reliance on the Bible) are unsatisfactory testimony to the shift toward Babylonia which took place in the mid-eleventh century, the first point is clear and stands independently. What factor led to the acceleration of this process at this precise time? Though we have no way of providing a clear-cut answer, we may approximate one, based on three factors:

1. The growing importance of Babylonia in other eleventh-century Diaspora centers. In Palestine, too, we find clear evidence of the growth of the influence of the Babylonian Talmud.[60] In fact, Palestine had lost that battle by the eleventh century, and it would not be surprising to find that this led to a weakening of the hold of Palestinian tradition on the Diaspora communities. Even in Italy, where the ties to the Palestinian tradition were relatively stronger, a similar increase in the influence of the Babylonian Talmud took place over the course of the eleventh century. A significant source preserved in manuscript in the Bodleian Library shows that some of Italy's most noteworthy rabbis had set out to study in R. Hai Gaon's academy. During a controversy among them concerning the matter of non-diseased adhesions (Aram. *sirkha beriya*), they turned to the halakhic works and responsa of the Babylonian sages.[61] R. Isaac

ben Judah, head of the Mainz yeshiva in the latter half of the eleventh century, learned the methodology of R. Hai Gaon from these rabbis.[62]

2.   The compilation of the responsa of the Babylonian sages and their dissemination among Torah scholars. These many responsa and other sources, transmitted mainly by merchants, were collated in a most valuable undertaking by R. Joseph Tov Elem and in other anthologies as well. This led to their wider dissemination and increased influence.[63]

3.   The sense of decline which characterized almost all the rabbis of Mainz in the latter half of the eleventh century. One cannot compare the self-confidence and self-esteem of these later rabbis to that of their forebears of the late tenth and early eleventh centuries. Clear traces of this sense of decline were already apparent in the works of R. Eliezer ha-Gadol and R. Jacob ben Yakar and even more so among those who followed them in the Mainz yeshiva.[64] One whose self-image is not high will hesitate to disagree with the rulings of the geonim of Babylon, and most certainly will not quarrel with the Babylonian Talmud. It would be far from correct to interpret biblical passages in an innovative manner for the purpose of rendering practical halakhic rulings, even if only by way of support, when these cases were in fact determined by personal judgment.

Linguistic Traditions and Practices

The influence of Palestine remained strong in two areas through the second half of the eleventh century and even afterwards: in linguistic tradition (mainly pronunciation), and in various customs (mostly those of certain families, and not those of the Jewish public in general).

There is no reason to be surprised by the preservation of ancient linguistic tradition. Pronunciation of the vowel symbol *kamatz* as *patah*, and of *zeireh* as *segol,* does not constitute a deviation from the halakhic tradition of Babylonia and its Jewish community. Moreover, it was hard for the Jews of Ashkenaz to change their linguistic traditions and abandon the ways of their forefathers, especially when the matter touched upon what they regarded as the central aspect of their spiritual endeavors—prayer. All the traditional religious poems that claimed a central role in their liturgy were built on their traditional system of pronunciation. It is a fact that even as late as the thirteenth century—when Babylonian practice is acknowledged by all to have clearly taken hold in Ashkenaz—the impact of the Palestinian linguistic tradition is still readily recognizable.[65]

Of greater importance is the preservation of Palestinian tradition in the customs of certain early Ashkenazi families and rabbis, in various areas but mainly in liturgy. More than in any other framework, Palestinian tradition was preserved in German liturgy up to 1096, and to a certain extent thereafter.

Notwithstanding, it is doubtful that we may interpret this as an actual link with Palestine, even in the latter half of the eleventh century. It seems more likely that those Jews of Ashkenaz who observed their families' traditions strictly merely sought the perpetuation of their forefathers' customs. It was loyalty to family tradition which brought about this conservatism, even when those who preserved such tradition knew that it differed from that of the Babylonian sources.

This reservation is related first and foremost to the question of whether the Jews of Ashkenaz were aware that they were observing Palestinian and not Babylonian practices. Such awareness would indicate their active interest in preserving those customs. It is difficult to suppose that they were unaware of the connection in at least two matters — the reciting of a blessing upon removing *tefillin,* and their custom of separating *halla* from dough.[66] But it seems that in the overwhelming majority of cases, the answer is negative. The best possible evidence of this is the great amazement expressed by the sons of Makhir concerning R. Judah ha-Cohen's ruling that one should sit in mourning even for an infant who had lived fewer than thirty days, a judgment which contradicts the Babylonian Talmud. Had they known that this was the practice in Palestine, it is hard to imagine that they would have reacted. Moreover, in all their extended and comprehensive treatment of customs, the sons of Makhir never noted that any custom was rooted in Palestinian practice, even though they struggled to fathom the nature of such customs.[67] Nor have we found reference to the customs of Palestine, or any attempt to link them to Ashkenazi practices, in the comments of other rabbis of the second half of the eleventh century. This strengthens our contention that Ashkenazi Jews preserved these customs out of deep attachment to family tradition and not out of ties with Palestine. In effect, these were merely rote practices. This holds especially true in the family of R. Judah ha-Cohen, a scholar who seems to have preserved Palestinian tradition more strictly than did others — although this may apply to the descendants of the Kalonymos family as well.[68] In any event, the extant sources do not enable us to indicate various schools of thought among the early rabbis of Ashkenaz regarding ties to the Palestinian or the Babylonian tradition.

The Situation in the Tenth Century

The significant change in the mid-eleventh century raises the question whether the accepted historiographical assumption concerning the hegemony of Palestine over Ashkenazi Jewry prior to 1096 is essentially valid, but should be restricted to the tenth and early eleventh centuries. The few surviving sources of that period do not enable us to provide a clear answer. It is apparent that the influence of Palestinian tradition was greater in the early period, for the growth of Babylonian influence was a gradual process which it is difficult to measure precisely. The few extant sources indicate that in this early period influences of both traditions existed. It is told of R. Moses ha-Zaken ben Kalonymos of Mainz, in the first half of the tenth century, that he was wont to recite the "Song of the Sea" daily during the morning prayer:

> And in the days of the early ones, when they would reach the words *le-shem tif'artekha,* the leader of the prayers would rise and begin reciting *yishtabaḥ shimkha.* And when our greatly learned Rabbi Moses of Lucca, son of our Rabbi Kalonymos, came to Mainz in the days of Charlemagne, he instructed those of his generation to continue reciting as far as *u-shmo eḥad.* For he was the greatest of his time, and nothing was hidden from him. This was our Rabbi Moses ha-Zaken, who founded the group [that recited] *eimat norotekha...*"[69]

It is clear that this practice deviated from that of Babylonia for in the *siddur* of R. Amram Gaon and in other Babylonian sources, the "Song of the Sea" is not included in the morning service. Yet one cannot state with certainty that its recitation is a Palestinian custom. A. Schechter was of this opinion, relying on the account in *Sefer ha-Manhig* which states that the "Song of the Sea" is recited in Palestine.[70] Can we, however, deduce the situation in ninth-century Palestine from a custom practiced there in the twelfth century, especially when Palestine was depicted together with Babylonia and other centers? Moreover, the selfsame source reveals that prior to R. Moses's arrival in Mainz, the Jews in Ashkenaz (at least those of that city) followed the Babylonian and not the Palestinian practice.

Of the five of R. Judah ben Meir ha-Cohen Leontin's halakhic rulings that have survived, three may have a bearing on the question of the ties with Palestinian and Babylonian tradition. In the case of reversing an oath, R. Judah explicitly disagrees with the Babylonian geonim and holds that an oath may be reversed even when the Torah obligation remains in force; it is still doubtful whether the Palestinian rabbis shared this view and whether he knew of such a tradition. Were it so, it would be hard to suppose that R. Gershom ben Judah, his student, who endeavored to explain and defend the methodology of his mentor, would have failed to mention it.[71]

Likewise, R. Judah ben Meir ha-Cohen Leontin taught that the monetary provisions of the Sabbatical year apply in post-Temple times. Various sources imply that this was both the position and practice of the Jews of Palestine. But some Babylonian rabbis also held this view, and we are thus unable to determine the source of his tradition.[72]

The third ruling concerns R. Judah's decision that a Torah scholar who has passed away during Hanukkah should be eulogized: "They did not acknowledge Divine judgment at the grave, nor did they eulogize during Hanukkah, and they said that our Rabbi ha-Cohen Leontin had already eulogized a Torah scholar."[73] The word "already" (Heb. *kvar*) demonstrates that there was a certain measure of innovation in his act, which elicited varying opinions. The odd aspect is that the Babylonian Talmud explicitly permits the practice: "R. Papa said that no festival stands before a great scholar, and *a fortiori* not

Hanukkah and Purim."[74] It clearly emerges that a eulogy is to be permitted.

It is nearly certain that the source of the problem was in a different judgment found in the Palestinian Talmud.

> R. Tanḥum b. Illai died on Hanukkah. R. Dosa died on the first day of Nissan. A feast was held....[75] They believed it to have been done in accordance with the views of Rabbanan, and investigated and found that it was not in accordance with the views of Rabbanan.[76]

This position of disagreement with "Rabbanan" (the Rabbis) relates to Hanukkah as well, for were it not so, there would have been no point in mentioning R. Tanḥum's situation. The two acts were paired and the reservation applies to both. It is of course possible that there was an alternate Palestinian tradition which permitted eulogizing on the intermediate days of festivals and on Hanukkah,[77] but from this source it is clear that the latter position had its opponents. Their use of the anonymous and collective phrasing "Rabbanan" (*Fragmentary PT:* "Rabbanin") had the additional effect of influencing some Ashkenazi Jews in the early period to follow this tradition and to oppose eulogizing. R. Judah ben-Meir ha-Cohen Leontin, in this case, tipped the scales in favor of the Babylonian (or alternate Palestinian) tradition.

The aforementioned ruling of R. Gershom ben Judah — that one should recite a blessing over spices when a festival enters with the exit of the Sabbath — may also be ascribed to this early period. His position testifies to a tradition observed in the generation preceding his as well. That is: he disputes the Babylonian Talmud and, in this case, chooses to follow the Palestinian Talmud, as did his predecessors. On the other hand, he noted that some did not recite the blessing; that is, some observed Babylonian tradition. Thence it holds that even in this early period it is hard to speak of a uniform halakhic tradition in the communities of Ashkenaz. In parts of the methodology of R. Meshullam ben Kalonymos as well (second half of the tenth century), we find close ties to Babylonian tradition and, as noted, a tendency to turn to Babylonian rabbis for counsel.[78]

The conclusion which emerges is that we lack the means to determine clearly which tradition exerted the greater influence in the tenth and early eleventh centuries, that of Babylonia or that of Palestine. There is no doubt that Ashkenaz felt close ties to both traditions, and there is no substantive reason to view Ashkenaz as subject to Palestinian hegemony in this formative period.

Nevertheless, acknowledgment of the primary influence of Babylonia, at least from the second half of the eleventh century onwards, does not mandate any devaluation of the ties of early Ashkenazi Jewry to the Palestinian tradition. The relationship of Ashkenaz to Palestine during the period under discussion was greater than that of any other Jewish community in Europe, with the exception of Italy. We have not set out to belittle this significant relationship, but rather to refute the claim that it was decisive and greater than the ties of early Ashkenazi

Jewry to Babylonian tradition, and in so doing to establish more precise time-frames for further study.[79]

Translated by Naftali Greenwood.

1   The Hebrew version of this article, which appeared in *Shalem* 3 (1981), included a comprehensive appendix which discussed two Palestinian customs that were transferred to Ashkenaz. A summary of this appendix has been included below, in note 66.

2   See especially, J. Mann, *The Jews in Egypt and in Palestine under the Fatimid Caliphs*, 1-2 (Oxford, 1920-1922); *Sefer haYishuv*, 2 (Jerusalem, 1944); also various studies by S.D. Goitein, *Palestinian Jewry in Early Islamic and Crusader Times* (Hebrew), ed. J. Hacker (Jerusalem, 1980).

3   S.J. Rapoport, *Biographies of the Great Figures of Israel*, 1 (Hebrew) (Warsaw, 1913), p. 246.

4   *Scroll of Aḥima'aẓ* (Hebrew) (Jerusalem, 1944), p. 144. He included the Jews of Italy and Ashkenaz among "those of the West." See also pp. 111-124. His views should not be restricted to the beginning of the period; the period of our discussion is included in the "first millenium" after the destruction of the Temple.

5   *Sefer haYishuv*, 2, introduction. See also the author's comments, pp. 43-44: "Concerning the ties between Palestine and the Jews of France and Germany, our knowledge is extremely limited, although the influence of Palestine upon them was most profound... Nevertheless these details — some presented here and others not — do not form a complete picture; indeed *they exceed those concerning relationships between Babylonia and France and Germany*" (emphasis mine; see below). Similarly in *HaShiloaḥ* 35 (1918):9 ff. See also A.M. Lifschitz, *Works*, 1 (Hebrew) (Jerusalem, 1947), pp. 16, 56.
For the attempt to link the development of various institutions in the medieval Jewish community to Palestine, see Y. Baer, "The Foundations and Beginnings of the Jewish Community Organization in the Middle Ages" (Hebrew) *Zion* 15 (1950):2: "It is a nearly certain supposition that in Palestine the democratic image of the community was preserved and revived in the 'geonic period,' and that here the foundations of the well-known organizational forms of the medieval European community were laid." Note also his continuation there, which refers to the customs of 'stopping the service'. However the custom has no connection to Palestine. See my article "The Origins and Essence of the Custom of 'Stopping the Service'" (Hebrew), in *Milet* (Tel Aviv, 1983), pp. 199-219. Agus upheld this without any reservations: "...However, this complex law, no doubt, was not developed in the Middle Ages... but every one of its numerous details was transmitted orally from the days of the Second Temple" (A. Agus, "The Oral Traditions of Pre-Crusade Ashkenazic Jewry," *Studies and Essays in Honor of A.A. Neuman* [Leiden, 1962], p. 4).
We should also make mention of a handsome illustration of the impact of this theory in the writings of a most esteemed and erudite scholar. L. Ginzberg questioned the ruling of R. Meshullam ben Kalonymos in a responsum found in the *geniza* along with his other responsa (and which explicitly bore R. Meshullam's name!), because it does not seem consistent — in Ginzberg's view — with the methodology of the Palestinian Talmud: "The view of R. Meshullam that the Levirate commandment takes slight preference is difficult to accept, for the influence of Palestine was greater upon Italy than upon the other lands of Europe;" *Geniza Studies*, 2 (Hebrew) (New York, 1929), p. 271. Though he chose his words carefully ("greater"), why should he have been amazed and perplexed if the influence of Palestine was not perceived as decisive? Concerning the essence of his discussion, it should be noted that the Jews of early Ashkenaz — and of Spain at the time — generally carried out Levirate marriage, rather than invoking *ḥaliẓa*. See, in the meantime, J. Katz, "Levirate Marriage (*Yibbum*) and *Ḥaliẓa* in Post-Talmudic Times," *Tarbiẓ* 51(1982):59-106.

6   A. Schechter, *Studies in Jewish Liturgy* (Philadelphia, 1930), pp. 33-40, goes too far in his conclusions. Among other things, he ignores some highly valuable sources which yield a different picture, including Neubauer's findings in the Bodleian Library MS (see note 61 below). Italy does not fall within the confines of this study, but the exaggerated conclusion

95

regarding Germany applies to Italy as well. See below.

7   Concerning the first, see A.S. Aescoli, *Messianic Movements in Israel* (Hebrew) (Jerusalem, 1956), pp. 133-136, and the sources cited there. The second is mentioned in various sources by Rashi's students, and was published in part from the *geniza* MS, by J. Mann (above, n. 2), pp. 221-222, and in full from the aforementioned MS by Marmorstein, *REJ* 73 (1921):84-92.

8   See Schechter (above, n. 6), and the comments of I. Davidson, *JQR* 21(1931):241-279, concerning Schechter's views. A number of important studies have been published on this topic in recent years. Consult the bibliography in A. Fleischer, *Hebrew Religious Poetry in the Middle Ages* (Hebrew) (Jerusalem, 1975), pp. 501, 510. The involvement with the Bible has no relevance here, although it is true that Assaf attempted to bring this element into the picture as well: "As in Palestine, there were people in France whose main preoccupation was with the Bible; ...readers from Palestine appeared frequently in Rashi's time as well..." (*Sefer haYishuv*, 2, p. 43). In fact, however, there is no proof whatsoever of a connection between the development of biblical exegesis in northern France and Palestine. In Spain and other centers as well—communities for which a Palestinian hegemony was not claimed—there were people preoccupied mainly with Bible. Rashi's comment concerning "melodies of biblical chant... (one) would move his hand according to the melody, as I have seen among those readers who have come from Erez Yisrael..." (*Berakhot* 62b) testifies to his having encountered such readers, but not to any ties with their custom. On the contrary, they appeared to constitute the exception which proves the rule. Thence it emerges that the custom in Rashi's locale—and certainly that of Ashkenaz, in which he studied—was different, for were it not so, he would have taken note of the fact and have called upon his mentors for support.

   The fact that biblical manuscripts from Ashkenaz often rely upon the Hebrew tradition and terminology of Tiberias is likewise no proof. Dr. Menahem Cohen, who specializes in this field, has informed me that a similar situation existed in Spain and in the entire Jewish Diaspora outside of Babylonia at the time—that is, in those communities in which Babylonian influence was greater by far. Instances of the terminology of Babylonian tradition in Ashkenazi manuscripts are even more numerous than they are in Sephardi manuscripts.

9   See A. Eldar, *Pre-Ashkenazi Recitation Tradition* (Hebrew) (unpublished Ph. D. dissertation, Jerusalem, 1977).

10 This is not the place to discuss this important topic. One example of the exaggerated belief that the ancient tradition of Ashkenaz is, as a rule, Italian tradition will suffice. R. Yakar ben Makhir asked R. Kalonymos ben Shabtai, who had emigrated from Rome to Worms c. 1075, to verify the customs of "our rabbis in Rome" concerning the Ninth of Av. These customs were known neither to him nor to his brother in Mainz. Furthermore, their examination reveals that these customs were somewhat different from those of Worms and Mainz (*Ma'aseh haGe'onim* (Hebrew), ed. Epstein [Berlin, 1909], pp. 35-36). Concerning the founding of the early Ashkenazi communities and the emigration routes thereto in the ninth, tenth and eleventh centuries, see Elbogen, "Siedlungs-geschichte," *Germania Judaica*, 1 (Tübingen, 1963²), pp. xviii-xx; S. Eppenstein, "Zur Frühgeschichte der Juden in Deutschland usw," *MGWJ* 63(1919):165-166. Sources which have since come into print enable us to expand the analysis, especially where Eppenstein's discussion is concerned, e.g. p. 167, concerning immigration to Mainz. See also A. Grossman, *The Early Sages of Ashkenaz* (Hebrew) (Jerusalem, 1981), pp. 4-9. See in the meantime, S. Schwarzfuchs, "L'opposition Tsarfat-Provence: la Formation du Judaïsme du Nord de la France," *Hommage à Georges Vajda* (Louvain, 1980), pp. 135-150; A. Grossman, "Emigration of Jews to Germany" (Hebrew), in *Emigration and Settlement in Jewish and General History* (Jerusalem, 1982), pp. 109-128. The influence of the Babylonian and Sephardic tradition on the customs, liturgy and general religious writings of the Jews of northern France was still apparent in the eleventh century See A. Grossman, "Nation and History" (Hebrew), *Proceedings Eighth World Congress of Jewish Studies* (Jerusalem, 1983), pp. 221-231.

11 L. Ginzberg, *Geonica,* 2 (New York, 1909), p. 57; B.M. Lewin, *R. Sherira Gaon* (Hebrew) (Jaffa, 1917), pp. 32-39.

12 Lewin, *ibid.,* p. 38. It is true that R. Meshullam regarded this as dependent on the interpretation in *Pesahim,* but this interpretation has clear ramifications concerning the custom as practiced. Agus's views were published in *Horev* 12(1957):196. Agus describes R. Kalonymos and R.

Meshullam in the nearly standard fashion, as personages of Mainz. See his *Urban Civilization in Pre-Crusade Europe,* 1 (New York, 1965), pp. 32-37. While we have no reliable information concerning R. Meshullam's father, R. Meshullam himself was by all appearances Italian. See my article, *Zion* 40(1975):154 ff.

13   *Responsa of Early Geonim* (Hebrew), ed. D. Kassel (Berlin, 1848), section 118; *Geniza Studies,* 2 (above, n. 5), pp. 219 (twice: once in the original and once in Ginzberg's commentary), 229, 231.

14   D. Goldschmidt, *Maḥzor for the High Holy Days according to the Ashkenazi Rite* (Hebrew) (Jerusalem, 1970), p. 15. See also I.M. Elbogen and Y. Heinemann, *Jewish Prayer in its Historical Development* (Hebrew) (Tel Aviv, 1972), p. 6; L. Lunz, *Die Ritus des synagogalen Gottesdienstes* (Berlin, 1859), p. 38.

15   Cited once by R. Meshullam ben Kalonymos of Lucca, *Ha'Itur, Get Ḥaliẓa,* 2 (Hebrew) (New York, 1955), p. 5d. A complete listing of citations of the Palestinian Talmud in the writings of the rabbis of Ashkenaz can be found in the Hebrew version of this article, in *Shalem,* 3 (Jerusalem, 1981), p. 68, n. 15.

16   See discussion of the blessing over removal of *tefillin* below.

17   A. Grossman, *Early Sages...* (above, n. 10), ch. 4, 5, 8, 9, and especially 10, sect. 1.

18   They have been partially examined in various portions of my book (above, n. 10). See also the discussion of the ties between the thought of R. Moses ha-Zaken ben Kalonymos and of R. Judah ben Meir ha-Cohen Leontin, and the schools of Babylon and Palestine respectively. See below concerning the ties between the Jewish community of Christian Europe and the Islamic world during the ninth, tenth and eleventh centuries, and the question of the autonomy of the early Ashkenazi communities; see also introduction to "The Origins... of 'Stopping the Service'" (above, n. 5). Analysis of this last subject reveals that apart from one case, there is no substantive testimony concerning relationships between the practices of the early Ashkenazi communities and Palestinian tradition.

19   "Cuidam Judeo mercatori, qui terram repromissionis sepuis adire, et inde ad cismarinas provintias multa praeciosa et incognita solitus erat afferre." J. Aronius, *Regesten zur Geschichte der Juden etc.* (Berlin, 1887-1902), No. 75. Richulf served as Archbishop of Mainz from 787 to 813.

20   See footnote 7 above.

21   See footnote 8 above.

22   J. Mann (above, n. 2), 2, p. 191; and more completely in N. Golb, *History and Culture of the Jews of Rouen in the Middle Ages* (Hebrew) (Tel-Aviv, 1976), pp. 163-170; see also pp. 3-12.

23   See Grossman (above, n. 12).

24   R.S. Lopez and I.W. Raymond, *Medieval Trade in the Mediterranean World* (New York, 1955), pp. 31-33, and M. Gil, "The Rādhānite Merchants," *JESHO* 17 (1974):299-328; see comprehensive bibliography on pp. 323-328. In contradiction to the view once commonly held that their origins were in Europe, Gil proposes that they be regarded as having stemmed from the district of Rādhān in the vicinity of Baghdad. This hypothesis better suits the wording of Ibn Khurradadhbah. This does not affect our suggestion that they served as conduits for transmitting cultural traditions. Ibn Khurradadhbah's description implies that their journeys were rather frequent.

25   This topic exceeds the parameters of our discussion, and must be considered within a broader survey of the economic and cultural ties between Jewish centers in Christian Europe and those in the Muslim Caliphate from the ninth through the eleventh centuries (the first clear evidence stems from the ninth). In any case, it is certain that the sources do not confirm S. Assaf's aforementioned conclusion that the details testify to closer relationships between the Jews of France and Ashkenaz with Palestine, than with Babylonia.

One of Assaf's quotations (see above, n. 5) may even be misleading. In his words: "R. Nathan ben Makhir, brother of Rabbenu Gershom, Light of the Exile, corresponded with R. Amram Yerushalmi, and R. Meshullam ben Moses of Mainz posed his questions to 'the Lions who reside in Jerusalem,' these being the Gaon R. Elijah and his son, R. Abiathar." R. Nathan did not direct his questions to Palestine! R. Amram Yerushalmi resided in Mainz and was among its foremost scholars. He may have emigrated there from Jerusalem; it is also possible that he had visited there, and was thus surnamed. In any case, this halakhic correspondence took place in Mainz, as clearly emerges in *Ma'aseh Makhiri*. See *Sefer haPardes,* section 23, and *Siddur*

Rabbenu Shlomo of Worms, ed. Herschler (Jerusalem, 1972), p. 277; this source, however, was unavailable to S. Assaf. R. Nathan ben Makhir was not the nephew of R. Gershom ben Judah, but rather his great-grandson. See my remarks in *Tarbiẓ* 45(1977):112-113.

26 See especially Aronius, *Regesten* (above, n. 19), Nos. 142-144, and H. Tykocinski, "Die Verfolgung der Juden Mainz in Jahre 1012," *Beiträge zur Geschichte der deutschen Juden. Festschrift... Philippsons* (Leipzig, 1916), pp. 1-5.

27 See P. Alphandéry, *La chrétienté et l'idée de croisade,* 1, ed. A. Dupront (Paris, 1954), pp. 43-56, and J. Prawer, "Christianity between Heavenly Jerusalem and Earthly Jerusalem," *Jerusalem Through the Ages* (Hebrew) (Jerusalem, 1969), pp. 179 ff. (esp. pp. 185-189).

28 See J. Mann, *HaTekufa* 23 (1925):253 ff.; A.S. Aescoli (above, n. 7), pp. 154 ff.

29 In general, the central role of the *piyyutim* in prayer and the messianic hope they expressed also strengthened the ties with Zion.

30 See A. Grossman (above, n. 10), chap. 1, 3, 4, that discuss the sources used by these rabbis.

31 The writers were not in proximity to R. Jacob ben Yakar (d. 1064) while composing their work; they were rather close to R. Isaac ben Judah and other scholars active in the 1070s and later.

32 Concerning this composition, see Sulzbach, *JJLG* 5 (1908):367-370, and Epstein, *ibid.* 8 (1911):447-451. My reasons for ascribing this book to R. Jacob ben Yakar are delineated in my book (above, n. 10), ch. 5. Even those unwilling to accept this contention will find it hard to disagree with the conclusion that this work was prepared and edited in Ashkenaz during the period under discussion.

33 See my commentary on this work in *'Alei Sefer* 1 (1975):7-34.

34 *Responsa of R. Meir of Rothenburg* (ed. Prague, 1895), section 263. See also the arguments which R. Gershom ben Judah raised in justification of his stance.

35 He ruled against the position taken in the Babylonian Talmud against the rulings of the Babylonian geonim in a number of matters (see footnote 68 below and, in greater detail, Grossman [above, n. 10], ch. 4).

36 *Shibbolei haLeket,* ed. Buber, order *Pesaḥ,* section 218, p. 92a.

37 The one exception was by R. Isaac ha-Levi of Worms, noteworthy for his originality and for a self-appraisal higher than that of any other Ashkenazi rabbi in the third quarter of the eleventh century. He chose, however, to envelop it in respectful rhetoric, unlike his aforementioned predecessors: "And that great man, who compiled *Halakhot Gedolot* is a marvelous scholar; but we have been unable to fathom his thoughts in several places... but one does not react to a lion after his death" (*Ma'aseh haGe'onim* [above, n. 10], p. 94). See also his response to Rashi: "Moreover, we have written above in the name of the undisputed (author of) *Halakhot Gedolot* (!) who provides instruction to all Israel..." (*Responsa of Rashi,* ed. Elfenbein [New York, 1942], p. 66). We must not associate this with the strictness with which the Jews of Ashkenaz preserved their forefathers' traditions, including those which contradicted Babylonian Talmud or geonic practice (e.g. *Ma'aseh haGe'onim,* p. 47 bottom) for, as will be proved, their motivation in such cases lay elsewhere.

38 See *Responsa of R. Gershom ben Judah,* ed. Edelberg (New York, 1956), sections 33, 63, 75, and *Shenaton haMishpat haIvri,* 2 (Hebrew) (Jerusalem, 1975), p. 198, among other such sources. There is no need to say that we learn nothing from them alone; we may only add them to the methodology which emerges from the very use of these sources.

39 See discussion of these scholars in my book (above, n. 10), ch. 2-4. An apt illustration of the point at hand is found in the fact that R. Meshullam ben Kalonymos chose to buttress his halakha that "Jewish martyrs who were handed over to the authorities and whose houses had been confiscated" had already despaired of retaining ownership—from a dubious tannaitic source and not from an explicit amoraic source, unlike his contemporary, R. Moses ben Hanokh in Spain (*Responsa of Geonim of Orient and Occident,* ed. Müller [Berlin, 1887], section 179). R. Meshullam is quoted in *Geniza Studies* (above, n. 5) 2, p. 213, section XV, and bases his comments on a *baraita* found in *Sanhedrin* 48b. This explains L. Ginzberg's query (*ibid.,* p. 198, section 15).

40 It is nearly certain that the early rabbis in Ashkenaz dealt in Mishna as a topic of learning for its own sake as well. See my book (above, n. 10), pp. 416-424.

41 Apart from Italy; for we have no substantial information concerning its rabbis' methodology of study nor of which talmudic sources they availed themselves in rendering halakhic rulings.

Nevertheless, we should note that in the *Scroll of Aḥima'aẓ* (above, n. 4), p. 33, the Mishna is cited by the rabbis of Bari as a source in their decision: "And the rabbis of Bari claimed before him in response: one who saves another from conscription, from the river, or from fire, acquires him as a subject, for so did Rabbi (Judah ha-Nasi) instruct in the Mishna" (ed. Klar [Jerusalem, 1973-1974], p. 33).

42   In his commentary on *Avot,* and not in practical halakha (*Sefer haArukh,* s.v. *sa'ad* and elsewhere). Notwithstanding, biblical passages there are juxtaposed and interpreted in an innovative manner which strays from the plain meaning. See also use of biblical passages in his missive to Constantinople concerning the Karaite disputations. A. Scheiber, in *Studies in Jewish History presented to Professor Raphael Mahler...* (Hebrew), ed. S. Yeivin (Merḥavia, 1974), pp. 19-23.

43   Thus, for example, he ruled that one is obliged to pay for a loan extended him although the home of the lender was plundered along with the city's other Jewish homes, and the money would have been lost had it remained there: "It is Divinely inspired, that they had pity on him and left him this measure, for it is written, '...and how few we are who once were so many...'" This issue recalls a similar topic and exegesis in *Baba Meẓia* 106a. See *Responsa of the Rabbis of France and Lorraine* (Hebrew), ed. Müller (Vienna, 1880), section 86.

44   In his permitting an apostate *cohen* to administer the priestly benediction: "If you were to say it, it is written: 'This is how they are to call down My name on the sons of Israel, and I will bless them.' Indeed, the *cohanim* bless the people, and the Holy One gives His consent. As for the *cohen* who has abandoned Him, so does He abandon him, as it is said, '...they will desert Me and break this convenant of Mine...'" (*Maḥzor Vitry,* section 125, p. 96).

45   See I.D. Gilat, "Exegesis of Verses in the Post-Talmudic Era," *Rabbi David Ochs Memorial Volume* (Hebrew) (Ramat Gan, 1978), pp. 210-213. Although not all the sources are included, its discussion clearly demonstrates the rarity of the phenomenon. (The early rabbis of Ashkenaz are not mentioned at all.)

46   Concerning the release of one who is half-slave and half-free, according to the *Beit Shammai* position. *Gittin* 4:5 (the verse is Isaiah 45:18).

47   *Responsa of R. Gershom ben Judah* (above, n. 38), p. 147. The verse is interpreted in *Baba Batra* 130a concerning a different matter — a father's right to bequeath his estate to anyone he wishes.

48   *The Responsa of R. Joseph Tov Elem; Responsa of R. Meir of Rothenburg,* Prague edition, section 941; *Kol-Bo,* section 142; numerous passages have been interpreted for this purpose.

49   "And many of the students of the holy yeshiva found (it) hard to accept... and Rabbenu Gershom responded: It there is no circumcision, there is never to be a blowing of the *shofar,* for it is said, 'If I have not created day and night...'" (*Or Zaru'a, Hilkhot Rosh Hashana* [Zhitomir, 1862], p. 125a). See also the following sources (most of the first type): *Responsa of R. Gershom ben Judah,* sections 4, 31, 33, 68 end, and 72; *Responsa and Decisions of the Rabbis of Ashkenaz and France,* ed. E. Kupfer (Hebrew) (Jerusalem, 1973), section 173 *et al.* It is enlightening to note that R. Gershom ben Judah and his colleagues were willing to rely on the order of the prayers in rendering halakhic rulings, although considering it in general (and apparently in a great majority of other cases) as no more than support: "And they brought evidence for their position from the fixed order of prayers: and God our Lord kept the Covenant... and behold the binding (of Isaac)... that is, the Covenant first, and only then the binding; thus the blowing of the *shofar*" (*Or Zaru'a, loc. cit.*).

50   *Maḥzor Vitry,* sec. 125; *Responsa of R. Gershom ben Judah,* p. 147.

51   R. Samson ben Ẓadok, *Sefer haTashbeẓ* (Cremona, 1556), section 575.

52   Concerning isolated cases in these centers and others, see Gilat (above, n. 45). These do not contradict our views here; rather, they confirm them.

53   "R. Samuel ben Judah ha-Cohen taught in the name of his father that one sits in mourning for a grandfather... for one is obliged to honor him, and this is the thrust of (the verse) 'Your ancestors will be replaced by sons...': But his friends disagreed, saying that the verse referred only to a blessing... And his father, too, the late R. Judah ha-Cohen, sought to instruct R. Meshullam to sit in mourning for his grandfather R. Itiel, and our late Rabbi R. Eliezer ha-Gadol and the other sages would not let him" (*Ma'aseh haGe'onim* [above, n. 10], pp. 49-50). We are dealing with a basic dispute concerning the right to interpret biblical passages for practical halakhic purposes, when the method proposed is at odds with that found in the

Babylonian Talmud. After all, it is absolutely clear that R. Judah ha-Cohen was familiar with the exegesis in *Baba Batra* 159b ("It is written in the blessing"); he rather held that one may generate new interpretations. It emerges from context that the opponents of the new exegesis were companions of the son, R. Samuel, and possibly for this reason a member of the previous generation, R. Eliezer ha-Gadol, and his colleagues, opposed this ruling of R. Judah ha-Cohen. From other sources as well, we perceive the general shift to the Babylonian tradition in the mid-eleventh century, as expressed clearly in the works of R. Jacob ben Yakar and R. Eliezer ha-Gadol, somewhat younger than R. Judah ha-Cohen, who headed the Mainz yeshiva towards the mid-eleventh century.

54 Concerning their relationship with early Ashkenaz, consult the sources cited by C. Sirat, *REJ* n.s. 91 (1961):11-12, and also E.E. Urbach, *Sefer 'Arugat haBosem by A. ben 'Azriel* (Hebrew) (Jerusalem, 1963), pp. 91 ff.; J. Dan, *The Esoteric Theology of Ashkenazi Hasidim* (Hebrew) (Jerusalem, 1967-1968), pp. 13-20; H. Soloveitchik, *AJS Review*, 1 (1976), pp. 311 ff.

55 Concerning *piyyut,* see A. Mirsky, *Yose ben Yose Poems* (Hebrew) (Jerusalem, 1977), pp. 42 ff.; I. Yahalom, *The Language of Piyyut* (in publication). Concerning apocalyptic literature, see I. Even-Shmuel, *Midrashei Ge'ula* (Hebrew) (Jerusalem-Tel Aviv, 1968).

56 A.I. Agus, "Responsa of the Geonim of Palestine and Babylonia," *Horev* 12 (1957):206.

57 "For in the Pentateuch and in the Prophets and in the Mishna and in the Talmud, we have found proof and halakha to the effect that one who performs under compulsion is exempt from (the penalties) of that act" (*Responsa of Geonim of Orient and Occident* [above, n. 39], section 22).

58 *Tarbiz* 2 (1935):395, see also Pirkoi's comments, *Geniza Studies* (above, n. 5) 2, p. 556, in his depiction of R. Yehudai, "who excelled in Bible and Mishna and Talmud and Midrash..."

59 His letter has been discussed in various places. An especially significant source is L. Ginzberg (above, n. 5) 2, pp. 504-573; also consult B.M. Lewin, *Tarbiz* 2 (1935):383-405; I.N. Epstein, *Jewish Studies* 2 (1928):149-161; J. Mann, *REJ* 70 (1920):113-148; S. Spiegel, *Harry Austryn Wolfson Jubilee Volume* (Hebrew) (Jerusalem, 1965), pp. 243 ff.

60 See M. Margaliot, *Palestinian Halakhot from the Geniza* (Hebrew) (Jerusalem, 1974), pp. 11-15. Margaliot contends that as early as in the tenth century, "the influence of the Babylonian Talmud had grown in Palestine, and it had become the most authoritative work in the instruction of halakha, not only among those of the Babylonian community in Palestine, but also among the natives there" (*ibid.,* p. 14). Here is clear evidence that the Babylonian Talmud had achieved a central role in the responsa of Palestinian scholars in the tenth and eleventh centuries.

61 A.B. Neubauer, *HaMaggid* 17, no. 5 (1874):41. Among the scholars he cites are R. Judah ben Elhanan, R. Menahem ha-Cohen, and others.

62 *Mordechai, Shabbat,* section 398.

63 Concerning the geonic sources assembled by R. Joseph Tov Elem, see *Tosafot Pesahim* 30a, beginning "Rava said..." See also *Tosafot Avoda Zara* 67b, beginning "Except for..." and *Tosafot Nazir* 69a, beginning "(He) said..."

64 I have discussed this in detail in my book (above, n. 10), ch. 5.

65 See A. Eldar (above, n. 9).

66 Both the Palestinian and the Babylonian Talmud make mention of a special blessing current in Palestine that was said after removing the *tefillin*. From the discussion (*Berakhot* 44b) it is clear that this was not the practice in Babylonia. This is also apparent from the responsa of the Babylonian geonim, although the Palestinians continued to follow this practice. In Ashkenaz, prior to 1096, this custom was widely—and perhaps universally—followed. Even after 1096, the practice continued although, like other customs, it gradually disappeared. The *hasidim* of the twelfth-thirteenth centuries, who tended to observe the early practices of Ashkenaz, continued to utter a blessing after removing the *tefillin*.

With regard to setting aside *halla*, the Babylonian Talmud (*Bekhorot* 27a) stated that two *hallot* were to be set aside, and that the High Priest's eating of the *halla* was a rabbinic (not biblical) decree. In Palestine the custom was to set aside only one *halla*. Prior to the twelfth century, Babylonia, Spain and Provence followed the Babylonian practice; in early Ashkenaz both traditions were followed, with many observing the Palestinian practice.

Both the above were daily practices that were widely observed, and it was clear to all that it was the Palestinian tradition that was followed (particularly in the case of the blessing after removing *tefillin*), for the difference was clearly spelled out in Babylonian Talmud. Thus, these practices have particular importance in establishing the community's ties to Palestine.

67 See my book (above, n. 10), pp. 369-386.

68 R. Judah's rulings in a number of matters contradicted the views of the Babylonian authorities: mourning for an infant who had not lived thirty days; allowing reversal of an oath even of Torah enforcement; reciting the *haftara* on Shabbat Hanukkah which falls on the first day of Tevet. Consult my discussion of each of these in *'Alei Sefer* (above, n. 33), p. 25. He likewise ruled that *halitza* may not be compelled—*Responsa and Decisions of the Rabbis of Ashkenaz and France* (above, n. 47), section 141 (compare the responsa of R. Hanoch ben Moses of Spain in *Responsa of Geonim of Orient and Occident* [above, n. 39], section 185). Apart from the first halakha, however, we have no evidence that his rulings were in accordance with Palestinian tradition.

Concerning the Kalonymos family, consult the aforementioned responsa which R. Meshullam ben Moses (a descendant of this family in the second half of the eleventh century) received from the Gaon in Palestine. On the other hand, another of this family's learned offspring, R. Itiel (apparently the grandfather of this R. Meshullam), cited a book from Kayrouan containing responsa of geonim. See *Responsa of Early Geonim,* ed. Kassel (Berlin, 1848), section 91. R. Moses (by all appearances the son of this R. Meshullam) possessed a book of the Prophets from Kayrouan in which the *haftarot* were marked. See also *Sefer haPardes* (above, n. 25), p. 353.

69 The matter has been preserved in two manuscripts. See my article (above, n. 12), p. 158.

70 A. Schechter (above, n. 6), pp. 52-55. The source in *Sefer haManhig* is sect. 24 (ed. Y. Raphael, Jerusalem 1978, p. 54); likewise, the custom is cited there as one found in both Palestine and the Diaspora.

71 *Responsa of R. Meir of Rothenburg,* ed. Prague, sect. 264.

72 See *Ozar haGeonim* to *Gittin, responsa* section, pp. 71-73 (especially concerning Maimonides's comments on Erez Israel, sect. 183, and the opinion of R. Natronai Gaon that the Sabbatical year provisions applying to finances have not been in force since the destruction of the Temple, *ibid.,* sect. 190); and ascribed to R. Paltoi Gaon, *Horev* 12 (1957):209.

73 *Ma'aseh haGe'onim,* p. 44.

74 *Mo'ed Katan* 27b.

75 A "healing feast" (for one emerging from his initial stage of mourning), held in public. The correct wording has been preserved in fragments found in the Cairo Geniza; see L. Ginzberg, *Yerushalmi Fragments from the Geniza* (Hebrew), 1 (New York, 1909), p. 207.

76 *Mo'ed Katan* 83d, particularly halakhot 7 and 8, "so as not to make the eulogy commonplace."

77 See *Tosefta, Mo'ed* 2:16 (ed. Sh. Lieberman, 1962, p. 372). If the phrasing is indeed "even in a city street," we are to infer that the reference is to a festival. However, a *baraita* in *Shabbat* 105b is lacking the word "even" (Heb. *afilu*); the topic at hand may thus be the requirement to mourn him at all.

78 See my book (above, n. 10), pp. 49-78.

79 In *Kiryat Sefer* 56 (1981):344-352, Y. Ta-Shma dealt with my conclusions regarding the ties of the Jews of Ashkenaz to Palestine, and supported the earlier scholars who gave greater weight to the Palestinian tradition than I did. In my response to Ta-Shma, *Zion* 47 (1982):192-197, I reiterated my position. This exchange appears in English translation in *Judaica in Jerusalem* 1(1984):3.

PROPHETIC KABBALA
AND THE LAND OF ISRAEL

MOSHE IDEL

*T*his essay by M. Idel concentrates on aspects of kabbala in thirteenth century Palestine. Idel, who has done pioneering research on the thought and influence of R. Abraham Abulafia, sees the latter's methodology as the central factor in the dissemination of kabbala in Palestine, where it merged with Sufic tendencies prominent among Jewish thinkers in the Near East. Idel brings conclusive evidence regarding the existence of an important group of Palestinian kabbalists who blended Sufic components with Abulafia's system. Ironically, this Palestinian school failed to contribute to the enrichment of the concept of "the Land of Israel" as a mystical symbol.

Although a number of Jewish mystics — kabbalists — settled in Palestine early in the thirteenth century, their presence did not contribute to the development of a kabbalistic school of thought. We know almost nothing of the outcome of R. Jacob ha-Nazir of Lunel's decision to visit Palestine.[1] Nahmanides, who exerted considerable influence among the Barcelona mystics, the followers of his kabbalistic views, was nonetheless unsuccessful in motivating his disciples to settle in the Land of Israel,[2] and it would seem that his migration to Palestine did not lead to the creation of an independent kabbalistic tradition. Similarly, R. Abraham Abulafia, who reached Palestine in 1260, left no imprint there. His principal aim was to search for the legendary Sambatyon River;[3] upon his reaching Acre, however, his search came to an end due to the war which then raged between the Mameluks and the Tatars in 'Ein Harod ('Ein Jalud).[4] He thereupon retraced his steps, leaving no description in his works of Palestine and/or Acre.

In the early 1270s, Abulafia began the study of the "kabbala of names," disseminating this method among his students and followers, both personally and in writing. In 1287, while traveling through Sicily, he composed *Shomer Mizva*[5] at the request of "that fine and learned young man, R. Solomon ha-Cohen son of the late Moses ha-Cohen of Galilee in the Land of Israel, who called upon me to compose a work on the procedures of the Priestly Blessing."[6] R. Abraham Abulafia testifies elsewhere that R. Solomon had been one of his students; "and in honor of the aforementioned fine student R. Solomon . . ."[7] This is clear evidence that one of the rabbis of Palestine had learned R. Abraham Abulafia's kabbalistic doctrines from Abulafia himself, as early as 1287.

Four years later, R. Isaac ben Samuel of Acre left for Spain, and an examination of this kabbalist's writings reveals clear indications of the influence of R. Abraham Abulafia's mystical thought. These are especially apparent in *Ozar Ḥayyim*, a work which includes descriptions of R. Isaac's visions and mystical practices.[8] Furthermore, MS Sassoon 919, which contains material from *Ozar Ḥayyim*, makes mention of "the mystic sage R. Joseph ben Solomon of blessed memory of Galilee, of the province of Safed" (p. 50). The three authors we have mentioned are identified with Galilee, and two of them are associated with the thought of R. Abraham Abulafia.

To these we should add a fourth scholar — the author of *Sha'arei Zedek*.[9] The title page of this MS reads: "This book was written by R. Shem-Tov of Spain among his other works; he is of the city of Leon and is a great kabbalist. This work was written in Upper Galilee."[10] However, in a different manuscript of the same work — MS Gaster 954 — we read: "This work of true kabbala, inspiring of wisdom and understanding, was completed in the year 55 *(heh-nun)* in the month of Marḥeshvan in Hebron."[11] Whether the year *(heh-nun)* referred to 1290 or 1295 and whether we accept the location either as Upper Galilee or as Hebron, we are in any case provided with additional evidence concerning the ties between R. Abraham Abulafia and his kabbalistic methods, and the kabbalists of Palestine. In less than a decade — between 1287 when *Shomer Mizva* was written, and 1295 — nearly all the evidence pertaining to kabbala in Palestine is associated with the methodology of R. Abraham Abulafia. This fact is particularly noteworthy in light of the minimal influence of R. Abraham Abulafia's mysticism among Spanish kabbalists at the end of the thirteenth and the beginning of the fourteenth centuries. Here it is most probable to suppose that R. Solomon ben Abraham Adret's sharp attack on Abulafia and his "prophetic kabbala" deterred Spanish kabbalists from following the path of "prophetic" mysticism.[12]

A more important question in the context of this discussion, however, is why the rabbis of Palestine were influenced by precisely this school of thought. It seems to me that at least a partial answer may be derived from perusal of the works of R. Isaac ben Samuel of Acre and of the author of *Sha'arei Zedek*. These kabbalists were greatly influenced by the teachings of R. Abraham Abulafia, but their writings contain a further characteristic lacking in Abulafia's thought — one that is of interest to us. In the writings of his Eastern followers in mysticism, the kabbala of R. Abraham Abulafia acquired a Sufic component.[13]

In practical terms, this phenomenon may be explained in two ways. The first holds that R. Abraham Abulafia's teachings reached Palestine and encountered various Sufic concepts. His students subsequently effected a synthesis between the two systems. The second possibility, however, seems to me the more reasonable; it assumes the existence of a Sufic-Jewish stream of thinking in the East prior to the dissemination of the kabbala of R. Abraham Abulafia. When word spread of this school of mysticism — which is similar in several aspects to Sufic and Yoga elements — scholars of Eastern lands sought ways to learn R. Abulafia's teachings. Consequently, R. Solomon ben Moses of Galilee went to Sicily to learn them. Thereafter, writers such as R. Isaac ben Samuel of Acre, and the author of *Sha'arei Zedek* emphasized the Sufic fundamentals within works in which R. Abraham Abulafia's influence is apparent.

The hypothesis that Sufic-Jewish tradition existed in the East, and likely also in Palestine, may well be supported by a series of studies undertaken in recent years which show clearly that an unbroken succession of writers in the Near East — principally in Egypt — were profoundly influenced by Sufic perceptions. S.D. Goitein[14] has shown that R. Abraham ben Moses ben Maimon and his colleague R. Abraham ibn Abu-Rabiya he-Hasid joined an existing Pietist circle. Sufic influence extended into R. Abraham ben Moses ben Maimon's circle itself,[15] and a clear mystic trend may be discerned in a work apparently written by R. Obadyah,[16] son of R. Abraham. Furthermore, an anonymous author who apparently lived in the fifteenth century continued to absorb Sufic influence.[17] We have, then, an unbroken chain of authors, all of Eastern communities, who developed a mystical trend under Sufic inspiration, starting from the first third of the thirteenth century. In this context, we should also mention *Perakim be-Hazlaha* (chapter on Beatitude) attributed to Maimonides, that was composed apparently in the East,[18] and in which Sufic principles are recognizable.[19] Given this environment, there is no reason to wonder why Abulafia's ecstatic kabbala merited distribution and why Sufic principles were blended with his techniques.

A different question worthy of expanded discussion here is whether the kabbalists we have mentioned absorbed R. Abraham Abulafia's views and superimposed them on Sufic concepts, each independently of the others, or whether there existed, in fact, a circle of Palestinian kabbalists in which Sufic principles were blended with the kabbala of R. Abraham Abulafia. It would appear that there was indeed such a distinctive circle in Palestine and that we are not dealing with a number of individuals of similar approach.

The geographic proximity of Acre where R. Isaac ben Samuel received his education, and Galilee, home of R. Solomon ben Moses, and the close time-frame (as we have noted) tip the scales in favor of the assumption that there was a relationship between the two authors. If the evidence concerning *Sha'arei Zedek* having been written in Upper Galilee is correct, it points further to a concentration of kabbalists in a relatively restricted geographic environment.

Ozar Hayyim written by R. Isaac ben Samuel and *Sha'arei Zedek* share certain similarities in several areas.

1. Ephraim Gottlieb has already remarked on an identical tale concerning Ibn Sina's usage of wine, which appears precisely in these two works.[20]

2.   Both works provide the same interpretation of the talmudic dictum found in *Shabbat* 152b, concerning study of kabbala after the age of forty.[21]

3.   Both of these kabbalists, unlike R. Abraham Abulafia, depict the danger of death while in a state of ecstasy, as if it were the experience of sinking into an ocean;[22] this may be a Sufic motif.[23] R. Abraham Abulafia, however, describes this peril in terms of being consumed by a great flame.[24]

4.   As I have tried to demonstrate elsewhere, the Sufic-influenced kabbalistic material available to R. Isaac of Acre, which is associated with his mentor, is similar to the approach in *Sha'arei Zedek*.[25]

Especially interesting evidence regarding the existence of the kabbalistic circle in which R. Isaac ben Samuel of Acre participated, and which dealt with the teachings of R. Abraham Abulafia, appears in *Ozar Hayyim*:[26]

> And I heard from my late teacher ... that "youth'" is an appellation for the ancient one, for he is the eldest of all creatures, and should be so called, and not called a youth. And he said that this is but an appellation, for in Arabic they call the elder "shekh" [*shin*=300, *khaf*=20, totalling 320], and the secret of youth [*no'ar: nun*=50, *ayin*=70, *resh*=200, totalling 320] is also "shekh". One of the students asked: "Surely, however, in Arabic one says "shekh" as if written with a *yod* — "sheikh". And what is done with the remaining "ten" [*yod*]?

It is not R. Isaac's response that concerns us here, but rather the evidence that R. Abraham Abulafia's teachings were studied in a teacher-student framework.[27] Furthermore, while the teacher either knew no Arabic or accepted R. Abraham Abulafia's tradition by which "shekh" was written without the letter "*yod*,"[28] the students did know Arabic; one was the anonymous student who had posed the question, and the second was R. Isaac of Acre himself. R. Isaac's testimony does not hint at where this discussion took place; he could in theory have learned Abulafia's teachings in Italy, while on his way from Palestine to Spain, or in Spain itself — though this possibility does not seem reasonable to me. I know of no evidence in relation to Spain concerning R. Abulafia's disciples' circulating his teachings there. Sicily, on the other hand, was R. Abraham Abulafia's bastion — but at present we have no evidence concerning his students' activities after 1291.[29] It is therefore more reasonable to assume that R. Isaac of Acre learned R. Abulafia's kabbala from one of his disciples in Palestine and not in Sicily. In this context, the fact that a possible son of R. Solomon ben Moses of Galilee — R. Joseph ben Solomon — is mentioned in a manuscript that includes material from *Ozar Hayyim* may be significant.

One further piece of evidence should be added to the arguments we have cited as proof of the existence of Abulafian kabbala in Palestine. In material belonging to R. Nathan (who was, in my opinion, R. Isaac of Acre's mentor and also, apparently, a disciple of R. Abraham Abulafia[30]) there appears a unique Sufic concept whose particulars are known to us only through Eastern Sufism. The first evidence concerning a system of five worlds, including one of the imagination —

'alam al-miṭal, or 'olam ha-demut in the phrasing of the collections based on R. Nathan's work — appear only in the thirteenth-century commentary of Abdel Rizak al-Kashani on a work of Ibn 'Arabi.[31] Thus R. Nathan's Hebrew material reflects a tradition put into writing in the East in the thirteenth century. It is difficult to assume that the synthesis between R. Abraham Abulafia's concepts and those of Sufism — which is undoubtedly of Oriental origin — found its way to the West within a short period of time and only there became known to R. Isaac ben Samuel of Acre. In my view, this kabbalist served as the main conduit for transmission of the kabbalistic-Sufic synthesis from the Orient to the Occident — a fascinating "migration" of kabbalistic theory which was locked into a restricted circle in thirteenth-century Barcelona.[32] R. Abraham Abulafia, who absorbed the teachings of this group, conveyed these concepts to Italy and Greece and developed them over the 1270s and 1280s. By the end of the latter decade, his teachings had reached Palestine where they blended with the Pietist-Sufic trend of thought and thence returned in the 1290s to Spain. There, the kabbalistic-Sufic synthesis had particular influence on the kabbalistic doctrine of worlds — an influence discernible in the writings of R. Elnathan ben Moses Kalkis and R. Abraham ben Solomon Adrutiel.[33]

It seems, however, that R. Abraham Abulafia's doctrines continued to bear fruit in Palestine itself after the thirteenth century as well. The work *Badei ha-Aron*, composed in Palestine by R. Shem-Tov ibn Gaon, contains a description of a vision of a Torah scroll in the form of a circle, a vision very similar to that witnessed by R. Isaac ben Samuel of Acre and described in *Oẓar Ḥayyim*.[34] R. Abulafia's Palestinian kabbalistic doctrines spread in an unprecedented fashion in the sixteenth century.[35] *Sulam ha-'Aliya*, written by R. Judah al-Botini in Jerusalem in the early sixteenth century, is based entirely on R. Abulafia's *Ḥayyei ha-'Olam ha-Ba* and on *Sha'arei Ẓedek*. R. Abulafia's influence is visible too in *Even ha-Shoham* by R. Joseph ibn Zaiaḥ (Jerusalem, 1539). The greatest of the kabbalists of Safed, such as R. Solomon ben Moses Alkabeẓ, R. Moses Cordovero, and especially R. Ḥayyim Vital were influenced by Abulafia's *Ḥayyei ha-'Olam ha-Ba* and *Or ha-Sekhel*. A sizeable collection of sections taken from R. Abulafia's mysticism, found in a manuscript copied by R. Menahem Papu (one of the Beit-El kabbalists[36]), is but one source of evidence of the deep impact Abulafia's techniques had on the Beit-El group. In addition, traces of the mystical-Sufic synthesis found in *Oẓar Ḥayyim* are apparent in the writings of R. Judah al-Botini[37] and R. Ḥayyim Vital, and in R. Elijah de Vidas's work *Reshit Ḥokhma*.[38]

It appears then that R. Abraham Abulafia's kabbala underwent a turning point toward Sufism with its acceptance by the kabbalists of Palestine in the thirteenth century. This development, and the extreme spiritualization of Judaism apparent in Abulafia's own writings, are apparently the factors responsible for the nearly total absence of discussion of the special status of the Land of Israel or of exceptional use of symbols linked thereto in prophetic kabbala. At first sight, this seems paradoxical; the Spanish kabbalists and especially the book of *Zohar* develop the symbolism of the Land of Israel and locate the central work of kabbala there, while the mystics of Palestine itself seem to have nothing to say on the subject! We say "seem to," because the mystical systems which stress extreme ecstatic experience tend to downgrade accepted religious ritual, while objects associated with that ritual, such as the Torah, the Temple and its appurtenances, become in the system of Abulafia, labels or symbols of internal events — stations in the spiritual life of the mystic.[39] This does not hold true in moderate mystical systems such as the kabbala of *sefirot* ("Divine Emanations") — systems in which the mystic's spiritual life revolves around ritual, draws sustenance from ritual and strengthens it. One who feels in direct proximity to the Deity has no further need for any such means of ascent; at least, such a "journey" cannot be essential.[40] But if ecstatic kabbala did not make an important contribution to the enrichment of the concept of "the Land of Israel" as a mystical symbol — as did the *Zohar* — it is nonetheless true that the Land of Israel, Palestine, made a great contribution to this school of thought. This contribution, ironically, was nurtured by Muslim mysticism.

Translated by Naftali Greenwood.

1   See G. Scholem, "From Researcher to Kabbalist" (Hebrew), *Tarbiz* 6 (1935): 96–97.
2   R. Solomon ben Samuel Petit is an exception; he expounded Torah in the yeshiva of Acre, though he left behind no kabbalistic writings. Evidence of his mystical teachings may be found in R. Isaac of Acre's *Me'irat 'Einayim*. See H. Graetz, *History of the Jews* (Philadelphia, 1956), pp. 626–628.
3   See text published by A. Jellinek, *Beit ha-Midrash*, part 3, p. XL.
4   J. Prawer, *A History of the Latin Kingdom of Jerusalem*, 2 (Hebrew) (Jerusalem, 1971), pp. 420ff. Concerning Acre as a gateway for travellers at the time, see A. Grabois, "Acre as the Gateway of Jewish Immigration to Palestine in the Crusader Period," *Studies in the History of the Jewish People and the Land of Israel*, 2 (Hebrew) (Haifa, 1972), pp. 93–106.
5   It has been preserved nearly in its entirety in MS Paris (BN) 853, fols. 38a–79a. I have recently identified three pages belonging to this book from Geniza material (MS Cambridge T-S, Ar. 48.194) sent to me by Dr. Paul Fenton for identification. It seems reasonable to assume that the existence of the leaves of precisely this Abulafian work in the Geniza material is relevant to the subject of this article, namely the assertion that Abulafia's treatise was in the hands of Oriental — perhaps Sufi-biased — Jews. Details on this treatise may be found in M. Idel, *Abraham Abulafia's Works and Doctrines* (unpublished doctoral dissertation, Hebrew, Jerusalem, 1976), p. 18.
6   MS Paris (BN) 853, fol. 44b.
7   *Ibid.*, 79a.
8   Concerning this work, see E. Gottlieb, "Illumination, *Devekut* and Prophecy in *Ozar Hayyim* by R. Isaac of Acre," *Studies in Kabbala Literature* (Hebrew), ed. J. Hacker (Tel Aviv, 1976), pp. 231–247.
9   Concerning this work, see G. Scholem, "*Sha'arei Zedek*: A kabbalistic Essay of the School of Thought of R. Abraham Abulafia, attributed to R. Shem Tov (ibn Gaon?)" (Hebrew), *Kiryat Sefer* 1 (1924): 127–139.
10 MS Jerusalem 148, 8°, fol. 18a.
11 See G. Scholem, *Catalogus Codium Hebraicum . . .* in *Bibliotheca Hierosolymitana* (Jerusalem, 1930), p. 34.

12 See *Responsa of Solomon b. Adret*, part 1, sect. 548.

13 See G. Scholem, "A Note on a Kabbalistical Treatise on Contemplation," *Melanges Offerts a H. Corbin* (Teheran, 1973), p. 670, no. 3; G. Scholem (above, n. 9), p. 132.

14 N. Wieder, *Islamic Influences on Jewish Worship* (Oxford, 1947); S.D. Goitein, "Abraham Maimonides and his Pietist Circle," *Jewish Medieval and Renaissance Studies*, ed. A. Altmann (Cambridge, Mass., 1967), pp. 150ff.; S.D. Goitein, "R. Abraham Maimonides and his Pietist Circle" (Hebrew), *Tarbiẕ* 33 (1964): 181–197. Concerning Abraham Maimonides's relationship with Acre, see Grabois (above, n. 4), pp. 102–103.

15 For a summation, see G.D. Cohen, "The Soteriology of R. Abraham Maimuni," *PAAJR* 35 (1967): 75–98; 36 (1968): 33–56.

16 G. Vajda, "The Mystical Doctrine of Rabbi Obadyah, grandson of Moses Maimonides," *JJS* 6 (1955): 213–225; see now, P. Fenton (ed.), *The Treatise of the Pool Al-Maqāla al-Ḥawḍiyya, 'Obadyāh b. Abraham b. Moses Maimonides* (London, 1981).

17 F. Rosenthal, "A Judaeo-Arabic Work under Sufic Influence," *HUCA* 15 (1940): 433–484. Concerning two Jewish-Sufic manuscripts in Arabic, see Vajda (above, n. 16), p. 222; Fenton (above, n. 16), p. 62 n. 89–90.

18 Ed. D.H. Baneth (Hebrew) (Jerusalem, 1939). On p. XXVII, Davidowich notes that Arabic and Hebrew manuscripts were written in "Syrian Mughrabi Rabbinic" hand. This work was little-known in the West. As Vajda has shown, of the two passages quoted by Steinschneider, only one (that of Don Benveniste ben Lavie, of the early fifteenth century) indeed parallels *Perakim be-Haẕlaha*. The second and later quotation was discovered by Vajda in R. Joseph Yaabeẕ's commentary on *Avot*. See G. Vajda, "Une Citation non Signalée du Chapitre sur la Beatitude attribué à Moïse Maimonide," *REJ* 130 (1971): 305–306. Wieder (above, n. 14), pp. 45–46, assumed that R. Abraham, the son of Maimonides, is the real author of this treatise, whereas Fenton (above, n. 16), pp. 44–46, proposed R. 'Obadyāh — R. Abraham's son — as the possible author. The present author pointed to a certain affinity between the concept "world of imagination" in R. Natan's — R. Isaac of Acre's master — *collectanaea* and the view of the imaginative faculty in the Chapter on Beatitude, see Idel, "R. Jehuda Hallewa and his book Ẕofenat Pa'aneah" (Hebrew), *Shalem* 4 (Jerusalem, 1984): 119–148.

19 *Perakim be-Haẕlaha*, p. 11; see also notes 22–23 below.

20 Gottlieb (above, n. 8), p. 233, n. 7.

21 See my article concerning the prohibition of study of kabbala before the age of forty, *AJS Review* 5, section B (1980): 8–10; see also the similar usage of the expression *adam katan* as microcosmos in Abulafia and R. Isaac of Acre, and the occurrence of the same phrase in *Sha'arei Ẕedek*. Cf. M. Idel, "The World of Angels in Anthropomorphic Shape" (Hebrew), *I. Tishby Festschrift* (Jerusalem, 1984), p. 57, n. 215; Idel, "Kabbalistic Materials from the School of Rabbi David ben Yehuda he-Hasid" (Hebrew), *Jerusalem Studies in Jewish Thought*, II, 2 (1982–1983): 177–178, n. 40.

22 See *Sha'arei Ẕedek*, MS JNUL 8° 148, fol. 65b, and *Oẕar Ḥayyim*, MS Moscow–Günzburg 775, fol. 161b; see also Gottlieb (above, no. 8), p. 237.

23 See *Perakim be-Haẕlaha*, p. 7, line 14. The meaning of *shekiya* (sinking) to both these kabbalists, and in *Perakim be-Haẕlaha*, is that of *devekut* with the spiritual world, the universal intelligence or the universal soul. We may find similar application of this concept in Ibn Tufayl's *Ḥai Ben Yoktan*. See S.S. Hawi, *Islamic Naturalism and Mysticism* (Leiden, 1974), pp. 150–151.

24 M. Idel (above, n. 5), pp. 322–323.

25 M. Idel, "The 'World of Imagination' and the Collectanaea of R. Natan" (Hebrew), *Eshel Be'er Sheva* 2 (Be'er Sheva, 1980): 170–171 and n. 30.

26 MS Moscow–Günzburg 775, fol. 131b. Cf. the extant fragments of *Oẕar Ḥayyim*, MS Sassoon 919, fol. 217: "One day during this month, I, a young man, was sitting in the company of veteran students who loved wisdom"; afterwards, R. Isaac relates a discussion concerning the *golem*. We should mention here the description of R. Isaac's teacher in *Oẕar Ḥayyim*, MS Moscow–Günzberg 775, fol. 100a: "... as I have received from the paragon of his age in matters of modesty, kabbalistic wisdom, philosophy, and secrets of the combinations of letters, he was most wont to instruct me in the ten *sefirot* of *belima* and in the ways ...." This

description, which is not in keeping with what we know about R. Abraham Abulafia himself — for he did not tend to deal in pneumatic contemplation of ten *sefirot* — is nevertheless in keeping with his theory, a blend of philosophy and combinations of letters. We should note that the addition of "kabbalistic wisdom" apparently refers to dealings in ten *sefirot*. Such study, in addition to philosophy and combinations of letters, is found in *Sha'arei Zedek*. In one surviving fragment of *Ozar Hayyim*, MS New York-JTS, micr. 2263, fol. 14b, R. Isaac discusses a conversation between himself and "a genuine kabbalistic scholar (who) came from Damascus with kabbalistic wisdom"; this sage reveals to him a method involving combination of the letters of God's name.

27 Idel (above, n. 5), pp. 320–321.

28 The discussion deals with a section of a work by R. Abraham Abulafia entitled *Hayyei ha-'Olam ha-Ba*. See MS Oxford 1582, fol. 53a, and Idel (above, n. 5), p. 348, note 125.

29 In that year, during which the traces of R. Abraham Abulafia were lost, R. Isaac left Palestine.

30 On this, see Idel (above, n. 25).

31 H. Corbin, *Creative Imagination in the Sufism of Ibn 'Arabi* (Princeton, 1969), pp. 360–361, note 19.

32 In 1270/1271, R. Abraham Abulafia participated in a circle to which R. Baruch Torgami belonged. It should be noted that R. Abraham ibn Hisdai had translated Algazali's *Ma'aznei Zedek* in Barcelona a generation earlier, and this work contains a brief description of Sufism. It is likely that Sufic concepts well-known in the West, such as in the quotations found in *Hovot ha-Levavot*, contributed to a certain extent to the consolidation of "prophetic" kabbala in the early 1250s. The impression these concepts left, however, is rather weak. Concerning Algazali's description of the Sufis, see G.C. Anawati, L. Gardet, *Mystique musulmane* (Paris, 1961), pp. 186–187.

33 See Idel (above, n. 25), pp. 165–166, 176.

34 See Idel (above, n. 5), p. 319, and *Even Sapir* by R. Elnathan ben Moses Kalkis, MS Paris (BN) 727, fol. 10a. Concerning R. Shem Tov Ibn Gaon's dealings in kabbala of letter-combinations, see D.S. Levinger, "Rabbi Shem Tov ben Abraham Ibn Gaon" (Hebrew), *Sefunot* 7 (1963):17. Concerning a possible relationship between the commentaries of R. Shem Tov and R. Abraham Abulafia on the dictum *min'u beneikhem min ha-higayon*, see Idel (above, n. 21), appendix, n. 17.

35 See G. Scholem, M. Beit Arié, *Introduction to the Book "Ma'amar Mesharei Kitrin" by R. Abraham ben-Eliezer ha-Levi* (Hebrew), (Jerusalem, 1978), pp. 15–16.

36 MS Musajoff 30, film 22858, Institute for the Microfilming of Hebrew Manuscripts, JNUL, Jerusalem.

37 See G. Scholem (above, n. 11), p. 226, n. 2. On the influence of a Sufic view on the Safedian kabbalist R. Jehuda Hallewa, see my article (above, n. 18).

38 Gottlieb (above, n. 8), p. 238, n. 14, p. 246, n. 25; M. Pachter, *Homiletic and Ethical Literature of Safed in the Sixteenth Century* (unpublished doctoral dissertation, Hebrew, Jerusalem, 1976), p. 370, n. 48; and see below, n. 40. The unpublished section of *Sha'arei Kedusha* by R. Hayyim Vital mentions R. Isaac explicitly. See, e.g. MS British Library, Margoliouth cat. 749, fol. 16b, in which the matter under discussion is the relationship between the soul and the Divine Presence. In his work *Sefer ha-Shemot*, R. Moses Zacut cites in the name of R. Hayyim Vital a tradition in the name of R. Isaac ben Samuel of Acre. See also R. Hayyim Joseph David Azulai's comments in *Midbar Kedemot*, part 8, section 17, item 11.

39 Idel (above, n. 5), pp. 174–177. Concerning the Ka'aba and the well-preserved tablet of the Sufis, see G.C. Anawati and L. Gardet (above, n. 32), pp. 59–60; see also Corbin (above, n. 31), pp. 384–385.

109

40 We should mention here R. Isaac ben Samuel of Acre's commentary on the dictum "Prophecy does not dwell outside the Land of Israel": "The secret of 'outside of the Land' (Israel) and of 'the Land of Israel' . . . The 'Land' *[erez]* does not signify the earth of dust (i.e. the geographic land), but the lump of dust (i.e. the human body) in which souls dwell. The 'Land' is the palace of the souls; it is flesh and blood. The soul that dwells in earth *[ba-arez]* which derives from Jacob's seed (i.e. stock) certainly dwells in the Land of Israel. Even if the soul dwells outside the Land (i.e. geographically), the Shekhina (i.e. the Presence of God) will rest upon it since it is

definitely in the Land (i.e. earth) of Israel. But the soul which dwells in the Land (i.e. geographically) which does not derive from the seed of Jacob . . . who is Israel, our father, certainly dwells 'outside the Land' even if it is in the Land of Israel, inside Jerusalem. Neither will the Shekhina dwell upon it, nor the spirit of prophecy, since it is certainly 'outside the Land'." (*Oẓar Ḥayyim*, MS Moscow–Günzburg 775, fol. 94a). Here, the Land of Israel has become an appellation for every member of the People of Israel; a Divine Presence capable of radiating only on these souls is a Sufic motif recurring in *Oẓar Ḥayyim* (fol. 71b). See Werblowsky concerning the appearance of this motif in the kabbala of Safed and its connection with R. Isaac ben Samuel of Acre and with Sufism: R.J.Z. Werblowsky, *Joseph Karo, Lawyer and Mystic* (Oxford, 1962), pp. 58–59. See also Gottlieb (above, n. 8), p. 242.

Concerning use of this Sufic motif in interpreting the Greek myth related by a Christian to R. Isaac of Acre, see Idel, "Prometheus in Jewish Garb" (Hebrew), *Eshkolot* 5 (1980): 119–121; and above, n. 38. See also my forthcoming article, "The Land of Israel in Medieval Kabbala," *Land of Israel: Jewish Perspectives* ed. L. Hofman (in press).

LINKS BETWEEN SPANISH JEWRY AND PALESTINE, 1391-1492

JOSEPH R. HACKER

H *istorical appraisal of the contacts between Spanish Jewry and Palestine in the fifteenth century has been impeded by the dearth of source material. In the following article, J. Hacker has scrutinized the existing sources and adduced new evidence to present a portrayal of this interrelationship that is convincingly different from previous historical research. Hacker maintains that Spanish Jewry emigrated to Palestine at different periods during the fifteenth century in numbers sufficient to enable its leaders to assume central positions in the Jewish community of Jerusalem by the 1460s and 1470s. He shows that the fall of Constantinople marked a turning point in the motivation of the emigrants, who were now drawn by a messianic awakening connected with the hopes in Europe for the destruction of Catholic Christendom. This migratory trend was part of the significant emigration of Spanish Jews (prior to the expulsion from Spain) to communities throughout the central and eastern Mediterranean area, which is also discussed here.*

T he study of the Jewish community in Palestine in the late Middle Ages has received new impetus in recent years, largely from the work of Israeli scholars. However, any attempt to study the ties of Spanish Jews to the Land of Israel and their settlement there during the fifteenth century is greatly hampered by the meagerness of the documents and manuscripts at our disposal.

Formerly, historians held that this immigration and settlement should be dated to the period after the Ottoman conquest of Palestine, that is, after 1516. Later, when it became evident that groups of Spanish and Portuguese exiles had arrived much earlier (we find them serving as community leaders in Palestine in 1503–1504),[1] scholars concluded that there was a considerable influx of Spanish Jews into the country following the Expulsion from Spain, largely in the first decade of the sixteenth century.[2] This immigration intensified when the entire eastern Mediterranean region came under Ottoman hegemony.

Scholars have noted the presence of Spanish Jews outside Spain and even in Palestine in the fifteenth century, especially several decades prior to the Expulsion.[3] Scholars of Spanish Jewry have also shown that Jews from Spain left for the Land of Israel shortly after the persecutions of 1391 and in the latter half of the fifteenth century.[4] Yet these new data did not change the commonly held ideas about the emigration of Spanish Jewry, and particularly its settlement in Palestine. This may, perhaps, be explained in terms of the scarcity of sources and the lack of actual evidence of the settlement of Spanish Jews in Palestine and elsewhere. However, it seems that research undertaken on the Diaspora communities and Palestinian Jewry went in different directions, and at times each field failed to take cognizance of what existed in the other.

Let us summarize what we know about Spanish Jews who left their homes before the sixteenth century to migrate to Palestine, their numbers, and their effect upon the Jewish settlement there. But first, note must be made that Spanish Jews migrated to the Land of Israel and settled there already in ancient times. Sources in the Cairo Geniza point to the migration of Jews from Spain to the East in general and to Palestine in particular. By the eleventh century there were apparently 'colonies' of Spanish Jews in Jerusalem and Ramla.[5]

Fourteenth Century Migrations of Spanish Jewry

Late fourteenth century sources illuminate the life of Spanish Jews in Palestine. One letter mentions a certain David, a Spanish Jew living in Egypt who "donated five coins (?) for oil for the House of the Prophet Samuel."[6] The writer of this letter, according to S. Assaf, was the caretaker of that sacred tomb, one "Y. [. . .] the son of Eli'ezer the Sephardi."[7]

A well-known Jerusalem figure of that time was R. Yosef ben Eli'ezer Tov 'Elem whose commentary on ibn 'Ezra, *Zofenat Pa'aneah*, was written in Jerusalem where he arrived in 1375 from Crete. R. Yosef left Jerusalem after 1380, probably because of financial difficulties, although in 1388 he resettled there, as we know from a letter which was sent to him. It was in Jerusalem that he copied a manuscript of *Tur Hoshen Mishpat*.[8] He relates that he "came to Zion from his native land — Spain," but he resided "in Jerusalem for many years."

A less well-known personage was Izhak ben R. Yosef HaSofer (the Scribe) "from the kingdom of Portugal from the city of Évora." He began to write a book "in the holy city of Jerusalem," completing the work "in Safed on Sunday, seven days after the New Moon Day of the month of Tevet in the year 5149 after the creation of the world."[9]

An examination of dated colophons of manuscripts written in Jerusalem between 1383 and 1391 reveals that a number of Spanish scribes, some of them well-known, were active in the city during this period, in addition to the authors mentioned above.[10] In responsa literature, too, we find references to Spanish immigrants to Palestine in this period. In one responsum, for example, mention is made of Avraham Farah who left Castile for the Land of Israel in 1373 and probably settled in Jerusalem.[11] From the responsum it is evident that a witness who testified before a court in Spain which was trying Avraham Farah, was of Portuguese descent and lived in Jerusalem for several years. It also emerges that during those years there was one Avraham Farah (not to be confused with the defendant), a teacher in Jerusalem, and he, too, hailed from Castile. The responsum also notes that the witness's journey from Portugal to Jerusalem had taken seven months.[12]

Even in these few examples dating from the twenty years before 1391, we see that a not inconsiderable number of Spanish Jews made their way to Palestine and Jerusalem,[13] and this despite the fact that in 1379–1380 Spanish Jews considered Jerusalem "the end of the earth." In the latter half of the fourteenth century, Jews came to the Land of Israel both as pilgrims to the holy places and as permanent settlers. However, the bulk of the Jews who arrived were either itinerant merchants making their rounds in the Mediterranean area,[14] students coming to visit or settle, or aged individuals going to die and be buried in the Holy Land. We possess very little evidence of entire families of Spanish Jews settling in Palestine in this period.

In addition to their religious, spiritual longings for and ties to the Land of Israel, Spanish Jews were probably influenced to migrate to the Holy Land by the fact that Catalan ships sailed regularly from Barcelona to the Ultramar, and especially to Beirut and Alexandria. This route was heavily used in the early fifteenth century for Mediterranean shipping and commerce.[15] Although soon thereafter Barcelona suffered a sharp decline as a center of maritime trade with the Middle East, and during the second half of the fifteenth century and afterwards there was no extensive Catalan shipping in the eastern Mediterranean,[16] Spanish Jews could still sail eastward in Catalan ships or go to Venice or Rhodes whence they could book further passage.

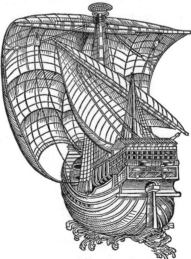

113

Sixteenth century woodcut showing type of sailing ship plying the Mediterranean routes

At first glance, this constant emigration of Jews seems surprising, for it became increasingly difficult for Jews to leave Spain after 1346, as a Catalan scholar tells us:

> ... with our own eyes we have seen and our fathers have told us, the learned men moved and performed a difficult feat. Among the nations it was heard and a herald loudly proclaims it, not surreptitiously and not leaving secretly for the Holy Land. And "some went to the land of Moab and strange lands," they made their way in the sea, a path in the mighty waters, with boats of reed, with all their gold and silver, their wives and children ... also among the Jews of Spain some people are leaving every year and no one says, 'Return!' And we have never seen anyone harrassing us or them, neither on the part of the crown nor of the communities.[17]

From this argumentation and other sources we see that the government authorities and interest groups within the Jewish communities both sought to prevent the free emigration of Jews in the mid-fourteenth century to other communities, whether near or far. Indeed this is apparent in the fifteenth century, primarily with regard to the departure of persons in a band. On the other hand, we do not possess sufficient information to judge whether these attempts did in fact hinder the rate of migration before 1391. At least until the 1420s, the authorities made it difficult even for individuals to leave via the kingdom of Aragon, granting permits only in isolated cases, although quite a few persons managed to leave even without a permit.

Motivations for Settling in Palestine

Numerous sources document the ties between Spanish Jews and the Holy Land, and their settlement there following the persecutions of 1391. The sentiments of Jews from the Spanish cultural sphere and their motives to settle in the Land of Israel emerge clearly from a responsum of R. Shim'on ben Zemah which overflows with praise of the Land and its religious importance:

> You asked whether a person who goes to the Land of Israel and enters it is absolved of all his light or serious sins by repentance; and whether in the case of a person who dies on his way to the Land of Israel, his intention atones as if he actually lived in the Land. Living in the Land of Israel is an important commandment and Nahmanides counted it among the 613 commandments ... And being buried in the Land of Israel is likened to being buried under the altar ... And rabbis would put themselves in danger, crossing rivers in order to enter the Land of Israel and would say: "This place which Moses and Aaron did not live to see, who can say that we are worthy of seeing?" And they would kiss the stones and roll in the dust following the verse ... [Psalms 102:15]. It is called "the beauteous land of the living" because people die there without

the agony of rolling through tunnels [as would the dead who had been buried in Exile, in the days of the Messiah — J.H.] ... It is forbidden to leave the Land of Israel, except for the purpose of studying the Law if one cannot find a teacher in the Land, or out of filial devotion. From the aforementioned, the [answer] to your question becomes clear, namely that a person who wants to repent his sins and wants to go to the Land of Israel, although it is repentance that absolves him, going to the Land of Israel speaks in his favor and saves him from sin all his life. And as to your question about a person who was unable to complete his commandment [i.e. who died on his way]... a good intention is considered by God as a good deed.[18]

This responsum indicates both directly and by inference the religious importance of visiting and settling in the Land of Israel. R. Shim'on ben Zemaḥ stresses the preeminence of the Land of Israel and ignores the difficulties of reaching it and settling there. He wrote similarly in other responsa,[19] in complete contrast to the responsa of the medieval scholars in Ashkenaz.[20]

Praise of the Land of Israel and its merits, following the style of Shim'on ben Zemaḥ but with the addition of some personal touches, may be found in the commentary on the Pentateuch written by R. Yosef ben David,[21] a student of R. Nissim Girondi. Based upon the teachings of the sages and the methodology of several medieval scholars, Yosef ben David emphasizes the difference between the Land of Israel and the rest of the world and elaborates the concept that the impurity of the gentile world causes Jews to "become dulled with sin," whereas the Holy Land has the special virtue of bringing about the intellectual perfection of man with God, and his devotion to the Lord. "The increase of seed" was another of the special virtues of the Land of Israel — an idea which was very far from the reality of life there in his day!

Royal permit issued on 21 April 1395, offering protection to three Jewish families from Castille, and helping them to sail to Jerusalem

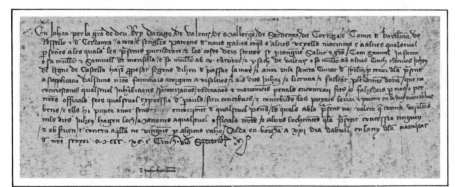

It is apparent that in light of the mood of the generation before and after 1391, Spanish scholars felt the importance of emphasizing the virtues of the Land of Israel and encouraging their fellow Jews to go there. To this end, they painstakingly gathered ancient praises of the Holy Land, even those which were ambiguous or incomprehensible. It is significant that such praise was accompanied by slurs heaped upon "the land of the nations," as found especially in the writings of the medieval Spanish scholars, Yehuda HaLevi and Nahmanides, in whose teachings the Land of Israel held a special place.[22] The persecutions of 1391 led to a change for the worse in the attitude of Spanish Jews to their homeland, and apparently made the Land of Israel seem more attractive.

In the writings of Hasdai Crescas (ca. 1407) we even find indications that the Jews had not abandoned hope that the changing political situation in Palestine might enable them to resettle there. His view was probably influenced as well by news that he received from Jerusalem in 1402 to the effect that an autonomous Jewish kingdom was battling the legendary Prester John. This probably led him to believe that the Mamluk sultan might be willing to negotiate with the Jews in Exile.[23]

From the writings of these late fourteenth century and early fifteenth century scholars in Spain and North Africa,[24] it becomes obvious that among the primary motives for visiting or settling in the Land of Israel were the fulfillment of a vow made in time of illness or trouble, or atonement for sins. During this period there is evidence that several persons who had converted to Christianity under duress but returned to Judaism, sought to expiate their sin by going to the Land of Israel.[25] In addition, the desire to be buried in the undefiled soil of the Holy Land was one of the most common motives for 'aliya among the Jews at that time, as we learn from R. Dossa of Vidin's commentary upon Rashi.

> And this is the custom among the Ashkenazi and Sefardi Jews, when they become old they go to the Land of Israel and dwell there so as to die and be buried there, and this would be their atonement. And they learn it from the verse, "He makes expiation for the land of his people" (Deut. 32:43).[26]

R. Dossa, who studied with R. Shalom ben Izhak of Neustadt and others in and around Vienna, also resided for a time in Venice, Bologna, and Candia, and was thus in a position to learn of these customs first-hand.

Medieval scholars were well aware of the perils of the journey to Palestine, whether by land or sea. This was especially true of North African scholars from whose writings it is clear that they received communications from Jerusalem with detailed information about life there.[27] R. Shim'on ben Zemah transmits an interesting report about the size of the Jerusalem community, the number of pilgrims there, and their country of origin in the first half of the fifteenth century:

> And there is proof that the holiness of the Temple and the city still exists, because [Jews] still go [there] on pilgrimage from Egypt and other places ... And it was said that some of the miracles that occurred in Jerusalem still occur, namely, that people never said, "The place is too

small for me," (TB *Yoma* 21a) because in the synagogue in Jerusalem the [seats] are needed for the local people throughout the year, but it fills up at the Festival of Weeks when more than three hundred people assemble there. They all come into [the synagogue] and sit comfortably, for [the land] is still holy and this is the sign for the third redemption.[28]

We assume that the majority of the residents of this modest sized community were Oriental Jews, probably in the main from Egypt and Syria.

Evidence regarding the motives for Jewish migration to Palestine, from Spain and the Spanish Jewish cultural sphere, does not differ substantially from what we know of other areas and earlier periods. However, here we encounter a new phenomenon: Jews leaving Spain after, and doubtless because of, the persecutions of 1391–1412. For example, in a group of letters which Rabbi Shlomo Da Piera wrote between 1391 and 1417,[29] and in several letters from Saragossa found in another collection from the same period,[30] we find expressions of the emigrants' desire to leave their native land, especially Aragon and Navarre, because of their revulsion against "the land of the nations" and what was perpetrated against the Jews there.

Page from the *Sassoon Haggada,* first half of the fourteenth century, showing Spanish and French influences. Probably executed in the eastern Pyrenees, Majorca, or southern France

The letters contain a striking comparison between the virtues of the Land of Israel as opposed to a detailed condemnation of the land of the nations, expressing the drastic change of heart that the Jews of Spain underwent in their attitude to their homeland and its native population. It is also instructive that the author of these letters generally attributes the desire to emigrate to the events that transpired in Spain, though around 1391 the Jews of Aragon suffered far less than those of Castile and Catalonia. Moreover, the new motivation alluded to in these letters connects the emigration of Jews from Aragon and Navarre to internal turmoil and the fear of the future, coupled with the impending redemption. All these point to a break with the past, at least for a few years.

Though it is difficult to discover anything definite about the nature of the migrants from Da Piera's letters, the fact that five of the letters[31] directly dealing with migration to the Land of Israel are addressed to persons who are obviously intending to depart with their entire family[32] may indicate that the social composition of Spanish immigrants changed after 1391, from individuals and old people to families.[33] One of the letters even singles out the wife for special praise for consenting to move to the Land of Israel (a subject which also appears in responsa literature).

We do not know about the extent or duration of this migration, nor have we any idea whether these people ever reached Palestine and how they adapted to life there. However, these facts, in conjunction with information about the flight of *conversos* from Majorca, Valencia, and elsewhere[34] is evidence of the growing dimensions of the exodus from Spain and of a change in motivation and social composition. No longer were the immigrants drawn solely from the ranks of the unfortunate, scholars, or the aged, but from persons of every class, including the wealthy.

There is, thus, special relevance to a responsum of R. Shlomo ben Shim'on indicating the presence of Jews from Spain in Jerusalem prior to 1441. R. Izhak al-Fara and his brother-in-law, the subjects of the responsum, died in Jerusalem before 1447.[35] In addition to these Jews, who came from Malaga[36] and maintained their ties with R. Shim'on ben Zemah's family, there was a certain "R. Hayyim Galipapa of Aragon" in Jerusalem at that time.[37] It was reported that R. Izhak al-Fara lived in Jerusalem for several years and even married there, though he had a wife in Malaga.[38]

In the first quarter of the fifteenth century another phenomenon appears, resulting from the trauma which Spanish Jewry suffered in 1391, namely the itinerant Spanish scholar who wanders from nation to nation, his ultimate goal the Land of Israel. One of these scholars, hitherto unknown, was Shem Tov ibn Puliya, a physician who travelled throughout the Greek mainland and islands after the persecutions of 1391, reaching Bulgaria.[39] He expresses the hope of reaching the Land of Israel, but does not know whether he will realize his wish. Similar years of wandering befell the far better known R. Izhak ibn al-Ahdab, exiled from Christian Spain to the "land of Islam" (probably North Africa, though possibly the state of Granada in the south), whence he made his way to Palestine after 1391. His travels also led him to Sicily where he probably settled for some time.[40]

Flight from the persecutions of 1391 is also the reason for the wanderings of another well-known scholar, R. Aharon ben Gerson Abu-al Rabbi of Sicily, several of whose relations are known to us in Spain. R. Aharon testifies to the trauma he suffered in his native land. He challenges God and attempts to ward off despair among the Jews during that trying time:[41]

> "But from there you will see the Lord your God," (Deut. 4:29). Woe to the ear that hears this. We did seek Him and we do not worship other gods; we suffer and are afflicted for maintaining our faith, "but He is like a man who does not hear" (Ps. 38:14). But there is no rebuke in any mouth, no doubt, though we suffer so many terrible troubles, with our hearts and souls we seek Him, and we did not stray from glorifying His Holy Law until "we are slain all the day long" (Ps. 44:23). And I write these words with much bitterness, an aching heart, and much shedding of tears, "God, His deeds are perfect" (Deut. 32:4), "for He will not fail you or destroy you" (Deut. 4:31) in such a way that you can not return to Him. Therefore, do not despair of repenting, even of the greatest sin that was committed willfully.[42]

R. Aharon wandered through the lands around the Mediterranean and even reached Jerusalem.[43] He and others like him[44] seem to have adopted this rootless existence because of the tragic events of the period. Thus we have what amounts to a class of "wandering scholars" whose peace of mind had been destroyed, never to be regained either in the Diaspora or in the Land of Israel.

Another factor strengthening the interest of Spanish Jewry in the Land of Israel during this period is the messianic movement which arose in Castile and elsewhere in Spain after the persecutions of 1391. The name of R. Ḥasdai Crescas is associated with such a movement which he seems to have supported passively in 1393.[45] A Castilian prophet, probably the well-known R. Moshe Botarel,[46] appeared on the scene during these messianic stirrings in which Jerusalem and events in that city occupied a special place.[47]

Most probably, these events were not fictitious, but a mixture of news and rumor which Spanish Jews then spread throughout the Diaspora in their letters.[48] In a group of manuscripts describing the wars between the Ten Tribes and Prester John, evidence exists of correspondence between the Jewish communities in Jerusalem and Catalonia in 1402.[49] The correspondence reveals a strong contact between scholars in the two places and the intention of those in Jerusalem to encourage the others to stir up messianic fervor. Rumors about miraculous events connected with the advent of the Messiah also made their way from Jerusalem to Spain and vice-versa, and raised the depressed spirits of the victims of the persecutions, though we do not know if these rumors were sufficient to increase migration to the Holy Land.

Yet another reason for migration during this period was forcible conversion to

Christianity after 1391. From various sources it becomes clear that those *conversos* who wished to return to Judaism preferred to leave Spain, either for North Africa or for eastern Mediterranean lands, including Palestine.[50] However, this was probably not a genuine movement of emigrants, but rather limited numbers of *conversos* who made their way to the Land of Israel or at least considered doing so.

Migratory Movements in the Early Fifteenth Century

The phenomenon of Jewish emigration eastward from Spain between 1391 and the 1420s can be properly understood only in the broader context of emigration from Spain after 1391 to other lands in the Mediterranean basin. Indeed, alongside the migration of Jews from Castile, Catalonia, and Aragon to Palestine, Spanish Jews are also found throughout the Mediterranean area in the first, and especially the second quarter of the fifteenth century. References to them appear in notarial documents and Hebrew sources studied in the last thirty years. When gathering all these scattered references together, a clear picture emerges. Jews left Spain at a steady rate after 1391, and between 1430 and 1450 this migration reached significant proportions and seems to have constituted a steady stream eastward. Examples of these migrants include R. Ḥanokh Saporta of Catalonia who settled in Istanbul,[51] and the Catalan and Provencal Jews who lived in Crete.[52] Furthermore, an examination of the data on the places where these Jews settled along the route which Spanish Jews took when migrating to Palestine shows a considerable increase in the number of Spanish Jews beginning in the 1440s. Although no precise numbers are available, one can say that in the first third of the fifteenth century our documents mention only individual Jews in some of these places, and that from the 1440s on, numerous Spanish Jews are mentioned in every place where archival documents and literary sources exist.

An excellent instance of this phenomenon is afforded by documents from Mediterranean islands which were ruled by Aragon, Venice, and Genoa in the fifteenth century, and the Italian colonial towns in Byzantium and the Balkans. In Sicily, which was ruled by Aragon, Catalan and Castilian Jews already constituted a sizeable proportion of the population in the 1430s.[53] A study of the *Takkanot* of Candia[54] shows a high incidence of names of Spanish immigrants in the 1440s in Crete, and of the sign next to these names indicating their Spanish origin. Data gathered from a study of archival documents confirm this picture.[55]

Spaniards and Spanish names in Byzantine Constantinople and in Genovese Chios are also encountered,[56] while in Venice and Mestre individual Jews from Spain were present from as early as the beginning of the fifteenth century.[57] The same applies to Cyprus in the 1440s;[58] and in 1447 in the well-known notebook of Balbo,[59] immigrants who reached Crete are mentioned.

A similar picture emerges on the Dalmatian coast, where Spanish Jews arrived via Italy, following a period of residence in various Italian cities. This phenomenon[60] may constitute one of the reasons for the development of the Jewish communities of Valona and Ragusa, and was especially obvious in Valona,[61] which already boasted a sizeable Jewish center in the fifteenth century. This may also explain why groups of *conversos* sailed from Spain to Valona in these years.[62]

Similar information exists about settlements of Spanish Jews in Italy in the fifteenth century. It is clear that beginning in the 1440s, an increasing number of Spanish Jews migrated to Italy and especially to Naples and the Neapolitan state which was ruled by Aragon. This migration, already sizeable in the 1440s,[63] grew in importance in the 1450s,[64] and greatly increased toward the end of the century.

At this point a unique source from Egypt must be mentioned. According to this Karaite document,[65] a group of some twenty-four wealthy *conversos* left Toledo no later than 1459 and probably travelled about before arriving in Egypt. Unable to decide whether to become Orthodox Jews or Karaites, they finally chose to embrace Karaism, according to this source, because of that religion's faithful adherence to the Bible and rejection of the Oral Law. Their leader went to the Land of Israel to atone for his sin of conversion, and his colleagues also intended to settle there.

A well-regarded source informs us not only of the departure of many Spanish Jews, but also of their arrival in Palestine in 1447.[66] These Jewish families, young and old, settled in Jerusalem and built homes there.[67] Here, then, is evidence that considerable numbers of Spanish Jews actually reached Palestine and began to settle in Jerusalem and environs as early as 1447.[68]

A Contemporary Source Depicting Messianic Fervor

A different picture emerges from a recently published letter.[69] Written by the *Muqaddims* (leaders of the Jewish community) of Saragossa in Aragon to the heads of the Jews of Castile, it describes the mass fervor, motivated by messianic impulses, to migrate from Castile via Aragon. The letter makes it clear that this is not merely an emotional phenomenon, but that Jews had actually set out and arrived in Aragon.[70] B.Z. Dinur proposed that this was a mass movement which began in the closing decade of the fourteenth century, or at any rate no later than 1404.[71] The letter itself contains no evidence of a specific date, but the collection in which it is found contains documents from after the persecutions of 1391 up to the sixteenth century.[72] Despite the fact that this letter is not dated, its nature and significance should be examined from several standpoints.

1. The letter says, "... it is now several years that when a Jew boards a ship in these countries *he must not let any of the passengers or crew know that he is a Jew ....*"[73] The danger evidently does not stem from the authorities on shore or pirates at sea, but from the people on board the ship. Nor is this danger confined to a specific place, but exists "in these countries" and "for several years now." The authors of the letter seem to be hinting at a state of affairs which arose in the

Mediterranean in the wake of the Pope's order of 1428 forbidding ships' captains to transport Jews to Palestine.[74] The order was in effect for several years and was apparently issued again ca. 1468, possibly even earlier, ca. 1452.[75] Aside from this papal order, the sources are silent as to other concrete dangers directed specifically against Jews in the course of a voyage. Of course, there is no proof that this papal initiative was obeyed in Spain as it was in Venice and her colonies, southern Italy, and elsewhere. It confirms the impression that the authors are not referring to any prohibition on Jewish voyages by the state; rather, they warn of the danger at sea when the crew is no longer subject to Spanish law and the Jews cannot save themselves with writs of protection and patronage from the Spanish authorities. For the letter to be intelligible, one must be aware of the fact that the sea routes to Palestine generally touched Sicily and either Venice or the coast of southern Italy,[76] and from there followed along the Greek coast of the Adriatic. Moreover, the anchorages along the route to Egypt or Beirut were in Venetian colonies, and there were probably no direct voyages from Spain to Palestine.

2.   The letter relates that "... the best of the gentiles say, ... It is well known that this is the beginning of an event referred to as the 'constellation of the stars,' which has recently become known in all the countries," From these lines it is evident that there is not only dependence upon an ancient prophecy, but also a reference to ideas and stories prevalent in contemporary Christian society "in all the countries," and that the Jews who wrote and received this letter are aware of them.

We should, then, ascertain what is known about the constellation of the stars that was so widely circulated in Spain and the neighboring countries, among Christians as well as Jews, and to which the messianic inspiration of the Jews to abandon their native land may be attributed.

According to Zunz,[77] Steinschneider,[78] and others, at the close of the fourteenth century and during the fifteenth, the expectation of the end-of-days and of redemption, fired by the constellation of the stars, found expression — especially from 1464 to 1468. There were occasional earlier reckonings of other messianic dates,[79] but no evidence has come down to us of the fervor of individuals or large groups connected with those dates. On the other hand, we have increasing information about events in 1456 in Italy which were accompanied by the appearance of a comet as predicted in the constellation of the stars, and its effect upon Jews and Christians.[80] Both the clergy and the public at large were caught up in the messianic fervor, and echoes of those events have been preserved by both Christian and Jewish sources.[81]

It is interesting that even R. Izḥak Abravanel attributed the establishment of the Inquisition and other fateful events in the history of Spanish Jewry to the stellar configuration of 1456, on the basis of R. Avraham Bar Ḥiyya's reckonings.[82] Despite his objections to astrological methods, Abravanel considers the configuration of 1456 and 1464 as beginning a fateful era,[83] and as Y. Baer has shown, he was not alone in his view. His writing represents the absorption and adaptation of a combination of popular ideas among Jews and *conversos* in the mid-fifteenth century.[84] Furthermore, even Abraham Zacuto in his astrological work, gave prominence to this constellation of stars. Like Abravanel and the *conversos* in the mid-fifteenth century, he saw a connection between the events predicted by the constellation of the stars and the rise of the Ottoman Empire and its impact upon the entire Christian world.[85]

Alonso de Espina testifies that the *conversos* during this period were imbued with a messianic faith which was based on astrology, and he also tells of a movement of returning to Judaism even before 1460. Similar reports about their contemporaries and about earlier generations also appear in the writings of the greatest scholars of Spain in the late fifteenth century.[86] Recently, additional evidence has come to light concerning the religious revival among *conversos* between 1453 and 1458 in the wake of celestial occurrences. Groups of these converts, imbued with the messianic fervor aroused by the comet, left their homes in Spain for the Ottoman Empire.[87]

Thus, in the years between 1453 and 1468, several phenomena and processes relevant to our discussion emerge. The great Spanish scholars report that a stellar configuration of that period was decisive in the history of Spanish Jewry, while individuals and documents testifying to popular messianic fervor linked to celestial occurrences and astrology appear during this period. This "configuration" is also well-known in the Christian world around the Mediterranean. On the other hand, none of our sources mention any other stellar configuration which was considered significant and which stirred up such excitement among Jews and Christians in the late fourteenth to mid-fifteenth centuries.

3. From the letter it is obvious that there was a mass departure of men, women, and children from their homes in Castile towards Aragon, from where they were to set sail for Palestine. Such a movement during that century is known from only one place, Sicily, where there was a Jewish community of considerable size. Sicily was a colony of the Kingdom of Aragon at that time, and the movement there occurred in 1455. A description of events in Sicily reveals that whole families from several communities on the island embarked together on a Spanish vessel which they had leased to take them to Palestine. However, they were arrested and imprisoned in the port on charges of being "servi camerae" of the royalty, who were leaving the country without permission and taking their property with them. The Jews who stayed behind were accused of aiding them to leave covertly and of secretly purchasing their property. The representatives of the Jews and the authorities finally reached an agreement in Syracuse according to which the Jews, after paying fines to the government, were permitted to leave for "Jerusalem" under certain conditions, *inter alia*, that no more than eight Jews would be permitted to sail at one time on any ship.[88]

It is reasonable to assume that the letter, which reflects a similar phenomenon, also deals with the same period and presents an analogous event to that which occurred in Sicily.[89]

4.   From various indications in the letter, it is obvious that the departure for the Land of Israel was linked with messianism. After the Ottoman conquest of Constantinople, messianic ferment and hopes were aroused in the Jews throughout the Mediterranean basin (especially in Palestine, Italy and her colonies, and Sicily).[90] Communities and individuals exchanged letters[91] concerning the messianic significance of political and military events of the day, with the resurgence of Islam and the conquest of Constantinople constituting the setting for new rumors and the revival of the popular belief, from 1400 to 1430, in the appearance of the Ten Tribes. The advent of the Messiah was imminent and the Children of Israel were being called to return to their faith. The fall of the Eastern Church was interpreted as the beginning of the end of Christianity and the first stage in the fulfillment of the prophecies of the redemption of Israel.[92]

Such ferment was also felt among the *conversos* and the lower classes of Jewish society in Spain and, as a result, some converts abandoned Christianity and left Spain for the Ottoman Empire.[93] In this setting we can understand the words of the letter: "... for tremendous hatred was stirred up against them in all these countries among the peoples who said, What are these wretched Jews doing? Do they intend to rebel against us? ..."[94]

In contrast to this popular ferment, the messianic fervor in Spain proper after 1391 was short-lived and, as far as we know, not attended by a mass movement.[95]

5.   It is difficult to attribute the letter to 1391 or shortly thereafter since it contains no hint of the terrible persecutions which Spanish Jewry suffered in 1391, nor is there any trace of revulsion for the "land of the nations" despite the fact that these two motifs regularly appear in letters originating in Saragossa in the fourteenth and early fifteenth century.

It is difficult to believe that so soon after the carnage, apostasy, and oppression of Castilian Jewry, the leaders of Saragossa could have found it in their hearts to write such a letter. For in that case, this would show that the Jewish leadership headed by Ḥasdai Crescas cold-bloodedly estranged itself from its brethren. Despite the danger to the Jews of Aragon and their difficult circumstances after such a migration, how could they reject the few survivors who were fleeing the ruins of their communities? And how could they have announced so summarily to the Jewish leaders in Castile (if any were still alive shortly after 1391) that they had stopped such a wave of migration without taking counsel?

Nor can this letter refer to the first quarter of the fifteenth century, before 1415, for by that time the Jews of Aragon themselves were being persecuted, and it is difficult to suppose that Castilian Jews should have chosen to flee to Aragon at this time. It seems more likely that the letter was written after the Tortosa controversy, some time after 1428. And it is not impossible that it dates from the 1440s.

In summation, each of the arguments in favor of one or another date for our letter encounters the same difficulty, namely, the meagerness of sources, which prohibits us from speaking of mass migration deriving from messianic motives before the Ottoman conquest of Constantinople. Some facts hinted at in the letter fit this period and confirm our knowledge of the widespread revival which began after 1453 among the lower classes of *conversos* and Jews. This revival fired an exodus from Spain to the Ottoman Empire, including Palestine. It is difficult, however, to determine with certainty exactly when our letter was written, for it could be dated to any time from 1453 to the 1470s.

We should also stress that the motives for leaving Spain to settle in the Land of Israel changed greatly beginning in mid-century. The main factor was the relatively more favorable conditions in the Islamic countries, together with the awakening of messianic hopes for the redemption of the Jewish people and its reestablishment in its Land. Political and military events stirred the imagination of Jews and Christians all over Europe. When an extraordinary event which upsets some of the fundamental conceptions of an entire generation nearly coincides with a date for which astrologers had predicted drastic changes, dramatic emotional outbursts and pragmatic actions are likely to result, such as the mass migration of Jews in Castile and of the community in Palermo, Sicily.

All this was clearly understood by the *conversos*, particularly in light of the tension resulting from the hostility and estrangement between them and the Christians. This hostility found expression in violent riots[96] and later led to the first trials of *conversos* by the Inquisition.

Despite the fact that during this period life in the Jewish communities had returned to normal, and cultural and educational activities were flourishing for the first time in many years,[97] the communities also experienced ferment and hope of messianic redemption,[98] though to a lesser extent than did the *conversos*. Hence, if we are in fact correct in assuming that this letter describes an attempt at mass migration to the Land of Israel on the part of Jews (doubtless including not a few *conversos*), then it must have been written after 1453, and constitutes evidence that Jews as well as *conversos* went beyond mere messianic hopes, calculations of the date of the end-of-days, preaching for religious revival, and the migration of individuals and a few families — to an attempt at mass migration to the Land of Israel, motivated by messianic fervor.

125

Spanish Jews in Palestine in the Late Fifteenth Century

This conclusion leads us to pose several additional questions: To what extent did this messianic fervor bring about an exodus from Spain toward the East? Where did these Jews go? Did their journey eastward end in Palestine? Did the presence of considerable numbers of *conversos* among them affect the Jewish community in

Letter sent by the Jewish court of Jerusalem in response to a communication from Crete, 1467

Jerusalem and other cities in Palestine? How did this immigration influence the Jewish community in Palestine, particularly its population of Spanish background?

We possess abundant evidence from Spain itself that *conversos*, both individuals and families, migrated eastward.[99] For example, seventy families of converts from Valencia left for Valona in Albania.[100] We also hear of their tendency to leave in groups[101] and of groups of *conversos* from Castile who embraced Judaism in Aragon and subsequently left for Palestine.[102]

Shortly after the conquest of Constantinople, there was a remarkable growth in the Jewish community in Jerusalem. The members of the rabbinical court of the city wrote in 1456: "... Furthermore, great scholars have recently arrived with their disciples ... and they enlarged the academy *(yeshiva)* and greatly enhanced the study of Torah."[103] Based on the letter of "Bnei Kedem" and on a letter written by the rabbinical court of Jerusalem,[104] it looks at present as if the bulk of the immigration was from Eastern countries rather than from Europe, although exact identification of the immigrants to Palestine at that period remains uncertain.

As noted above, sources indicate that individual Jews left Spain and came to the Land of Israel during this period, and that Jews of Spanish origin held important public posts in the Jerusalem community at that time. A newly discovered document from the years 1467–1468 points to a Spanish scholar at the head of the rabbinical court in Jerusalem.[105] In his response addressed to Candia on behalf of the Jerusalem court, Yosef ben Gedalia ibn 'Immanuel emphasizes the Spanish tradition and extols the teachings of his masters, the scholars of Spain. It is reasonable to assume that the composition of the rabbinical court of the Jerusalem community reflected not only the personal qualities of its members, but also the composition of the local population.

Moreover, in a group of documents from the notebook of R. Michael Balbo of Candia, we learn of the mission of R. Yosef *HaDayan* (the Judge), an emissary *(shaliah)* from Jerusalem to Candia in 1473.[106] Although Freimann regularly calls him "the Ashkenazi", this epithet is nowhere found in the manuscript.[107] Meanwhile, we have information about a *shaliah* from Jerusalem, R. Yosef *HaSefaradi*, in Italy during this period,[108] so it is quite possible that they are one and the same person who was twice dispatched to Jewish communities in the Diaspora.[109]

Be that as it may, we have additional evidence of a Jew of Spanish origin serving as a representative of the Jerusalem community in the Diaspora during these years; and if this was indeed the same individual, he was also a *dayan*, a rabbinical court judge, apparently in Jerusalem. It would seem that the broad representation of Spanish Jews in the institutions and leadership of the Jerusalem community which emerges from the few sources which we possess,[110] may reflect the existence of larger numbers of Spanish Jews in Palestine than was formerly thought, though their exact number is still unknown.

127

Several pieces of information from the last decades of the fifteenth century also indicate that Jews as well as *conversos* from Spain and Portugal resided in Palestine during this period. Rabbi Izḥak Laṭif tells of "that old man who relied on the testimony of Spanish youngsters regarding the graves of Hillel and Shammai."[111] 'Ovadia of Bertinoro tells us of Spanish widows, students, and *conversos* in Jerusalem,[112] though he also remarks that all the rabbis and scholars who were in Jerusalem, both Ashkenazim and Sefardim, fled for their lives from the city.[113]

Hebrew script and example of language spoken by the Jews in the Holy Land in the fifteenth century

Befinna	גבינה	lehem	לחם
betzim	ביצים	jojen	יין
hometz	חומץ	moim	מים
semen	שמן	boissar	בשר
balbaes	בעל־בית	tangol	תרנגול
beyueren	שתיה	tangoles	תרנגולת
dormen	שינה	daegim	דגים

128

From the writings of travellers in Palestine in the 1480s it becomes apparent that the number of Jews had increased considerably since the beginning of the century. If sources of the earlier period speak of three hundred Jews praying in the synagogue during a festival (and we know that pilgrims from Eastern lands were numerous at those times), in the 1480s Christian travellers speak of five hundred Jews on an ordinary day.[114] This growth is confirmed by Meshullam of Volterra who speaks of two hundred and fifty Jewish *families* in 1481.[115]

Though the numbers are small, this phenomenon is remarkable, for during this period we witness a general decline in the size of the population in Eastern lands, a decline which included the Jewish population.[116] In Palestine, however, the process was reversed. Despite its modest size and the persecution to which it was subjected, the Jewish population was clearly increasing. One sign that Jerusalem had become a center for the absorption of immigrants from various lands is the fact that for daily purposes the Jews of that city spoke Hebrew among themselves.[117]

In light of this increase in numbers and influence, why was the social position of the Spanish Jews in Jerusalem between 1450 and 1470 not mentioned at all in the writings of Jewish travellers from Italy in the 1480s and 1490s? The explanation may lie in a decline in the number of Jewish immigrants from Spain during this period, coupled with the death or departure of those who had lived there from the 1450s through the 1470s. This may also explain why Meshullam of Volterra does not mention Spanish Jews explicitly, even though he names the *parnassim* (community heads) and scholars of Jerusalem.[118] The answer may also lie in the depressed state of the Jerusalem community on the eve of 'Ovadia of Bertinoro's arrival. We have evidence of the flight of Jews, including the rabbis of Jerusalem, "around 1480–1488."[119] One of these, R. Shmuel Minir, may have been of Spanish origin.[120] This phenomenon, then, may have been part of the general decline of the Jerusalem community during these years until it was rehabilitated by 'Ovadia of Bertinoro. Only after the expulsion from Spain do we hear once more of the ascendancy of Spanish Jews in the city. On the other hand, in the 1480s and 1490s, Jews of Ashkenaz and Italy are prominent in Jerusalem.

*

In summation, we conclude that at least some of the *conversos* and Jewish emigrants from Spain during this period made their way to Palestine despite the perils and hardships of the journey, though it is certain that most of the migrants settled in the cities of Italy and their colonies and in the Ottoman Empire. After the fall of Constantinople, the reasons for leaving Spain and migrating to the Land of Israel changed, and with them the pattern of the migration. Thus, the years immediately following the expulsion from Spain do not represent the true beginning of Spanish Jewry's settlement in Palestine though, of course, it was during this period that the group became dominant in the Jewish population of the country. A further increase in emigration took place after the Ottoman conquest of Palestine. We have noted that Jews from Spain held respected positions in the Jerusalem community in the 1460s and 1470s, a fact which indicates the existence of a sizeable group of Spanish Jews in that city. We also know of Spanish Jews in Jerusalem in the late 1440s and the late 1480s.

Although we do not know the precise number of Spanish migrants to the East, they were not isolated individuals; in the second third of the fifteenth century they apparently numbered in the hundreds. In the terms of that period, they constituted an important factor in Jewish settlement of the central and eastern Mediterranean basin, and are significant for an understanding of the impact of the tradition and culture of Spanish Jewry upon those communities. Spanish Jewish migration is also apparent in the relatively large (for that period) number of Spanish Jews in Palestine in the second half of the fifteenth century, several decades before the expulsion from Spain.

Translated by Carol Kutscher.

This article is a reworked and updated version of one published in Hebrew in *Shalem* 1 (1974), pp. 105–154. The appendices have been omitted here.

1   See M. Benayahu, "A Document from the First Generation of the Expelled Spanish Jews in Safed" (Hebrew), *Sefer Assaf* (Jerusalem, 1953), pp. 109–125; see p. 119: "...We should mention that the first sabbatical year after the Expulsion was 1497, but the issue arose, acrimoniously, in the next sabbatical year, 1504, a fact which reflects an increasing number of scholars coming to Erez-Israel immediately after 1497..."; idem, "Rabbi Yehuda ben Rabbi Moshe Albotini and his Book, *Yesod Mishneh Torah*" (Hebrew), *Sinai* 36 (1955):240–241: "It was commonly thought that nearly all the Spanish and Portuguese scholars who settled in Erez-Israel came there only after the Ottoman conquest in 1517, and that the spiritual center in Erez-Israel was established in Safed soon after the right to grant ordination was restored. Recently discovered sources show that very shortly indeed after the Expulsion, renowned rabbis settled in Jerusalem and Safed, and already before 1504 scholars who had been among the leading rabbis in Spain and Portugal were at the head of the communities of Jerusalem and Safed."

2   This is the opinion of the leading historians of the Jewish settlement in Palestine during this period; see *e.g.* the writings of I. Ben-Zvi, A. Ya'ari, and I. Braslavski, and the studies by E. Ashtor, M. Benayahu, and D. Tamar.

3   S. Assaf, "The *Conversos* of Spain and Portugal in the Responsa Literature" (Hebrew), *Me'Assef Zion* 5 (1933):41–42 (=*Be'Ohalei Ya'akov* [Jerusalem, 1943], pp. 164–165), thinks that most *converso* emigration from Spain took place "only in the last decades of the fifteenth century at the start of the Inquisition". Assaf also notes that "... we possess some facts about the settlement of Spanish Jews in Erez-Israel after the persecutions of 1391 even before the Expulsion"; "On the History of the Last *Negidim* in Egypt" (Hebrew), *Sources and Studies* (Jerusalem, 1950), p. 191; and see *ibid.*, n. 8: "The names of several individuals are known to us, and 'Ovadia of Bertinoro found a few Spanish *conversos* who had embraced Judaism." A. Freimann is also of the opinion that the exodus of Spanish and Portuguese exiles began "even before the official Expulsion, beginning in 1492"; see "Emissaries and Immigrants" (Hebrew), *Zion* 1 (1936):192. In the appendices, *ibid.*, Freimann also cites documents concerning the migration of several of them to Palestine. See also E. Ashtor, *The History of the Jews in Egypt and Syria*, 2 (Hebrew) (Jerusalem, 1951), p. 438f., on the *conversos* who migrated to Eastern countries in the second half of the fifteenth century. He maintains (p. 442) that most of these persons were *conversos*. "However, in the final analysis, the Spaniards of every description who fled to Egypt and Syria before the Expulsion were few."

4   See Y. Baer, *A History of the Jews in Christian Spain*, 1–2 (Philadelphia, 1971), 2, pp. 158f., 292f., and notes.

5   See S. Assaf, "Sources for the History of the Jews in Spain" (above, n. 3), pp. 103–114; *ibid.*, p. 50. See also S.D. Goitein, *Palestinian Jewry in Early Islamic and Crusader Times* (Hebrew), ed. J. Hacker (Jerusalem, 1980), p. 105f.

6   See S. Assaf (above, n. 3), p. 113f.

7   As M. Beit-Arié has recently shown in "Hebrew Manuscripts Copied in Jerusalem or by Jews who Hailed from Jerusalem up to the Ottoman Conquest" (Hebrew), *Jerusalem in the Middle Ages: Selected Papers*, ed. B.Z. Kedar (Jerusalem, 1979), p. 258, n. 46, he should not be identified with the Yosef whom we shall discuss below.

8   See A. Marx, "From the Geniza," *The HaDoar Commemorative Volume*, ed. M. Ribalow (New York, 1927), pp. 186–188; and following his lead, N. Ben-Menahem, "Yosef Tov 'Elem and his Book *Zofenat Pa'aneah*" (Hebrew), *Sinai* 9 (1942):353–355; and Beit-Arié (above, n. 7), No. 10.

9   From the colophon of a biblical commentary by Ya'akov ben Asher, Manuscripts of the Jewish Community of Mantua (No. 32 in The Mortara Catalogue, p. 35). Film No. 812 in the Institute for the Microfilming of Hebrew Manuscripts, JNUL, Jerusalem (hereafter, Microfilm Institute). See also Beit-Arié (above, n. 7), No. 12.

10 *Ibid.*, p. 247. According to Beit-Arié, there were ten persons, but apparently this is too many. 1) MS No. 7 was written, according to Beit-Arié, by four scribes. The colophon explicitly states "completed in Jerusalem," but this does not prove that all the scribes worked in Jerusalem. 2) In addition to the two persons mentioned in our article, Moshe ben Ya'akov and Avraham HaLevi are also named. The other three remain anonymous, and further investigation is required before we can determine whether they are different individuals and whether any of these manuscripts was written by one of the scribes whose names are known. At any rate, here is evidence of a surprisingly lively literary activity during this little known period.

11 Responsa of Rabbi Isaac ben Sheshet (Ribash) (Constantinople, 1547), no. 508.

12 A. Ya'ari's contention (*Emissaries from the Land of Israel* [Hebrew], [Jerusalem, 1951], p. 211) that the witness is (an emissary) from a *yeshiva* in Jerusalem has no foundation in the responsum in question. This individual simply passed through several European countries on his way home and collected money for his personal needs, not for the Jewish community in Palestine. The witness's testimony was obtained in 1380, not 1390, as the responsum clearly shows. These details are correctly described in H.J. Zimmels, "Erez Israel in der Responsenliteratur des späteren Mittelalters," *MGWJ* 74 (1930):61–62.

13 At the same time, Beit-Arié's conclusion (above, n. 7), p. 247, seems questionable: ". . . On the one hand, these findings confirm the vague information and unfounded assertions regarding the migration of Spanish Jews in the fourteenth century before the persecutions of 1391. On the other hand, they call into question the data on their migration in the fifteenth century before the Expulsion, while confirming the commonly accepted view that the main migration of Spanish Jewry began after the Ottoman conquest." But all this is beside the point. No one would dispute that after 1492 and 1516 the emigration of all segments of Spanish Jewry increased, perhaps motivated by new considerations. The real issue is whether or not there was a steady, sizeable flow of migrants eastward from Spain, particularly to Palestine, after 1391 and prior to 1492. Likewise, the fact that we possess several dated manuscripts from the close of the fourteenth century, whereas very few have survived from the fifteenth century, only means that we do not know very much about the extent of the Spanish community in Palestine in the fifteenth century. By the same token, why does Beit-Arié's list not include even a single manuscript from the period 1492–1516, while we have six from 1383–1391? Are we to conclude that more Spanish Jews resided in Jerusalem during that single decade than in the first quarter-century after the Expulsion from Spain and Portugal? Or is it the result of pure chance and the scribal custom of recording the year and place in which the manuscripts were written? The colophons with the date and place of composition or copying are of great value for the historian, especially in the absence of any other data, but we must beware of drawing *ex silentio* conclusions from the lack of dated manuscripts!

131

  Incidentally, we should mention that dated manuscripts have survived from the period following the Expulsion, such as JTS, R1030, completed in Jerusalem in 1503; see J. Hacker,

"A Group of Contemporary Letters on the Expulsion of the Jews from Spain and Sicily" (Hebrew), *Studies in the History of Jewish Society . . . Presented to Prof. J. Katz* (Jerusalem, 1980), p. 77 and n. 78.

14 Although it is commonly accepted that their numbers, and those of the Jews especially, declined in the latter half of the fourteenth century, by contrast with the thirteenth and early fourteenth century. See E. Ashtor, "New Data for the History of Levantine Jewries in the Fifteenth Century," *BIJS* 3 (1975):69–70.

15 See e.g. F. Melis, "Note sur le Mouvement du port de Beyrouth d'après la documentation Florentine aux environs de 1400," *Actes du Huitième Colloque International d'Histoire Maritime*, ed. M. Mollat (Paris, 1970), pp. 371–373. According to the lists, in just a few years 224 Catalan, 262 Genovese, and 278 Venetian ships arrived in Beirut. After Tamerlane's invasion and conquest of Syria, there was a considerable decline in maritime traffic to Syria in 1400, and the number of the Catalan ships drastically decreases from the second decade of the fifteenth century. See C. Carrère, *Barcelone centre économique a l'époque des difficultés, 1380–1462* (Paris, LaHaye, 1967), pp. 639ff., 851ff.; idem, "Barcelone et le commerce de l'Orient à la fin du Moyen Age," *Actes du Huitième Colloque . . .* (see above), pp. 365–369; J.M. Madurell Marimón; A. García Sanz, *Comandas Comerciales Barcelonesas de la Baja Edad Media* (Barcelona, 1973), pp. 19–32.

16 See in Carrère (above, n. 15) and E. Ashtor, "The Venetian Supremacy in Levantine Trade: Monopoly or Pre-Colonialism?" *Journal of European Economic History* 3 (1974):10, 14–15, 46–47; idem, "The Volume of Levantine Trade in the Later Middle Ages (1370–1498)," *ibid.* 4 (1975):586–591, 593.

17 F. Baer, *Die Juden im christlichen Spanien*, 1 (Berlin, 1929), pp. 316–317.

18 *Responsa of R. Shim'on ben Ẓemah Duran* (Amsterdam, 1738), part 3, no. 288; for quotations of sources cited in the responsum, see Zimmels (above, n. 12), p. 55.

19 See, e.g., *Responsa of R. Shim'on . . . op. cit.*, part 1, no. 21; part 2, no. 128; part 3, no. 169, 201, etc. And see Zimmels's quotations, pp. 54–55, 59, 63. On the Land of Israel in those responsa, see also part 3, no. 152 concerning the man who donates his money to an alms-house in Jerusalem.

20 See the sources quoted by Zimmels (above, no. 12); I. Ta-Shema, "Inyanei Ereẓ Israel" (Hebrew), *Shalem* 1 (1974), pp. 81f., 85–88. According to the interpretation of R. Ḥayyim Cohen which is cited in the *tossafot* to *Ketubot* 110, 2 ("Now there is no commandment to live in the Land of Israel because there are several commandments which depend on the Land and certain prohibitions which cannot be carried out") — nowadays no one is compelled to go to the Land of Israel. Yet, despite the difficulty of this question and the widespread debate in rabbinical literature, R. Shim'on ben Ẓemah does not deal with it at all. On the thinking of R. Ḥayyim Cohen, see R. Moshe Ḥagiz, *Sefat Emet* (Amsterdam, 1707), fol. 14; Y. Baer, "The Land of Israel and the Diaspora in the Eyes of Medieval Generations" (Hebrew), *Me'assef Zion* 6 (1934):164 and n. 1; E.E. Urbach, *The Tosaphists: Their History, Writings and Methods* (Hebrew), (Jerusalem, 1980), p. 126; A. Rivlin, "A Chapter in the History of the Land of Israel" (Hebrew), *Mada'ei HaYahadut* 1 (1926):102–106. I. Schepanski, *The Land of Israel in Responsa Literature*, 1 (Hebrew), (Jerusalem, 1967), pp. 34–35, 135–161, 309–400; D. Tamar, "*'Ollelot*" (Hebrew), *Areshet* 6 (1981):263–264.

For example, even R. Shim'on's emphasis upon the commandment to live in the Land of Israel as one of the 613 commandments follows Naḥmanides and ignores Maimonides and his followers' approach. This, too, is evidence of his thinking and outlook.

21 L. Feldman, *Commentary on the Pentateuch by R. Yosef ben David of Saragossa* (Hebrew), (Jerusalem, 1973), pp. 5–16. See also pp. 25–27: ". . . and also the Land [of Israel] creates more fertility . . . [and] a person can impose on his family to migrate to the Land of Israel, and even a wife can impose on her husband to go and live there. Although some of the commentators wrote that this is so only when the voyage is not dangerous, and one does not have to cross the sea, because seafaring is dangerous." Cf. p. 37 and see p. 95: "One should make an effort to be buried in the Land of Israel, just as Jacob did when he made Joseph and his other sons, and Joseph made the Children of Israel, swear to this . . . ."

22 Here we should also mention R. Ya'akov the Sicilian who lived in the first half of the fourteenth century and hailed from the same cultural sphere. He also lived for a time in Spain, finally

settling in Damascus. In his writings, the Land of Israel holds a special place, though we can not interpret his writings here. For more about him see S.H. Kook, *Iyyunim UMehkarim*, 2 (Jerusalem, 1963), pp. 273–290; A. Hurvitz, *Sinai* 59 (1966):29–38; A. Kupfer, "An Erez Israel Notebook" (Hebrew), *Kovez al Yad*, new series 7(17):103–123.

23 See J. Hacker, "The Despair of Redemption and Messianic Hopes in the Writings of Solomon Le-Beit HaLevi of Salonica" (Hebrew), *Tarbiz* 39 (1970):206 and n. 59. See also n. 49.

24 See, e.g., the responsa of R. Isaac ben Sheshet, R. Shim'on ben Zemah, and R. Shlomo ben Shim'on; also the works of Spanish scholars from the first half of the fifteenth century.

25 See e.g., the case of Profet Duran and his friend Bonet Bonjorn, in Baer, 2 (above, n. 4), p. 151. Other instances occur in the literature of the period.

26 A. Neubauer, "Commentar zu Raschi's Pentateuch-Commentar von Dossa aus Widdin," *Israelitisches Letterbode* 8 (1882–1883):37–55. For the quotation see p. 48 (from the weekly Torah portion *Ha'azinu*, fol. 261). Dossa's commentary was written at the beginning of the fifteenth century.

27 See notes 19–20 above and cf. Zimmels's quotation from the *Responsa of R. Shlomo ben Shim'on*; see also Abraham Zacuto, *Sefer Yuhasin*, ed. Filipovsky (Frankfurt a.m., 1925), pp. 228–229 (a description of the travels of Izhak ibn Alfara of Malaga, despatched in 1441 to R. Shim'on ben Zemah and R. Shlomo ben Shim'on).

28 *Responsa of Shim'on ben Zemah*, part 3, no. 201. This is a very interesting source of information on the history of the Jews of Jerusalem during this period which has thus far escaped scholarly notice. 1) It is now clear that the Jews of Jerusalem probably possessed only one synagogue at this time. 2) It also shows that the community was very small, no larger than about 100 families, perhaps fewer, though during festivals, with the arrival of pilgrims, the number of Jews increased to some 300 worshippers (men — young and adult?). Information from later periods indicates that considerable numbers of pilgrims from the East came to celebrate the festivals in Jerusalem. See, e.g., in A. Neubauer, "Collections on Matters Pertaining to the Ten Tribes and the Sons of Moshe" (Hebrew), *Kovez al Yad* 4 (1888):45–50, on pilgrims after 1453; *The Pilgrimage of Meshullam of Volterra* (Hebrew), ed. A. Ya'ari (Jerusalem, 1949), p. 74, on pilgrims ca. 1481.

29 H. Brody, *Beiträge zu Salomo da Pieras Leben* (Berlin, 1893), pp. 16–27. On R. Shlomo see most recently *Encyclopaedia Judaica* (Jerusalem, 1971), vol. 5, p. 1299, and bibliography. Also, Y. Baer (above, n. 4), index. And see now another letter in A. David, "An Epistle regarding Migration to the Land of Israel from Spain" (Hebrew), *Tarbiz* 52 (1983):655–659.

30 See H. Beinart, "A Fifteenth-Century Hebrew Correspondence from Spain" (Hebrew), *Sefunot* 5 (1961):81–83; 116–117, 126.

31 In another collection of letters from this period we found a reference to Izhak ben Makir "whose heart prompted him ... to go and see the beauteous land for himself ..." See film 17844, fol. 33a–b, Microfilm Institute.

32 On the other hand, the letters in the collection (see n. 30) are different in that they do not deal with families, but with financial aid. This is obvious from the nature of this collection whose main topic is "letters seeking compassion," to be written by needy Jews.

33 We also draw this conclusion from a document dated April 21, 1395 which contains the king's orders to the commanders of the fleet and other royal officials to protect three Jewish families and their children from Castile and help them sail to Jerusalem. See J. Vielliard, "Pèlerins d'Espagne à la fin du Moyen Age," *Analecta Sacra Tarraconensia* 12 (1936):270.

34 See e.g., in S. Assaf, *Be'Ohalei Ya'akov* (above, n. 3), pp. 164–165.

35 See *Responsa of R. Shlomo ben Shim'on* (Leghorn, 1742), no. 512; cf. A. Neubauer, *HaMaggid* 15 (1871):53 who did not know that the text was a published responsum. See also E. Ashtor, *A History of the Jews in Egypt and Syria, etc.* (Hebrew), Vol. 2 (Jerusalem, 1951), pp. 168–169. As to the date of the responsum: 1) From the responsum itself it is clear that Izhak Alfara and his brother-in-law left Malaga "one after the other for the Land of Israel." 2) In Zacuto's *Sefer Yuhasin*, p. 228, it is written: "R. Izhak ibn Alfara of Malaga who sent to Shim'on Duran in the year 1441, and to Shlomo my son [i.e. Alfara's son] concerning what he had seen with his own eyes in the Land of Israel." On the basis of this datum it is obvious that he travelled there before 1441. 3) On the other hand, in the *Responsa of R. Shlomo ben Shim'on* in MS Escorial G IV,7 (and the photostats in the Microfilm Institute, JNUL), which

were written in 1447 (see e.g. leaf 143a in the manuscript), we found the responsum in question. Hence our responsum was written before 1447. 4) Since the name of the author's father in the signature on the responsum is followed by the blessing for the dead, the responsum was probably written between 1444 and 1447. On the basis of the present discussion, we should amend A. Ya'ari, *Travels to the Land of Israel* (Hebrew), (Tel Aviv, 1946), p. 108.

36 For another immigrant who travelled via Malaga during those years, see MS JTS Mic. 2242 (Film 28,495, Microfilm Institute, JNUL), leaf 41b: "completed is the book *Hovot HaLevavot* with the help of God and I wrote it for myself, I, Yihye the Levite son of Moshe ibn al-Saft, and I finished it in Malaga on the fifth of Elul 1442 when I was on my way from Fez to the Land of Israel". L. Schwager and D. Frankel, *Catalogue of Rare Books and Manuscripts*, No. 11 (Husiatyn, 1906), mistakenly read "Persia" *(Paras)* for "Fez" *(Fas)*.

37 This is not the Hayyim Galipapa who is well-known for his opinions (see Yosef Albo, *Sefer ha'Ikkarim*, ed. J. Husik [Philadelphia, 1930], part IV 2, p. 418). Fragments of his works have survived in manuscripts. See also Y. Baer (above, n. 4), index; *Encyclopaedia Judaica* (Jerusalem, 1971), vol. 7, pp. 271–272.

38 According to this responsum, the migration of North Africans throughout the Mediterranean basin was especially conspicuous, and was most likely the result of commercial enterprise. In the course of their travels, many of these Jews came to Palestine, as we see from this responsum. See also n. 27, 36 above.

39 On ibn Puliya and his travels see my Hebrew article in *Shalem* 1 (Jerusalem, 1974), pp. 133–137.

40 See his introduction in *Klal Katan*, Cambridge MS Add. 492,1 (Film 16,786 Microfilm Institute, JNUL), fol. 2a, which contains information on the Jews of Sicily: "... And later, when I was travelling on the sea to the Land of Israel ... [we ran into a terrible storm but God] calmed the sea and brought us safely to the famous city of Syracuse in Sicily, and I found there great, honorable people, learning the Torah and performing *mizvot*, and their children with them, among them four lovely, learned lads. I enjoyed their affection and company, and they read for me from our Torah. And in their free time some of them studied mathematics ...." Apparently Izhak did not go to Palestine, but settled in Sicily. In 1428 he was still in Palermo.

41 He wrote his book after 1447, as I have shown in my article "The 'Nagidate' in North Africa at the end of the Fifteenth Century" (Hebrew), *Zion* 45 (1980):127. Shem Tov ibn Puliya (see n. 39 above) wrote with the same end in mind, although in an entirely different style.

42 *Commentaries on Rashi* (Hebrew) (Constantinople, no date). This section was published by J. Perles, "Aharon Ben Gerson Aboulrabi," *REJ* 21 (1890):246–269; see p. 249 with slight changes in the original and incorrect division of the sentence. This error led him to conclude that this section shows that *htp* = *hqp*, and that the work was written in 1420. He did not realize that *htp* is the acronym of *HaZur Tamim Po'alo* ("God, His deeds perfect," as S.D. Luzzatto, in *Kerem Hemed* 8, p. 84 interpreted it), not a date. On the basis of Perles's date see, e.g., E.E. Urbach, "Rabbi Abraham ibn Daud's Critique of Rashi's Commentary on the Pentateuch" (Hebrew), *KS* 34 (1949):103.

43 Perles, *op. cit.*, pp. 253, 257.

44 See the story of Shabbetai HaCohen the Byzantine who lived under Ottoman rule; MS Paris 707, published by Israel Isser Perah Zahav (=Goldblum), in *Talpiot* (Berditchev, 1895), from where it was copied by Z.H. Jaffe in the Appendices to Graetz's history, *Divrei Yemei Yisrael* (Hebrew), vol. 6 (1898), p. 489.

45 A description of the events appears in Baer, 2 (above, n. 4), pp. 160–162, and in notes 46–47 on p. 476 where the relevant literature is cited.

46 See I. Sussmann, "Two Fascicles on *Halakha* by Moshe Botarel" (Hebrew), *Kovez al Yad*, New Series 6 (16):271–342, especially 295–297.

47 See A. Jellinek, *Beit HaMidrash* 6 (Hebrew), (Jerusalem, 1938), p. 142.

48 See Baer, 1 (above, n. 17), p. 419: "and they proclaimed throughout the Hebrew's camp, and sent letters on eagles' wings."

49 These events, too, are connected with the scholars of Catalonia and Aragon, especially R. Hasdai Crescas. This will be dealt with in a forthcoming book by M. Idel and J. Hacker.

50 See, e.g., Baer, 2 (above, n. 4), pp. 158–160; Assaf, *Be'Ohalei Ya'akov* (above, n. 3), pp. 164–165; and see also n. 25 above.

51 See *Responsa of Eliahu Mizrahi* (Istanbul, 1560), no. 57.

52 As already noted by J. Starr, "Jewish Life in Crete under the Rule of Venice," *PAAJR* 12 (1942):103, n. 131. And see in *The Takkanot of Candia*, ed. M.D. Cassuto (Jerusalem, 1943), pp. 83–85, though he was not exact in certain details.

53 E. Ashtor, "Palermitan Jewry in the Fifteenth Century," *HUCA* 50 (1979):223–224, 235 n. 15, 237 n. 178, 241 n. 205.

54 See n. 52. See also A. Freimann, (above, n. 3), pp. 192–193, 202–207.

55 D. Jacoby, "Quelques aspects de la vie juive en Crète dans la première moitié du xv e siècle," *Actes du Troisième Congrès International d'Etudes Crétoises*, 2 (Athens, 1974), pp. 111–112.

56 Idem, "The Jews in Chios under the Rule of Genoa (1346–1566)" (Hebrew), *Zion* 26 (1961):186–187; idem, "Les quartiers juifs de Constantinople à l'époque byzantine," *Byzantion* 37 (1967):213–214.

57 See e.g. n. 49 above and D. Jacoby, "Les juifs à Venise du xiv e au milieu du xvi e siècle," in: *Venezia centro di mediazione tra Oriente e Occidente (secoli xv–xvi), Atti del II Convegno internazionale di storia della civiltà veneziana* Venezia, 1973, (Firenze, 1977), pp. 184, 199; E. Ashtor, "Gli inizi della Comunità ebraica a Venezia," *Rassegna mensile di Israel* (1978):694.

58 V. Polonio, "Famagosta genovese a metà del'400: Assemble, armamenti, gride," *Miscellanea di Paleografia e Storia Medievale, Fonte e Studi* 12 (1966):231–232; B. Arbel, "The Jews in Cyprus: New Evidence from the Venetian Period," *JSS* 41 (1979):23 ff.; B.Z. Kedar, "Jews in Genovese Famagusta, 1388" (Hebrew), *Jerusalem in the Middle Ages: Selected Papers*, ed. B.Z. Kedar (Jerusalem, 1979), p. 200.

59 Freimann (above, n. 3), pp. 205–206. Further sources on Spanish emigrants in Greece are to be found in the Balbo Manuscript which served as the basis for Freimann's article, and in other manuscripts as well.

60 See J. Tadić, *Jevreji u Dubrovniku* (Sarajevo, 1937), pp. 20–35 on Jews from Catalonia who settled in this city and in Valona. For additional material on Dalmatia and Valona, see *Zbornik* 1 (Beograd, 1971), published by Jevrejski Istorijski Muzej. On p. 195: two *converso* physicians (one from Salamanca, the other from Toledo) in Zadar in 1480.

61 See Hrabak, in *Zbornik (ibid.)*, p. 64 on the surprising number of Jews in that city in the fifteenth century.

62 See the document quoted in Baer (above, n. 17), vol. 2, p. 440.

63 Hacker (above, n. 13), pp. 73–78. To this data we should add, for example, the rich material in the correspondence of the Zarko family which I shall soon publish; and see also R. Bonfil, "Una lista di libri ebraici della fine delo XIV° secolo" (Hebrew), *Scritti in Memoria di Umberto Nahon* (Jerusalem, 1978), pp. 51, 53, 56, 61–62.

64 The present state of documents and sources does not permit us to speak of the emigration of considerable numbers of Jews before the 1440s. All that has been found to date on these regions during the years following 1391 is that some Jews who had come from Spain were there, whether because of the persecutions of 1391 or for economic and commercial reasons (bearing in mind that only individuals left before 1391, while their numbers increased after that date). Furthermore, some of the names mentioned by Starr and Jacoby might belong to Jews from Provence as well as Catalonia, but there is no certainty that the bearers were natives of either place.

65 See H. Hirschfeld, "A Karaite Conversion Story," *Jews' College Jubilee Volume* (London, 1906), pp. 81–100; E. Ashtor, 2 (above, n. 35), p. 107f. This document was not discussed by Baer and Beinart in their treatment of this issue (see below). Prof. E. Ashtor kindly informed me, after examining this source, that instead of Hirschfeld's "We have been living six years in this country . . ." (p. 87), the translation should read, "We have been travelling around [various] countries for six years . . ." This dovetails nicely with other sources and shows that *conversos* and Jews did not settle down in the first place they came to, but wandered great distances after leaving Spain.

66 B.Z. Kedar, "On the History of Jewish Settlement in Erez-Israel in the Middle Ages" (Hebrew), *Tarbiz* 42 (1973):413–418.

67 *Ibid.*, pp. 413, 417.

68 Kedar cites the words of Gascoyne as evidence that the emigration of Spanish Jews was motivated by a revival of messianic fervor and that, "according to Gascoyne, those who came

135

to Jerusalem were imbued with messianic hopes" (pp. 413, 414). However, this is apparently untenable, since Gascoyne's words on the thoughts and hopes of the Jews are his own reflections as he himself explicitly states. Furthermore, can vague expressions of the hope of rebuilding the Temple or faith in the coming of the Messiah after its rebuilding tell us anything concrete about the reasons for emigrating to the Land of Israel or serve as evidence of a revival of messianic fervor? After all, the expression of such hopes and beliefs was common to Jews everywhere during the Middle Ages, as every Christian scholar knew. At most, Gascoyne's words show that these particular Jews hoped for the rebuilding of the Temple and the coming of the Messiah. Moreover, we need not link the information concerning 1440 and 1447 or consider it evidence of the same wave of migration (see *ibid.*, pp. 414–415), especially since Gascoyne himself does not link them. There is no proof that the migration in 1440 was also from Spain. From a letter dated 1456 it becomes clear that the travellers going to the Land of Israel, whether for permanent residence or a temporary pilgrimage, came from the East (Egypt, Syria, Persia, etc.). See notes 90, 103, below.

69 B.Ẓ. Dinur, "A Wave of Emigration from Spain after the Persecutions of 1391" (Hebrew), *Zion* 32 (1967):161–174.

70 *Ibid.*, p. 163: "... that from now on [they] cannot pass through this country ... and [they] cannot stay here with us ...."

71 *Ibid.*, p. 165.

72 In the first collection of letters in the manuscript from which the above letter was published (MS Montefiore 488 and its photostat in the Microfilm Institute, JNUL) a document by Don Benvenist ben Labi of Saragossa (leaf 22a–b) was found. This was published by Y. Baer (above, n. 17), pp. 986–992, from other manuscripts and is a post-1391 document. However, there are also letters from the fifteenth and sixteenth centuries.

73 Dinur (above, n. 69), p. 162. This source stresses that it is dangerous when many sail "in one or two boats and it becomes known on sea and land ...." Thus it is the notice which a large group of Jews attracts which makes it dangerous, rather than the mere fact of their leaving; when individuals set sail, they attract no notice and there is no danger.

74 On the setting and consequences of this order see J. Prawer, "The Franciscan Monastery on Mt. Zion and the Jews of Jerusalem in the Fifteenth Century" (Hebrew), *Yedi'ot* 14 (1958):15–24. See also p. 16 and n. 7, citing the literature on the situation in various parts of Italy, and Jacoby (above, n. 55), p. 117 and n. 51. For the text of the Venetian prohibition which was transferred to Corfu, Methone, Coron, Crete, and Negroponte, see *MGWJ* 22 (1873):282–284. We should note that the captain and his ship were punished.

75 Prawer, *op. cit.*; M. Ish-Shalom, *Christian Travels in the Holy Land* (Hebrew), (Tel Aviv, 1966), pp. 102–103. This is still a conjecture and needs further proof.

76 See e.g., the description of the route from Venice in the late fifteenth century which appears in *Iggeret 'Orḥot 'Olam* by Abraham Farissol (Venice, 1586), ch. 11–12, and in the text published by Neubauer in *HaMazkir* 21 (1881/1882):136. On these descriptions and their date, see M. Artom, "An Italian Travelogue of the Fifteenth Century" (Hebrew), *Italiyah* 1 (1945):21–23; M. Shulvass, "On the Italian Travelogue" (Hebrew), *KS* 23 (1946):73–74; D.B. Ruderman, *The World of a Renaissance Jew* (Cincinnati, 1981), pp. 139, 234, n. 46. We find similar descriptions in the writings of travellers in Palestine in the late fifteenth century. See Inquisition documents concerning the exodus of *conversos* from Spain, e.g. Baer, 2 (above, n. 17), no. 392, p. 440.

77 L. Zunz, "Eine merkwürdige Medaille," *Israelitische Annalen* 18 (1840):156 (=*Gesammelte Schriften* 3 [Berlin, 1876], pp. 94–95); idem, "Erlösungsjahre," *ibid.*, p. 228.

78 M. Steinschneider, *Catalogus Librorum Hebraeorum ... Bodleiana* (Berlin, 1852–1860), coll. 1575; idem, "Meir Daspira," *JJGL* 9 (1889):79–81; idem, *Die hebräischen Uebersetzungen des Mittelalters und die Juden als Dolmetscher* (Berlin, 1893), pp. 636–637. See also A. Posnanski, *Schiloh* (Leipzig, 1904), p. 180.

79 They based their argument largely on A. Bar Ḥiyya's calculations that the end-of-days would occur in the year 1358 (during which, in the forty-fifth year of the constellation of stars [1403] Israel would enjoy a respite), or 1444. See A. Bar Ḥiyya, *Megilat HaMegaleh* (Berlin, 1924), p. 151f.; they also based their reckoning on calculations of the end (*qeẓ*) in the year 1430 (*qẓ*), without any reference to the constellation of stars.

80 See, e.g., U. Cassuto, *The Jews in Florence during the Renaissance* (Hebrew), (Jerusalem, 1967), p. 195f. and also concerning southern Italy. On the comet sighted over Spain at this time see n. 90. The identity of the Izhak of Florence whom Zunz quotes in *Annalen* is unclear, as are the sermons according to which Zunz found his calculations for the constellations of 1464 and 1469. He is not listed among the scholars of Florence in Cassuto's book or even in Zunz, *HaDerashot B'Israel* (Jerusalem, 1954). Perhaps Zunz was referring to Moshe Ben Yoav (see Cassuto, *op. cit.*). None of those involved in these calculations, nor their writings and letters, are mentioned in A.H. Silver, *A History of Messianic Speculation in Israel* (New York, 1927).

81 See references and works quoted above. Also the work published in an appendix in my article in *Shalem* 1 (1974), pp. 137–147. On the opposition to the widespread calculations and prophecies inspired by the stellar configurations, see also G. Pico della Mirandolla, "Disputationes in astrologiam divinatricem," *Opera Omnia, 1557–1573*, vol. 5 (ed. Hildesheim, 1969), especially chapters 1 and 12 on the Jews. The author attacks the astrologers, their methods and computations, and devotes a special place in his work to a refutation of the *prognosticatores* who referred their prophecies to the changes which would occur in Europe and all Christendom.

82 *Shalem* 1 (1974), pp. 152–153, 154.

83 Various scholars (Zunz, Guttmann, Silver, etc.) have already treated this point at length; see also Y. Baer, "The Messianic Movement in Spain During the Period of the Expulsion" (Hebrew), *Me'asef Zion* 5 (1933):71–77.

84 *Ibid.*, pp. 76–77. See also Baer's remarks on p. 71: "From the documents of the Inquisition, we see several clear signs of an extensive messianic movement among *conversos* as well as Jews, a movement which began in the mid-fifteenth century."

85 His words have been preserved in MS 8° Heb. 3935, JNUL. As the text is garbled in several places and seems to have been cut off at the beginning, I have restored it in the Hebrew version of this article, p. 121, no. 53. On Zacuto's work, see H.H. Ben-Sasson, "The Reformation in Contemporary Jewish Eyes," *Proceedings of the Israel Academy of Sciences and Humanities* 4 (Jerusalem, 1970), pp. 261–264, and see there the reference to earlier literature. Zacuto's work has been recently published by M. Idel and M. Beit-Arié, "Treatise on Eschatology and Astrology by R. Abraham Zacuto" (Hebrew), *KS* 54 (1979):174–194, 825–826.

On messianic hopes and calculations regarding the period close to the fall of Constantinople see also Alonso de Espina, *Fortalicium Fidei* (Nuremberg, 1494), Liber 3, consideratio 4, argum. 21 (fol. 98b): Et ideo dicunt moderni iudei quod ille erravit qia ubi posuit quia debuit ponere ria [r-y-h] quae facit in numero ducenta decem et octo . . . See also Y. Guttmann in his introduction to *Megilat HaMegaleh* (above, n. 79), p. xxviii.

86 Baer (above, n. 83), p. 77 and n. 1; idem (above, n. 4), pp. 284–292, 488 and n. 28.

87 H. Beinart, *Conversos on Trial* (Jerusalem, 1981), pp. 13–14, 59–60. And see *Shalem* 1, pp. 137–147 on the impact of the appearance of the comet among Jews and Christians in Italy during those years.

88 C. Roth, *A History of the Jews in Italy* (Philadelphia, 1946), pp. 242–243; A.Z. Aescoly, *Messianic Movements in Israel* (Hebrew), (Jerusalem, 1956), pp. 289–295.

89 Interestingly enough we also hear of the fervor for group emigration which seized members of the community of Dra' in Morocco on an unknown date in the latter half of the fifteenth century. The event is described in the Responsa of R. Zemah ben Shlomo Duran (the son of R. Shlomo ben Shim'on), *Yakhin UVo'az* (Leghorn, 1782), part 1, no. 58. For more on this event, see L. Zunz, *Zur Geschichte und Literatur* (Berlin, 1845), pp. 497–498. (Zunz thought that the event occurred in 1430, but this is ruled out by the authorship of the responsum); S.H. Kook, "R. Halafta and his Faction" (Hebrew), *Iyyunim . . .* (above, n. 22), pp. 146–149; I. Schepanski (above, n. 20), pp. 145–147. From the responsum it is clear that the authorities prevented them from going to Palestine as happened elsewhere during this period, in Spain and Sicily. Although there is no resemblance between this group and the mass migration in Castile and Sicily, their banding together and emigration may also be linked to the influence of the conquest of Constantinople and its aftermath.

90 See A. Neubauer (above, n. 28); J. Prawer, "An Examination of Letters from Jerusalem from the Fifteenth and Sixteenth Centuries" (Hebrew), *Jerusalem* 1 (1948):144–150; *Shalem* 1 (1974), pp. 137–147. On Sicily, see n. 53 above.

137

91 *Ibid.* Baer (above, n. 83), p. 71 thinks: ". . . letters of this type were unquestionably received in Spain as well," and see idem, (above, no. 17), 2, pp. 384–385 and see also n. 49 above.

92 See Baer (notes 84, 86 above) and Beinart (n. 87 above).

93 I intend to deal separately with the influence of the fall of Constantinople on the state of mind of the Jewish communities in Europe and in Muslim countries.

94 Dinur (above, n. 69), p. 162.

95 *Ibid.*, pp. 171–172. Dinur also tries to find some connection between the letters of reference which were given to emigrants after 1391 in Saragossa, and the letter in question, and even views them as evidence of mass emigration (p. 165 f.). These letters were given to persons from Aragon and Navarre, and not from Castile. The data in the present letter are totally different from those in the others, and the migration which they reflect is confined to families, not large groups of persons.

96 On Toledo see Y. Baer (above, n. 4), p. 277f.; on Ciudad Real see H. Beinart (above, n. 87), pp. 16f., 55f.

97 See e.g., A. Marx, *Studies in Jewish History and Booklore* (New York, 1944), pp. 88–89. And cf. e.g. *Sefer Yuhasin*, ed. Filipovsky (above, n. 27), p. 226; Responsa *Zera Anashim* (Husiatyn, 1902), no. 42, and other sources.

98 See n. 85 above, the words of Alonso de Espina and the reference to the writings of Izhak Abravanel, Baer (above, n. 83), also A. Zacuto, (above, n. 85), and the testimony of Abraham ben Eli'ezer HaLevi (*KS* 7 (1931):448). We should mention an exegetical tradition which arose among Spanish scholars in the latter half of the fifteenth century, according to which Lamentations 4, 21–22 was thought to predict the fall of Constantinople in their own time. This momentous event was seen as a sign of the imminent redemption of the Jews. This tradition may also show how prevalent the idea was among the Jews of Spain, for the belief found its way into various scholarly circles; it was by no means exclusively held by Izhak Abravanel. See, e.g., R.I. 'Aramah's commentary on Lamentations in *Tora VeHamesh Megilot 'im Perush Rashi* (Riva di Trento, 1561); Don Yosef ben Don David ibn Yachya, *Perush Hamesh Megilot* (Bologna, 1530), leaf 23a; Abraham ben Eliezer Ha-Levi, *Mashre Kitrin* (Constantinople, 1510), leaf 9. And see the text which I published in *Shalem* 1, p. 147.

99 See Baer (above, n. 4), p. 390f.; Beinart (above, n. 87), pp. 59–60.

100 See n. 62 above.

101 Beinart (above, n. 87) p. 60 and n. 50.

102 Baer (above, n. 17), No. 410, p. 484f.

103 A. Neubauer (above, n. 28), pp. 45–50; J. Prawer (above, n. 90), pp. 144–148. See also D. Tamar, "An Epistle from Jerusalem Scholars (1455)," *Sinai* 86 (1980): 55–61.

104 *Shalem* 1 (1974), pp. 147–154.

105 *Ibid.*

106 Freimann (above, n. 3), pp. 187–188, 194–198.

107 D. Tamar has already commented on this in "A New Responsum of Yosef Colon Concerning the Land of Israel" (Hebrew), *Zion* 18 (1953):127–135. For this discussion, see p. 129, n. 23. Cf. also E. Gottlieb, *Studies in the Kabbala Literature* (Hebrew), ed. J. Hacker (Tel Aviv, 1976), p. 370, no. 1, on the erroneous identification of Moshe HaCohen Ashkenazi with Moshe 'Esrim Ve'Arba'.

108 D. Tamar, *op. cit.*, p. 129f. Because the second Yosef was a Sefardi Jew, Tamar admits, n. 23a, "I have particular doubts regarding this matter because it makes better sense to assume that Yosef the *Dayan* was a Mustariba or a Jew from the Maghreb, rather than a Sefardi," and thus he hesitates to identify him with the Yosef the *Dayan* in the documents found in the Balbo Manuscript. See also idem, *Tarbiz* 39 (1970):98. However, he tends to think that they are one and the same person. In light of the document from the court and other sources which testify that there were Spanish Jews in the East and in Palestine at that time, we are inclined to think that these two Yosefs were one and the same. On other *dayanim* in Jerusalem in the fourteenth to the fifteenth centuries, see G. Scholem, *KS* 21 (1944):291; J. Prawer (above, n. 90), p. 148.

109 There is no specific date for Yosef the Sefaradi's mission to Italy. D. Tamar thinks that it was before 1467, and that it was his first mission, which is hinted at in Yosef the *Dayan*'s writings (Freimann, above, n. 3, p. 194). However, we should not rule out the possibility that this was

part of his 1473 mission, if in fact this was a single individual.

110 We possess no documents concerning the Jerusalem community during this period, aside from the sources connected with the destruction of the synagogue in 1475, namely, the letters and documents published by Freimann. Other sources concerning the Jerusalem community between 1466 and 1480, such as the writings of travellers, references in responsa, and the works of scholars in the Diaspora, are extremely meager.

111 A. Ya'ari, *Letters from Erez-Israel* (Hebrew), (Ramat Gan, 1971), p. 96.

112 *Ibid.*, pp. 127, 128, 139, 142.

113 *Ibid.*, p. 122. On the *conversos* and their emigration eastward during this period, see also Ashtor, 2 (above, n. 3), pp. 438–447, especially p. 441; also Assaf (above, n. 3), pp. 164–165. I am in possession of evidence from Hebrew sources and documents regarding the migration of Jews from Spain to Istanbul after the conquest of Constantinople and before the Expulsion from Spain, but will discuss the subject elsewhere.

114 For a summary of the travellers' estimates, see M. Ish-Shalom (above, n. 75), pp. 104–105.

115 A. Ya'ari (above, n. 28), p. 71.

116 See Ashtor (above, n. 3), pp. 428–437.

117 See M. Ish-Shalom, "On the History of Hebrew Speech" (Hebrew), *Areshet* (Jerusalem, 1944), pp. 390–391.

118 Of course, we do not know whether Meshullam's list (above, n. 28, p. 77) includes Sefardi Jews, though the Ashkenazi element is conspicuous and clearly defined. As to the rest of the persons mentioned, we can not at present tell who they are. (This also applies to the names which S. Assaf mentions. See n. 119 below.)

119 S. Assaf, "Miscellaneous Manuscripts" (Hebrew), *KS* 11 (1935):397–398; idem, "On the History of the Last *Negidim* in Egypt" (Hebrew), *Zion* 6 (1941):114 and n. 13. On the decline of the Jewish population in the city, see the well-known figures cited by 'Ovadia of Bertinoro who found seventy families there.

120 On individuals from the Minir family, see Baer (above, n. 17), index.

SYMPOSIUM

MESSIANIC CONCEPTS AND SETTLEMENT IN THE LAND OF ISRAEL

Participants: *Arie Morgenstern*
Jacob Katz
Menachem Friedman
Isaiah Tishby
Israel Bartal

MESSIANIC CONCEPTS AND
SETTLEMENT IN THE LAND OF ISRAEL

ARIE MORGENSTERN

*A*t the turn of the nineteenth century, Palestine witnessed several significant waves of immigration which changed the nature of its Jewish community. The followers of the Gaon of Vilna, who began settling in Palestine early in the century, constituted one of the more important trends. Basing himself on sources that have been but scarcely utilized by historians, A. Morgenstern has developed a strong case for the messianic nature of this immigration which focused its expectations on the year 1840. Morgenstern's provocative thesis has raised queries from various perspectives: to what extent the Gaon's disciples were in fact imbued with messianic views; whether the texts discussed truly express a direct connection between messianic language and actual settlement of the Holy Land; what historical implications may be derived from certain ritual emendations effected by the Gaon's disciples. The following symposium brings together experts from different fields, who explore these and other methodological and textual problems.

Historians have not paid sufficient attention to the immigration and settlement of the disciples of the Gaon of Vilna in Palestine between 1808 and 1847.[1] In general, their immigration has usually been considered an integral part of what historians of Palestine call the "old yishuv". This lack of attention may be ascribed to two main factors. First, the leaders of the Ashkenazi community in Palestine in the second half of the nineteenth century deliberately obscured the ideological motivations of the Vilna Gaon's disciples, for these were based on the principle of messianic activism and thus stood in opposition to the traditional stance of passive waiting for the Messiah. Second, extreme secrecy characterized the activities of the Gaon's followers, who feared arousing Russian and Ottoman opposition to their immigration, and who were also wary of openly engaging in messianic activity. It is likely that the failure of previous messianic movements led the Gaon's disciples to refrain from recording their views in writing; thus their activities were not accompanied by a systematic ideological platform.

An overview of Jewish history during the first half of the nineteenth century reveals little indication of the immigration of the Gaon of Vilna's disciples to Palestine, not only because they did nothing to publicize their activities, but because the attention of European Jewry was then focused on the advent of the Reform movement in Judaism and the ensuing debates. Indeed, that period is marked by the physical and ideological distancing of the Jews from the Land of Israel, and by their efforts to entrench themselves in the Diaspora. Furthermore, of some three million Jews throughout the world in the early nineteenth century, only about 5,000 lived in Palestine, and most of these were Sephardic Jews. Thus, the ideological detachment of European Ashkenazi Jewry from Palestine was noticeable and significant.

The Reform movement in Judaism, which arose during the period of struggle for the political emancipation of European Jewry, was characterized, *inter alia*, by a detachment of the traditional messianic beliefs from the hope for the ingathering of exiles and the restoration of a Jewish Kingdom in the Land of Israel. Reform also transformed Jewish messianic beliefs from a particularistic faith to a universalistic *Weltanschauung* focusing on the idea of *tikkun 'olam be-malkhut Shaddai*, reforming the world according to a Divine plan. The talmudic statement that the messianic period would be distinguished merely by an end to Jewish political enslavement was reinterpreted and applied to the drive to obtain equal rights for Jews living among the gentiles, rather than to the aspiration for Jewish national liberation.

It should be noted that it was not Reform alone that infused new meaning into the traditional Jewish messianic expectations; Orthodox groups also sought to bridge the gap between the desire to acquire citizenship in the general society and the traditional messianic view. However, while Reform made no mention whatever of an existential return to Zion, Orthodoxy postponed the return to a future "messianic period", thus neutralizing any current, concrete political ambitions. The Orthodox position was based on talmudic and midrashic tales forbidding the Jewish people to hasten their redemption, retake the Land of Israel by force, or rebel against the gentile nations,[2] until the time comes for their miraculous redemption, as they were earlier redeemed from slavery in Egypt. This view, including an express sanction against those attempting to speed the redemption process, was widely accepted in Orthodox circles in both Eastern and Western Europe. The disciples of the Gaon of Vilna were exceptions to this rule; they favored messianic activism and claimed that the way "to raise up the *Shekhina* from the dust" was not solely by worship — observing the Torah and its precepts, as was generally accepted — but by settling the Land of Israel.

The Gaon
of Vilna

The Messianic Views of the Vilna Gaon's Disciples

The messianic philosophy of the Gaon of Vilna and his disciples has, by and large, not been a subject of historical investigation. Nonetheless, sources such as the facsimile letters of the *Pekidim* and *Amarkalim* (clerks and treasurers) of Amsterdam from 1825 to 1870, and other contemporary works, can provide an insight into their thinking. Two additional books which have come to my attention in recent years are primary sources of information regarding the messianic approach of this group.

The first of these books, *Hillel ben Shaḥar*, was written by R. Hillel of Kovno,[3] one of the earliest of the Gaon's disciples to immigrate to Palestine. His name is signed to a letter written on the 10th of Adar II, 5570 (1810) in Safed.[4] The second book, *Sha'arei Ẓedek*,[5] was written by R. Aviezer of Tykocin who went to Palestine in 1832 and became one of the leading scholars in the Perushim community of Jerusalem.[6]

Both books express, as the basis of their messianic views, belief in the existence of "favorable periods of time" as mentioned in the *Zohar*. R. Hillel explicitly notes the belief in two such "favorable periods" which should have brought redemption to the Jewish people:

in the year תתנ"ו (856) of the fifth millennium (=1096), indicated in the verse גאולה תתנו לארץ... and in the year ת"ח (408) of the sixth millennium (=1648), of course, hinted at in the verse בזאת יבא אהרן אל הקדש... all this being completely true, were it not for the lack of repentance, which kept us from it [redemption].[7]

R. Aviezer of Tykocin also assumes the validity of "favorable periods":

All Jews should realize that there have been a number of times for redemption which were cancelled because of the lack of repentance, i.e., times explicitly appearing in the holy *Zohar*... but the Messiah did not come because, as we are forced to admit, Israel did not repent fully at that time.[8]

The belief in "favorable periods" leads us to the next step in the ideology of the disciples of the Gaon of Vilna, namely that the nearest favorable period to their days would be in the year ת"ר 5600 (1840), as the *Zohar* states:

When the sixth millennium comes, in the 600th year of the sixth millennium, the gates of wisdom above and the founts of wisdom below shall be opened... and God will raise up the nation of Israel from the dust of its Exile and will remember it.[9]

This is an explicit reference to a favorable period, mentioning the year without referring to alphabetic calculations based on biblical verses.

R. Hillel's book makes no specific reference to the year 5600, due to the restrictions on *hishuvei hakez*. R. Aviezer, whose book was published in 5603 (1843), admits that the advent of the Messiah had been awaited in 5600:

From now on we shall have to explain how it is that the reference of the holy *Zohar* to the year 5600 did not materialize... for it clearly meant that he [the Messiah] should have come in the year 600 of the sixth millennium... and if so, why has our Messiah yet to come, for [the year] 6[00] has already passed.[10]

The Vilna Gaon's commentary on the book *Sifra Di-Zeni'uta* includes an allusion to the time of the redemption and to the fact that there are people who know when it is to come to pass:

All these days are an indication of six thousand years which are six days... all the details of these six days conduct themselves in the six millennia, each in its appointed day and at its appointed hour. Hence one can calculate the advent of the redemption coming at its appointed time, and I call upon the reader, in God's name, not to reveal this.[11]

The Gaon's disciples viewed contemporary history in the light of their messianic conception, thus discerning in the events of their day signs of the *'ikveta de-Meshiha* (footsteps of the Messiah), the last stage of the Exile. R. Hillel saw in the

Page from the Venice Haggada, 1609, showing the Messiah arriving at the gates of Jerusalem

decline of Torah and Torah scholars and their replacement by unrestrained materialism clear proof that this period had arrived: "Alas for those who witness the decay of that generation, seeking peace and quiet in royal palaces and secure dwelling-places ... Anyone who looks can see that these times are *'ikveta di-Meshiha* ...,[12] and "The day God is to redeem His people is near."[13] He held that the pursuit of materialism causes Jerusalem to be forgotten and the Divine Presence to go into Exile; this is why the Exile was still in effect, because "the reason for the prolonging of the Exile is that we refuse to partake of the taste of Exile and prefer a high standard of living; if there is no Exile there can be no Redemption."[14]

R. Hillel did not believe that repentance would come about from love of God, but only from pain and affliction. He viewed the troubles besetting the Jewish people as an early, necessary stage in the redemption process, and so he awaited them almost joyfully:

> We shall not escape repentance out of fear, when the nations oppress us and
> money is no more, God willing, shortly [sic!] ... every day we shall await
> the coming of that hour, and we shall pray to the Lord, God of our fathers.[15]

Contrary to the later view expressed by Rabbi Z.H. Kalischer, whereby the civil emancipation and equal rights granted to the Jews in several European states were seen as signs of the approaching redemption, the Vilna Gaon's disciples looked upon the persecution of the Jews as the direct route to the final redemption. As the Gaon himself says:

> All the persecutions the Jews undergo in Exile bring the Redemption
> nearer ... and so all the maledictions [listed in the Mishna, at the end of
> Tractate *Sota*] are beneficial, in that they shorten the way to Redemption.[16]

R. Hillel, too, noted the mutual relationship between the improvement of the conditions under which the Jews lived and their forgetting the Land of Israel:

> We all have luxurious tastes, seeking delightful clothing and royal palaces ... and we unthinkingly ignore the fact that our land is desolate, with gentiles exulting in its Temple's being burnt to the ground; what has become of the vow we swore, "may my tongue cleave to my palate" ... we ignore the sorrow of the Holy One and His Presence.[17]

It is clear that R. Hillel thus linked his view of the contemporary period as *'ikveta di-Meshiḥa* with the redemption process which, in his opinion, had to follow the path of affliction:

> The earth has caved in, it has crumbled, as changes take place daily in the world, for in my opinion and in that of anyone of perception, it is clear that the day the Lord will redeem His people is near.[18]

This pre-messianic era would be marked not only by political revolutions and wars, but also by the increasing oppression of Israel by the nations of the world.

> When He unleashes a gentle wind from above to redeem us, liberation and repentance being denied us, then God will command the Heavenly Host ... that is, He will also order earthly kings to increase their evil decrees ... with the promise of setting up a king as terrible as Haman.[19]

In his discussion of the approaching redemption, R. Hillel mentions the kabbalistic principle that the redemption itself is to be hastened by "an awakening from below":

> When the time of the redemption comes, as it must, either at its set time or speedily, with only strict justice holding it back ... and God desires to arouse mercy to counter-rising justice, the holy *Zohar* lays down the rule that there is never an awakening up above *(hit'aruta di-le-'eila)* without a previous awakening from below *(hit'aruta di-le-tatta)*.[20]

R. Hillel does not explain exactly what steps are required, though the expression of his desire to go to the Land of Israel suffices to indicate the direction:

> If God pardons me ... and takes me out of this pit in the desert of the gentile nations, to bring me to the land of sanctity, of life, where my heart and eyes dwell constantly, waiting and anticipating going there ....[21]

R. Hillel's desire to go to the Land of Israel was linked to his expectation of redemption, and was for him a practical conclusion to be drawn from the ideas and aspirations he preached.

However, the messianic views expressed in the books of R. Hillel of Kovno and R. Aviezer of Tykocin do not necessarily lead to a deviation from the traditional concept that nothing should be done to hasten the coming of the redemption, other than observing the Torah and its precepts. Only the authority of a figure like the Gaon of Vilna, or a movement based on such an authority, could reverse that concept, and rule that the practical interpretation of "an awakening from below" in the redemption process is not merely spiritual, but is rather linked to clear messianic activism requiring settling the Land of Israel — and not by individuals alone, but by organized groups, which implied taking back the land by force.

It indeed seems that the appearance of the Vilna Gaon on the Jewish scene was interpreted by his disciples as marking the beginning of a new era in Jewish history. An analysis of their statements on this topic shows that they perceived in him a figure whose spiritual greatness and absolute command of all branches of Jewish thought, both simple and occult, was inexplicable in rational terms, but was rather a phenomenon that in itself constituted a Divine revelation:

> God seems to have sent us an angel from Heaven, the famed Vilna Gaon, our teacher R. Eliyahu of blessed and righteous memory, to begin the restoration of Torah to its pristine glory ... until the process reaches completion, when we are all worthy of the Divine light and abundance to be bestowed by the Messiah.[22]

In similar fashion the Gaon's disciple, R. Israel of Shklov, wrote of him:

> Secrets were revealed to him by our father Jacob, our teacher Moses and our prophet Elijah; and we are sending some of his holy mystic writings, and several secrets he uncovered, which had been completely concealed until he came.[23]

Map attributed to the Vilna Gaon, showing the Division of Ereẓ Israel among the tribes (Vilna, 1802).

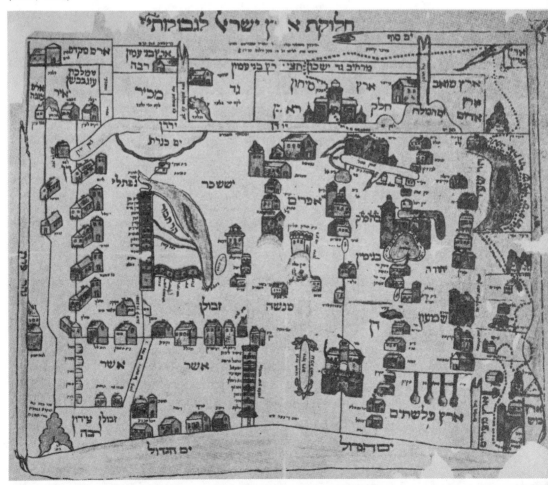

Thus, within the framework of the belief in the year 5600 as the imminent "favorable period", the Vilna Gaon's presence was a historic event marking the arrival of the *'ikveta di-Meshiḥa* period and confirming the validity of the entire messianic concept.

Against the background of these beliefs, one can understand why five of the six leading disciples of the Vilna Gaon emigrated to Palestine between 1808 and 1810,[24] and why 511 people closely associated with the Gaon's disciples arrived in Palestine by 1812,[25] filled with a sense of obligation to devote themselves to rebuilding the land and expanding the Jewish community therein. This feeling was shared by his followers who remained in Europe.[26]

The letter drafted in 1810 by the Gaon's disciples in Safed for the purpose of propagating their teachings gave expression in no uncertain terms to their special attitude toward the situation in the Land of Israel which signified, by its ruin, the exile of the Divine Presence:

> Good are its rocks and its dust; good are its grain and its fruits and its vegetables ... Forgetting the Holy Land means — God forbid — prolonging the Exile, forgetting one's right hand ... How long will it be before Jerusalem is pitied ... with the Holy City, once a source of joy for the entire land, still delivered into foreign hands.[27]

Since "in this hidden redemption the Divine Presence cannot rise of its own accord from the dust,"[28] they felt it necessary to hasten the redemption process by human endeavor defined as *tikkun ha-Shekhina* "restoration of the Divine Presence," as opposed to a miraculous redemption. One of the most important of the Gaon's disciples even defines this as a "natural" redemption. R. Yehuda Halevi Edel claims that if, during the Second Commonwealth period, no overt and renowned miracles took place, obviously none can be expected during the third redemption either, the whole process being natural, taking place by means of human activity: "For in the future, the matter [the redemption process] will be conducted in a natural way, without miracles."[29] R. Israel of Shklov, who dispatched a messenger from Safed in 1831 to seek out the Ten Lost Tribes and ask their sages to officially recognize the jurisdiction of the rabbis in the Land of Israel, wrote them that it was obligatory to further the redemption process by human endeavor, "for everything first requires an awakening from below ... Thus we have strengthened ourselves ... and we are hereby dispatching a fair and honest representative ...."[30]

148   Abrogation of the "Three Oaths"

How did the Vilna Gaon's disciples circumvent the prohibitions connected with the "three oaths", such as the prohibition of hastening the redemption or that of mass settlement "by force" in the Land of Israel?

A cursory glance at their writings suffices to prove that they engaged in calculations of the time of redemption by means of alphabetic letter-values (*gematria* and *notarikon*). Their positive approach towards this activity contrasts sharply with the traditionally negative attitude towards any calculations of this type:

> It is certain that anyone taking the trouble to give expression to his feelings and calculate the time of redemption will be rewarded additionally, for by means of these calculations the belief of the redemption is reinforced in one's heart, and God desires to bring the Messiah by virtue of this belief.[31]

R. Aviezer of Tykocin ruled that the prohibition against hastening the redemption process does not hold during "favorable periods", when not only is it permissible to hasten this process, but it is actually obligatory to do so:

> When ruling that the redemption should not be hastened, our Sages were referring ... to other times, not during favorable periods, when Israel is expected to make a strong effort to repent, lest the Evil Inclination overcome them. For during favorable periods it is very easy to achieve redemption.[32]

R. Israel of Shklov presented another reason for abrogating this prohibition. He claims that the "three oaths" are a kind of "package deal" concluded by God with Israel and the gentile nations. Israel was forbidden to hasten the redemption process or to return forcibly to the Land of Israel, while the nations were forbidden to subjugate the Jews too severely, lest they have no alternative but to take action concerning their redemption. When the gentile nations violate their part in the "three oaths", Israel is no longer bound by them either:

> ... He was only slightly angry at the sins of His people, but they [the gentiles] exaggerated in increasing the weight of their yoke, thus violating the prohibition they were sworn by God to uphold, not to oppress Israel too severely lest Israel act to hasten the redemption process.[33]

Settling the Land of Israel by "An Awakening from Below"

The move of the Gaon's disciples to the Land of Israel was not the final stage in their efforts to "restore" the *Shekhina* and hasten the coming of the redemption by means of an "awakening from below", but merely a first step. R. Israel of Shklov, who headed the Safed Perushim (as the Vilna Gaon's disciples were known) community, guided it toward spiritual endeavors expressed mainly in supreme efforts to hasten the redemption process through study of Torah and kabbala, observance of the *mitzvot* valid only in the Land of Israel, elevating the spirits of righteous departed souls, and especially through attempts to restore *semikha*, the juridical validity of the rabbinate, with the help of the Ten Lost Tribes who were traditionally considered to have passed on such ordination in an unbroken chain of succession from Moses himself. Restoration of Torah jurisprudence following the renewal of *semikha* was a recognized way to hasten the impending redemption, and R. Israel of Shklov gave it precedence even over the rebuilding of Jerusalem.[34] Accordingly, in 1831 he dispatched a messenger to Yemen to search for the Ten Tribes.[35]

149

Seal of R.
Menahem Mendel
of Shklov

The main body of the Gaon's disciples settled in Jerusalem and under the guidance of R. Menaḥem Mendel of Shklov adopted a different goal, one of practical projects aimed at hastening the advent of the redemption and arousing the *Shekhina* from the dust. Beginning in 1816, this group concentrated tirelessly on efforts to gain control of the compound of the "Ḥurva of R. Yehuda He-Hasid", in order to rebuild the apartments, synagogue, and public institutions within it. These attempts included lobbying at the Sultan's court in Constantinople, and seeking the intervention of foreign consuls, missionaries and the leaders of the local community. They also tried to come to a satisfactory arrangement with the heirs of the creditors of the early eighteenth century Ashkenazi community that had owned the Ḥurva and had gone bankrupt, and with the local governors of Jerusalem. The Ḥasidic community in Palestine also claimed ownership of the Ḥurva compound in Jerusalem, but they did nothing to establish their case. In contrast, the Gaon's followers worked unceasingly to bolster their claim.[36]

150

An expression of their approach to the rebuilding of the Ḥurva compound is to be found in a letter sent to the Diaspora announcing the beginning of the reconstruction:

> ... those in whom there burns the sacred flame of the Love of Zion and of Jerusalem. And to awaken to the sorrow of the Divine Presence ... to raise up the Divine Presence so it can find a place to rest in our study hall; rise up and have mercy on Zion for the time has come for its reprieve, to favor its

rocks and pardon its soil. It all depends upon the awakening from below to stir up the awakening from above, to rebuild the ruins . . . .[37]

In their fervent messianic expectations as the year 5600 (1840) grew nearer, the Perushim referred to sources in the *Zohar* and the Midrash which mention that Ishmael's (Muslim) rule of the Land of Israel would last a specific period, after which the land would come under Edom's [Christian] control, to be handed over finally to the Jewish people.[38] They did not consider Egyptian rule over Palestine an extension of Muslim rule, but rather subject to European-Christian control; as such it should not be considered as a mere change of government, but rather constituted an upheaval of theological-messianic significance.[39]

The improved legal status of the Jews in Palestine under Muhammad Ali's rule, and their increased economic activity, reinforced this concept. R. Eliezer Bergmann's letter from Jerusalem demonstrates this clearly: "The Ishmaelites are greatly humbled, whereas the Jews, especially the Ashkenazi Jews, enjoy impressive status . . . so that it can almost be said that the Redemption has already begun."[40] Messianic expectations intensified alongside the increased freedom of worship, for the Jews had been given permission to worship in public, mainly public prayers at the graves of holy rabbis, and to rebuild the Sephardi synagogues that were falling into ruin — privileges which the Jews had been denied during the period of Ottoman rule.

When the Perushim of Jerusalem were granted the right to rebuild the Ḥurva compound in the summer of 1836 — that is 5596 in the Jewish calendar, equivalent to the letter value of בונה ירושלים, "He who rebuilds Jerusalem" - they were seized by messianic ecstasy: "When has such an event befallen Zion ever since the Exile began? . . . to rebuild a glorious synagogue . . . this is a sign of the start of the Redemption . . . ."[41] In similar fashion R. Eliezer Bergmann wrote to Z.H. Lehren, head of the *Pekidim* and *Amarkalim* Fund (a European society to administer funds for the benefit of the old yishuv), that people in Jerusalem were saying that the redemption had already begun. This attitude did not remain in the realm of theory, but assumed a concrete and most dramatic form in the theology and liturgy of the Perushim. On the basis of their belief that the redemption had already begun, the disciples of the Vilna Gaon made changes in the order of their prayer services and in the wording of the prayers. They dropped the "shake off the dust, rise up" verse from the *Lekha Dodi* prayer welcoming the Sabbath, and ceased reciting the lamentations over the destruction of the Temple in the *Tikkun Ḥazot* (midnight prayers), for they held that the *Shekhina* had already risen from the dust. Z.H. Lehren protested this bold step, writing:

> Regarding the omission of "shake off the dust", etc. and the lamentations from *Tikkun Ḥazot*, I would like to know who introduced this innovation . . . I suspect him of having been misled by Shabbetai Ẓevi, since the book *Ḥemdat Yamim* also rules that this should be omitted.[42]

The reconstruction of the Ḥurva compound was not merely symbolic. Heading the priorities of the Perushim was the desire to augment Jewish settlement in

The Ḥurva synagogue and surrounding buildings

Jerusalem, to extend its residential areas, and to develop additional economic resources. Under the rule of Muhammad Ali their activities in these realms were accelerated. From the controversy which developed between Z.H. Lehren, who adhered to the traditional messianic views, and the disciples of the Vilna Gaon, we learn of the diversified activities of the latter group. One letter refers to the purchase of buildings far from the Jewish Quarter by the leaders of the Perushim who used their community's funds:

> Concerning the news from Jerusalem of the purchase of houses cheaply from Gentiles in areas previously not allowed . . . without the approval of the Sephardi Rabbis and scholars, but the heads of the Ashkenazim hasten to do so.[43]

The collectivist-future orientation of the leadership of the Perushim, who were interested in acquiring additional buildings and courtyards so as to expand the area of Jewish settlement, is apparent in another letter — where it stands in contrast to the here-and-now traditional orientation expressed by Lehren, who argued that all the available funds should be devoted to the maintenance of the Jewish residents of Jerusalem:

> Let him [R. Nathan Nata', the son of R. Mendel, a leader of Jerusalem *Perushim*] decide if buying up those courtyards is such a wise move, and if it

opens up hope of a large settlement in that area ... it will be good for the community if Jewish settlers are soon included in that project too.[44]

From a letter from Z.H. Lehren to R. Arye, a trustee of the Perushim community, we learn of that community's involvement in activities aimed at providing Jews with a more balanced economic base: "... regarding the projects of negotiations or agriculture or purchasing property, let whoever has the means make the attempt and even succeed, but in my opinion doing this in the name of the community is nonsense."[45] Even R. Israel of Shklov who, as we have noted, favored a spiritual approach to the redemption process, came to the conclusion at the end of 1837 that land should be acquired in Palestine, and sought to convince his friend, Z.H. Lehren, in this regard. Lehren's reply was that "the whole business of buying up fields and vineyards seems mad to us. I am especially surprised that you, my esteemed friend, have been taken in by E. Bergmann's ideas, so as to write this ... can you imagine basing all life in the Land of Israel on agriculture?"[46]

The letters sent to Moses Montefiore by the Perushim in the summer of 1839 also show that they wanted some of their members to engage in practical agricultural work, as an expression of their messianic approach in which settling the land and making its desolation bloom was one of the signs of the Redemption:

> We were happy to hear that Sir Moses has spoken of having them work their own plots in the Holy Land, the land of our forefathers ... We await and expect the love to awaken and the land to bring forth its fruit for the Jewish people living on it. For it all depends on the awakening from below to arouse the awakening from above. How long is our Holy Land to remain desolate and abandoned by its inhabitants.[47]

In light of their collectivistic-futuristic orientation, the leaders of the Perushim Kolel in Palestine and in Russia strove, in an organized fashion, to bring groups of immigrants from various social strata to the country, so as to enlarge the Jewish community and to establish it there firmly.

The Crisis of 5600 (1840) and the Conversions to Christianity

As 5600 (1840) drew nearer, tension in the Jewish world grew stronger and messianic expectations were rife. Great expectations permeated the Perushim community in Jerusalem as well. Though sources indicate that not all the Perushim were agreed that the Messiah would appear in 5600, some preferring to view the redemption as a gradual process, even those who were doubtful tensely awaited some event that would clearly mark the beginning of the new era. The Messiah did not appear in 1840, and instead of this joyous event the year was darkened by the Damascus blood-libel. The Messiah not having arrived by the end of 5600, everyone realized that this "favorable period", like those of 4856 (1096) and 5408 (1648) before it, had proved false. Without doubt, the more zealous the people's faith in the coming of the Messiah in 1840, the greater was their disappointment and disillusionment. Not everyone could remain steadfast in this period of spiritual turmoil and carry on his life as before. There seems to have been some truth in the writings of the Christian traveller who told of the confusion of the Jews:

> We are sure they want to return to the land of their forefathers with all their heart, and they believe that their hour of redemption is nigh. But after their prophecies failed, they began to realize that they had made a mistake. A few rabbis did not hesitate to proclaim this publicly, and many have recently converted.[48]

As early as 1839, we find evidence of a link between three scholars of the followers of the Vilna Gaon, and missionaries of the "Society for Promoting Christianity among the Jews" who were active in Jerusalem. In March 1842, the decision of these three rabbis to convert to Christianity was made public. We may assume that the crises preceding 1840, especially the suffering endured by the inhabitants of Jerusalem during the famine and the epidemics of 1838–9, raised doubts concerning what the future had in store for them. There is, however, no doubt that their final decision to convert was taken as a result of the failure of the Messiah to appear. A missionary delegation and the Protestant bishop, Michael Solomon Alexander, himself a convert from Judaism, provided the necessary encouragement for them to carry out their resolution.

Early in October 1842, a veritable war was waged in Jerusalem between the heads of the Perushim community, and the missionaries and Bishop Alexander, for the souls of the three rabbis. The missionaries exerted every effort to convert the three — in the very heart of Jerusalem, where Jews had in the past rejected the messianic claims of Jesus. The leaders of the Perushim did all they could to prevent such a step which was liable, above all, to blacken the name of the Jews of Palestine.[49] On May 21, 1843, the missionaries chalked up a victory: five Jews, including R. Eliezer Luria, of a distinguished rabbinical family, and R. Benjamin Goldberg, were baptized and accepted Jesus as their Messiah in the very heart of Jerusalem.[50] The third rabbi, who changed his mind at the last moment, was also a scion of one of the founding families of the Perushim, R. Abraham Nissan Wolpin. He was the son of R. Reuben of Mohilev, one of the first Perushim to settle in Palestine and one of the heads of the community during the 1830s, and son-in-law of R. Menaḥem Mendel of Shklov, the foremost disciple of the Vilna Gaon in Palestine.[51]

R. Aviezer of Tykocin testifies to the causal connection between the religious crisis and the conversions:

> From now on we must clarify the words of the holy *Zohar* on *Vayyera* 117 . . . why its explicit reference to the year 5600 did not materialize, and if so . . . why is our Messiah delayed, for six ([5]600) has already come; several people have already abandoned their faith because of this, saying that as the year 5600 has already passed and the Messiah has not come, he will surely not come any more.[52]

R. Aviezer maintained that the people who converted to Christianity because of their disappointment at the nonappearance of the Messiah were the descendants of the 'erev-rav, the "mixed multitude" who formed the golden calf in the desert. On the basis of the belief that everything written in the Torah refers equally to the past, the present and the future, he held that the verse "The people saw that Moses was delayed in descending from the mountain" referred to the mixed multitude who said that since the sixth hour had already passed, Moses would no longer return; and so they told Aaron: "Rise, and make us a god...". He concluded: "...the sacred Torah surely hints at the people of this last generation who arrogantly revile and curse because of six ([5]600)."[53]

R. Aviezer of Tykocin sought not only to justify the expectations that had been held for the year 5600, but to bolster the faith of those who had been disillusioned. He constructed a whole set of proofs to justify the hopes they had had for 5600. However, he continued, it must be remembered that 5600 marked the start of the redemption process, which would be reaching its climax in 5606 (1846). The years between were to be years of trial, even extremely difficult ones. R. Aviezer's thesis was based on fundamental concepts of Luria's kabbala and on alphabetical calculations. Every such calculation indicating the year 5600 he automatically adjusted to 5605. This adjustment was only an attempt to extend the messianic expectations as much as possible, and prevent at any price the crisis he saw developing before his very eyes. An outstanding example is provided by the way he referred to verses of the "Song of Songs", which were interpreted by kabbalists and by the Vilna Gaon's disciples as a song of the future redemption. He interpreted chapter two, verse twelve — "The blossoms have appeared in the land, the time of pruning has come; the song of the turtledove is heard in our land," as follows: "This will only take place up above, and not yet reach down below ... i.e. the blossoms have begun to be seen in the land above, but human beings know nothing of it." However, he interpreted "the song of the turtledove is heard in our land" to mean that when the year of the dove (תור = 5606) would come, the song of redemption would be heard in the land below as well.[54]

As the year 5606 (1846) came nearer, it became clear that this would not be the year of redemption either. 1845 was one of the most oppressively hot and dry years that Palestine experienced in the nineteenth century. It was a year of severe famine which led to complete demoralization in the Jewish community, and a number of its leaders, who were unable to shoulder the burden of feeding the community's members, fled the country.[55] In Russia, too, the land of the Perushim's origin, the Jews were finding life very difficult. The decrees promulgated by Tsar Nikolai I to "improve" the lot of the Jews grew more frequent. These decrees affected the attire of the Jews, their autonomous organization, and their traditional educational system. Their economic position worsened, tens of thousands were recruited into the army, and many had their freedom of movement severely curtailed.[56] It was apparent that the attempts to move the period of redemption from 5600 to 5606 had failed completely. In 5605

(1845), Z.H. Lehren complained that Jews in Jerusalem still awaited redemption, assuming that the settlement of the Land of Israel marked the rising of the *Shekhina* from the dust, "for in the Holy City Jews do not recite 'until when is Your strength in captivity, and Your majesty in enemy hands', because the *Shekhina* has already arisen from the dust."[57] It is, however, very doubtful if by 5606 they still held that belief.

Spiritual Means of Bringing Redemption Nearer

Following the crisis of 5606, it was increasingly argued that settling the Land of Israel was not the legitimate way to hasten the coming of the Redemption; emphasis should rather be placed on spiritual activity.

R. Aviezer of Tykocin's book, *Sha'arei Ẓedek*, expresses this approach. R. Aviezer already (5603 — 1843) blamed the opponents of R. Israel of Shklov for the failure of the Perushim in hastening the redemption. They had favored the rebuilding of Jerusalem as a major act of "awakening from below", but he maintained that all the building they had urged merely resembled the deeds of the generation of the Tower of Babel whose only aim was to make a reputation for themselves:

> Concerning them it is said, "Let us build us a city and make a name for ourselves, and build synagogues and study-halls and put Torah scrolls in them with crowns upon them" — not for God's sake, but rather to make a name for themselves; this is the Evil Inclination overcoming Israel.[58]

He went still further and accused the veteran leadership of the Perushim community which had disagreed with the ruling of R. Israel of Shklov, of responsibility for the devastation of Safed at the hands of rioting Arab peasants in 5594 (1834), for the casualties suffered in the destruction of the Galilee in the earthquake of 5597 (1837), and for the epidemics which plagued Jerusalem in 5598–5599 (1838–9). He maintained that their desire to rebuild Jerusalem and restore the compound of the Ḥurva was wrong from the very beginning. Even if they had desired to rebuild the Temple itself, it was doubtful if this was the right thing to do:

> We shall yet come to learn for what main purpose the Temple was built; it cannot be for the building itself, for wood and stone have no sanctity. Thus it must have been in order to house something of sanctity, that is, the Ark in which the Torah was placed ... all the more so since the main reason for the *Shekhina* visiting this world was not for the Temple, but only for the Torah.[59]

R. Aviezer emphasized the importance of Torah and kabbala study as a means of "restoring" the *Shekhina*: "That is, one must study the secrets of the Torah, for this study is what raises the *Shekhina* up from the dust ... for this study Israel will be redeemed from their exile."[60]

156

Reinstating the Recitation of Tikkun Ḥazot

As early as 5603 R. Aviezer called upon Jewry to repent, repentance centering around the reciting of *Tikkun Ḥazot*:

> In this regard, my fellow Jews, take my advice . . . and rise up to fulfill these three major commandments, *i.e.*, to love your fellow man as yourself, to honor the Sabbath . . . and the third one — to rise at midnight to lament the exile of the *Shekhina* . . . and the destruction of the Temple.[61]

The call for the resumption of reciting *Tikkun Ḥazot* and upgrading it to the level of two other precepts upon which the redemption depended, was in essence a call for a total withdrawal from the messianic belief fundamental to the activities of the veteran leadership of the Perushim, namely that the reconstruction of the Ḥurva compound would raise the *Shekhina* from the dust.

Two concrete signs of the spiritual crisis affecting the Perushim were the strengthening of the leadership status of R. Isaiah Bourdaky, the son-in-law of R. Israel of Shklov, who opposed the reconstruction of the Ḥurva, and the weakening position of R. Abraham Solomon Zalman Zoref, a leading supporter of the Ḥurva's restoration. In Iyyar 5607 (May 1847), after the deaths of two leaders of the community, R. Nathan Nata' and R. Moses Maggid-Rivlin,[62] the new leadership had the courage to ask the members to sign an agreement reinstituting the custom of reciting *Tikkun Ḥazot*:

> The princes of the people have gathered to confer as to what steps to take concerning the cessation of the daily sacrifice in our Temple . . . ever since its destruction, God only has room in this world for halakha . . . only this Torah is left for us.[63]

Correcting this situation entailed setting up Torah study groups and, in particular, reciting the *Tikkun Ḥazot* —

> . . . even greater than intensive Torah study and bewailing the Destruction at night, upon which both the upper and lower worlds depend, one of the most important things upon which all the Jews depend.[64]

The apologetics in the agreement seem to indicate that not everyone was happy with the reinstitution of this recitation, and not everyone agreed with the view that everything the Vilna Gaon's disciples, the first Ashkenazi settlers to return to Jerusalem, did was invalid and was not the right way to hasten the redemption process. The thirty-two signatures on the agreement do not include that of R. Abraham S.Z. Zoref, for he was out of the country at the time, and his absence may indeed have been taken advantage of by the heads of the community in order to present the agreement and get it signed. R. Arie, a trustee of the community, and R. Shmuel Salant did not sign the agreement either.

In 1849, another retreat from the views of the founders became apparent. When the leaders of the Perushim appealed to Moses Montefiore concerning the establishment of workshops to help support the community, their appeal was written rationally, with no use whatever of kabbalistic motifs linking the

Signature of R. Abraham S. Zoref

development of the country with the redemption, such as were to be found ten years earlier in almost all the letters sent to Montefiore in 5599 (1839).[65]

"If God Does not Build the House, Its Builders Labor in Vain"

The reinstitution of *Tikkun Ḥazot* was not the last stage of the retreat from the views of the founding Perushim. A new slogan was needed that would anchor their conception in the Holy Scriptures. A source dating from 5610 (1850) reveals for the first time that the Ashkenazim of Jerusalem maintained that the construction and development of the Land of Israel not only did not contribute to the hastening of the redemption process, but was lacking in all value. This was to be understood from the verse in Psalms, "If God does not build the house, its builders labor in vain." In none of the letters dating from the early 1840s, arguing for the establishment of a hospital, is there any sign of anyone having made use of this verse, not even Z.H. Lehren. Lehren's opposition to the building of the hospital was mainly based on his fear of the influence this modernizing process would have on the community, lest Jewish doctors introduce a spirit of heresy or atheism among the local residents. However, the quotation from Psalms in the aforementioned source is quite extreme and forbids all practical steps:

> [The Polish Jews] have no interest in the philanthropy of Rothschild, and always say, "If God does not build the house..." though the 8,000 Sephardi Jews and their sages do not accept this verse, written by King David, for they request that various repairs be made by Sir Montefiore or by others.[66]

It is evident that this verse did become an ideological slogan in Jerusalem. In a private letter R. Naḥman Nathan Coronel sent to R. Solomon Zalman Ḥayyim Halberstam on 23 Kislev 5625 (December 1865), he expressly refers to this verse as of ideological import while writing of R. Isaac Rosenthal of the Dutch-German community:

> Though he belongs to the sect (!) striving for the settlement of the Holy Land, I think it will remain forever in ruins as long as the leadership of the kingdom of Ishmael [the Muslims] does not change, and until God agrees, for if God does not build, etc....[67]

Jacob Saphir, too, in an open letter to Rabbi Alkalai, rejected the practicality of settling the Land of Israel as a means of natural redemption:

> These inferences will not be of any use to us, for those who believe in the redemption of Israel fully believe, as our reliable tradition holds, that it will be wondrous and miraculous... and by means of Torah, repentance and charity... If God does not build the house, its builders labor in vain. There is no point in getting up early, before dawn, to eat unripe fruit, before the time God fixes has come... so as to fulfill... I, the Lord, have rebuilt the ruins and replanted the desolation.[68]

R. Meir Auerbach also expressed, in a reply to Rabbi Z.H. Kalischer, his opposition to the latter's position that the settlement of the Land of Israel was a means to hasten the redemption. In my opinion, R. Auerbach was referring to the failure of the disciples of the Gaon of Vilna to hasten the redemption in this manner when he wrote:

> But this is not the way to reach our goal, and let us not be disgraced, God forbid, like some of our predecessors who thought similarly and erred, though they too thought their intentions were honorable; but they were wrong, and many followed them, and this led to laxity and weakness in our faith in the True Redeemer.[69]

In summation, the practical settlement of the Land of Israel seems to have been the ideal of the disciples of the Gaon of Vilna. They immigrated to Palestine at their rabbi's behest, and out of a sense of imminent redemption; they sought to hasten its advent or to bring it about by a natural process. In the 1830s, at the beginning of Egyptian rule over Palestine, their basic ideology meshed with the dynamics of contemporary events and with the increasing opportunities for building and economic projects. However, following the failure of the Messiah to appear in 5600 (1840), the Perushim community underwent a crisis accompanied, among the fringe elements, by a number of conversions to Christianity. The attempts made by the veteran leadership to continue with the rebuilding projects met opposition on the part of those who claimed that the true way to hasten the redemption process was spiritual in character — through study of Torah and Kabbala and recitation of *Tikkun Hazot*.

By the end of the 1840s, when the founders of the community had all passed away, a new leadership took over, reinstituting the reciting of *Tikkun Hazot* and thereby expressing its reservations regarding the rebuilding of Jerusalem as a means of raising the *Shekhina* from the dust. In place of the ideology of "rebuilding ruins" as an "awakening from below", there developed an ideology of "If God does not build the house, its builders labor in vain." This ideology underlies the opposition of the leadership to proposals for productivization and modernization and to the settlement of the country in the second half of the nineteenth century.

As time went by, this opposition was reinforced by other factors, including the fear of cultural "Enlightenment" influences, the inroads of the Reform movement, growing limitations on the distribution of funds within the *halukka* system, the problems involved in observing Torah commandments tied to the Land of Israel, etc. But the nucleus of the Perushim ideology remained the belief that the rebuilding of the Land did nothing to hasten the coming of the redemption, and that the only legitimate ideology was faith in a miraculous redemption.

Fearing that the supporters of settlement of the Land of Israel in the 1880s would seek to base their activities on the ideology that had motivated the followers of the Vilna Gaon to immigrate to Palestine, the leaders of the Perushim sought, from the 1860s on, to obliterate traces of that historical episode, even deliberately refraining from specifying the names of those earlier immigrants.

This symposium was translated by Yoel Lerner, with the exception of the article by I. Bartal, which was translated by Naftali Greenwood.

1 For a more complete treatment of this subject, see my book *Messianism and the Settlement of Palestine* (Hebrew), in print.
2 B, *Ketubbot* 111a: "Why these three oaths? One so that Israel would refrain from taking the land by force, another, where God had Israel vow not to rebel against the gentile nations, and the other, where God had the idolators swear not to oppress Israel too severely ... also not to reveal the time of the redemption and not to delay [Rashi reads: not to speed up] it and not to reveal the secret to the idolators."
3 The book *Hillel ben Shahar*, containing twenty-six sermons, was compiled (1804) by the famed Rabbi of Kovno, the son of the Rabbi Ze'ev Wolf of Ratzki.
4 See A. Ya'ari, *Letters from the Land of Israel* (Hebrew) (Tel Aviv, 1943), p. 337.
5 *Sha'arei Zedek le-Zera Yizhak* was printed in Jerusalem in 1843.
6 His name appears in the list of scholars of the Perushim community in Jerusalem. MS. Montefiore 528, dated 5599 (1839), The Institute for the Microfilming of Hebrew Manuscripts, JNUL, Jerusalem (hereafter, Microfilm Institute).
7 *Hillel ben Shahar*, p. 23b. The years were derived by application of *gematria* to biblical verses.
8 *Sha'arei Zedek*, p. 24b.
9 *Zohar* (trans. *Ha-Sullam*), *Vayyera* I, 117.
10 *Sha'arei Zedek*, p. 56b.
11 The Vilna Gaon's commentary on *Sifra di-Zeni'uta*, Vilna 5580 (1820), p. 33b. Also in B, *Sanhedrin* 99a: Rabbi Dosa says, [The Messianic period] is four hundred years. Here it is written, "and they shall slave for them and they will oppress them four hundred years," and there it is written: "Let us rejoice [for as long] as the days you oppressed us, etc."
12 *Hillel ben Shahar*, Introduction, p. 6b.
13 *Ibid.*, p. 7b.
14 *Ibid.*, p. 21a.
15 *Ibid.*, p. 42a.
16 Commentary on the Prophets and Hagiographia, attributed to the Gaon of Vilna, Microfilm Institute, JNUL, 3426, p. 21a. The ms. was written during the lifetime of the Gaon's disciple, R. Hayyim of Volozhyn.
17 *Hillel ben Shahar*, p. 21b.
18 *Ibid.*, **p. 7b.**
19 *Loc. cit.*
20 *Ibid.*, **p. 17b.**
21 *Loc. cit.*
22 Menasseh of Ilya, *Sefer Alfei Menashe* (Hebrew) (Vilna, 1822), p. 73b.
23 Ya'ari (above, n. 4), pp. 350–351.
24 The Vilna Gaon's son, R. Abraham, lists the names of his father's thirteen foremost disciples. Six or perhaps seven of them were still alive in 1808. Five came to live in Palestine: R. Menahem Mendel, R. Sa'adia, R. Israel — all of Shklov; R. Zevi Hirsch of Simyatitz; and R. Hayyim Katz. Sh.Y. Finn, *Kirya Ne'emana* (Hebrew) (Vilna, 1914), pp. 163–170.

25 See J.J. and B. Rivlin, critical edition of *Letters of the Pekidim and Amarkalim of Amsterdam 5586–5587* (Hebrew) (Jerusalem, 1965), p. 93.

26 The organization which arranged for the immigration and support of the members of the Perushim community is known officially as *Roznei Vilna*, and was initially headed by R. Hayyim of Volozhin.

27 Ya'ari (above, n. 4), pp. 330–333.

28 *Sha'arei Zedek*, p. 64a.

29 R. Yehuda Halevi Edel, *Sefer Afikei Yehuda* (Hebrew) (Zloczow, 1819), p. 109a.

30 Ya'ari (above, n. 4), p. 352.

31 *Sha'arei Zedek*, p. 46b.

32 *Ibid.*, p. 26a.

33 Ya'ari (above, n. 4), p. 352.

34 R. Israel of Shklov, *Sefer Tiklin Hadtin* (Hebrew) (Minsk, 1812), Introduction; and also B, *Megilla* 17b; *Rosh Ha-Shana* 31a; Maimonides' *Commentary on the Mishna, Sanhedrin*, ch. 1.

35 Ya'ari (above, n. 4), p. 352.

36 For the activities of the Perushim in Jerusalem during the period 1816–1837, see my article, "Reconstruction of the Compound of R. Yehuda He-Hasid's Hurva" (Hebrew), *Shalem* 4 (Jerusalem, 1984), pp. 271–305.

37 P. Grajewsky, *From the Archives of Jerusalem*, 2 (Hebrew) (n.p., n.d.), pp. 2–3.

38 See *Zohar* (trans. *Ha-Sullam*), *Bereshit, Vayyera*, 13; *Vayikra Rabba* 8, end of section 13; Letters of the *Pekidim* and *Amarkalim* of Amsterdam, ms. in Yad Izhak Ben-Zvi library, 5, 86a.

39 See my article, "Messianic Expectations for the Year 5600 (1840)" (Hebrew), in *Essays in Messianism and Eschatology* (Jerusalem, 1983), pp. 343–364.

40 Eliezer V. Bergmann, *Yis'u Harim Shalom — Letters of Travel and Aliya 1833–1836* (Hebrew) (Jerusalem, 1968), p. 76.

41 See above, n. 37.

42 *Letters of the Pekidim . . .* (above, n. 38), 8, p. 7a. For the liturgical changes made by the followers of Shabbetai Zevi, see M. Benayahu, "The Innovations Introduced by Nathan ha-'Azzati in his Circle in Kastoria and Salonika," *Sefunot* 14 (1978): 297 (10), 299–300 (20).

43 Z.H. Lehren's letter dated 12 Elul 5596 (August 25, 1836), Letters of the *Pekidim . . .* (above, n. 38), 6, p. 233b.

44 *Ibid.*, 8, p. 26a.

45 *Ibid.*, 8, p. 61a, dated 26 Av 5597 (August 25, 1837).

46 *Ibid.*, 8, p. 46a, a letter dated 20 Sivan 5597 (June 23, 1837). R. Eliezer Bergmann went to Palestine from Germany, actively expecting messianic developments. He frequently expressed himself in favor of a natural process of redemption. His significant activities during the 1830s and his connections with the Perushim in Jerusalem are a separate topic deserving special study.

47 S. Baron, "On the History of the Jewish Community in Jerusalem" (Hebrew), *Klausner Jubilee Volume*, ed. N.H. Torczyner, A.A. Kabak, A. Tcherikover, and B. Shohetman, (Tel Aviv, 1937), p. 304, note 2. Similarly the statement made by the heads of the community: "They almost all desire to earn their own livelihood by cultivating the Holy Land, eating of its fruit and being sated with its goodness," MS. Montefiore (above, n. 6), 528.

48 Quoted from M. Ish-Shalom, *Christian Travellers in the Holy Land* (Hebrew), (Tel Aviv, 1966), p. 554.

49 See Albert H. Hyamson, *The British Consulate in Jerusalem*, 1 (London, 1941), pp. 56–77; *Jewish Intelligence*, 1842, pp. 60–63.

50 See *Jewish Intelligence*, 1843, p. 280.

51 I am grateful to the Jerusalem genealogist, R. Shmuel Gur, for assisting me in the exact identification of those involved in this affair.

52 *Sha'arei Zedek*, p. 56a.

53 *Ibid.*, p. 56b.

54 *Ibid.*, p. 60b.

55 See M. Benayahu, "The Famine in Jerusalem in 5606" (Hebrew), *Jerusalem Quarterly for the Study of Jerusalem and its History* 2, A–B (1949): 72–88.

56 For a further discussion of these developments, see M. Stanislawski, *Tsar Nicholas I and the Jews. The Transformation of Jewish Society in Russia, 1825–1855* (Philadelphia, 1983).

57 Letters of the *Pekidim* ... (above, n. 38), 11, p. 122.

58 *Sha'arei Zedek*, p. 40a.

59 *Ibid.*, p. 15a.

60 *Ibid.*, p. 7a.

61 *Ibid.*, p. 31a.

62 R. Nathan Nata' died on 22 Tishre 5607 (1846); R. Moshe Maggid-Rivlin died on 28 Elul 5606 (1846). See A.L. Frumkin, *The History of the Sages of Jerusalem*, 3 (Hebrew) (Jerusalem, 1929), p. 224.

63 P. Grajewsky (above, n. 37), 13 (1931), p. 3.

64 *Ibid.*, p. 4.

65 See above, n. 47.

66 M. Weinstein, "Plans for improving the conditions of the Jews of Jerusalem in the mid-nineteenth century" (Hebrew), *Bar-Ilan: Annual of Bar-Ilan University* 6 (1968): 349; Israel Freidin, "'Bikur Holim Perushim' in Jerusalem — From Society to Hospital" (Hebrew), *Cathedra* 27 (1983): 117–140.

67 Microfilm Institute, JNUL, ms. 29459.

68 *Ha-Levanon* 8 (1872): 338, 346.

69 *Ha-Levanon* 1 (1863): 8.

MESSIANISM AND THE
DISCIPLES OF THE VILNA GAON

Menachem Friedman

he *aliya* of the disciples of the Gaon of Vilna to the Land of Israel between 1808 and 1812 is undoubtedly an event of special historical significance; Morgenstern's claim that this move was linked to messianic ferment is therefore in need of serious consideration. When Dr. Morgenstern made it known that he had proof that the migration of the followers of the Gaon of Vilna was linked with an ideology of messianism developed under the inspiration (if not more actively) of the Gaon himself, this seemed to me to be a sensational discovery, opening up the social and spiritual world of the Vilna Gaon and his disciples for new study. Morgenstern's thesis is very convincing, and it does support the hypothesis that the disciples of the Gaon who moved to Palestine were part of a wider circle which viewed settlement of the Land of Israel as a fateful religious mission within a framework of messianic expectations.

Morgenstern's proof is intriguing and challenges accepted notions in current research. My comments are not intended to disprove his thesis, but rather to consider whether systematic study of the sources leads only to the interpretation Morgenstern gives these events. I do not wish to rule out the thesis that there was a connection between the migration of the Gaon's disciples to Palestine and messianic activity; on the contrary, it seems difficult to explain so significant a step without a background of messianic expectation and hope of redemption!

This, however, does not necessarily lead to the conclusion that the Vilna Gaon developed a systematic ideology of messianism. Despite all the evidence Morgenstern adduces, it is difficult to draw such a conclusion. The idea of a period especially favorable to redemption, with everything depending solely upon repentance, is not new; similar explanations have been adduced in connection with other significant historical developments in Jewish history, even in recent years. R. Hillel of Kovno makes no mention, in his book *Hillel ben Shaḥar*, of the hopes linked to the year 5600 (1840). Morgenstern maintains that he refrained from doing so "for obvious reasons," mainly the secret concepts that forbade mentioning a definite date. This is possible, but only if the assumption of the existence among the Gaon's disciples of a systematic messianic ideology specifically relating to the year 5600, is a fact. It is normal to mention '*ikveta di-Meshiḥa* in times of trouble for the Jews; such reference by R. Hillel is thus no proof of Morgenstern's basic premise. At any rate, if the Gaon of Vilna had a systematic messianic philosophy that was adopted by his followers, no expression of this can be discerned in R. Hillel's writings.

Morgenstern maintains that it is possible to explain the *aliya* of the Gaon's disciples in 5568 (1808) only in terms of an explicit command on the part of the Gaon within the framework of messianic activity. This, in his opinion, is the source of the emphasis placed on the obligation to resettle the Land of Israel, an obligation that was to be fulfilled to the point of martyrdom; as R. Israel of Shklov testifies, he "sacrificed his very soul for the Holy Land, its founding and its reconstruction . . ." Here too, I believe, things should be interpreted cautiously. If the first assumption regarding the Gaon's command is accepted, then this indeed constitutes evidence; however this excerpt can also be understood as a stylistic device frequently employed by those engaged in settling and rebuilding the Holy Land.

The preference shown to Safed over Jerusalem is an important element in Morgenstern's work, which maintains that this is a messianic view of the order in which the redemption is to unfold — firstly, in reintroducing the *semikha*, the ordination, which is to take place in the Galilee, where Israel's redemption is to begin. However, a study of the evidence raises a number of questions. Morgenstern himself deals with this topic thoroughly and with insight. He notes that according to traditions held by the Perushim, the Gaon himself wanted to move to Jerusalem, and R. Israel of Shklov's grandfather, R. Azriel, tried to establish an Ashkenazi community in Jerusalem. However, contemporary conditions there made it difficult to do so: the previous Ashkenazi settlers (followers of R. Yehuda He-Ḥasid) had left considerable debts behind them; the Sephardim feared that support of their community would diminish; nor were the Ḥasidim in favor of such an undertaking. After the 1812 epidemic in Safed, the Perushim split up, the faction headed by R. Menaḥem of Shklov settling in Jerusalem, and R. Israel of Shklov remaining in Safed. This dissension is evident from the letters of the *Pekidim* and *Amarkalim* dated 5591–5600 (1831–1840). Yet those letters contain no vestige of a messianic argument concerning the initial importance of the Galilee for the reinstitution of *semikha*. If this really was the reason R. Israel of Shklov objected to settling in Jerusalem, it should have been the decisive argument, all else being of secondary importance. Why was it not mentioned or even hinted at in the letters? If one suggests that, because of the great secrecy, it could not be mentioned in public or before outsiders — we may reply that R. Israel himself mentions the reinstitution of *semikha* in his letter to the Ten Lost tribes. Why should it be permissible to mention *semikha* there, yet forbidden here?

The episode of the Ten Tribes can be given a different interpretation than the one Morgenstern offers. R. Israel of Shklov's letter to the Ten Tribes includes a section incompatible with Morgenstern's central thesis. R. Israel wrote:

> Lest there still be more time until we are redeemed from our oppression, and the troubles preceding the advent of the Messiah be plentiful, take

> pity on us and assist us every year ... so that the scholars worshipping
> God in the Holy Land and studying His Holy Torah in poverty day and
> night in our academies and study-halls grow stronger in Torah.

This is not the style of someone who is convinced of the messianic experience to which he is witness, that is rooted in so powerful a personality as the Gaon of Vilna. Nor is this the style of someone who senses it is already "Sabbath eve," that "the *Shekhina* has already risen from the dust," and that the most important thing is to reinstitute the *semikha* so as to hasten the redemption process. R. Israel's doubts and requests for support show that he is still living "during the secular week," and by the notions of the traditional Jewish society. Furthermore, there were some who opposed the mission and the emissary, both among the Hasidim and the Perushim. And, since the discovery of the Ten Tribes is known to be a sign of the redemption, why should the Perushim in Jerusalem who followed the tradition of the Vilna Gaon be opposed to such a step, fearing that messianic unrest would result from it? Wasn't this already a period of *'ikveta di-Meshiḥa* and hadn't the *Shekhina* already risen from the dust?

The messianic fervor connected with the year 5600 is a well-known phenomenon which has been widely investigated a number of times, and Morgenstern has undoubtedly made a praiseworthy contribution to this study. Indeed, this fervor in itself can explain several apparently surprising facts, such as the decision to stop reciting *Tikkun Ḥaẓot* in Jerusalem, just before the year 5600. However, must this step really be viewed in the perspective of the messianic views which the Vilna Gaon's disciples inherited from their teacher?

These questions require further study and discussion.

1840 AS A "YEAR OF REDEMPTION"

JACOB KATZ

I should like to begin by commenting on the year 5600 (1840) as a messianic year. The apostate Benjamin Be'eri wrote in his book that when he was a student at the Volozhin Academy in 5600, they discussed the coming of the Messiah who was expected there, as he was expected elsewhere. This testimony enlarges the geographic scope of the areas where messianic expectations were a subject for discussion. I would like to point to yet another source, as yet unnoted, namely excerpts from the writings of Moses Hess, published by Dr. R. Michael.[1] There we read as follows:

> A short time ago people spoke of the political revival of the Jews, an idea they [the Jews] themselves had already given up. As for myself, I tended, at the time, to favor the hope, which the Jews had aready abandoned, that one day they would be reunited in their ancestral homeland. This is the point: According to an old Jewish prophecy the Messiah should come this year [1840], to reunite the dispersed Jews and gather them together in their homeland. To this one may add the infamous incident in Damascus. Thus, while I was embittered at the brutal tendencies of the mobs both in the East and the West, as was evident in the Damascus affair, I was ready to add my voice to the pious requests on behalf of the Jews. However, after studying the question more thoroughly, I soon reached the conclusion that despite the prophecy of redemption in 1840, the Jews are at present farther from their political revival than ever before. Who, then, can cherish this hope, when the Jews themselves reject it?

This, of course, means that Hess, living at the time in Bonn and Cologne, knew that the year 5600 was considered a messianic year. He admits that for a moment he considered this a real opportunity to get the Jews to work for a hastening of the redemption process. Hess clearly did not expect a miraculous redemption, but thought this an opportunity to work toward the political revival of the Jews. When he realized that this hope had no real meaning for the Jewish masses, who showed no signs of yearning for political liberation, he set it aside. Twenty years later, in *Rome and Jerusalem*, he mentioned the Damascus affair, but not the messianic excitement of 1840.

And now for the main topic. Undoubtedly, two trends existed at the time. One of these was that the very rebuilding of the Land of Israel, that is, the expansion of the Jewish community in Palestine, was a preparatory step for the advent of the Redeemer. The evidence for this is very clear. Rabbi Kalischer, who held a similar view, clearly said that the settlement of the country was a precondition for the

166

redemption. Something of this kind seems to have characterized the thinking of the disciples of the Gaon of Vilna. That they were serious in their expectation is, in my opinion, clearly proved — as Dr. Morgenstern has shown — by the fact that they made changes in the prayer ritual. I tend to view the omission of the verse from *Lekha Dodi* as more significant than the omission of *Tikkun Ḥazot*, as the latter was never an obligation accepted by all Jews, but was only incumbent upon various groups who took pride in this liturgical custom. When one abrogates a generally-accepted custom, and does so in public, this is a significant step in the orthodox world. Such an omission undoubtedly had a demonstrative nature; making manifest that the era of redemption has already begun.

Dr. Menachem Friedman raised a serious question: Were these people really acting upon the instructions of the Gaon of Vilna himself? From a historical point of view I don't think that is overly important. It is questionable whether one can regard this large group as real disciples of the Gaon, for we know that the Vilna Gaon actually had very few disciples, not all of whom joined the group emigrating to Palestine. It is doubtful if all of the migrants had studied at the feet of the Gaon himself. It is a common phenomenon in traditional circles to cite impressive sources, and those who seek to innovate prefer to view themselves as acting in accordance with the instructions of the outstanding scholar of the time. It is also not very important whether the Jews in Vilna were aware of the messianic question, for in other matters as well there was no direct public fulfillment of the Gaon's teachings. The Perushim practiced customs that were unfamiliar outside the Gaon's immediate circle and were not intended for public consumption.

The letter sent by R. Israel of Shklov to the Ten Tribes is important. One of the requests contained in this letter was to dispatch sages whose ordination stemmed directly from the traditional *semikha* of Temple days, in order to establish an ordained rabbinic court in Jerusalem. Such a step was a form of preparation for redemption. It was a repetition of the attempt made in Safed in 1538 by R. Ya'akov Berab to renew the *semikha*, based on the ruling of Maimonides who said that, in accordance with the verse (Isaiah 1:26): "I will restore your magistrates as of old ... after that you shall be called City of Righteousness, Faithful City," before the beginning of the messianic era there will first have to be an ordained rabbinic court in the original sense of the term; only thereafter will the redemption be able to begin. Maimonides himself had no intention of taking a step to prepare the way for the redemption, but merely sought a way to facilitate the establishment of the rabbinic court before the redemption; since only an ordained sage can ordain another, and since we have no ordained sages at present, Maimonides ruled that all the rabbis of the Land of Israel could gather and select a single leader who could then reinstitute the *semikha*. R. Ya'akov Berab, who in the spirit of the times also had messianic tendencies, turned this ruling into a means for preparing the way for redemption. That attempt is known to have failed, but another attempt was made by R. Israel of Shklov. It was hoped that somewhere, across the River Sambatyon, there were still ordained sages; if some

167

of them would come to Jerusalem, Maimonides's precondition for the redemption would be met, thereby bringing the Messiah.

Actually, the situation must be more clearly defined. This attempt was not part of the existential activities favored by the Jerusalem group. Dispatching that letter represented a different sort of messianism that linked the advent of redemption with definite preconditions. There are talmudic traditions to the effect that the Messiah will come if the Jewish people observe two successive Sabbaths halakhically. A certain sage did indeed try to persuade the Jews of Italy to observe two Sabbaths with all their regulations. Another attempt to fulfill such a precondition literally took place in the days of Shabbetai Zevi, when the redemption was felt to be near. A talmudic statement was recalled whereby the redemption would come only after all the souls destined to be born in the future had already been born. People hurried to marry off their sons and daughters, so as to hasten the birth of all the souls. It is surprising, however, that the disciples of the Gaon were also subject to this kind of thinking, for this was already the nineteenth century, when sections of the Jewish people were beginning to take action, identifying such positive steps as the rebuilding of the Land of Israel as realistic stages leading to redemption. These people, however, did not detach themselves completely from the expectation of a miraculous redemption, but added to it, introducing practical action into the picture. This approach reappears in similar fashion a generation later in the theses of Kalischer and Alkalai.

I find it amazing that Kalischer and Alkalai and their contemporaries, active a single generation later, did not know of the activities of the Vilna Gaon's disciples. At least, so it would seem; for if Kalischer and Alkalai had known of them, they could have based their own ideas on those of their predecessors. Sometimes, of course, a movement which fails, buries itself. Perhaps this is what happened in this case, which is why the activities of the Perushim were not known to those who would have continued their work.

1   R. Michael, "Vier Unveroffentlichte Manuskripte von Moses Hess," *Bulletin des Leo Baeck Instituts* 7, 25–28 (1964): 312–344. These fragments are drafts of Moses Hess's book, *Die Europaische Triarchie*, which appeared in 1841, and were apparently written in 1840.

REDEMPTION OF THE *SHEKHINA* AND IMMIGRATION TO THE LAND OF ISRAEL

Isaiah Tishby

aising up the *Shekhina* as a motive for coming to live in the Land of Israel was already known in the sixteenth century when R. Solomon Alkabeẓ and R. Joseph Caro settled in Palestine; this was, I believe, an innovation. In the narrative of the revelation of the *Maggid* in the *Tikkun Leil Shavuot* we learn that Alkabeẓ appealed to his colleagues in Salonika whom he was leaving behind, to go to the Land of Israel for one clear purpose: to raise up the *Shekhina*. It was clear that it was not sufficient to prepare for the raising of the *Shekhina* abroad; Jews must go to the Land of Israel and take action there.

The non-recital of *Tikkun Ḥaẓot* and the omission of the verse from *Lekha Dodi*, which Professor Katz also emphasized in his comments, are important innovations that have parallels in Sabbateanism. In my opinion, these changes make it very clear that the immigration to the Land of Israel had a messianic dimension; they strongly indicate the existence of an obviously messianic trend. But this is also very surprising, since these are features that were known to be characteristic of the Sabbatean movement, and people had been warned to beware of them. I find it hard to comprehend how these groups dared to take steps characteristic of Sabbateanism; not only did they do away with accepted customs but, in the light of their historical connotation and context, these innovations might very well have aroused suspicions of heretical tendencies.

Of course, the Gaon of Vilna and his disciples dared do many things the Ḥasidim never dared do, except in private. The Gaon and his disciples felt completely sure of themselves, unlike the Ḥasidim who were suspected of Sabbatean leanings and were afraid of being indicted. An outstanding example of the difference between the approaches of the Gaon of Vilna and the Ḥasidim is in their attitudes toward the early eighteenth century book, *Ḥemdat Yamim*, which was of Sabbatean composition. In *Shivḥei Ha-Besht* (Praises of the Besht) we find that the Ba'al Shem-Tov proclaimed that anyone reading *Ḥemdat Yamim* would be considered on the verge of idolatry. In actual fact, this charge was baseless and purely apologetical, for the Ḥasidim used to read and study *Ḥemdat Yamim*; however, because of R. Jacob Emden's attacks, they were forced to disguise their study of this controversial book. The Gaon of Vilna and his circle acted differently, and in a *Siddur* published by one of them with the Gaon's approval, *Ḥemdat Yamim* is openly mentioned with no fear whatsoever.

It seems then that the disciples of the Vilna Gaon were not afraid to omit *Tikkun Ḥazot* or a verse of *Lekha Dodi* because they felt they were immune even to attacks on matters far more closely and openly linked to Sabbateanism such as the book *Ḥemdat Yamim*.

MESSIANIC EXPECTATIONS
AND THEIR PLACE IN HISTORY

Israel Bartal

> *I have heard Rabbi Kossovsky relate a story he had heard from his father, that after the passing of the Vilna Gaon anyone publishing in the Gaon's name statements he had never made, was declared excommunicated.*
>
> (S.Y. Agnon, *Pinkas Katan*)

There is nothing more difficult in Jewish historical research than distinguishing between the yearnings of those engaging in the prediction of impending redemption, the position accorded them by scholars, and the actual role of those yearnings in the existential complex of history. One of the sources of this difficulty is the generally murky style of the relevant literary texts; another is the adjustment of past expectations and hopes to current opinions and beliefs. Dr. Morgenstern's method engenders difficulties of the latter type. He studies the sources diligently, reconstructing missing sections; he adduces new material of great importance for the history of messianic expectations concerning the year 5600 in traditional Jewish society and among Christian millennarians; his method has the beauty and integrity of logical thought — which explains well known facts and events in a new light. However, he seems to have simplified matters and "smoothed over" rough spots, so that the entire structure presented in his article suffers from several fundamental flaws that threaten to undermine the whole impressive edifice.

The article opens decisively, stating that "historians have not paid sufficient attention to the immigration and settlement of the disciples of the Gaon of Vilna," those having been "considered an integral part of what historians of Palestine call the 'old yishuv'" — thus strangely overlooking the fact that most of the studies on the immigration of the Perushim, though unscientific and based on unsatisfactory sources, clearly emphasized its messianic character! It suffices to open a recent book on Palestine in the nineteenth century and to read the following:

> A considerable portion of the Vilna Gaon's teaching was devoted to the consideration of the impending redemption and to the calculation of its appointed time, based on kabbalistic lore the Gaon was engaged in studying. The Vilna Gaon considered it his task to prepare for the redemption. Before the advent of the Messiah there would be a period similar to that of Cyrus, a kind of *hit'aruta di-le-tatta* ... While the

171

hasidim were stressing the need for a life of holiness in the Holy Land, expressed in Torah study and worship of God, the Gaon and his disciples placed settlement of the Land at the heart of their efforts, in addition to the establishment of a Torah center.[1]

It is true that serious doubts have arisen as to the validity of the sources attributing a redemption thesis to the Gaon and his disciples,[2] especially with regard to the book *Kol HaTor*, and the 'Ḥazon Zion' movement said to have existed in Shklov. Nevertheless, one cannot deal with the messianism of the Gaon's disciples as a previously unnoticed phenomenon. On the contrary *their messianist yearning is generally accepted*, even though it may be based on controversial sources!

In making his opening statement, Morgenstern completely obscures all differences between the terms 'traditional' and 'orthodox' as accepted at present by historians of the Jewish society of Eastern Europe,[3] and creates a distinction not validated by any historical criterion, namely, the traditional immigration of the 'old yishuv' which was synonymous with passivity, as against 'non-traditional' immigration characterized by messianic activism. This results in the characterization of all the eighteenth century movements of Jewish immigration of Palestine as 'non-traditional'. Messianic activism, which is interpreted as an innovation because of the call for human action to precede the redemption process, is identified by the author with the school of thought represented by Rabbis Y. Alkalai and Z.H. Kalischer. This means that messianic activism was actually the forerunner of the modern national-religious movement. However, though the texts considered by Morgenstern do contain various elements which may lead to such conclusions, it is doubtful just how widespread the ideas themselves were, what the practical intentions of their originators were and, especially, how continuous this activity was over a period of almost forty years.

It seems that despite his utilization of sources which make his research far more reliable than that of previous scholars, Morgenstern is *a priori* enslaved by his conclusion that every expression hinting at 'realistic action' automatically links up with some real act. Many years ago, G. Kressel established that the struggle to build the compound of R. Yehuda HeHasid's Ḥurva was a significant step in the development of the concept of the productivization of the yishuv,[4] and linked this with the involvement of the Perushim in Moshe Montefiore's activities for agricultural settlement.[5] This he did from a modern Zionist-Socialist point-of-view, and attributed to the Perushim many qualities which, in my opinion, they never had.[6] Morgenstern has done the same, and by adding 'messianic activism' has introduced a kind of religious-nationalism into the historiography of the 'old yishuv', even claiming that "the leaders of the Perushim Kolel in Palestine and in Russia strove, in an organized fashion, to bring groups of immigrants from various social strata to the country, so as to enlarge the Jewish community and to establish it there firmly." This statement is astounding in light of the clearly elitist stance of the Perushim Kolel and the elitist character of the immigrants who joined it throughout the nineteenth century, in sharp contrast to the Ḥasidic immigration of the same period.

It appears to me that the various phrases adopted by Morgenstern to demonstrate his claims are often taken out of their linguistic-ideological context and pressed into the service of his thesis. The phrase *hit'aruta di-le-tatta*, so central in Morgenstern's thesis, is always interpreted in accordance with the messianic concepts of the Perushim, and is even used to demonstrate the identity of concrete steps taken to settle the land, such as agricultural activities, with the Vilna Gaon's teaching of 'messianic activism'. Morgenstern has failed to notice that the Ḥabad Ḥasidim in Hebron used the same expression when corresponding with Montefiore in connection with his settlement projects;[7] had they, too, adopted 'messianic activism' in the year 1839? Or, perhaps, this expression was one they were accustomed to using, just as it was used by R. Menaḥem Mendel of Vitebsk, a leader of the Ḥasidic immigrants in 1777?[8]

However, it is not only the writer's use of messianic expressions that is problematic, but rather his grasp of the position of messianism in the philosophies of that generation of immigrants from Eastern Europe. There undoubtedly were some among them who were steeped in messianism and engrossed in kabbala and

Tombstone of R. Menahem
Mendel of Vitebsk

in calculating the year of redemption. Neither is there any doubt that they viewed contemporary events as heralding the advent of the messianic epoch. But the difference between this and what Morgenstern attributes to them, is still considerable. The second half of the eighteenth century suffered no lack of redemption-calculators who compiled books, such as that written by R. Hillel of Kovno, and who predicted the dates of the coming redemption. R. Israel Harif of Satanov, one of the disciples of R. Israel Baal Shem-Tov, for instance, expected the redemption to dawn in the year 1767/1768, and then in 1777/1778, and later yet in 1787/1788 — yet his book was published in Eastern Europe three times in the 1860s and 1870s.[9]

Is there not a continuity of such calculations in the eighteenth century, from those spearheaded by the hopes pinned on the year 1739/1740, to those of several of the Gaon's followers? Why is R. Hillel of Kovno to be considered a forerunner of the unrest in Jerusalem in the 1830s, rather than an integral part of the messianic unrest extending in an unbroken sequence throughout East European kabbalistic study circles ever since the Sabbatean movement? On the contrary, he was even more careful in his worship than R. Israel Harif, and fixed no definite date; neither did he interpret the expression "awakening from below" in an explicit fashion. In this he was not very different from R. Menahem Mendel of Vitebsk!

Furthermore, R. Aviezer of Tykocin's book, Sha'arei Zedek, the second major source of Morgenstern's thesis, appeared in 1842/1843, but how many books of that nature appeared in Jerusalem in that period? We have a detailed list of all the books printed in Jerusalem, and no volumes of that kind appear in it. If it is claimed that others covered the matter up, why then was R. Aviezer's book printed? And if no one hid anything, then the conclusion must be that the issue of messianism was not as acute as Morgenstern makes it out to be, for otherwise we would have at least one additional source describing the feelings of someone whose messianic expectations were disappointed.

The idea of concealment is itself flawed, for according to the sources adduced by the author, including proclamations of emissaries, letters that were made public, and a printed book, it seems unlikely that any attempt at concealment was made. It appears to me that the importance of the issue among traditional circles in Palestine is reflected in the amount of publicity it received.

I would like to present additional arguments against Morgenstern's explanation of the events in the 1830s and 1840s.

Omissions from the Sabbath Eve Liturgy

Morgenstern claims with certainty that in Jerusalem the verse "shake off the dust" was omitted from the Sabbath eve liturgy once permission was given to rebuild the Hurva compound in the summer of 1837. Without saying so explicitly, he attributes this omission to the Perushim, for afterwards, he believes, they reinstated that verse. This he learns from Z.H. Lehren's reply to R. Eliezer Bergmann.[10] Unfortunately, we do not have R. Eliezer's missive, but merely Lehren's response; I find it difficult to adduce from the reply that it referred to the Jerusalem Perushim and not some other group. Moreover, even though the letter includes the words "[that one] who ... introduced this innovation," we must not overlook the fact that in the Sephardi prayer-books printed at the same time or close thereto, which undoubtedly were available to immigrants from Turkey and Greece, such omissions were common. Moreover, in those that followed the version of *Hemdat Yamim*, other verses were included.[11] The complete text of Lehren's comment does say:

> And concerning what they say there about the redemption having begun, may it be God's will, I do not believe that liberties granted are proof of this, for this is the mistake the Jews made in light of the liberties of France ... and regarding the omission of "shake off the dust," etc. and the lamentations from *Tikkun Hazot*, I would like to know who introduced this innovation, if not some eminent person making the same mistake as Shabbetai Zevi — God will devour the wicked — then I suspect him of leaning to Shabbetai Zevi, since *Hemdat Yamim* also rules that this should be omitted and substitutes another verse in its stead, as well as in place of *mikdash melekh*.

How can we be sure that Lehren is not referring to the Sephardim? In addition, the Sephardi Jews of Jerusalem were not reluctant to use *Hemdat Yamim* even after 1840, as shown by the 1842/43 printing of the second part of the Sephardi prayer book by R. Israel Bak's press, which explicitly included "... prayers taken from *Hemdat Yamim* and festival readings for the eve of *Hoshana Rabba* ... now reprinted here ... with many additions ... with all the merits ... of the Salonica, Leghorn and Vienna prayer-books ..."[12] In 1872/73 the same Jerusalem press published *Sefer Marpe la-Nefesh*, a collection of excerpts from the Sabbath regulations cited in *Hemdat Yamim* which "had been published two or three times in Jerusalem ...", for the earlier editions were no longer extant.[13] The omission of verses from *Lekha Dodi* might thus have been an old Sephardic custom (with its parallel, incidentally, among the Hasidim).[14] Indeed, this is the way R. Yehoseph Schwartz's letter to his brother, dated 23 Iyar 5597 (1837), should be interpreted: "Only the verses *lekha dodi, shamor vezakhor, likrat shabbat, mikdash melekh, hit'oreri*, and *bo'i beshalom* of the *Lekha Dodi* poem are actually sung."[15] This letter makes it clear beyond doubt that the old prayer customs of the Sephardim were being discussed, for immediately thereafter Schwartz writes: "On Sabbath afternoons, at about two o'clock, the rabbis preach on points of morality and religion in the large synagogue called Kehal Stampoli (Constantinople)."[16] We thus have evidence of an old Sabbatean custom still observed by the Sephardim of Jerusalem; evidence of this custom being followed by the Perushim is still lacking.

175

Reinstitution of the Lamentations of *Tikkun Ḥaẓot*

According to Morgenstern's interpretation: "... the new leadership [of the Perushim] had the courage to ask the members to sign an agreement reinstituting the custom of reciting *Tikkun Ḥaẓot*" in 1846/47. He infers this from a text taken from the ledger of a society called 'Mishmorim Or Torah' founded in 1847 by members of the Jerusalem Perushim community. This society engaged in nightly Torah study in the Menaḥem Zion study hall in shifts *(mishmarot)*, and was actually an already existing organization called 'Mishmorim'; the name 'Or Torah' was added in the text under consideration.

The text opens with various verses and quotations concerning nightly Torah study, and concludes: "And many other rabbinic rulings ... even greater than intensive Torah study and bewailing the Destruction at night...,"[17] i.e., that there are other verses and quotations stressing the importance of Torah study and mourning the Destruction. In other words, the passage does not deal primarily with lamentations, but rather the whole text concerns the institution of night shifts for the study of Torah, and the matter of lamentations is only peripheral. Morgenstern remarks that since they gathered to reinstitute this recitation, Torah had not been studied at night earlier; but this is not so. All that is said concerns learning together in the *beit midrash* and not individually at *home*, as is actually stated at the beginning of the text: "Indeed everyone has specific hours for the study of Torah at home, yet we regret the [abandonment of] *beit midrash*."[18] From the reactivation of a society for the nightly study of Torah in shifts — it being explicitly stated that every member studied privately at home — we can hardly infer anything about the reinstitution of reciting the lamentations of *Tikkun Ḥaẓot*! Because the text mentions "bewailing the Destruction" the author links it with the words of R. Aviezer of Tykocin in his book *Sha'arei Ẓedek*,[19] which he interprets as a "call to reinstitute the recitation of *Tikkun Ḥaẓot*." It seems, however, that R. Aviezer's words are themselves not such a 'call'. *Sha'arei Ẓedek* says that one must repent and fulfill three precepts: love one's fellow Jew, observe the Sabbath, and lament the exile of the *Shekhina* at midnight. Are we also to interpret his "call for the reinstitution" of the lamentations as a call to the people of Jerusalem to reinstitute Sabbath observance?[20]

R. Zundel of Salant in the Perushim Kolel in Jerusalem

One wonders why there is no mention, not even a hint, in Morgenstern's research of the position taken by a central figure at the Perushim Kolel, R. Zundel of Salant, concerning the redemption theories of the Vilna Gaon. R. Zundel reached Palestine at the beginning of 1837/38 and became a central figure in the spiritual life of the Perushim community. He was the principal founder of the aforementioned 'Mishmorim Or Torah', and was the first to sign the society's regulations. In R. Eliezer Rivlin's book *The Righteous Joseph Zundel of Salant and his Teachers*, there is occasional mention of his stand regarding the redemption as interpreted in the Gaon's commentary on *Sifra de-Ẓeniuta*. R. Zundel is quoted as saying:

> ... Once when I met Rabbi Avraham, the Vilna Gaon's son [i.e., in Europe, before R. Zundel's arrival in Palestine], we spoke a great deal about the Gaon's commentary on *Sifra de-Ẓeniuta*. I then had a dream about an old man with an angry visage, and on the morrow I asked what the Gaon had looked like. The description I received was very similar to that of the figure I had seen in my dream, and the conclusion I drew was that I was unworthy of studying this matter either.[21]

This story and others show that the redemption question really did concern R. Ḥayyim of Volozhin and his circle. But this was certainly not acute messianism; rather it sought to avoid taking action and trying to speed up the process. The story adduced by R. Zundel's pupil, R. Nathan Friedland, about R. Ḥayyim of Volozhin is typical:

> ... *for the Messiah will come*, that is, while he is sitting alone in his room studying (Torah), his wife will come in suddenly and say: "Oh Ḥayyim, are you sitting here and studying!? Behold, the Messiah has come!" Then he will look shocked, he will expectorate three times and ask her: "Who told you?" And she will say: "*Go outside and see for yourself*; not even the babies in the town are in their cradles — for everyone has gone out to meet the Messiah ..."[22]

The position adopted by R. Ḥayyim of Volozhin and R. Zundel of Salant seems to me to have been dominant among the Perushim in Jerusalem, though definite messianic overtones were added to it. In other words: Torah study comes first and, as R. Ḥayyim of Volozhin taught, even if the Messiah really comes, he will not stop studying until the whole town has gone to meet him. These sources precede the late 1830s; it can thus not be said to signify a later retreat from 'messianic activism', which Morgenstern attributes to the Perushim in the 1840s.

Our reservations concerning the definitive assumption of the 'messianic activistic' position are strengthened by another type of source frequently used by Morgenstern in his various studies — namely the testimony of missionaries regarding the expectations of the Jews concerning the year 5600 (1840).[23] It is true that Christian missionaries diligently collected material concerning Jewish messianic hopes throughout the Diaspora, and the information they provide is considered reliable. The article under consideration here does not, however, contain other testimony regarding the moderation of the messianic expectation and the avoidance of designating a definite date for the redemption. Here is an outstanding and instructive example: the American missionary Isaac Bird, in his book about the mission in Syria, reports a fragment of a conversation between his fellow Christian Pliny Fisk, and rabbis Yitzḥak ben Shelomo and Joseph Markovitz of the Perushim Kolel, held in the mid-1820s. Answering Fisk's question about the date of the redemption, R. Joseph said:

... There were two things about which it was not permitted to inquire: one was what took place before the foundation of the world; the other was *when the Messiah will come.* Daniel said: "The time is sealed," and what fool would presume to be wiser than Daniel? But are there not Jews who *do* endeavor to ascertain the time when the Messiah will come? Yes; there are some such. but they are not upright. They are wicked Jews ...[24]

The similarity between this answer and R. Zundel of Salant's position as adduced above is more then coincidental. It seems that along with those sages, scholars, and emissaries who so enthused the missionaries, there were others, including some of the Perushim in Jerusalem, who expressed reservations concerning the actualization of the messianic idea and took pains to expand this viewpoint. This contrasting testimony must, therefore, be amassed as well and weighed carefully to decide which, if either, stand was dominant among the Lithuanian immigrants to Palestine in the 1820s and 1830s.

Other questions concerning various points in the writer's arguments arise after carefully scrutinizing the texts in their concrete historical contexts. I should like to deal with a number of substantial matters concerning his view of the 'old yishuv' in the nineteenth century. Morgenstern does not explain why immigration to Palestine continued after the year 5600 (1840), and even grew in numbers — he even claims that many immigrated (even in an "organized" fashion) as a result of the Messianic tension![25] If the claim is made that other types of immigrants came later — it is difficult to discern differences between the immigrants from Eastern Europe, North Africa and the Near East who arrived in 1830s, and those thousands who came between 1840 and 1870. It is also difficult to comprehend why the East European *Haskala* literature, so sensitive to any fault, deficiency or failure in traditional society, makes no mention — not even a hint — of so central a phenomenon among East European Jewry. Alleged attempts at concealment cannot explain this, for what any Christian missionary in a Polish or Russian town was aware of, the local *maskilim* certainly knew as well. If Abraham Mapu of Kovno devoted considerable time to his anti-Shabbetai Zevi composition called *Hozei Hezyonot,*[26] it is clear that the subject was not uninteresting for his contemporaries.

Morgenstern's view of the retreat from the 'messianic activism' of the 1830s to a more subdued messianism in the 1860s and 1870s is also open to debate. Eager to emphasize the contrast between the dream and its shattering and to underline the attempts at concealment, he interprets the later "Jerusalem leadership" as holding a homogeneous stand against all active settlement of Palestine. The actual situation was very different, for the standpoints taken by R. Shmuel Salant or R. Joseph Rivlin indicate almost the exact opposite.[27] Y. Kaniel's view of Jewish settlement in Palestine in the second half of the nineteenth century also contradicts such a simplistic generalization.[28]

Setting the messianic expectations of the year 5600 at the center of 'old yishuv' life, and explaining all the changes which took place in it in the second half of the nineteenth century as resulting from these dashed hopes, seems to me to be exaggerated and subject to refute. It is true that messianic expectations motivated the immigrants, but the central development in the Jewish community in Palestine seems to have been its transformation from a traditional society to an orthodox one. The confrontation with the modernization developments in European society was decisive in that ideological and social shift.

My thanks are hereby extended to Elḥanan Reiner, with whom I analyzed topics related to this subject, and upon whose knowledge I drew.
All bibliographical references, with the exception of note 24, are in Hebrew.

1 M. Eliav, *Ereẓ Israel and its Yishuv in the Nineteenth Century, 1777–1917* (Jerusalem, 1978), p. 85.
2 The writings of A.R. Malachi are characteristic of this criticism: "Messianic yearnings are attributed to this immigration. It was undoubtedly permeated with longing for the redemption of the *Shekhina* from its exile . . . [but] in essence this immigration bore an imprint of realism, and it was based on the love of the Land [of Israel] in and of itself. Nor should we read into this immigration any hint of the political Zionist movement known as 'Ḥazon Zion', as Dr. J. Rivlin attempted to do based on the article of that name written by H.M. Rivlin and printed in *HaZefira* (1889)"; see Malachi, *Chapters in the History of the Old Yishuv* (Tel-Aviv, 1971), p. 19. On the other hand recent studies have utilized this material, in particular, *Kol HaTor* attributed to Hillel ben Benjamin of Shklov (Bnei Berak, 1969), see Tova Cohen, "From 'Love of Zion' to Petaḥ Tiqva — Descriptions of Ereẓ Israel in the Writings of Yoel Moshe Salomon," *Cathedra* 10 (1979):164; idem, *From Vision to Reality, Ereẓ Israel in Haskala Literature* (Ramat Gan, 1982), pp. 39–41.
3 Cf. J. Katz, *Tradition and Crisis* (Jerusalem, 1958), pp. 11–18; idem, "Traditional Society and Modern Society," *Megamot* (1960):304–311; M.S. Samet, "Orthodox Judaism in the Modern Age," *Mahalkhim* 1 (1969):29–40; idem, "Orthodoxy" in *The Hebrew Encyclopedia*, 32 (Jerusalem, 1981), pp. 193–200 (Change and Tradition); idem, "The Conflict Surrounding the Institution of Jewish Values in the State of Israel," *Sociological Research* (The Hebrew University, Jerusalem, 1979), pp. 39–60; E. Etkes, *R. Israel Salanter and the Beginning of the Musar Movement* (Jerusalem, 1982), pp. 147–164, 271–310, 345–346; I. Bartal, "The *Pekidim* and *Amarkalim* and their Letters, an outline for the study of the organization and the sources," in B. Rivlin (ed.), *The Letters of the Pekidim and Amarkalim of Amsterdam, 1829* (Jerusalem, 1979), pp. 14–16; Y. Salmon, "The Confrontation between *Maskilim* and *Ḥaredim* in the Ḥibbat Zion Movement," *HaẒiyyonut* 5 (1979):43–47.
4 G. Kressel, "Palestine-Settlement Policies in the Generation of the Emancipation," *Aḥdut HaAvoda* 2 (1943):181–184.
5 Compare his views in *Potḥei HaTiqva: From Jerusalem to Petaḥ Tiqva* (Jerusalem, 1976), pp. 76–81 with those of I. Bartal, "Settlement Proposals During Montefiore's Second Visit to Ereẓ-Israel (1839)", *Shalem* 2 (1976): 258–259.
6 A characteristic example is his definition of what was shared by the students of the Vilna Gaon and of the Ḥatam Sofer: ". . . but what united them primarily was their common purpose: the settlement of Ereẓ-Israel through immigration and productive labor; for the purpose of increasing the Jewish community — and not necessarily the Ashkenazi community alone." See *Potḥei HaTiqva* (above, n. 5), p. 36.

179

7   Bartal (above, n. 5), pp. 259–260. See note 136 there, which deals with the significance of using kabbalistic expressions such as *hit'aruta di-le-tatta*, and draws attention to the 'realistic' intentions of the writers: "Underlying [these expressions] was the goal of acquiring the holy land of Israel, of plowing and sowing it and of reaping it in joy; of each man sitting in peace and security under his vine and fig tree, studying Torah and worshipping God. Those who are God-fearing in their actions and diligently serve Him would study Torah and worship in shifts, and the others, the common people, would work the holy land . . .".

8   *Peri HaArez* (Kopys, 1914), commentary on *Shemot*: "As is known, there is no possibility of redemption other than through the 'awakening from below' . . . for the essence of the Exile is the lack of faith, which has been forgotten . . ." This was stressed by Israel Halpern who noted, following G. Scholem, the blurring of the messianic tendency in Menaḥem Mendel of Vitebsk's theory of redemption; see Halpern, *The Early Immigration of the Ḥasidim to Erez Israel* (Jerusalem and Tel-Aviv, 1947), pp. 38–39.

9   A. Ya'ari, *Ta'alumat Sefer* (Jerusalem, 1952), pp. 136–137.

10   Letters of the *Pekidim* and *Amarkalim* of Amsterdam, ms. in Yad Izḥak Ben-Zvi library, 8, 7a.

11   Until 1843/1844 when Israel Bak began to print the Sephardi prayer book *Seder Tefillat Israel* in Jerusalem, the prayer books in use were printed in various centers of Sephardic population, or in the large printing establishments (Vienna) which catered to the demands for prayer books throughout the Sephardi world. My investigation of various versions of *Lekha Dodi* in Sephardi prayer books printed outside of Palestine before 1840 indicates that some of them followed the *Ḥemdat Yamim* liturgy and changed those verses, or included them side-by-side with the *Ḥemdat Yamim* version. See Salonica community's *Seder Tefillot* (1773/74) and prayer book compiled by Abraham ben Shalom Tubiana, *Sefer Ḥesed LeAvraham* (Izmir, 1763/64). On the other hand, the traditional version appears unchanged in the *Sefat Emet* prayer books (Safed, 1831/32); in the above mentioned *Seder Tefillat Israel* (1841–1844) despite the fact that its title page indicates the addition of "customary prayers from *Ḥemdat Yamim*; and in various Leghorn printings of *Sefer Mo'adei HaShem* of the nineteenth and twentieth centuries, despite the explicit imprint: ". . . and prayers and customs from *Ḥemdat Yamim* . . . ." In general, *Ḥemdat Yamim* and the Shabbetai Zevi issue were less repudiated by the Sephardim than by Eastern and Central European Jews, and with the approach of the year 5600 (1840), messianic hopes were associated with old practices. Cf. Ya'ari (above, n. 9), pp. 147–149.

12   It is no. 20 in the listing of Shoshana Halevi, *Sifrei Yerushalayim HaRishonim* (Jerusalem, 1976), pp. 11–12.

13   No. 196 in Halevi, *ibid.*, p. 85. Hundreds of pamphlets based on excerpts from *Ḥemdat Yamim* were printed and distributed throughout the Sephardi communities.

14   *Siddur haGeonim vehaMekubbalim*, 2 (Jerusalem, 1971), p. 58.

15   A. Ya'ari, *Letters from the Land of Israel* (Tel-Aviv, 1943), p. 771. Morgenstern considers the citation by Schwartz as being unimportant, and suggests that the Hebrew translation may differ from the German text (Morgenstern, *The Pekidim and Amarkalim of Amsterdam and the Jewish Community in Palestine in the First Half of the Nineteenth Century* [unpublished doctoral dissertation, The Hebrew University, Jerusalem, 1981], p. 162, n. 63); idem, "Messianic Expectations for the Year 5600 (1840)," in Z. Baras (ed.), *Essays on Messianism and Eschatology* (Jerusalem, 1983), p. 360, n. 96. However, a reading of the original version in *Orient* (1840) reveals that no change appears in the translation.

16   Ya'ari (above, n. 15), p. 771.

17   "Mishmorim Or Torah," in P. Grajewsky, *From the Archives of Jerusalem*, 13 (1931), p. 4b. Cf. n. 7. A reading of the society's by-laws (Jerusalem, 1895) reveals that paragraph four mentions *Tikkun Ḥazot*, but that most of the activities were study of Torah and Talmud.

18   *Ibid.*, p. 3.

19   *Sha'arei Zedek*, p. 31a.

20   It should also be noted that in certain years the lamentations in *Tikkun Ḥazot* were not said in Palestine. In the Sabbatical years *Tikkun Raḥel* was not said because "the land was resting" and the exaltation of royalty rested upon it.

21   A. Rivlin, *The Righteous R. Joseph Zundel of Salant and his Teachers* (Jerusalem, 1926/27), p. 18.

22   *Ibid.* For R. Ḥayyim of Volozhin's opinion regarding study, see Etkes (above, n. 3), pp. 45–48.

23 Morgenstern went into detail on this issue and presented significant material in his doctorate, pp. 150–153, and in his article, pp. 353–357 (both above, n. 15).

24 I. Bird, *Bible Work in Bible Lands, or, Events in the History of the Syria Mission* (Philadelphia, n.d.[1872]), p. 57.

25 Morgenstern presents an extremely important compilation of information about Jewish immigration to Palestine in the first half of the nineteenth century in his doctorate (above, n. 15), pp. 26–31. From missionary reports and Jewish sources he adduces that messianic hope was a major element in such immigration prior to 1840.

26 B.Z. Dinur (ed.), *The Writings of Abraham Mapu* (Jerusalem, 1970), pp. 31–33, and glossary, *Hozei Hezyonot*. Regarding the disinterest of the enlightened Lithuanian Jews in messianic anticipation of the year 5600, it should be noted that Jacob Lipschitz, the orthodox historian of East European Jewry, made no effort to conceal these hopes, and considers that year the beginning of the modern period in Jewish history. J. Lipschitz, *Zikhron Ya'akov* 1 (Kovno Slobodka, 1924), pp. 84–85.

27 Compare Joseph Rivlin who writes with messianic fervor about the establishment of new Jewish neighborhoods in Jerusalem in the 1870s; "... all of us can see that a marvellous awakening is occurring these days in our holy land. The children of Israel are taking hold of it, and one leads us with assurance toward the desired goal of settling the Land of Israel." See letter to Y.M. Pines, 19 Kislev 5636 (1875) in A.R. Malachi (above, n. 2), p. 145. See in this regard, I. Bartal, "Petah Tiqva — Between Ideological Roots and Contemporaneous Circumstances," *Cathedra* 9 (1979):66–67.

28 Y. Kaniel, "The Controversy between Petah Tiqva and Rishon LeZion concerning Primacy of Settlement, and its Historical Significance," *Cathedra* 9 (1979):39–40. Incidentally, Kaniel presents the attitude of the rabbis of Jerusalem toward agricultural settlement in a fashion different from that of Morgenstern. Rabbi Auerbach, for example, viewed the purchase of fields and orchards and the establishment of settlements in a positive fashion, following the views of Rabbis Alkalai, Guttmacher and Kalischer; but he was doubtful regarding the link between messianic redemption and practical activities to settle the holy land (*ibid.*, p. 40). Nonetheless, in greetings sent to the founders of the Ge'ulat HaArez Society, he expressed this link in a familiar fashion: "*Hit'aruta di-le-tatta* will arouse the promise that the Holy One blessed be He gave to you — and I will remember the land" (*ibid.*, p. 50, n. 102). See the complete letter in A. Druyanow (ed.), *Hibbat Zion and the Settlement of Erez Israel*, vol. 1, 1870–1882 (S. Laskov edition), (Tel-Aviv, 1982), pp. 55–56. In contrast, Morgenstern seems to hold that the dominant trend among the Perushim was opposition to all materialistic activities involved in building the land, in accordance with the slogan "if the Lord will not build the house, its builders will labor in vain."

RESPONSE

Arie Morgenstern

D r. Menachem Friedman questioned the substance of the messianic views held by the disciples of the Gaon of Vilna. Undoubtedly there was no uniformity in the messianic concepts held by the disciples of the Gaon, as Professor Katz has indicated. One must also remember that the Gaon of Vilna had quite a number of disciples whose relations with him date from different periods in his life, and that whatever he is reported to have said is phrased in ambiguities and hidden meanings, and not in explicit terminology. Moreover, since his doctrines were never written down in a systematic fashion, but were transmitted by word of mouth, it is not surprising that various approaches to the redemption process may be distinguished among his disciples.

For example, two approaches to the year 5600 are apparent. According to the testimony of the apostate, Benjamin Be'eri, R. Aviezer of Tykocin and the scholars at the Volozhin academy believed that the Messiah himself would come during that year. Others viewed 5600 not as the year of destiny in itself, but rather as the beginning of the messianic era. This group believed that redemption was a developmental process. From the letters of R. Israel of Shklov to Z.H. Lehren we see that he held with the second viewpoint.

However, a significant source attributed to one of the Gaon's disciples expresses the author's strong reservations concerning the belief in 5600 and, incidentally, reflects the serious disagreements apparently rife among the followers of the Gaon regarding this matter. It is a section located in the writings of R. Manasseh of Ilya, who was known for his rationalist approach and his opposition to studying kabbala:

> ... and whoever is so stupid as to hold false beliefs ["false" in Hebrew — שקר, which is numerically equivalent to ת"ר — (5)600] is holy in his own eyes; but whoever wants to consider seriously if there is any truth in these things will be said to belong to the mixed multitude who did not have it in their nature to believe, whereas Israel are believers and the descendants of believers ... what happened in the days of the false messiah Shabbetai Zevi is well-known, and we have not yet managed to rid ourselves of the poison he left in the land. At any rate, we want our words to make true sense ... and not that the Torah and its *mitzvot* be opposed to common sense.[1]

We have also noted the disagreement within the Perushim in Palestine — between R. Israel of Shklov, who favored spiritual activity as a means to bring the redemption nearer, and R. Menaḥem Mendel of Shklov and the Jerusalem

Perushim who viewed the "raising of the *Shekhina* from the dust" accomplished by rebuilding the ruins of Jerusalem. In this respect, the fact that R. Hayyim of Volozhin refrained from going to Palestine might be interpreted as his taking a stand in favor of the first concept of the redemption process. But from the letters of the *Pekidim* and *Amarkalim* we learn of his involvement in the affairs of the Perushim of Palestine. This included a profound obligation to provide for them financially, and to support their activities spiritually and ideologically. Nonetheless R. Hayyim of Volozhin appears to me to have been closer in his outlook to R. Israel of Shklov than to R. Menahem Mendel.

Hand-embroidered Sabbath cloth, gift from the Perushim community in Jerusalem to Akiva Lehren, an official of the *Pekidim* and *Amarkalim* Fund

The question of whether the Gaon did or did not command his disciples to go to Palestine was answered by A.M. Luncz who wrote that they came in order "to fulfill the desire of their teacher." This can be interpreted as a practical conclusion based on his own experience! However, in one of the letters of the *Pekidim* and *Amarkalim*, I found explicit reference to the fact that the move was linked to a kind of mission or legacy. In one of his letters, Z.H. Lehren referred to R. Abraham S.Z. Zoref, the rebuilder of the Hurva and a person he particularly disliked. He wrote that he knew that Zoref came to Palestine as aide to R. Elija Bialystoker, but in no way "at the behest of the Vilna Gaon." In my opinion, we may deduce from this that to the best of Lehren's knowledge the others did come at the Gaon's behest.

Dr. Friedman asked why the Perushim did not explain their messianic views to Lehren. This is not true. For lack of time I did not mention in connection with the dispatch of R. Baruch to the Ten Tribes in order to bring about a renewal of *semikha* that there was a discussion regarding the messianic concepts of the Perushim. Moreover, R. Israel of Shklov apparently did explain his messianic views to Z.H. Lehren. R. Israel wrote to him in the spring of 5594 (1834) of his intention to make another attempt to reach the Ten Tribes. This was after the emissary R. Baruch was murdered by the Imam of Yemen in the month of Shevat 5594 (February 1834). The subject comes up again several times, when Lehren refers to what will happen to the debts of the community when the Messiah comes, and when he begs R. Israel of Shklov in 5599 (1839), to tell him exactly when the Messiah will appear. There was, however, little trust between the Jerusalem Perushim and Z.H. Lehren — mainly, I believe, because of ideological differences — and they refrained from discussing matters of redemption and messianism with him.

Dr. Menachem Friedman correctly states that we learn from a section of the letter to the Ten Tribes that R. Israel of Shklov was unsure of the exact date of the redemption; he repeated this explicitly in his letters to Lehren. I have already mentioned that R. Israel of Shklov held that redemption was a gradual process, and that after the reinstitution of the *semikha* there would come the day of judgment for the wicked, to be followed by the rebuilding of Jerusalem, and only thereafter — the advent of the Messiah, son of David. Until he came, it would be necessary to maintain the community, which is why he requested economic support from the Ten Tribes. There is no contradiction between this outlook and the feeling that he was living in the period of "Sabbath eve, after mid-day." The opposition of the Perushim in Jerusalem to the dispatching of the emissary to the Ten Tribes seems to reflect a dispute regarding the order of the redemption process. They apparently held that the rebuilding of Jerusalem preceded the renewal of the *semikha*. At any rate, it is to be remembered that the strong messianic expectations characterizing the Perushim in Jerusalem came later, in the wake of Muhammad Ali's rule over Palestine, the *firmān* permitting the reconstruction of the Hurva compound, and the destruction of Safed in the 1837 earthquake — which they believed was referred to in the mishnaic statement at the end of Tractate *Sota*: "Prior to the coming of the Messiah, the Galilee will be laid waste."

Elsewhere, Dr. Friedman has claimed correctly that kabbala was not studied at Volozhin when R. Ḥayyim Soloveitchik was head of the yeshiva, and holds that this indicates that they had no acute messianic expectations; but I believe that one must draw quite different conclusions from this. It is true that the yeshiva neglected the study of kabbala during the second half of the nineteenth century. The reason for this, in my opinion, was the crisis of 5600, for we have definite evidence that they did study kabbala during the first half of the century, quite apart from R. Ḥayyim of Volozhin himself, who studied, published and discussed kabbalistic questions.

Professor Katz raised the difficult question of the absence of references to the disciples of the Gaon in the writings of R. Kalischer. This point has bothered me as well, and Professor Katz's answer seems valid: a movement which has failed buries itself. The leaders of the Perushim during the second half of the nineteenth century apparently tried to ignore the Gaon's disciples, and Rabbi Kalischer preferred not to rely upon an attempt which failed.

Concerning the problem raised by Professor Tishby — the boldness of the Gaon's followers in adopting Sabbatean customs — I definitely accept his point that it was easier for them to do so than for the Ḥasidim. This found extreme expression in the faith of those disciples who saw in the Gaon a spark of "Messiah son of Joseph" — a point also made by the English missionaries then active in Palestine. In this regard, a tradition should be noted that in 5566 (1806) a meeting of disciples in Europe resolved to migrate in an organized fashion to the Land of Israel. According to its letter-values, the year 5566 is equivalent to משיח בן יוסף [Messiah son of Joseph], and the serious attitude of this group to such calculations is extremely well-known. The difficulty Professor Tishby raised also appears with regard to the attitude of the Vilna Gaon's disciples to the personality of R. Yehuda He-Ḥasid. It may be assumed that they were aware of the fact that R. Yehuda He-Ḥasid and his circle were suspected of Sabbatean leanings. From the letters of the *Pekidim* and *Amarkalim* we learn that R. Israel of Shklov refrained from visiting the Ḥurva of R. Yehuda He-Ḥasid and its compound until 5598 (1838), because he claimed the site was accursed, with Satan ruling there. On the other hand, the Perushim in Jerusalem, following R. Menaḥem Mendel of Shklov, treated R. Yehuda He-Ḥasid in their documents as a most positive character.

My dispute with Bartal indeed focuses on substantial matters connected with the overall view of the nineteenth century old yishuv. Bartal's point of departure — that the fundamental purpose of the Ashkenazi community in Palestine was study and labor of God — is mistaken. Bartal then goes on to infer that the Perushim community in Palestine was elitist *in all its stages*. To this I would respond that the range of activities in which the Perushim engaged to realize their goal leaves

185

no doubt concerning their messianic intentions. In order to solidify and expand their community, they engaged in the organization of immigration; to strengthen the community's economic foundations they labored to obtain broad financial support to be invested in plots of land and residential and institutional buildings; and they tried to diversify their sources of livelihood by engaging in handicrafts, commerce, and even (later, in the 1830s) agriculture. All these attempts on their part were undertaken *in absolute and utter confrontation* with the officials of their fund in Amsterdam, who preferred to regard the yishuv as an elitist community composed exclusively of religious scholars. This was the state of affairs *a priori*, and not *a posteriori*. These activities were contradictory in principle and in practice to the character of an elitist community.

Very briefly, we now turn to matters in need of clarification.[2] *Hit'aruta di-le-tata* is a well-known kabbalistic concept, but its practical expression takes many forms. R. Menaḥem Mendel of Vitebsk uses it to refer to *tikkun ha-'olam*, "correction of the world" by observing the commandments between man and man. On the other hand, the Vilna Gaon's disciples, chiefly those in Jerusalem, relate to this concept in terms of activity linked to the building of Jerusalem, the redemption of the Land of Israel and fructification of its desolate soil, in the spirit of the famous talmudic dictum concerning the "revealed end." Is it forbidden to imagine that the Ḥabad Ḥasidim of Hebron were also swept up in messianic ecstasy as the year 5600 approached, and that they identified with the Perushim community of Jerusalem which regarded Muhammad Ali and his activity to improve the Jews' situation as the first stages of Redemption?

In contradiction to Bartal's claims, I believe that no common thread runs between the eighteenth century calculations of the Messiah's coming, and those of the Vilna Gaon's disciples. The fundamental difference is rooted in the fact that the year 5600 (1840) is explicitly and prominently cited in the *Zohar*, and that year can in no way be compared to other speculative dates. Furthermore, a number of revolutionary historical events took place at the end of the eighteenth century following the great wave of Hasidic immigration to Palestine, which served the faithful as pragmatic proof of beliefs derived from the words of the holy *Zohar* — that the great and awesome day was indeed drawing nigh. Moreover, the Vilna Gaon's disciples were aware of the historical upheaval involved in their deeds, and they coped consciously with theological questions that stemmed from their messianic activism, such as whether the "three oaths" that prohibit man's taking action to hasten Redemption, remained in force. In contrast, the relatively numerous letters we possess from the Hasidic immigration from 1777 onward do not reflect any such self-awareness.

Bartal's unwillingness to accept the sources in *Sha'arei Ẓedek* as sufficient proof that belief in the year 5600 indeed played a central role in the community's conciousness is not legitimate. To bring further evidence, another book which mentions the feelings of those whose messianic expectations were crushed is *Ohalei Yehuda*, by R. Yehuda ben R. Shlomo ha-Cohen, printed (as was *Sha'arei*

Zedek) in 1843, by R. Israel Bak in Jerusalem. Another work in MS, *Pi Moshe* by R. Moshe Turgeman a leader of the North African Jewish community in Jerusalem, was apparently written late in 1840 and, like the previous works, is devoted in its entirety to discussion of the results of the disappointment likely to result from the failure of the Messiah to arrive that year.

Bartal claims that omission of the phrase "Shake off your dust, arise" from the Sabbath introductory service is attributed in Lehren's letter to the Sephardim, and that it precedes the period in which we are dealing and even extends beyond it. Bartal's mistake lies in his ascribing Lehren's comments to a Sephardi practice. Lehren, familiar with Sephardi customs, dealings and halakhic practices from his youth, did not require Eliezer Bergmann's testimony in that realm. But Bergmann's testimony took Lehren by storm. Anyone who reads the missive sees clearly that the letter deals with the nullification of two sections of liturgy — the phrase "Shake off your dust, arise" and, chiefly, the kabbalistic *Tikkun Hazot* rite — after Muhammad Ali issued *firmāns* for the construction of synagogues in Jerusalem in 1833–1836. When Lehren relates to these two deletions, he links them in such a way that they appear to have been effected at the same time. Bartal does not relate to the two customs, but selectively chooses between the topics of the sentence. He ascribes the deletion of "Shake off your dust, arise" to an early period, and totally ignores the nullification of the midnight custom of reciting *Tikkun Hazot*.

Bartal bases all his discussion of the cancellation of *Tikkun Hazot* on the declaration of the resumption of that custom in 1847. Though the document speaks explicitly of two elements — ". . . even greater than intensive Torah study and *bewailing the Destruction at night*" — Bartal contends that the text does not speak mainly of lamentations, but of renewing the study of Torah. If so, the document's hesitant manner of calling for renewed Torah study seems curious. Moreover, the regulations cited by Bartal state explicitly that the practical purpose of convening the night-watches is the reciting of *Tikkun Hazot*.

It seems to me that *some* of the members of the Perushim *Kolel* regretted having cancelled the *Tikkun Hazot* rite after the crisis of 1840, and therefore sought to downplay its reintroduction by appending it to a call for prodigious Torah study. Moreover if, as Bartal claims, we are dealing only with an innocent ordinance concerning study of Torah in the *beit midrash*, why does the document lack the signatures of several of the most active participants? Did those figures oppose the study of Torah in the *beit midrash*? Or did they rather oppose the resumption of *Tikkun Hazot* because this expressed a retreat from the view that the Holy Presence had already "risen from its dust" — a view accepted by Jerusalem's Perushim since permission was granted to reconstruct the Hurva compound?

Inasmuch as my research linked the reinstatement of *Tikkun Hazot* with R. Aviezer of Tykocin's call for the resumption of that custom, Bartal tries to ignore his call by equating Sabbath observance with the renewal of *Tikkun Hazot*. I would claim that R. Aviezer of Tykocin's call for the resumption of *Tikkun Ḥazot* is absolute, while his call for preservation of the Sabbath and love of one's fellow-man is a matter of relative observance; in our case, R. Aviezer speaks explicitly of people who make light of the strictures regarding the laws of Sabbath boundaries. Further evidence for his call for the reinstatement of *Tikkun Ḥazot* can be found in his book and in other letters of the *Pekidim* and *Amarkalim* fund which deal with the question of why the Messiah had not arrived in 5600, which of the Perushim's sins had delayed the Messiah's advent, and how to correct the situation so that he would appear, as they hoped, in the year 5606.

Bartal has failed to evaluate the sources properly in his reliance on the testimony of the American missionary Isaac Bird. The American missionary Pliny Fisk was unfamiliar with the language spoken by the Jews. In the end, Isaac Bird copied the missionary newspaper's account of the meeting under discussion into his book. We should now analyze the details.

First, Isaac ben Solomon (Pah) did not take part in the conversation but rather accompanied the apostate missionary Joseph Wolff. Second, if Bartal had gone to the primary source — that is, to Joseph Wolff's diaries — he would have discovered that we are dealing with an unusual and strange figure in terms of behavior and expression. Wolff describes R. Joseph Markovitz as a "Master of the Name" from Poland who had healed a woman in Constantinople through use of the "explicit Name" and had even revealed the phrasing of the "explicit Name" to him — to the displeasure of the Jews of Jerusalem. Markovitz, according to Wolff, told him that according to the Talmud the Jews would not escape their fate as long as they did not believe in Jesus as the Messiah. Furthermore, Markovitz revealed that he was favorably inclined to Christianity, and his son Meir admitted that he wanted to convert.

Identification of Markovitz's deviant personality becomes possible through an 1833 account of a missionary named Nicolayson who relates that he met a man then eighty-eight years old, who gave him his book, *Birkat Yosef*. Nicolayson also describes the unusual and eccentric characteristics of this man, who voiced his contempt of the rabbis and whose views were close to Christianity, and then relates facts of great importance to our subject. The man had followers in Poland and supporters in Leghorn, Italy. Markovitz claimed that R. Menaḥem Mendel of Shklov regarded his erudition and familiarity with mysticism highly, although he did not belong to the Perushim community in Jerusalem. In my view, it is also doubtful that he belonged to the Ḥasidic community which already existed in Jerusalem in the 1820s, but evidently operated as a lone wolf who wandered between Jerusalem and Safed. The comments of R. Joseph ben Ze'ev Eidles (i.e., Markovitz, Ben-Mordechai or Ben-Meir) in condemnation of believers who wished to hasten the advent of the Messiah, paradoxically cast light on the world of the Perushim in Jerusalem. Bartal therefore relies on a source which contains only part of the evidence concerning Markovitz's identity, and has on that basis determined definitively that he was a member of the Perushim community.

Bartal also regrets my not having referred in my study to R. Zundel Salant's position on Redemption in the Vilna Gaon's thinking, inasmuch as his view and that of R. Ḥayyim of Volozhin appear to have been the dominant position among the Perushim in Jerusalem. To confirm his opinion that both R. Zundel and R. Ḥayyim objected to acute messianism, he quotes a story based on a dream from Eliezer Rivlin's book. I find it curious that Bartal overlooked another story, actually adjacent to the one he quotes, which proves acute messianism.

I thank Bartal for raising the question of why Enlightenment literature makes no mention — not even a hint — of so central a phenomenon as the messianic anticipation of the year 5600. Is it not reasonable to suppose that Abraham Mapu, exposed in his youth to the thinking of the Vilna Gaon which he learned directly from one of the Gaon's disciples, R. Elija Ragoler, was referring in fact to *his own time* in speaking obliquely of Shabbetai Zevi in his *Ḥozei Ḥezyonot?* Furthermore, severe censorship, decrees, and persecution discouraged authors from messianic expression, whether favorable or adverse.[3]

Finally, a comment regarding the deeds of the Perushim leadership in Jerusalem in the 1860s and 1870s. In my opinion, it is clear that this leadership was passive in all matters related to future-oriented activity; its motives focused exclusively on the solving of immediate problems of existence, i.e. fundraising for the various *halukka* enterprises. Only a small group, operating independently of the leadership although many of its members belonged to the establishment, took initiatives. The Naḥalat Shiv'a quarter, for example, was established through the enterprise of seven individuals, and not by the initiative of the Ashkenazi community leadership. So it was with the Mea She'arim and Even Yisrael neighborhoods. The events which took place in the Ashkenazi community in Jerusalem in the latter half of the nineteenth century were the results of a number of influences. I have never ascribed *all* the changes which took place exclusively to disappointment related to messianic hopes, although in my view this was a central factor of influence.

---

1 *Sefer Alfei Menashe*, 2 (Hebrew) (Vilna, 1905), pp. 51–52.
2 My detailed response, together with additional sources and references was published in *Cathedra* 31 (1984):172–181.
3 Anti-kabbalistic attitudes and opposition to calculating the date of the Messiah's arrival can be expressed through anti-Sabbatean writings. Examples are provided by *Sippur Ḥalomot ve-Keẓ ha-Pela'ot*, a pamphlet composed of various anti-Sabbatean excerpts, printed in Lemberg (1804) and Kopys (1814), and *Me'ora'ot Zevi*, which appeared in Warsaw in two printings, both in 1838. Were these polemics written to combat ghosts, or real and existing figures? We also find literature relating to the Ten Tribes, which constitutes expression of acute Messianism, as a counterpoint to literature expressing opposition to Sabbateanism. We may cite *Mikve Israel* by R. Manasseh ben Israel, printed in 1712, and then again in 1807 (Shklov), 1837 (Vilna, two printings), and 1841 (Warsaw).

BRITISH POLICY IN PALESTINE: THE "CHURCHILL MEMORANDUM" OF 1922

EVYATAR FRIESEL

*T*he British Mandate period in Palestine has engaged historians during the last four decades. Nonetheless, a seminal document, the "Churchill Memorandum" of 1922, has not been treated in all its ramifications. E. Friesel unravels the background to the Memorandum, analyzes its relationship to the draft mandate, and discusses Zionist and Arab responses to it. Friesel sees the source of the Memorandum in Herbert Samuel's reappraisal of the Palestine situation soon after taking up office as High Commissioner, and discusses its significance for Zionist-British relations.

British policy and administration in Palestine rested upon three main political documents up to 1939. The first was the Balfour Declaration of November 1917; the two others, each related to the Declaration in its own way, were the Churchill Memorandum and the text of the Mandate for Palestine.[1] Both documents came into effect at almost the same time, June–July 1922, the accepted idea being that the Memorandum was an 'interpretation" of the Mandate, aiming to explain certain points that might have remained unclear or controversial.

A quick look at the Churchill Memorandum immediately raises doubts about the supposed harmony between the two documents. To begin with, there is the accompanying letter of Sir John Shuckburgh, head of the Middle Eastern Department of the Colonial Office, delivered to Weizmann together with the Memorandum. Iron fist carefully wrapped in the silk of good manners and well-rounded sentences, Sir John explained that "... it appears to Mr. Churchill [the Colonial Secretary] essential, not only that the declared aims and intentions of your Organization should be consistent with the policy of His Majesty's Government, but that this identity of aim should be made patent both to the people of Palestine and of this country.... Mr. Churchill feels sure that you will appreciate this consideration and will be anxious to do all in your power to remove any misunderstandings that may have arisen."[2] Privately, Shuckburgh's assessment of Weizmann's situation and feelings was more explicit: "He was on the whole in good spirits, and is taking his basin of gruel with a better grace than I expected," he commented in a note to Herbert Samuel.[3]

The Churchill Memorandum and the terms of the Mandate for Palestine were *not* complementary, neither in the formal sense nor in content, even if they dealt with the same issue (Palestine, the Jewish National Home), originated from the same source (Great Britain), and became operative at almost the same time. Formally, the Mandate was certainly more important. The Mandate was a document of official standing in international law, determining the terms and conditions on which Great Britain was to administer Palestine for the League of Nations which held sovereignty over the country. The Memorandum, on the other hand, was only an internal document issued by the Colonial Office, although it was officially communicated to Parliament and to the Mandates Commission of the League of Nations.

The meaning of each document was quite different. The terms of the Mandate were a direct outgrowth of the Balfour Declaration, which was included in its Preamble. Besides establishing some general principles for the administration of Palestine, the outstanding theme of the Mandate text was the development of a Jewish National Home in Palestine. It is true that on several occasions various British officials had tried to read a "double obligation" in the very general text of the Balfour Declaration.[4] But it took, apparently, too much of an effort of imagination to understand the second part of the Declaration ("... nothing shall be done which may prejudice the civil or religious rights of existing non-Jewish communities in Palestine...") as being of equal weight to the first part. The Palestinian Arabs, in any case, seemed to lack that capacity of imagination entirely.

To proclaim the principle of the "double obligation," to Arabs as to Jews, as the foundation of British policy in Palestine, to explain it and to elaborate on it — was the main objective of the Churchill Memorandum. In the perspective of past history, it becomes evident that the Memorandum, more than the Mandate, oriented British policy in Palestine up to 1939. What were the origins of the Memorandum? How did it happen that Great Britain's administration in Palestine, from 1922 on, functioned under the aegis of two different and even diverging sets of obligations? What were the consequences of this situation?

Drafting the Mandate for Palestine

191

At the root of our theme lies that most extraordinary document in the history of the modern Middle East, the Balfour Declaration. How the Declaration was born and what it meant, has interested politicians and historians ever since the publication of those fateful few lines, on November 2, 1917.[5] Differences of opinion about the meaning of the Declaration arose between the British and the Zionists (or among the British and among the Zionists) immediately after its publication. All sides agreed, nonetheless, that the Balfour Declaration represented an opportunity. It was up to the Zionists to try to make the best of it. In the unsettled conditions of Europe and of the Middle East after World War I, Palestine was only one of the many'issues — and certainly not one of the more important ones — that had to be settled by the harassed leaders of the victorious powers and their assistants. But for the Zionists it was *the* issue. Led by Weizmann who combined conviction, steadiness, cunning and, above all, singlemindedness of purpose, the Zionist leadership set forth to establish the foundations of the Jewish National Home in Palestine.

The Zionists acted in different places and on several levels. One of these levels was the political-juridical one: to participate in the preparation of the terms of the Mandate, the document to be formalized by the League of Nations establishing the rights and duties of Britain's rule in Palestine, and the conditions for the development of the Jewish National Home there.

Direct or indirect work on the text of the British Mandate went on from the end of 1918 until the end of 1920,[6] and the terms were formally approved by the League of Nations only in 1922. Ideas and corrections were suggested or prepared by various people, British and Zionists: Aaron Aaronsohn, Herbert Samuel, Arthur J. Balfour, Felix Frankfurter, Chaim Weizmann, and others. The main work of drafting and re-drafting was done between May and December 1919 by a small group of middle-echelon officials, Eric Forbes-Adam and H.W. Malkin on the British side, Benjamin V. ("Ben") Cohen — a young, highly-gifted American-Jewish lawyer — on the Zionist side. By December 1919 a provisional draft had been agreed upon by both sides.[7] Lord Curzon, who in the meantime had succeeded Balfour as Foreign Secretary, subjected the draft to closer scrutiny in March 1920. He was upset by what he considered, and quite rightly, a pro-Zionist document. "I want the Arabs to have a chance and I don't want a Hebrew State. I have no idea how far the case has been given away to the Zionists" — he scribbled, among other peppery observations, on the margin of the text.[8] Curzon ordered changes, and by June 1920 a watered-down version was shown to the Zionists.[9] The wrangling about articles, sentences, and words — Balfour, Weizmann and others now participating too — went on for several months more, and by the end of 1920 the compromise crystallized that was to remain the unchanged draft of the Mandate of Palestine, finally approved by the Council of the League of Nations in July 1922.

Even in its diluted version, the terms of the Mandate remained one of the outstanding political achievements in the history of Zionist diplomacy. The basic structure of the document had not been changed by the Curzon-ordered revision, and some of the expressions and sentences dear to the Zionists were later restored. The draft was a product of one of the better periods in British-Zionist relations. Zionists could find in the text of the Mandate an even more explicit expression of their hopes than in the Balfour Declaration:

The Mandatory shall be responsible for placing the country under such political, administrative and economic conditions as will secure the establishment of the Jewish national home ... (article 2)

An appropriate Jewish agency shall be recognised as a public body for the purpose of advising and co-operating with the Administration of Palestine in such economic, social and other matters as may affect the establishment of the Jewish national home and the interests of the Jewish population in Palestine, and, subject always to the control of the Administration, to assist and take part in the development of the country. (article 4)

The Administration of Palestine, while ensuring that the rights and position of other sections of the population are not prejudiced, shall facilitate Jewish immigration under suitable conditions and shall encourage, in co-operation with the Jewish agency referred to in Article 4, close settlement by Jews on the land, including State lands and waste lands not required for public purposes. (article 6)

The Arab population of Palestine went even less mentioned in the mandate draft than in the Declaration. In 28 articles the word "Arab" appeared only once, in article 22, and even then only in connection with the Arab *language*.

Not that the British were unaware of that somewhat surrealistic aspect of the draft mandate. If in 1917, when the Balfour Declaration was discussed and prepared, the Palestinian Arabs had been either forgotten or disregarded, the situation was certainly different by the end of 1920. The pressure of British administrators in Palestine and in the Middle East, conscious of the political weight of the local populations, the restlessness of the Arab population in Palestine itself which had erupted in violent riots in April 1920, the negotiations with Faisal regarding an Arab state, all this together was bound to impress upon British statesmen the existence of a significant Arab dimension in the question of Palestine. The British were also warned in unequivocal terms by their European allies. Robert Vansittart, member of the British delegation to the Paris Peace Conference, wrote to London that the Italians had reacted to the terms of the Mandate for Palestine like the French: "They think us foolish and asking for trouble...."[10]

The Zionists, therefore, had many reasons to be satisfied with the political situation that existed at the end of 1920. The draft mandate appeared to be settled. Back in April, at the same time of the San Remo Conference, the British leaders had decided to abolish the unfriendly (for the Zionists) military administration in Palestine and to establish instead a civil administration headed by none other than Herbert Samuel, a Jew, a man of high-standing in British political circles, and a staunch supporter of Zionism. Samuel had arrived in Palestine in July 1920, and had started his administration most propitiously. There remained the bothersome question of the lands on the eastern side of the Jordan — or Transjordan, as the region came to be called. The Zionists did not know what exactly British intentions were with regard to these lands, after the collapse of Faisal's regime in

HIGH COMMISSIONER
SIR HERBERT SAMUEL   סיר הרברט סמואל   السر هربرت صوئيل
לשנה טובה

Damascus, in July 1920. But it may be said that the issue did not bother them too much. The Zionists were fortunate to have settled their major political issues with the British when they did, for in August 1920 the Zionist leadership embarked on the fratricidal conflict known as the "Brandeis–Weizmann struggle" that paralyzed the leading organs of the movement for an entire year.

194

The Riots of May 1921 — Samuel's Political Reassessment: Phase One

The Palestine idyll of Herbert Samuel came to an abrupt end on May 1, 1921. A local clash in Jaffa between two different Jewish political groups celebrating Worker's Day precipitated an outbreak of Arab violence against Jews that spread throughout the country. Taken by surprise, the British authorities reacted clumsily. By the time the riots were suppressed there were more than one hundred dead, Jews and Arabs, and additional hundreds of wounded.

Seeking to understand the outbreak and its causes, the High Commissioner underwent, during May, what gradually became a soul-searching reassessment of his ideas regarding Zionism, the character of the Jewish National Home, and the conditions for collaboration between Jews and Arabs in Palestine. Samuel had been one of the most influential figures in the development of the political relationship between the Zionist leadership and the British government. More than anyone else, Samuel was well connected with both sides and symbolized the logic and the harmony of such a double attachment. As member of the British Cabinet he had argued for the Zionist case among his colleagues, and he later helped the Zionists in their political contacts with the British and participated in the drafting process of the Mandate for Palestine.

Nevertheless, Samuel's ideas about the future of Palestine were ambiguous, Zionist hopes running parallel to sober thoughts about the political situation due to the country's large Arab population. Thus Samuel wrote privately, shortly after being designated as High Commissioner for Palestine:

> For the time being, there will be no Jewish state; there will be restricted immigration; there will be cautious colonisation. In five years, the pace will probably be accelerated, and will grow after that progressively in speed. In fifty years there may be a Jewish majority in the population. Then the Government will be predominantly Jewish, and in the generation after that there may be what might properly be called a Jewish country with a Jewish state. It is that prospect which, rightly, evokes such a fine enthusiasm, and it is the hope of realising that future which will make me ready to sacrifice much in the present.[11]

At the same time, since his visit to Palestine in February–March 1920, Samuel had become aware of the seriousness of the Arab question, and in his conversations and correspondence with Zionists in London and in Palestine the matter was repeatedly raised.[12] In Samuel's public utterances during his first months as High Commissioner there were hints that indicated his continuing reflections on the balance between Jews and Arabs in Palestine. The riots of May 1921 brought this process of reassessment to maturation, in the form of conclusions that were, for Samuel, far from easy.[13]

On June 3, 1921, the occasion of King George V's anniversary, Samuel presented his new views to representatives of the population of Palestine in a carefully prepared statement, corrected and approved by the Colonial Office in London.[14] The essence of the statement was the formulation of the principle of "double obligation" as directing the British administration in Palestine. First Samuel spoke about the practical improvements his administration had brought to Palestine. Then he turned to the political tensions in the country. He stated that many Palestinian Arabs thought that the establishment in Palestine of a national

195

home for the Jewish people, as mentioned in the Balfour Declaration, "meant that their lands, houses and Holy Places would be taken away from them and given to strangers . . . ." Samuel stressed that this was not the meaning of the Declaration, but

> that the Jews, a people who are scattered throughout the world but whose hearts are always turned to Palestine, would be enabled to found here their home, and that some among them, within the limits that are fixed by the numbers and interests of the present population, should come to Palestine in order to help by their resources and efforts to develop the country, to the advantage of all its inhabitants . . . the British government, the trustee under the Mandate for the happiness of the people of Palestine, would never impose upon them a policy which that people had reason to think was contrary to their religious, their political, and their economic interests.

Samuel announced that Jewish immigration, suspended after the riots, would be allowed again, to the extent that work was available for the newcomers. "But it must be definitely recognised that the conditions of Palestine are such as not to permit anything in the nature of a mass immigration." More vaguely, Samuel also mentioned the development of frames of consultation between the government and representatives of the population.

The reaction in Zionist circles was stormy. Samuel's new conceptions narrowed the scope of the Zionist program and struck at the very heart of the Zionist idea, its political dimension. For Jews living in Palestine the situation created had an appalling significance. One month after a veritable pogrom, which in many of its characteristics reawakened painful East-European memories, the government clamped down limitations — on the Jews! Samuel's pronouncements were considered apologetic, his behavior panic-stricken.[15] "The Arab rabble . . . try the whole time to blackmail Samuel, who is afraid of them," Weizmann had written to his wife three months before, after a visit to Palestine.[16] Now, apparently, the Arabs had succeeded.

Perhaps it was fear that impelled Samuel. Or perhaps the riots brought him to an understanding and a decision about the Palestinian situation that had been maturing in his mind anyhow. Both possibilities deserve consideration; however, Samuel's behavior after the statement of June 3, like his next steps, or his correspondence with Weizmann, leave the impression of somebody not necessarily afraid, but rather in the hold of a new set of conclusions.

Weizmann was in the United States at the time of the riots in Palestine and during their aftermath. He participated there in the internal struggle in the American Zionist movement that ended with the withdrawal of Louis D. Brandeis and his followers from the affairs of the Zionist Organization of America. On his return to London, towards the end of June 1921, Weizmann began dealing with the new situation arising from the Palestinian developments. He sought written contact with Samuel, and in the new correspondence that developed between them we find the most expressive statements of two different conceptions about the situation in Palestine and the political steps to be taken there.[17]

Writing on July 19, Weizmann stated that in spite of his longstanding friendship with Samuel and their close association in Zionist work, he was forced to oppose his actions in Palestine after the May riots. "It seems that everything in Palestinian life is now revolving round one central problem — how to satisfy 'and to pacify' the Arabs. Zionism is being gradually, systematically, and relentlessly 'reduced'. Jewish public opinion is not reckoned with, we have ceased to exist as a political factor." Weizmann mentioned the delegation of Palestinian Arabs that was coming to London for political conversations, and whom Samuel had asked him to contact. In Weizmann's opinion, the Zionists were placed at the outset at a disadvantage. "Why should the Arabs argue with us at all?" he asked. "They feel that they are in a position to enforce their will on the Government by threats of an uprising or by a Jewish pogrom, and that they can extract all the 'guarantees' they can possibly wish. What chance have we in these discussions?"

Weizmann also dealt with what he considered the roots of the tensions in Palestine. He argued that in spite of Samuel's interest and good will, many of the officials of his administration continued to be negatively disposed towards Zionism. Nevertheless, he added, it was not the Palestinian administration that was, in the last analysis, responsible for what he considered a wrong political direction:

> The causes in my humble opinion lie deeper. There has, it seems to me, been a shifting of political values, due to transient phenomena which momentarily obscure the vision of British statesmen. This is doubtlessly only a passing phase, but the fact remains nevertheless that there is a tendency for the Balfour Declaration and the San Remo decision to be either ignored, or interpreted in a manner which may possibly give a certain amount of temporary satisfaction to the Arabs but which destroys the political foundation on which we have been building.

Weizmann finished his letter asking for guarantees from the Palestinian administration and from the government that the Zionists might continue their work. "We are all anxious to help you in your difficult task, but we must be given a fair chance."

Samuel answered on August 10. He stated that the year he had spent at the head of the Palestinian administration had strengthened his view about the importance of the Arab problem in the country: "Unless there is very careful steering it is upon the Arab rock that the Zionist ship may be wrecked." Contrary to what the Zionists supposed, he went on, the difficulties in Palestine were not due to the bias of this or that British official, or the machinations of individual Arab leaders. The fact was that a very large number of Arabs, many of them well educated, considered Zionism as a danger to their political predominance and to their possessions in Palestine. The speeches of Zionist leaders, including those of Weizmann himself, only indicate that their worst fears may be fulfilled. These

197

people, continued Samuel, would not accept the fate which they thought in store for them without a fight which might take different forms, including armed revolt that would have to be put down by force. Such a development would discredit the Zionist movement and alienate British public opinion.

"The Zionist policy is not based upon such stable foundations in Great Britain that it can afford to see those foundations shaken," he continued, "and troubles in Palestine would almost certainly be followed by debates in Parliament and by speeches in the Constituencies, which, if they did not induce the present Government to change its course, would certainly incline any succesor to do so." Samuel explained that these were the reasons behind his new political line, and although he knew that many of his Zionist friends would be deeply disappointed, he was sure that in the long run it was in the best interests of the Zionist cause. [18]

Weizmann's Political Efforts in London

Although approved by the Colonial Office, Samuel's statement did not, so far, represent the accepted and recognized policy of the British government. Political maneuvering now developed in London around the policy in Palestine: Samuel trying to broaden the acceptance of his approach, Weizmann working to maintain the existing position. Samuel acted through the Colonial Office, headed by Churchill; Weizmann sought contacts in high levels of the government.

It was soon apparent that Samuel was laboring under several disadvantages. He was too far way to exert personal influence; the political redefinitions he asked for seemed too radical; worst of all, Churchill, the Secretary of State for the Colonies, surprisingly turned out to be an ineffective spokesman for the new approach.

Churchill had acted most impressively during the Cairo Conference, in March 1921, when he had consolidated the frames of British rule in the Middle East that were to hold until the aftermath of World War II.[19] But when it came to dealing with Palestine, Churchill's positions were inconsistent, sometimes inclined towards the Zionist wishes, sometimes not, and gradually developing to a point where he apparently thought it better to keep his hands off the Palestinian issue. At the time of his visit to Jerusalem in March 1921 he made a blunt statement before a delegation of Arab notables that had asked him to repudiate the Balfour Declaration and to stop Jewish immigration into Palestine:

> It is not in my power to do so, nor, if it were in my power, would it be my wish. The British Government . . . view with favour the establishment of a Jewish National Home in Palestine, and that inevitably involves the immigration of Jews into the country . . . Moreover, it is manifestly right that the Jews who are scattered all over the world should have a national centre and a National Home where some of them may be reunited. And where else could that be but in this land of Palestine, with which for more than 3,000 years they have been intimately and profoundly associated?[20]

Later on, after the May riots, Churchill adopted a position that was almost

Winston Churchill, Secretary of State for the Colonies, visiting the future site of the Hebrew University on Mt. Scopus, Jerusalem, 1921

opposite; he became gloomy and pessimistic about the British presence in Palestine and in Iraq as well. Writing to Lloyd George, he commented on the growing difficulties with Turkey, and the tendency of the League of Nations to postpone the approval of the Mandate. Churchill thought that it might be "impossible for us to maintain our position either in Palestine or in Mesopotamia," and consequently "the only wise and safe course would be to take advantage of the postponement of the Mandates and resign both and quit the two countries at the earliest moment, as the expense to which we shall be put will be wholly unwarrantable." Some days later he suggested to the Prime Minister to turn the Palestinian and Mesopotamian Mandates over to the United States, adding that he was prepared to bring up his proposal at the next meeting of the Cabinet. Both Lloyd George and Curzon, the Foreign Secretary, rejected the idea, the impression being that they did not take it too seriously.[21]

Yet only a week later Churchill found himself capable of presenting in the House of Commons a most spirited and forceful defense of the government's policy in the Middle East and in Palestine.[22] That double attitude — outer optimism, inner pessimism — was to characterize Churchill's position on Palestine over the next period. His indecisiveness meant that the Colonial Office was unable to present a coherent and well worked-out position when the Palestinian question came up during the next months. It seems that the only two men with clear ideas

199

about what to do in Palestine were Samuel and Weizmann. But Samuel was away in Palestine. Weizmann was on the scene in London, and he proceeded to make the best of his advantage.

The next chapter in the political discussions about Palestine was uncommon in character, to say the least. Seeking to neutralize the effects of the political steps adopted by Samuel, Weizmann went to see Balfour, Churchill, Smuts and others. Balfour, still a member of the Cabinet, promised significant help; he would call a private meeting at his home, with the Prime Minister, the Colonial Secretary, and others, where Weizmann would present his arguments against the political changes in Palestine introduced by Samuel with the support of Churchill.[23]

The meeting took place on July 22 with the participation, besides the host and Weizmann, of Lloyd George, Churchill, and the Secretary of the Cabinet, Maurice Hankey. It is remarkable that the Foreign Secretary, Lord Curzon, was apparently not invited. The impression given by the material available is that it was Weizmann's day. He made a forceful presentation of his case, and the tenor of the meeting was very much in his favor. Both Lloyd George and Balfour agreed that the Balfour Declaration meant that a Jewish majority should develop in Palestine, leading to an eventual Jewish state. Samuel's declaration and attitude were criticized; Churchill found himself on the defensive and out-played.[24]

The line of Weizmann's argument was typical of his more optimistic days. As he stated in a conversation with Gen. Smuts, the day after the meeting at Balfour's house:

> [if Great Britain holds Palestine for the Jews] does she do it out of pure political altruism, or because she thinks that a Jewish Palestine might be of value to the British Empire? In other words: *Is there or is there not* a coincidence of Jewish and British interests? If, in the opinion of British statesmen, there is no such coincidence, then we should be told so honestly and straightforwardly. We are an old people, full of sores. We bleed out of every pore and it is a great sin, which will bitterly revenge itself, if we are simply put off by pious promises.[25]

It was Weizmann at his best — and Weizmann at his best, it had been said, was a master.

Nothing was or could have been decided at the encounter. But the atmosphere of mutual understanding between Weizmann and the British leaders was reaffirmed. More practical consequences were soon felt. Weizmann's standing was enhanced. Most important, on August 18, the question of Great Britain's policy in Palestine was discussed by the Cabinet. The presentation of the case by the Colonial Office was strange, to say the least. A memorandum was delivered, preceded by a chillingly pessimistic statement by Churchill:

> The situation in Palestine causes me perplexity and anxiety. The whole country is in a ferment. The Zionist policy is profoundly unpopular with all except the Zionists. Both Arabs and Jews are armed and arming, ready to spring at each other's throats.... Meanwhile Dr. Weizmann and the

Zionists are extremely discontented at the progress made, at the lukewarm attitude of the British officials, at the chilling disapprobation of the military, and at the alleged weakening of Sir Herbert Samuel. It seems to me that the whole situation should be reviewed by the Cabinet. I have done and am doing my best to give effect to the pledge given to the Zionists by Mr. Balfour on behalf of the War Cabinet and by the Prime Minister at the San Remo Conference. I am prepared to continue in this course, if it is the settled resolve of the Cabinet.[26]

Thus far, Churchill. But then came the memorandum proper, and it did *not* match the gloomy tone of the introductory statement. The proposals run parallel to many of the Zionists' suggestions, although formulated in a more moderate fashion. Moreover, some of the accompanying comments written by officials of the Colonial Office and approved by the Colonial Secretary himself were entirely out of tune with the policies both of Churchill and of Samuel: "The problem which we have to work out now is one of tactics, not strategy, the general strategic idea, as I conceive it, being the gradual immigration of Jews into Palestine until that country becomes a predominantly Jewish State. There is no half-way house between this conception and total abandonment of the Zionist programme."[27] No Zionist leader could have formulated it better.

The tendency of the Cabinet was highly satisfactory, from the Zionist viewpoint: "The honour of the Government was involved in the Declaration made by Mr. Balfour, and to go back on our pledge would seriously reduce the prestige of this country in the eyes of the Jews throughout the world," said the main sentence of the conclusive considerations drafted at the meeting of the Cabinet.[28] Due to Balfour's absence, the discussion in the Cabinet was not summed up, and the question remained formally open, although it was not considered again in the near future. The intention of the Cabinet had been clearly stated. It seems that a certain amount of ambiguity and even confusion with regard to Palestine reigned in the Colonial Office, evidently a result of the diverging political conceptions and pressures that had been raised during July and August. As Shuckburgh, the head of the Middle Eastern Department, admitted privately later on:

The Zionist Organization, in the person of Dr. Weizmann, enjoys direct access to high political personages outside the Colonial Office .... It is clearly useless for us to endeavour to lead Doctor Weizmann in one direction, and to reconcile him to a more limited view of the Balfour pledge, if he is told quite a different story by the head of the government. Nothing but confusion can result if His Majesty's Government do not speak with a single voice.[29]

The Zionists in London: New Political Problems

Although Weizmann had successfully curbed the efforts of Samuel and Churchill to change the government's policy in Palestine, he had little respite from his worries about the political situation of the Zionists. Three new problems developed from the second part of 1921 on: complications with the confirmation of Britain's Mandate over Palestine by the League of Nations, the visit of a Palestinian Arab delegation in London and its activities there, and a general shift in British public opinion with regard to Palestine. Moreover, in the fall of 1922 there was a resurgence of the efforts on the part of the Palestinian administration and the Colonial Office to introduce changes in the constitutional basis of the British rule in Palestine.

The League of Nations' delay in confirming the British Mandate over Palestine was now perhaps the most troublesome problem bothering the Zionists. As long as the Mandate was not approved, the political situation in Palestine and in London would remain unstable and uncertain, open to doubts and re-evaluations. The heads of the Palestinian administration were as interested as the Zionists in a settlement of these uncertainties. Herbert Samuel stressed at every possible opportunity the need to reach a decision at the League of Nations with regard to the Mandate, since it would calm the mood of the country. The decision was also essential in that it would provide a basis for new domestic measures which he wished to take, such as drafting a constitution, holding elections for a legislative council, scheduling municipal elections, and regulating fiscal matters.[30] When Herbert Samuel accepted the position of High Commissioner at the end of April 1920, he had not expected such a lengthy transitional period to precede the confirmation of the British Mandate.

It should be remembered that the juridical basis of Palestine's civil administration was, so far, rather doubtful. The category of the mandates within which Palestine fell had been created by the Charter of the League of Nations in June 1919. According to article 22 of the Charter, responsibility for certain countries whose population was considered as still unable to govern itself and which, as a consequence of the war, had ceased to be under the sovereignty of the states which had formerly ruled them, had been transferred to the League of Nations. Article 22 established that the League would turn these countries over to the tutelage — or mandate — of more advanced states who were to administer them on its behalf. Rights and duties of each mandatory government were to be defined by the Council of the League of Nations.[31]

Another document affecting Palestine's legal situation was the Peace Treaty between Turkey and the Entente Powers signed at Sèvres in August 1920, in which Turkey had relinquished its sovereignty over Palestine (article 132). The signatories established that the administration of Palestine was to be transferred to a mandatory power that would act in accordance with article 22 of the League of Nations' Charter and would take upon itself the implementation of the Balfour Declaration (article 95). Earlier, at the San Remo Conference in April 1920, the representatives of the Entente Powers had agreed that Great Britain was to be the mandatory power governing Palestine. But this decision lacked international-legal validity as long as the British Mandate was not confirmed in all its details by the

Council of the League. Moreover, the fact that the Turkish regime which had signed the Sèvres Treaty had since been overthrown, and a new regime headed by Mustafa Kemal had repudiated the treaty, did little to strengthen the legality of the British civil administration in Palestine.

In February 1922 the British press published the draft of the Mandate for Palestine that was to be considered at the coming session of the League's Council. The topic was actively discussed in the press, which was far from supportive of the Jewish National Home policy. Two large newspaper networks, that of Lord Northcliff which included the important *Times* and *Daily Mail*, and that of Lord Beaverbrook, expressed reservations not only about the draft of the Mandate, but about the Mandate itself. Northcliff's position, in particular, was very negative; he had visited Palestine and severely criticized British policy there.[32]

In May 1922 the issue of the British Mandate over Palestine was brought before the Council of the League, but the decision was postponed. The reasons were unrelated to the increasingly hesitant attitude toward Zionism in Great Britain. The Vatican had exerted pressure behind the scenes, due to dissatisfaction with the articles of the draft dealing with the holy places.[33] The matter would have to be brought up again at the Council session in July 1922.

During the interim between the two sessions of May and July, the opponents of the British policy in Palestine managed to initiate a debate in Parliament. The first debate took place in the House of Lords on June 21–22, 1922. Lord Islington opposed acceptance of the Mandate in its proposed form, stating that it did not accord with various commitments which the British government had made to the Arabs in the past, and that its formulation was in contradiction to the wishes of a large majority of the country's population. Balfour, who had just been raised to the peerage, defended the government's policy regarding the Zionist aspirations in Palestine in his maiden speech in the House of Lords. Nonetheless, the motion criticizing the government was carried by a large majority.

Two weeks later the subject was raised in the House of Commons, where the debate was more important than that in the House of Lords. Churchill skillfully led the debate and with the help of other members of the House who supported the government's traditional policy towards Zionism and Palestine, succeeded in having the anti-Mandate proposal rejected by a large majority.[34] The Zionists breathed more freely, but the discussion in the Council of the League of Nations was still to take place. Weizmann and his colleagues feared that any additional postponement in the international forum might well lead to the collapse of the existing policy.[35]

203

The Palestine Arab Delegation in London

The Palestinian Arab delegation arrived in London in August 1921. It represented the Fourth Palestinian Arab Congress, which had met in Jerusalem the preceding May. The delegation included both Christians and Muslims and was headed by

Musa Kazem Pasha al-Husseini, a former mayor of Jerusalem and one of the outstanding Arab personalities of Palestine. The purpose of the delegation's visit to London was to discuss the position and present the demands of the Arabs in Palestine. The trip had the blessing of the High Commissioner; as we have seen, Samuel was convinced that an understanding with the Arabs was the only guarantee for ensuring peace in the country and for preventing a new outbreak of riots.[36]

The Zionists took an interest in the delegation,[37] although Weizmann tried to minimize its importance. At the meeting in Balfour's home on July 22, he described the Arabs as "political blackmailers" and said that he had little interest in meeting with them. The Zionists also expressed doubts that the delegation and the Arab Congress that had chosen it were representative of the population in Palestine. If this argument was intended as a tactical measure, if was of doubtful effectiveness: the Arab Congress consisted of members of the ruling class of the population, namely, the *effendis*, both Christian and Muslim, and no other group had emerged capable of speaking in the name of the Palestinian Arabs.

The first discussions between the Arabs and the officials of the Colonial Office, held during August, proved unproductive. The Arabs expressed strong opposition to Zionism and to the British policy regarding Zionist aspirations. They stressed the irreconcilable contradiction between the two parts of the Balfour Declaration and vehemently demanded their rights. The British explained that if the Arabs were to practice restraint, the different interests in Palestine could be accomodated. Churchill suggested that for the sake of mutual understanding the members of the delegation should meet with Weizmann, but the Arabs replied that their business was with the British government and that they did not recognize Weizmann.[38]

Talks continued, since neither the British nor the Arabs wanted the delegation to return to Palestine empty-handed. At the end of October the Arabs and the Zionists were invited to attend a meeting at which the Secretary for the Colonies intended to read a statement of policy. As we shall see later, the idea was actually Samuel's, who had written to Churchill suggesting the main points to be presented.[39] The draft, prepared by Shuckburgh, was a cautiously worded document which adhered to the draft mandate and was therefore closer to the Zionist position than to that of the Arabs. It stated that British policy in Palestine was based on the Balfour Declaration, but it emphasized that the Declaration had a two-fold even-handed significance. On the one hand, it promised Britain's assistance in establishing a Jewish National Home; on the other, it stressed the civil and religious rights of the non-Jewish communities in Palestine.

The meeting, scheduled for November 16, was postponed to November 29 because Churchill became "ill".[40] On November 28 Weizmann met with Churchill and was informed of the contents of the planned statement. Apparently the conversation went well, but it is hardly to be believed that Weizmann was happy with the new initiative of the Colonial Office, or that he failed to recognize the long hand of Samuel behind it. As it turned out, however, Churchill decided not to participate in the meeting on the following day, and consequently no statement was read out.[41] It was Shuckburgh who received the two delegations. The occasion had symbolic importance, being the first meeting between Arab and Zionist leaders since the agreement between Faisal and Weizmann in January 1919. Although the atmosphere of the conversation was polite, the participants never entered into a real discussion but maintained two separate dialogues with Shuckburgh. Weizmann and the Arabs each voiced their arguments, and despite Shuckburgh's efforts there was no interchange between them. Thus the practical results of the meeting were nil.[42] The approach adopted by the Arabs was similar to that taken at the meeting with Churchill in Jerusalem at the end of March 1921. In both cases they avoided direct contact with the Zionists and put their case in an uncompromising manner. This time, however, the Arabs were much more skillful in the presentation of their arguments.

The failure of the meeting led to mutual recriminations. Weizmann held that in the absence of an unequivocal stand on the part of the Colonial Office, making clear that the Balfour Declaration and the draft of the mandate were not subjects for bargaining, the Arabs would adopt extreme tactics in order to extract political advantages from the British government. Several of the British participants, on the other hand, criticized Weizmann's conduct during the encounter.[43] Among themselves, the British officials expressed a poor opinion of the Arab delegates. Shuckburgh commented:

> Experience has shown that they are a hopeless body to deal with. In the first place, hardly any of their number can speak English, and everything has to be translated by an interpreter. Secondly they are very slow of understanding, and probably rather suspicious of one another. At any rate they will never commit themselves to anything in the course of conversation. All that happens is that, after much inconclusive talk, they go back to their Hotel and wait till one of their British advisers comes and tells them what to say.[44]

The Palestine Arab delegation remained in England until the summer of 1922. After their first talks with the Colonial Office had not produced results, the Arabs started a publicity campaign to influence British public opinion, and sought to explain their views through newspapers sympathetic to their case.[45] It is questionable whether at that stage the Arabs were in a position to significantly sway British public opinion in their favor. There is no doubt, however, that their propaganda activity, through the press, brought home to the British public that the situation in Palestine was complex and many-sided, and might entail large expenses which would have to come out of the pockets of the British tax-payer. The Arabs also continued in their negotiations with the Colonial Office. With the Zionists, there was no further contact.

It is apparent that Herbert Samuel had hoped that the very presence of a group of Arab Palestinian leaders in London, their contact with British officials, with the

205

British public, and with the Zionist representatives, would lead them to develop a more pliable and compromising frame of mind with regard to Palestine and its problems. With regard to contacts with the British, this may indeed have been one of the indirect and non-declared results of the Arab delegation's stay in London. With regard to the Zionists, the chasm between both sides only grew wider.

Samuel's Political Reassessment: Phase Two

Although Weizmann had been successful in thwarting the High Commissioner's new proposals with regard to Palestine, Samuel did not give up. On October 14 he wrote a long and thoughtful letter to Churchill, in which he stated that "the uneasy political situation in Palestine is a matter of constant preoccupation, and the possibility of adopting measures for its improvement is continually under my consideration."[46] Samuel was also worried about the lack of any results, so far, from the contacts between the Palestinian Arab delegation and the Colonial Office.

In his letter Samuel concentrated on two main themes: the urgency of a settlement of Great Britain's Mandate over Palestine; and the necessity of a redefinition of the government's policy regarding Zionists and Arabs. It was Samuel's assumption, based more on wishful thinking than on concrete facts, that politically moderate trends leading towards mutual understanding were developing among the Arabs and the Zionists. As for the Arabs, he believed that they were prepared to accept the policy of the Jewish National Home as explained in his June 3 speech and in Churchill's June 14 speech in Parliament. With regard to the Zionists, Samuel pointed to the decision of the Twelfth Zionist Congress to maintain relations of respect and cooperation with the Arabs in order to ensure the national development of both peoples.[47] Samuel intended to make additional demands on the Zionists. In his letter he suggested that they be required to declare that their aim was "not the establishment of a State in which the Jews would enjoy a position of political privilege, but a Commonwealth built upon a democratic foundation." Samuel also dealt with the immigration of Jewish workers (proportional to employment opportunities in new enterprises), and guarantees for the holy places. Most of these ideas had been mentioned in his June 3 statement.

Now Samuel continued with what may be considered as the first step later to lead to the Churchill Memorandum: "As all these points have already appeared in Zionist pronouncements at one time or other" — he wrote, rather surprisingly — "there should be no insuperable difficulty in securing their embodiment in a formal declaration. But the effect of such a declaration in clearing the political atmosphere in Palestine would be very great."

Last, almost as an afterthought, came another suggestion of far-reaching meaning:

> If it were possible in addition for the Zionist Organization to agree to limit the functions of its Commission at Jerusalem to economic and cultural

questions, leaving political action to the Elected Assembly of the Jewish population and its Executive Committee and to the Zionist Committee in London, the prospect of an accommodation with the Arabs would be greatly increased.

The Commission, i.e., the Zionist Commission, had by then changed its name to Palestine Zionist Executive, and was the body that under article 4 of the draft mandate enjoyed a special status in Palestine prior to the formation of the Jewish Agency. Samuel was considering, it turns out, to deprive that body of its privileged status.

Samuel's letter did not remain without results. The planned November 16 meeting in London (later postponed to November 29) was one direct outcome. The draft of the memorandum prepared by Shuckburgh that Churchill was supposed to have read before the Arabs and the Zionists was an elaboration of the ideas and the approach expressed in Samuel's letter. As noted, however, Churchill evidently had second thoughts about the initiative, and no statement was presented. Nevertheless, the process of reconsideration of the situation in Palestine and the policy there continued to be fanned by Samuel through letters and conversations with Colonial Office officials who came to Palestine, or by members of the Palestinian administration who visited London.[48] The fact that the Cabinet discussion of August 18 had not ended with a formal resolution, and that contacts between the Colonial Office and the Arab delegation continued, provided a formal basis as well as a continuing stimulus for these political considerations. One suggestion that came up again and again in these internal discussions was the idea, mentioned by Samuel, to change the special position accorded the Zionist Organization in article 4 of the draft mandate.

Weizmann knew about this process of re-thinking going on between Jerusalem and London, and was deeply disturbed.[49] At a given moment the Central Zionist Office in London considered calling for popular demonstrations by American Jews against the introduction of changes in the draft mandate.[50] For once, Weizmann was too pessimistic. The Colonial Office did not accept the more extreme propositions emanating mainly from Jerusalem.[51] The result of all these labors in the Colonial Office was a political draft sent by Shuckburgh both to the Zionists and to the Arabs on December 17. In attached letters Shuckburgh asked each side to consider the draft as a basis for discussion with the other.[52]

The draft was an elaboration of the text of the intended declaration prepared for Churchill a month earlier. It presented four main points: 1. British policy in Palestine is based on the Balfour Declaration; 2. The rights of the present population will be preserved; 3. Jewish immigration will be fixed according to the country's economic capacity; 4. A legislative council will be set up. The Colonial Office tried once again to reduce the fears of the Arabs about the significance of the Balfour Declaration and the concept of the Jewish National Home — an exercise as repetitive as it was unconvincing. The text emphasized that the national home "does not mean the creation of a state in which Jews will be in a

207

position of political ascendancy or enjoy political privileges denied to other inhabitants of the country. It does not mean the unrestricted admission of Jewish immigrants." But in continuation, the document was equally emphatic about Jewish rights in Palestine:

> But it does mean that His Majesty's Government recognize the historical and religious associations that connect the Jewish people with the soil of Palestine, and that Jewish immigrants will be given special facilities as compared with immigrants of non-Jewish origin for entering the country. The intention is that immigration of all kinds should be strictly proportionated to the capacity of the country to receive new inhabitants. Stated in other words, the policy is to build up in Palestine a commonwealth, based upon a democratic foundation, in which all sections of the community will enjoy equal political rights.

It is not to be believed that the Zionists were pleased by the document. But since it was rejected by the Arabs, the burden of non-acceptance fell upon them.[53] The Colonial Office probably tried another way to clarify its intentions in Palestine; it prepared a draft of a future Constitution for Palestine, to be published after the ratification of the Mandate by the League of Nations. Drafts of the document were delivered during February 1922 to the Zionists and to the Arabs for consideration.

The draft was necessarily an elaborate document. It comprised ninety articles grouped into eight parts, specifying the organization of the Palestinian government, its various institutions and departments, their powers and competences.[54] In terms of the political discussion among the Jews, the Arabs and the British, the Preamble to the Constitution was significant. It repeated the first two paragraphs of the draft mandate, including the Balfour Declaration. Outstanding among the provisions were those dealing with the formation of a Legislative Council (part three) — the establishment of representative institutions in Palestine being one of the major hopes of the High Commissioner. The Legislative Council was to consist of 22 members and the High Commissioner, *ex officio*[55] — ten officials (departmental heads of the Administration) and twelve representatives to be elected by the local population. The proportional division of the twelve representatives was not specified, but the composition of the existing Advisory Council, formed by Herbert Samuel in the fall of 1920, would probably serve as a precedent, since it had also consisted of official and elected representatives: four Muslim, three Christian, and three Jewish delegates. The Legislative Council could not propose laws that contradicted the terms of the Mandate, and its proposals required confirmation by the High Commissioner.

A lengthy correspondence ensued from February through April 1922 between the Colonial Office and the Arab delegation regarding the terms of the Constitution.[56] The manner in which the Arabs framed their arguments had improved considerably during the delegation's stay in London. The experienced hand of British advisors (sympathetic British military personnel, journalists and politicians) was clearly visible. A new argument was brought up: the correspondence between McMahon and Sharif Hussein in 1915.The Arabs now pointed — rightly or wrongly — to a second promise made by Great Britain which, in their view, affected Palestine and was equal to the Balfour Declaration in importance. After consultation with McMahon himself, the Colonial Office clarified that Palestine west of the Jordan was not included in the British promise to Hussein. In spite of this, the new argument was not dropped by the Arabs.[57]

The exchange of letters, which continued until the middle of April, again achieved nothing. The Colonial Office was prepared to accommodate the Arabs with details and explanations, but it adhered to the government's basic political stand regarding Zionist aspirations in Palestine. The Arabs adamantly refused to enter into a discussion related in any form to the Balfour Declaration, maintaining that it would be a useless exercise.[58]

Towards the Churchill Memorandum

By the end of April 1922 it seemed that Samuel's efforts to bring about a redefinition of British policy in Palestine had again reached a dead end, this time because of the Arabs' intransigence. But now chance intervened; the Council of the League of Nations was supposed to approve the British Mandate on Palestine at its meeting in Geneva, on May 13. It had seemed that the whole procedure would be purely formal, but difficulties arose during the meeting, as the Foreign Office seemingly had not done its preparatory work adequately. To the surprise of the British delegates and the chagrin of the Zionists, the decision on the Mandate was postponed until mid-July.[59]

Samuel, who happened to be in London, saw his opportunity: to prepare a statement of policy based on his ideas, and to force the Zionists to accept it. Thus the Churchill Memorandum was born. The text was drafted by Samuel himself, in consultation with the Middle Eastern Department.[60] Churchill, in whose name it was going to appear, received the draft on May 24 and confirmed it three days later, without any corrections or remarks.[61] During these months Churchill had not taken any initiative concerning Palestine, and according to Robert Meinertzhagen, then an official in the Middle Eastern Department, Churchill had lost interest in Palestine: "Winston does not care two pins, and does not want to be bothered about it . . . He is to wrapped up in Home Politics," he recorded in his diary.[62]

Formally, Samuel and the Colonial Office hoped to prevail upon the Arabs and upon the Zionists to agree to the new definition of British policy in Palestine prior to the publication of the document.[63] But there was a fundamental difference between what was demanded, or could have been demanded, from each party. The Arabs were given the text accompanied by explanations, and they rejected it in the same way they had rejected all the other formulations of the Colonial Office.[64] The Zionists, on the other hand, were caught in an hour of political

209

weakness: postponement of the confirmation of the Mandate, the impending debate in Parliament on British policy in Palestine, and mounting doubts in British public opinion about the situation in Palestine. A pessimistic mood pervaded Zionist and pro-Zionist circles. Even as favorably disposed a British politician as David Ormsby-Gore, then the head of a pro-Zionist group in the House of Commons, told Leonard Stein in March:

> ... there could be no doubt that the situation had undergone an unfavourable change. There was growing up a body of [British public] opinion which was inclined to view Zionism with scepticism, if not with positive dislike. Some of those who had supported the Balfour Declaration when it was issued were tending to change their minds now that it appeared to them to be giving rise to serious difficulties which they had not at the outset foreseen. There was a disposition in some quarters to fear that what was going on was an attempt on the part of a body of powerful and aggressive Jews to tread down a weak and helpless little people.[65]

For the Zionists then, the situation warranted orderly political retreat and measured concessions. In Shuckburgh's introductory letter to the Memorandum there was not so much an insinuation as a veiled implication that non-acceptance of the Memorandum by the Zionists might result in unforeseen consequences. Commenting privately on the document, Shuckburgh wrote:

> The Arabs will be given to understand that this is our last word, and that if they cannot accept it off-hand they had better go back to Palestine and take counsel with their supporters on the spot. There can be little doubt, I think, that the Zionists will accept the statement. It contains certain passages that will not be at all to their liking. But they are beginning to realize clearly that they must modify their ambitions; that the patience of His Majesty's Government is not inexhaustible; and that by claiming too much they run serious risk of losing everything. The Arabs doubtless will not be satisfied, but they may be glad of the opportunity that will be given them of returning to Palestine not entirely empty-handed.[66]

The stated purpose of the Memorandum was to define the rights of the Jews and the rights of the Arabs in Palestine, and how the rights of one party were compatible with the rights of the other. In practice, the document was a redefinition of Britain's policy regarding Zionist aspirations in Palestine, because the rights of the Arabs tended now to be determined by placing limitations on the Zionists. For example, the document defined what the Jewish National Home was *not* intended to be: It was not intended that Palestine become wholly Jewish, nor that it be made "as Jewish as England is English." "His Majesty's Government," it stated, "regard any such expectation as impracticable and have no such aim in view." It stressed that a Jewish National Home was to be established *in* Palestine, to the dissatisfaction of the Zionists who wanted *all* of Palestine to be recognized as a National Home. It stated that the Zionist Organization would not participate in governing the country and that article 4 of the draft mandate did not imply any such function.

At the same time the Memorandum stressed that the government had no intention to renounce the policy implied in the Balfour Declaration, as now interpreted. The Jewish community developing in Palestine was recognized as having national characteristics, but it was stated that the development of the Jewish National Home did not imply the imposition of Jewish nationality on all the inhabitants of Palestine, "but the further development of the existing Jewish community, with the assistance of Jews in other parts of the world, in order that it may become a centre in which the Jewish people as a whole may take, on grounds of religion and race, an interest and a pride." And here came the part that mollified the Zionists somewhat:

> But in order that this community should have the best prospect of full development and provide a full opportunity for the Jewish people to display its capacities, it is essential that it should know that it is in Palestine as of right and not on sufferance. That is the reason why it is necessary that the existence of a Jewish National Home in Palestine should be internationally guaranteed, and that it should be formally recognized to rest upon ancient historic connection.

The document dealt briefly with the question of whether Palestine had been promised to the Arabs in the negotiations between McMahon and Sharif Hussein in 1915, and determined that the country was not included in the promise.

Regarding Jewish immigration, it was established that the Jewish community in Palestine should be enabled to grow through immigration, on condition that the numbers would not exceed the country's economic capacity. Since that subject seriously worried the Arabs, the Memorandum spoke of the establishment of a special committee for matters of immigration, to consist of members of the planned Legislative Council, that would discuss with the administration questions connected with the regulation of Jewish immigration.

The Memorandum anounced that His Majesty's Government intended, in due time, "to foster the establishment of a full measure of self-government in Palestine. But they are of the opinion that, in the special circumstances of that country, this should be accomplished by gradual stages and not suddenly."

The summation of the Memorandum expressed the hope that the political steps mentioned, along with the insistence on full religious freedom in Palestine and the safeguarding of the holy places of every community, would foster increased cooperation between all sectors of the population on whom the prosperity and progress of the Holy Land depended.[67]

The characteristics of the preliminary contact between the British and the Zionists regarding the text of the document bore the unmistakable signs of a new period in the political relations between both sides. Gone were the days when documents were elaborated in close collaboration between British and Zionist officials. Still, Weizmann received a confidential copy of the statement on May 27, *after* its approval by Churchill, so as to enable him to study it and consult with his advisors.[68] Weizmann met with Samuel a few days later and tried to persuade him to have some changes made in the Churchill Memorandum. For example, he requested deletion of the sentence criticizing his statement that Palestine be "as Jewish as England is English." The conversation must have been tense and difficult; not only did Samuel reject any changes in the Memorandum, but he expressed his opinion that it would be desirable to eliminate article 4 from the draft mandate. Weizmann answered that without article 4 the whole Mandate ceased being of any significance for the Zionists.[69] The British reaction to Zionist pleas to change the draft was vividly described in a letter of Leonard Stein to Nahum Sokolow, then in the United States:

> The reply was that in the case of Palestine, as in many other matters, things were not what they were two or three years ago, and that many hopes which had then been entertained had been found to be incapable of full realization. The situation must be taken as it was and it must be realized that what was set forth in the statement represented what the Government was actually prepared to do . . .. As we have now exhausted our efforts to get the statement modified in our favour, nothing remains but to accept it with the best grace we can, and to turn the acceptance to our advantage by the frank and loyal answer in which our assurances are conveyed to the Government.[70]

Weizmann understood that there was no way but "to take his basin of gruel with good grace."[71] On June 3 the Zionist Executive got the Memorandum with the accompanying letter of Shuckburgh. Was the date merely a coincidence? The letter was sent exactly one year after Samuel's first statement announcing his new political approach with regard to Palestine, which Weizmann had later succeeded in thwarting.

The letter and the Memorandum were discussed by the Zionist Executive at a regular meeting on June 9 and at an expanded meeting on June 18, attended by members of the Executive and by members of the Zionist Council who had been summoned from Europe. Weizmann explained the situation: The Zionist reply must reach the Colonial Office the following day, in time for the debate in the House of Lords that was to take place within a few days. A delay in the decision, Weizmann continued, might influence the debate and could endanger the approval of the Mandate. As during the previous discussion, it was felt that the Memorandum was a bitter pill that had to be swallowed. Even Jabotinsky (then a member of the Zionist Executive) said that on the eve of the debate on the Mandate, the Executive was obliged to compromise. The positive answer of the Zionists reached the Colonial Office the next morning.[72]

In spite of the Arab delegation's negative reply, the Colonial Office, after some hesitation, decided to carry out its original intention and publish the political statement by the Secretary of State for the Colonies, along with the correspondence that had preceded it or was connected with it.[73] The material, in the form of a White Paper, was put before Parliament on July 1, 1922.

At the meeting of the Council of the League of Nations, which opened in mid-July 1922, the British Mandate over Palestine was confirmed with no additional debate or excitement.[74] There were still unresolved questions regarding a number of formal matters, and certain points connected with the northern border remained to be fixed, but this did not deter the decision to hand the Mandate over to Great Britain.

The reactions of the British and of the Zionists were restrained. The *New Statesman* commented approvingly in its editorial that the matter was concluded and that the Mandate was now a *fait accompli*.[75] Most people seemed to share this opinion.

The Churchill Memorandum: Appraisal and Consequences

Acceptance of the Churchill Memorandum by the Zionists, and its publication within the framework of a White Paper, represented a significant victory for Samuel's position. Nevertheless, there are indications that from Samuel's point of view the Memorandum was not ideal and that he would have preferred instead (or in addition) to introduce changes in the draft of the mandate. From the British point of view, the disadvantage of the situation now created was that one more document of political weight was added to the series of pronouncements, agreements, and declarations which complicated Britain's political position in the Middle East after World War I. The connection between the text of the Mandate and the Memorandum was problematic, with each document reflecting a different conception and emphasis.

From the Zionist point of view, a careful examination of the text of the Memorandum revealed nothing that contradicted the Balfour Declaration, while it referred positively to the Jewish presence and to the Zionist aspirations in Palestine. However, the document also contained obvious changes for the worse. In defining the status and purposes of the Zionists in Palestine, it detracted from the explicit or implicit Zionist political achievements after the Balfour Declaration. It was built on the principle of the "double obligation" interpreted in its fullest meaning, something found neither in the Balfour Declaration nor in the draft mandate. It checked the Zionist aspiration that one day the National Home would become a Jewish Commonwealth. Its interpretation of the special status of the Jewish Agency was restrictive. It specifically negated any interpretation according to which the right of the Jews to Palestine might be understood as being superior to the right of the Arabs.

The Arabs were neither pleased with the Memorandum nor were they appeased by it; the declared policy of His Majesty's Government continued to be the establishment of a Jewish National Home. The document dwelt at length on the civil and religious rights of the Arabs, but nothing very explicit was said about their political rights. Possible limitations on Jewish immigration were mentioned,

213

due to economic reasons, although the document stated that so far this problem had not arisen.

In theory, nothing improved in Palestine as a result of the publication of the Churchill Memorandum within the framework of the 1922 White Paper. Samuel had intended to initiate a policy which, in his view, would be more "balanced" and acceptable to both Jews and Arabs. But the Zionists acknowledged the document only under duress, and the Arabs rejected it outright.

In practice, matters worked out differently, and after the publication of the White Paper and the approval of the Mandate, quiet reigned in Palestine. Samuel's policy built no bridges between the three corners of the Palestine triangle, but it created the conditions in which each party was able, for some time, to go its own way and to develop its own institutions — not together, but side by side. Palestine remained calm until the end of the 1920s and even later on, despite the fact that during those years the neighboring countries — Syria, Egypt, Iraq — were in continuous turmoil.

Finally, in terms of the political relationship between the Zionist movement and Great Britain, the Churchill Memorandum signaled the beginning of a new period. From 1917 until August 1921 the tenor of Zionist political behavior had been active, self-assured, and sometimes even aggressive. Now a new pattern was established, essentially defensive, that was to continue until the publication of the MacDonald White Paper in 1939.

Although defensive, the new political approach of the Zionists was far from negative. Leonard Stein expressed the new feeling, writing in the aftermath of the Churchill Memorandum:

> ... it depends upon the Jews themselves in the long run, as in fact it has always depended upon them, what they make of their opportunities. With the guarantees now given, it remains, as it has always remained, for the Jews to succeed in Palestine on their merits, and no limit is set to what they may accomplish there.[76]

In their political relationship with the British, the Zionists now labored not to attain new achievements, but toward a holding operation. They sought to avoid or at least to delay the gradual erosion of British adherence to the original spirit of the Balfour Declaration. During this new period, the leading conductor of Zionist foreign policy was, as in the past, Chaim Weizmann. His qualities as a statesman enabled him to recognize when it was in the best interests of Zionism to advance, and when it was unavoidable to retreat, in as orderly and slow a fashion as possible. That he was capable of leading the movement in *both* directions offers a positive measure of his political stature.

1 The Churchill Memorandum was published under the title "British Policy in Palestine," as part of the so-called Churchill White Paper of June 1922. The official name of the White Paper was: *Palestine — Correspondence with the Palestine Arab Delegation and the Zionist Organization*, Cmd. 1700 (1922). The White Paper contained nine documents. The Memorandum appeared as an enclosure to document no. 5. The Mandate for Palestine was published as Cmd. 1785 (1922).

2 The Colonial Office to the Zionist Organization, June 3, 1922, letter signed by John Shuckburgh. The letter was document no. 5 of the Churchill White Paper, to which the Memorandum was enclosed.

3 June 3, 1922, PRO CO733/34, p. 320.

4 See the Military Chief Administrator's proclamation of April 28, 1920, "To the Heads of All Sects," Israel State Archives 141/2.

5 Two different directions of explanation are to be found in L. Stein, *The Balfour Declaration* (London, 1961), and M. Vereté, "The Balfour Declaration and Its Makers," *MES* 6 (1970):48–76.

6 For a more detailed description of that theme, see E. Friesel, *Zionist Policy After the Balfour Declaration* (Hebrew), (Tel Aviv, 1977), pp. 72–80, 120–125, 186–196; J.J. McTacue Jr., "Zionist-British Negotiations over the Draft Mandate for Palestine, 1920," *JSS* 42 (1980):281–292.

7 The text is in *Documents of British Foreign Policy 1919–1939*, 1st. series, eds. E.L. Woodward, R. Butler, J.P.T. Bury, vol. IV, pp. 571–591, (Hereafter, *DBFP*.)

8 Palestine Chapter, March 11, 1920, PRO FO 371/15199/E1447.

9 Draft Mandate for Palestine, June 10, 1920, CZA A18/40/2.

10 Vansittart to Hubert W. Young, June 29, 1920, *DBFP*, XIII, p. 299; see also *ibid.*, p. 292.

11 To Lucy Franklin (Samuel's sister-in-law), May 3, 1920, Herbert Samuel Papers, Library of the House of Lords, London B/12.

12 Israel Sieff to Weizmann, Jan. 29, 1920, CZA Z4/16033; Weizmann to Vera Weizmann, March 29, 1920, in *The Letters and Papers of Chaim Weizmann*, series A (hereafter, *Letters*), IX, no. 300; Samuel to Weizmann, June 20, 1920, CZA, Benjamin V. Cohen Papers.

13 Arthur Ruppin, Diary, June 4, 1921, CZA; David Eder (political officer of the Zionist Commission) to London Zionist Executive, June 4, 1921, WP.

14 Statement of the High Commissioner, WP; Churchill's comments on Samuel's draft, June 2, 1921, PRO CO733, vol. 3; parts of the statement and an analysis of it are to be found in Aaron S. Klieman, *Foundations of British Policy in the Arab World* (Baltimore–London, 1970), pp. 182–183; Doreen Ingrams (ed.), *Palestine Papers 1917–1922* (London, 1972), pp. 128–129.

15 Eder to the Zionist Executive, letters from May 8, 15, 29, WP; Samuel Landman to Churchill, May 5, 1921; meeting of the Zionist Executive with Sir Alfred Mond, May 13, 1921, CZA Z4/16055.

16 February 9, 1921, *Letters* X, no. 117.

17 The two main letters were Weizmann to Samuel, July 19, 1921, *Letters* X, no. 213; Samuel to Weizmann, August 10, 1921, CZA Z4/16151.

18 Samuel's attitude toward Zionism deserves special attention, and it is the author's intention to deal with the issue in a separate article.

19 Aptly described in Klieman (above, n. 14).

20 For the full text, see *ibid.*, pp. 269–273.

21 Churchill to Lloyd George, June 2, June 9, 1921; to Curzon, June 9, 1921; Curzon to Lloyd George, June 10, 1921; Lloyd George to Churchill, June 11, 1921; the original letters are in the Beaverbrook Library, London, files F/8/48–54; see also Lord Beaverbrook, *The Decline and Fall of Lloyd George* (London, 1963), pp. 252–254.

22 Middle East: Mr. Churchill's Statement, June 14, 1921, CZA Z4/16055.

23 Weizmann to Balfour, July 8, 1921; to Shmarya Levin, July 15, 1921, *Letters* X, nos. 208, 210.

24 Notes of the conversation, WP; most of the text is reproduced in Robert Meinertzhagen, *Middle East Diary 1917–1956* (London, 1959), pp. 103–106; for descriptions of the meeting, obviously based on the notes but with personal comments, see Weizmann to Ahad Ha'am, July 30, 1921, and to Wyndham Deedes, July 31, 1921, *Letters* X, nos. 227, 228. The notes were

probably written by Edward Russel, a friend of Weizmann, who participated in the meeting.

25 To Deedes, July 31, 1921, *Letters* X, p. 236.

26 PRO CAB24/CP3213/127; partially reproduced in Ingrams (above, n. 14), pp. 142–143. Churchill's pessimism was apparently deepened by information he got from Palestine. Both the High Commissioner and the military authorities stated that although the country was quiet, new outbreaks of violence were quite possible, Samuel, "Political Report for June," July 17, 1921, PRO FO371/6376/8940; Memorandum, General Staff: "The Military Aspect of the Present Situation in Palestine," July 7, 1921, PRO CAB24/CP3129/126.

27 Ingrams (above, n. 14), pp. 140–141.

28 PRO CAB24/CP3213/127; reproduced in Ingrams, *ibid.*, pp. 146–147.

29 Shuckburgh to James Masterton–Smith, Nov. 7, 1921, *loc. cit.*; see also the highly interesting comments of British officials, *ibid.*, pp. 154–157.

30 Samuel to Churchill, Oct. 14, 1921, CZA Z4/16055.

31 The Charter of the League also appears as an introduction to the Peace Treaty with Turkey, signed at Sèvres, August 10, 1920, Cmd. 964 (London, 1920).

32 Weizmann at the meetings of the Zionist Executive, Feb. 21, 1922, May 5, 1922, WP.

33 Weizmann to Vera Weizmann, May 16, 1922; to Sokolow, May 24, 1922, *Letters* XI, no. 98, 102.

34 Ingrams (above, n. 14), pp. 169–170.

35 Weizmann to Julius Simon, July 16, 1922, *Letters* XI, no. 158.

36 Samuel to Churchill, July 18, 1921, Lloyd George Papers, Beaverbrook Library, F/9/3/92; for an excellent brief description of the delegation's visit and talks, see Klieman, pp. 190–197; see also Ingrams, pp. 137–150 (both above, n. 14).

37 Discussion at the meeting of the Zionist Executive, June 28, 1921, CZA Z4/302/4/I; meeting of the Zionist Commission, August 3, 1921, with a description of the delegation and of its composition, WP.

38 Klieman (above, no. 14), pp. 192–194; minutes of conversation between Major Young (Colonial Office) and Leon Simon, Samuel Landman (Central Zionist Office), Aug. 23, 1921, WP.

39 WP.

40 According to Weizmann, Churchill became doubtful about the presentation of the statement; letter to Deedes, Dec. 13, 1921, *Letters* X, p. 328.

41 Weizmann to Nahum Sokolow, Nov. 28, 1921; to Colonial Office, Dec. 1, 1921; to Eder, Dec. 8, 1921, *Letters* X, nos. 291, 296, 308; Richard Lichtheim to Sokolow, Nov. 30, 1921, CZA A18/53/2.

42 Weizmann to Eder, Nov. 27, 1921, *Letters* X, no. 288; Klieman (above, no. 14), pp. 195–196. Klieman is based on a report in the Colonial Office files. Another report, of similar content, but apparently recorded by one of the Zionist delegates who participated in the meeting (perhaps Stein), is found in WP.

43 See remarks of Mills, in *ibid.*, pp. 196–197.

44 Nov. 7, 1921, PRO CO733/15.

45 See, for example, the pamphlet *The Holy Land – The Moslem–Christian Case Against Zionist Aggression*, official statement by the Palestine Arab Delegation (London, February 1922). The Central Zionist Office generally replied to Arab publications and interviews. See L. Stein, *The Truth About Palestine – A Reply to the Palestine Arab Delegation* (London, 1922).

46 CZA Z4/16055.

47 Protokoll ... XII Zionisten-Kongress, p. 769. It may be said that this paragraph of the resolution was of a rather declaratory character.

48 See Major H.W. Young's impressions after a visit to Palestine, Shuckburgh, Memorandum on Palestine, Nov. 7, 1921, PRO CO733/15; about Ernest T. Richmond's (Palestine administration) visit to London in December 1921, see Bernard Wasserstein, *The British in Palestine* (London, 1978), p. 143; see also Deedes to Shuckburgh, Nov. 22, 1921, Ingrams (above, n. 14), pp. 154–156; Deedes to Weizmann, Nov. 26, 1921, WP.

49 See minutes of conversation between Landman and Alfred Mond, Dec. 16, 1921, CZA A18/43/4; Lichtheim to Sokolow, Dec. 14, 1921, CZA A56/18; Weizmann to Balfour (cable),

Dec. 13, 1921; to Deedes, Dec. 13, 1921, *Letters* X, nos. 316, 315, 318; Lord Rothschild to Balfour, Dec. 13, 1921, CZA Z4/16055.

50 Weizmann to Sokolow (cable), Dec. 13, 1921, *Letters* X, no. 318.

51 Weizmann to Sokolow (cable), Dec. 19, 1921, Weizmann, *Letters* X, no. 326; see also Sokolow to Weizmann, Dec. 18, 1921, CZA Z4/16055.

52 CZA Z4/16055.

53 See Wasserstein (above, n. 48), pp. 115–118.

54 The approved version was published on Sept. 1, 1922 under the heading *Palestine Order in Council, 1922* (Statutory Rules and Orders, 1922, no. 1282), in Robert Harry Drayton, *The Laws of Palestine*, III (London, 1934), pp. 2569–2589.

55 The first draft mentioned 25 members, together with the High Commissioner, who should also appoint the two additional members.

56 Included in the 1922 White Paper (Cmd. 1700).

57 Letters from April 11, 1922, June 17, 1922; 1922 White Paper, documents no. 4 and 6. On the McMahon–Hussein correspondence, see I. Friedman, "The McMahon–Hussein Correspondence and the Question of Palestine," *Journal of Contemporary History* 5 (1970):83–122; E. Kedourie, *In the Anglo-Arab Labyrinth* (Cambridge, 1976), pp. 244–248. Kedourie levels serious criticism at the Colonial Office reply to the claim made by the Arabs. Regarding the guidance the Arabs received from various people in Britain, see Meinertzhagen to Shuckburgh, Nov. 17, 1921, PRO CO733/15, p. 246.

58 See the end of the Arab delegation's letter from March 16, 1922; 1922 White Paper, doc. no. 3.

59 Weizmann to Vera Weizmann, May 11, 13, 16, 1922, *Letters* XI, nos. 96, 97, 98.

60 Shuckburgh to Vansittart, June 7, 1922, PRO CO733/34, pp. 322–323.

61 See the material on the Statement of Policy, May 30, 1922, PRO CO733/34.

62 Meinertzhagen (above, n. 24), p. 112.

63 A copy was sent to the Arab delegation on May 30, and to Weizmann on May 27; Statement on Policy, PRO CO733/34.

64 June 17, 1922; 1922 White Paper, document no. 6.

65 Interview, March 7, 1922, WP; see also Albert M. Hyamson to L. Stein, March 7, 1922, WP.

66 PRO CO733/34, pp. 296–299.

67 British Policy in Palestine, enclosure in document no. 5, 1922 White Paper.

68 Shuckburgh to Weizmann, May 27, 1922, PRO CO733/34, p. 317.

69 Minutes, meetings of the Zionist Executive, May 31, 1922, June 9, 1922, CZA Z4/4020.

70 June 13, 1922, CZA A18/47/3.

71 See above, no. 3.

72 1922 White Paper, document no. 7.

73 Churchill was doubtful about the publication, and the decision was taken due to Balfour's intervention. See Shuckburgh to Vansittart, June 7, 1922, PRO CO733/34, pp. 322–323.

74 S. Landman, "The Struggle for the Mandate," *Jewish Chronicle*, Aug. 4, 1922, p. 81.

75 July 29, 1922, issue no. 485, pp. 453–454.

76 To Sokolow, June 13, 1922, CZA A18/47/3.

THE KLADOVO-DARIEN AFFAIR — ILLEGAL IMMIGRATION TO PALESTINE: ZIONIST POLICY AND EUROPEAN EXIGENCIES

Dalia Ofer

E uropean Jewry's attempts to reach Palestine during the period of Nazi occupation and the British White Paper became all the more dramatic when an arm of the Haganah—the underground Jewish defense organization—began to organize illegal immigration, with the consent of prominent Zionist leaders. D. Ofer concentrates on the complications involved in bringing over 1,000 Jewish refugees from Europe (Kladovo group) to Palestine in 1940, which had tragic consequences. She places this episode within the Zionist dilemma of the war period, i.e., whether to support illegal immigration unequivocally and thus clash with the British, or to make common cause with the British, Germany's chief enemy, at the expense of Jewish immigration.

The fate of the immigrant group that spent ten months in Kladovo, Yugoslavia waiting for transport to escape Europe in 1940, and another year in Sabac until it fell into the hands of the Nazis, is one of the saddest episodes in the history of illegal immigration to Palestine.[1] Many attempts were made to bring this group of more than one thousand refugees to Palestine, and each met with failure. The Kladovo affair became a painful topic in the complex relations between the Jewish communities throughout the world and the heads of the Zionist institutions in Palestine. For a long period of time it was held up as an example of the latter's irresponsible attitude toward the Diaspora.

The Kladovo episode, which is tied to the affair of the ship "Darien", touches on the central problems of Zionist policy during the Holocaust, and on basic questions regarding the rescue of European Jewry. The two intermeshed tales present us with the dilemma of the Zionist leadership: whether to attempt the immediate rescue of a group of refugees from war-torn Europe (despite the uncertainty of a successful conclusion), or to carry out an operation that was one small link in a broad political program promising wide-scale rescue of refugees in the future — and that also had no guarantee of success.

The affair begins in the summer of 1939 in Vienna, when the so-called "Kladovo group" was first formed by *He-Ḥalutz*, an organization that trained Jewish youth to settle on the land in Palestine (in 1939 it had a membership of 100,000 throughout eastern and central Europe), and *Mossad l'Aliyah Bet*, an organization set up by the Haganah (the underground self-defense organization of the Jewish community of Palestine) to carry out "illegal" immigration activities in the face of the British restrictions on Jewish entry into Palestine.

The original plan was for the group to be transported from Vienna to a Black Sea port on the Danube; the Mossad agents were to arrange for a sea-going vessel to continue to Palestine.[2] After war broke out it became increasingly urgent to get Jews out of the areas under the control of the Reich. Future exit possibilities were questionable, and the Germans' first expulsion of Jews to Lublin[3] created a great sense of emergency. However, difficulties in obtaining boats for illegal immigration during wartime delayed the group's departure. Late in October and early in November, the group was transferred from Vienna to Bratislava. Ehud Avriel, the representative of He-Ḥalutz received temporary entry visas into Slovakia by bribing the Slovakian consul in Vienna, with whom the Mossad had maintained contact since pre-war days. In Bratislava, the group took up lodgings in a small hotel and awaited notification of the arrival of a ship at Constanza, when they would continue the journey to Palestine. Only after the ship had arrived at Sulina or Constanza would the group be transported further. However, at this stage the Mossad had no ships at its disposal.

Keeping the group in Bratislava was both extremely costly and risky. The police threatened to send the Jews back to the Reich, which meant only one thing — concentration camps. Still, the Mossad agents decided it would be better to wait in Bratislava than in Rumania, for Rumania was flooded with groups of immigrants waiting for ships. Adding another group would not be in the interests of any of the refugees, and their own security would be jeopardized.[4]

As the weeks passed and the Mossad agents were still unable to get hold of a sea-going ship, staying in Bratislava became more dangerous. The group leaders pleaded with the Mossad agents in Geneva to arrange for their departure to a Rumanian port whose proximity to the Black Sea and the Mediterranean seemed to promise a better chance of embarking with their possessions and reaching Palestine. But the Rumanian government would not permit the group to enter its territorial waters unless a ship was waiting to continue the journey. By early December 1939 the weather was turning cold and there were very real fears that the Danube would soon freeze over. But still the Mossad agents failed to charter a sea-going ship. Finally, Moshe Agami, the Mossad representative in Geneva, agreed to allow the group to continue south on riverboats although no deep-water ship was in sight. He hoped that the Rumanian authorities, seeing the group approaching, would not deny them permission to enter its territorial waters. Meanwhile, he was relying on the possibility that somehow a boat would be obtained by Mossad agents in Greece. In December, the group left Bratislava on the German boat "Uranus", but the German Danube Company would not take the people to Rumania unless a ship was waiting there.

Despite disagreement with other Mossad agents, Agami arranged with Sima Spitzer, the general secretary of the Jewish communities in Yugoslavia and a veteran Zionist, to charter three Yugoslav riverboats and sail the people to Constanza. The group, numbering almost 1,000 by this time, embarked on the boats at the border town of Benzian, hoping to reach Rumania in a few days. But permission to enter territorial waters was not granted. While waiting at the Iron Gate for the entry permit, fears that the river might freeze over became a reality and the boats were ordered by the company to enter Kladovo harbor for the winter. Spitzer obtained government permission to keep the people on the boats, promising that the Jewish community would provide for their needs. Kladovo harbor gave its name to the group.

The "winter stay" lasted until the summer of 1940 when the group, still unable to sail, was moved 225 kms. to the north to the town of Sabac on the Sava river. It was still there when the Nazis invaded Yugoslavia, and the unfortunate people found themselves once again under Nazi rule. Only three small groups of children — 206 in all — reached Palestine on Youth Aliyah certificates. Their departure took place in March 1941 at the last possible moment. The rest were murdered by the Nazis — first the men, and then the women and children — during the fall of 1941.

Why was the group not transported by the Mossad as planned? Why were the refugees not rescued by other means? What were the circumstances that hindered and prevented their departure from Kladovo and Sabac? Finally, what conclusions can be drawn from these events?

In order to answer these questions one must reveal the efforts made to ensure that the voyage continued and analyze the reasons for their failure. This will throw light on some of the basic problems of Zionist policy with regard to the rescue of European Jews at that time, and in particular on the difficulties inherent in illegal immigration.

The Kladovo–Darien affair can be divided into four stages: (a) from the winter of 1940 to June 1940; (b) from July to September 1940; (c) from October 1940 to January 1941; (d) from January to October 1941.

Those involved in the effort to bring the Kladovo affair to a successful conclusion were the Jewish Agency, the Joint Distribution Committee and the Organization of Yugoslav Jewish Communities represented by Sima Spitzer. Each of these attempted to assist the group in its own way — the Agency by trying to get immigration certificates from the British, the JDC by financial assistance, and the Organization of Yugoslav Jewish Communities by appealing to the government and by organizing the daily routine of the refugees. They all carried out their tasks faithfully, but all saw the Mossad as responsible for finding a solution to the problem. Thus, the core of the Kladovo affair consists of the attempts made by the Mossad agents to acquire a ship to transport the immigrants to Palestine.

The Mossad L'Aliyah, Zionist Policy and Illegal Immigration[5]

The Mossad L'Aliyah was an organization set up by the Haganah to help young He-Ḥalutz members enter Palestine despite the British immigration restrictions. Its origins were in dissent groups within the He-Ḥalutz pioneering movement in 1934, and aroused many debates and disagreements within the labor movement and its leadership. But in the last months of 1938 and the beginning of 1939, in view of Britain's new anti-Zionist policy, it received the blessing of the Zionist political leadership and established itself as a branch of the defense organization, the Haganah. In this sense it was under the control of the Jewish Agency. It was headed by Shaul Meirov (Avigur) and had its headquarters in Paris. From the end of 1938 until the beginning of World War II it brought some 5,000 people to Palestine — approximately one boat per month. Many of the boats succeeded in landing clandestinely with the help of another branch of the Mossad that was set up in Palestine for the purpose of assisting in the landing operations. But the concepts of illegal immigration as understood by its activists and by the political leadership were not identical.

Women's demonstration in Jerusalem, against the British White Paper. Flag-bearer, Rahel Yanait Ben-Ẓvi; second row left, Sarah Herzog, wife of the Chief Rabbi

Zionist policy during that period approved of illegal immigration, regarding it as a tool to be used against the implementation of the White Paper policy of May 1939. This policy limited Jewish immigration to Palestine, narrowed the area where land was allowed to be purchased by Jews, and planned to establish Arab majority rule within five years. Prior to the outbreak of World War II, Zionist leaders supported illegal immigration in various degrees. Some Zionist leaders, among them Ben-Gurion, thought that they could control illegal immigration totally and maneuver it according to the political needs of Zionism. They wanted to organize an open demonstration to protest against Great Britain. At one time they planned an impressive voyage of Jewish refugees on hundreds of vessels, an immigration revolt which would embarrass the British. They assumed that the British would not be able to oppose the entry of these people into Palestine without resorting to force. However, using force against Jewish refugees who were escaping Nazi persecution would be very unpopular in Britain and throughout the free world, so the demonstration was considered an effective means of opposing the British without the use of force. Mossad operatives rejected this plan. They regarded their work as a covert and secret operation, the aim of which was first and foremost to bring He-Halutz members safely to Palestine. A demonstration such as that envisioned by Ben-Gurion was too risky. It would be a one-time operation and if it failed it would destroy the future of illegal immigration. The British would uncover the agents and governments that were supporting illegal immigration and punish them, thus destroying the whole movement.

Others understood that Zionism could not totally control illegal immigration since it grew out of the needs of the people rather than from a political decision. However, Zionism would gain if it were to take part in helping to get the desperate Jews to Palestine. They understood illegal immigration as an ideal means by which an honorable but weak Jewish community could oppose a great empire. It should therefore remain an underground movement. Its very existence represented protest, so an open demonstration was unnecessary. The Zionist movement should contribute by supporting the Mossad financially and morally, and not by changing its strategy. Berl Katzenelson, leading ideologist of the Labor Party, accepted this line. He considered illegal immigration to be an actualization of a trend in Jewish history, showing the rescue of the Jewish people to be dependent on Zionist fulfillment.[6] Other figures, among whom were Chaim Weizmann and leaders of German Jewry, were more hesitant since they were afraid to alienate the British — almost the sole friend of European Jewry in spite of the White Paper. These hesitations were supported by other leaders who were concerned with the economic burden of illegal immigration on the Jewish community in Palestine, and by some figures who opposed it altogether, such as A.H. Silver, the leader of American Zionism.

After the outbreak of war, the misgivings about illegal immigration grew. The political aims were no different but new strategies and tactics were developed. Zionist leaders planned to bring about a change in British policy through strong

Jewish Agency recruiting poster for auxiliary police

Calling on Palestinian Jews to enlist in the war effort:

"For freedom, for the people and the land"

support for and cooperation with Great Britain in the war effort. The formation of a Jewish military force became a prime goal. This force would achieve many goals. It would strengthen the defense of the *yishuv*, it would fight Hitler in the name of the Jewish people, and it would prove to the British how important the *yishuv* was to the Empire's security. In the long run, if everything turned out as was hoped, Zionism would gain a major tool which could be used in the rescue of European Jewry. If this conception was to be implemented, the areas of conflict between Britain and Zionism had to be minimized without concealing the continuing strong opposition to the White Paper.

Illegal immigration suffered acutely from this new strategy. Its detractors developed new arguments for attacking it, and its supporters became ambivalent. Its strongest defense was the moral argument: illegal immigration was a practical way of rescuing the European Jews. But even this became more and more difficult to put into operation for tactical reasons. On the theoretical level, the debate on illegal immigration was never settled decisively. On a practical level, the issue was no less complicated. The difficulties involved in the organization of illegal immigration, and the constant uncertainty regarding the success or failure of an operation, led to the abandonment of illegal immigration even as a means of rescue. This will be demonstrated by the Darien affair.

223

Maritime Transport and Other Difficulties

When war broke out, the Jews of Germany and those living in the occupied territories were declared enemy subjects by the British and were denied entry into British territories. This meant that legal immigration to Palestine would almost come to a halt. The British defended their decision on the grounds that the Germans might plant spies and fifth columnists among the immigrants and use their families in Germany as hostages. The fear of spies and enemy agents amounted to hysteria in Great Britain during the first year of the war, and the Home Office was inflexible in dealing with this problem.

Mossad agents in German territories had to leave since they were British subjects, and thus the work became even more difficult. The Mossad had less control over the operation for it was no longer able to work according to the centralized pattern developed before the war. The agents could not foresee what changes would be made in German policy toward emigration, nor how long it would be permitted at all. They also wished to participate in the selection of emigrants in order to prevent the Germans from using the departing Jews for their own purposes. The matter of selection of immigrants to Palestine was thus distorted; no longer an internal Zionist question of the candidate's education and suitability for life in Palestine (legitimate considerations on the part of He-Halutz), it became a question of exercising control over possible Nazi pressure vis-à-vis the emigration list. Decentralizing the work was essential under the new conditions, but the inherent dangers were very real because of the changed situation and the attitude of the British. In addition, the practical difficulties of organization in wartime became overwhelming.

As a result of the war there was an increased demand for ships. Countries forbade the sale or transfer of vessels from one flag to another, and closely supervised their use. Only ships which had officially been retired from service were available to the *aliyah* (immigration) activists for sale or lease. These vessels required repairs as well as adaptation to the needs of immigration, yet despite their poor quality their prices soared, occasionally to three or four times their true value. Governments increasingly kept an eye on ship captains and shipping agents who maintained contacts with *aliyah* agents. It was also hard to find crews for these ships, for the British empowered the Palestine administration to confiscate those that reached its shores and imprison their crews.[7] Only sailors in difficult straits were candidates for jobs on the immigrant ships.

Additional factors contributed to the sky-rocketing costs of the journey. The shipowners and their agents, seeking to increase their profits from these hazardous ventures, insured the ships at exorbitant rates, thus creating an excuse to damage the ships maliciously before they could reach shore. Agents would demand, shortly before the ships were due to leave, high bank guarantees which the *aliyah* organizers had difficulty arranging. Agents and shipowners also broke contracts, knowing that the organizers of *aliyah*, engaged as they were in illegal activity, could not appeal to the courts.

The matter of passing through several countries in order to reach a port of departure became more complex as well. The British effectively increased their political pressure on the Balkan states to refuse passage through their countries for refugees on their way to Palestine. It was difficult to get transit visas, and visas with fictitious destinations also became rarer and, consequently, more expensive.

This complex of difficulties created almost insurmountable obstacles. Some Mossad people proposed purchasing ships and training Jewish crews to man them. In January 1940, one of them wrote, "All our failures with the 'goyim' prove the necessity of finding another way." Under these circumstances the Mossad policy was to complete the voyage of groups who were ready before war broke out but who were not shipped out because of it. Some 2,500 people came under this category, among them the so-called "Kladovo Group". After a few weeks of confusion during the month of September and part of October, the Mossad envoys turned up again in the shipping market only to discover that the two boats they had obtained during the summer of 1939 had been lost and they would therefore have to start again from the beginning.

Leaders of the *yishuv* undertake a hunger strike in protest against Britain's immigration policy and its preventing the departure of immigrant boats from the port of La Spezia, Italy

Mossad Attempts: January–April 1940

With the acquisition of a ship having first priority, Mossad agents Zeev Schind and Zvi Yeḥieli left for Italy in an attempt to establish contact with ship agents in Genoa. Shemarya Ẓameret, another Mossad agent, was in Athens negotiating for a small ship. J. Barpal and Ruth Klüger-Aliav, both Mossad agents in Rumania, were negotiating for a large Turkish vessel, "Vatan", to take some 3,000 passengers. Mossad agents remained in contact with Dr. Baruch Confino from Bulgaria who was planning to buy a ship in Bratislava.[8] All these agents sought to buy or rent a vessel to transport 3,000 people in the near future, of whom the largest group was the 1,100 people in Kladovo.

In January and February 1940, Mossad representatives met in Geneva with leaders of the Jewish communities of Prague and Berlin, who demanded that more decisive steps be taken to organize Jewish emigration. They described the cruel fate of the Jews who had been expelled to Lublin, a fate they expected to be visited on all Jews not leaving the Reich very shortly. The Czech authorities were willing to permit the Jews to acquire foreign currency to finance their journey, and the Mossad agents undertook to help 2,000 Jews leave Prague. The Prague community would forward to the Mossad foreign currency to finance acquisition of a ship and fit it out for passengers. The amount agreed upon was £25 per head, a reasonable sum in January. But the program had to be carried out as soon as possible, because costs were rising at a giddy rate. In this way the Mossad agents hoped to help Czech Jewry and to have the communities themselves finance their emigration.

Late in February and early in March the best chance seemed to be the Turkish deal for the "Vatan", through Pendelis, a Greek agent known as the "Fat Man" who worked with the Mossad and other illegal immigration agents for a long time.[9] The Mossad believed it could overcome all the formal problems, including the Turkish government's negative attitude. Although the dealings with Pendelis were more like an obstacle course than negotiations, a group of Mossad representatives left for Istanbul to sign a contract with Vatan's owner. The day of their arrival, March 1, 1940, the press announced a new regulation prohibiting Turkish ships from being transferred to foreign owners. The law also required increased government supervision of the work carried out by the ships, in order to plan transportation resources during the war. The trip made by the Mossad people seemed to have been in vain, but they were told that the law was to be applied in time of emergency, and that since no such emergency had yet been proclaimed in Turkey, the law was not yet in force. They decided to go ahead and complete the deal.[10]

The owner of the "Vatan", after receiving an advance payment of $12,000, informed the Mossad that he was raising the price of the boat from $30,000 to $60,000. The Mossad agents, who wanted to guarantee that the ship would be put at their disposal, agreed to this as well, intending to transport a larger number of refugees on the ship to cover the new price. Since the purchase of the "Vatan" was to be carried out with the money from Czechoslovakia, Yeḥieli now contacted Y. Edelstein of the Czech Zionist Organization, asking for the rest of the money. The transfer of funds, however, was delayed, and the Mossad agents did not understand why. Only later did it become evident that these delays were deliberately caused by Storfer, who had been placed in charge of emigration from the Reich by the Germans.[11]

Without the Czech money the Mossad had insufficient resources to buy the "Vatan". The delay in payment was endangering the deal, and the Mossad agents searched feverishly for alternate financial sources. Meanwhile the Mossad office in Geneva received $35,000 from American Zionists, earmarked specifically for the Kladovo refugees. The question then arose as to whether this money could be used to acquire the "Vatan". This sum was inadequate to complete the purchase, nor would it enable the ship to be fitted out for transporting immigrants. On the other hand, it was sufficient to buy a smaller vessel capable of serving the Kladovo group alone. However, the Mossad was interested in the larger enterprise of which the Kladovo group would be a part.

The decision regarding the use of these funds was dependent upon the authority of those handling the money, and on the moral justification for its use — one way or another. Besides transferring money from one budgetary category to another, which seems to have been a mere formality, there was another problem connected with foreign currency regulations in Turkey. If the dollars were transferred to Turkey they could not be withdrawn, because it was impossible to take foreign currency out of Turkey even if it had been brought into the country with the intention of leaving it for only a short period of time. Thus, if and when the dollars were transferred to Turkey, they could not be transferred back to Geneva in case of a sudden collapse of the "Vatan" deal. It seemed to be easier to conclude the "Vatan" deal with Czech funds transferred from the Czech Central Bank. But if the Czech money did not arrive, despite promises, even the smaller vessel could not be purchased, and the Kladovo people would be stranded without a boat.

The dilemma was painful. Should the "Vatan" deal be endangered by waiting for the money from Czechoslovakia, or should the Kladovo money be risked by transferring it as part of the acquisition of the "Vatan"? In the complex situation then prevailing, a simple answer was not forthcoming. The dividing line between irresponsible speculation and successful maneuvering was very faint, and definitely not under the control of the Mossad agents. Those in charge tried to postpone a decision and to seek an interim solution.

Yeḥieli returned to Geneva and tried to guarantee the Turks their money without actually transferring the money to Turkey, but he failed. He had to make an immediate decision; the ship's owner would wait no longer, and further hesitation would lead to cancellation of the deal. Information from Prague was not clear. Yeḥieli summed up the affair as follows:

Though we had all agreed that everything should be done to avoid losing this ship, it was difficult to decide to transfer the money. Once again we contacted Dani and Kadmon who were in Istanbul. They explained that the completion of the deal was only a hair's breadth away from disaster, and that if the contract was not signed immediately, the ship might well be lost. On this basis we transferred to Istanbul all the money we had at our disposal, including the Joint's advance on the money for Danzig ($6,000) . . . I want to emphasize that we were all responsible for this decision, some hesitating more, others less. We all realized that in the situation we found ourselves, there was no choice. The money was transferred at the end of March.[12]

A few days after the transfer of the money something happened which had long been feared. A new obstacle (or perhaps more stringent implementation of existing regulations) prevented the transfer of the "Vatan" from its owner to Pendelis.[13] The available sources do not explain what the difficulty was, nor why it could not have been surmounted by fictitious transference of ownership or by leasing the ship under contract. Neither do we know why the obstacle was not foreseen, or whether immediate transfer of the money would have acquired the ship for the Mossad. All we know is that the Mossad was left with neither money to be used for another purpose nor a ship.

The failure of the deal aroused a series of negative reactions among those working with the Mossad and supporting its activities. In America the group's reliability became suspect, and this hindered further appeals for financial support. In Yugoslavia it caused deep depression and added to the tension between the Mossad and the Organization of Jewish Communities. The Yugoslav government pressed for the refugees to move on, the shipping company wanted its riverboats released, and there seemed to be no practical way for the potential immigrants to continue their journey. The representatives of the JDC who had until then supported the Mossad, were also in a difficult position, not knowing how to evaluate the reliability of the *aliyah* operations. And the Mossad people themselves were unable to undertake any serious negotiations for other vessels. Thus the month of April passed with no progress made, despite the opening of the Danube River to traffic. Throughout the German-occupied areas pressure increased to get Jews out, but there were no practical suggestions of how to do this.

In April Agami travelled to Kladovo to meet with the refugees. He felt the full weight of the Mossad's failure and of his responsibility. It was difficult for him to explain the simple truth to the Kladovo group. They had been all ready to set out when they received word of the "Vatan" fiasco, and they were depressed by the knowledge that they were at a dead end.[14] Agami assured them that he would keep trying to get a ship and promised them financial assistance. This can, to all intents, be viewed as the completion of one stage in the Kladovo affair. The agents of the Mossad now set out in a renewed assault on the ship market.

The "Darien" Enters the Picture — Rescue, War, and Political Maneuvering

The next stage of the story begins in May 1940, with Shemarya Zameret and Moshe Agami in Athens inspecting the ship later to be known as the "Darien 2". The ship flew a Panamanian flag and belonged to a retired sea-captain who wanted to sell it. Agami and Zameret negotiated with the man through Pendelis, who already owed the Mossad money from the advance paid in connection with the "Vatan" ($12,000). In order to buy the "Darien", which would cost some $60,000, money would have to be raised by the Zionist movement in the United States, and by the Jewish Agency. The $42,000 invested in the "Vatan" deal had not yet been returned to the Mossad. Small sums were being sent daily from Istanbul to Geneva, but most of the money was still in Turkey. The Mossad activists initiated a special fundraising campaign whose main purpose was to rescue the Kladovo group. After the "Darien" was repaired it would be able to transport most — but not all — of the group which now numbered 1,250. The series of cables sent to the Mossad centers in New York, Jerusalem and Geneva from May 22 on, reflect the anxiety that this deal would also fall through because of lack of funds. The feeling was that if this were to happen, the Kladovo problem might never be resolved.[15]

Anxiety grew with Italy's pending entry into the war. This could become a significant turning point. Could attempts to bring Jews to Palestine continue while the Mediterranean became an area of hostilities? The JDC made the transfer of money conditional upon the Mossad's guaranteeing a way to leave Yugoslavia, i.e., acquiring a ship.[16]

On May 28, 1940, a meeting was held in Bern between M. Troper and Saly Mayer of the JDC, representatives of the Agency, and the Mossad, on the subject of the Kladovo refugees. Yehieli spoke strongly against the JDC's refusal to provide the $45,000 needed to conclude the "Darien" deal. He warned that the Mossad would relinquish all responsibility for the Kladovo affair if the JDC's position did not change.[17]

On May 29, 1940, Agami informed Yehieli that the negotiations for the acquisition of the "Darien" were successful; Yehieli was to transfer $30,000 to Pendelis to conclude the deal. On May 31, Yehieli planned to transfer the money to Athens — but at the last moment he decided to consult first with Mossad headquarters in Tel Aviv. He cabled Palestine, asked their opinion about the transfer, and received a positive reply. The money was to be invested in the ship on the condition that Shemarya Zameret would be registered as its new owner. (His American passport made this possible.) On June 2,[18] the money was transferred and a few days later the "Darien" was purchased in the name of Zameret. Now it had to be fitted out for the transport of immigrants. Continued JDC participation in the expenditures was made conditional upon similar participation on the part of the Agency and the American Zionist institutions. In

229

answer to Yehieli's cable requesting the support of all the groups, E. Kaplan cabled (June 10, 1940)[19] that the Agency would pay its share, and thus guaranteed the resources for the rest of the enterprise. Towards the end of June, everyone hoped, the Kladovo refugees would board the "Darien" on their way to Palestine.

On June 10, 1940, Italy announced her entry into the war. This caused the Mossad agents and community leaders further problems. Agami cabled to Palestine for advice (June 13, 1940), and was told to halt *aliyah* plans and arrangements for the Kladovo group (June 14–15, 1940). Agami disagreed with the decision, realizing how deeply disappointed the refugees would be and how strongly they would question the reliability and sincerity of the Mossad in resolving the Kladovo affair. He also knew that other *aliyah* activists (such as Storfer in Vienna and Confino in Bulgaria) were continuing with their operations and that sea traffic in the Mediterranean was proceeding unhindered. He believed that there was still enough time to see the Kladovo affair to its conclusion. Knowing all this, Agami decided to go to Palestine in the last week of June and talk directly with the Mossad leaders there, in order to change their decision. Zameret, who was with him in Athens, and was now the legal owner of the "Darien", remained behind to maintain contact with shipping agents concerned with fitting out the "Darien" to carry the immigrants.[20]

Agami did not succeed in swaying the opinion of the Mossad agents. Nevertheless, a short time after his arrival in Palestine (July 17, 1940), the "Darien", which was intended for the Kladovo refugees, was transferred from the Mossad to Yehuda Arazi, for £15,000. Arazi was a Haganah member who was organizing sabotage work for the British and who sought to use the ship in cooperation with them.

How can one explain these two decisions — to halt *aliyah* plans and to transfer the "Darien" to Arazi? Were they related to one another; did the idea of transferring the ship to the Haganah for cooperation with the British influence the decision to halt the Kladovo affair in the middle of June? An answer to this question is essential if one is to understand the position of Mossad and Haganah leaders with regard to illegal immigration, in view of the enormous difficulties inherent in organizing such an operation during wartime. In seeking an answer one must also keep in mind the Mossad's moral and financial obligations to resolve the Kladovo affair, their difficulties in obtaining a ship suitable for illegal immigration before finding the "Darien", and what alternatives to illegal immigration existed. Finally, it should be noted that the decision to halt the arrangements for the Kladovo transport was taken by the Mossad and Haganah people in Palestine who, without a doubt, cared deeply for the physical safety of the immigrants, but whose opinions conflicted with those of the Mossad agents in Europe.

The sources provide three different answers to these questions; generally they do not link the two decisions. The decision to halt immigration was regarded as

230

temporary, pending an examination of the results of Italy's entering the war. Thus the sources are mainly concerned with the decision to sell the "Darien" for use in cooperation with the British. This was a very difficult question of conscience for the Mossad, and it was in this decision that Agami and Zeev Schind (a central figure in the Mossad) participated.

Two explanations were offered by the Mossad people regarding the transfer of the "Darien", one by Agami and one by Ruth Klüger-Aliav.[21] They claim that it was never intended to hand the ship over either to the British or to the "cooperation" group. The deal was a ploy to get money for Mossad activities from the British, while continuing to use the ship in defiance of their immigration policy. Schind offered another interpretation;[22] a new strategy for illegal immigration had been created. Since the same Haganah people were participating in both cooperation and illegal immigration operations, and since immigration had to be halted for the time being, they could play a double role and take advantage of their contacts with the British to advance illegal immigration operations. Whenever an immigration plan was likely to be endangered because of this double role, the goal of immigration was to be preferred. The "Darien" transfer was the first test of this strategy. It was adopted at a special meeting between Haganah, Mossad, and "cooperation" people in Jerusalem. The majority, among whom were Shertok and Golomb, approved of it; some, like Yehuda Braginsky (a veteran Mossad activist) opposed it.

A completely different explanation was offered by the two major "cooperation" people, Yehuda Arazi and David Hacohen.[23] They claimed that the transfer of the "Darien" was made because illegal immigration was not feasible. The Mossad needed money desperately and the transfer provided it. For several months, the cooperation people had been looking for a ship to be used for sabotage and espionage operations. Mossad people in Greece had helped in the search, but a good ship could not be found. The "Darien" would suit their requirements and they wanted to examine it. Hacohen and Arazi differ as to the specific plan designed for the "Darien" and their personal role in the transfer arrangement.

One version stressed the particular value of the "Darien" because it could be used for illegal immigration as well. The idea was to send the boat up the Danube with explosives and station it at the Iron Gate to block the traffic on the river. This would stop the regular supply of oil from Rumania to Germany. However, if the "Darian" were first to undertake an illegal immigration voyage, the Germans would not suspect that it was being used for sabotage, and thus its real purpose would be concealed. Whether this version is accepted or whether our conclusion — that there was no single specific program for the "Darien" that could be put into operation[24] — is considered more likely, an immediate problem arises. Could such divergent aims as illegal immigration and actual anti-German activities be carried out by the same people? Until then, Germany had encouraged the emigration of Jews, and this was what made the illegal immigration possible. But would they continue to permit the departure of Jews if this served to further anti-

German (i.e., pro-British) activity? The Mossad operatives were well aware of this dilemma; notwithstanding, they chose this dual line of action. Collaboration with the British, and immigration activities that defied them, were carried out by the very same people within a single institutional framework. Could such contradictory activities be combined without a conflict of interests? In the summer of 1940, after weighing the feasibility of immediate immigration and simultaneous cooperation with Britain for the duration of the war, the latter course of action seemed more practical. The rather small regional operations in which Hacohen's group was involved seemed to succeed. The services that Hacohen could render the British that summer were invaluable. The Haganah was very interested in supporting them. In case of open conflict, the guideline was that laid down by Berl Katzenelson: in every case, the rescue of Jews and their immigration to Palestine was to be preferred over any other goals.[25] How this guideline was implemented in the Kladovo–"Darien" affair can be seen in the next stage of the story.

Spring followed a long winter spent by the refugees in the riverboats in Kladovo, and then the hot summer days approached, making it almost unbearable to remain on the crowded vessels. It became imperative to improve the accommodations as the journey to Palestine no longer appeared to be imminent.

In July 1940 the Yugoslav government permitted the Kladovo group to disembark from the riverboats and move into a tent camp in the town.[26] This was a slight improvement in their situation. At the end of August they were moved to another transit camp near the town of Sabac, 225 kms. northwest of Kladovo on the Sava River, where they were housed in buildings. There they were able to establish a daily routine and organize social and cultural activities.

The greatest immediate enemy of the Kladovo group was idleness. They were not permitted to work and only occasional temporary employment in town was available. Many were depressed and could only see a dead-end ahead. Jewish Agency efforts to obtain certificates to Palestine for them in order to legalize their immigration did not succeed, and promises to get some of the young people out with Youth Aliyah (a special immigration program for children between the ages of 11 and 16) dragged on until March 1941. Relations between the refugees deteriorated as despair intensified and hoped faded. The leaders of the community pleaded for help.[27]

During the summer of 1940, too, the use of the "Darien" remained in limbo. Throughout these months the hesitations of the Mossad operatives regarding the purpose for which the ship was to be devoted are clearly discernible, as is the apparent obscurity of the plans of the British and their Palestinian partners. The agent of the maritime company "He-Atid", which represented the new owners of the "Darien", arrived in Piraeus to examine the boat and arrange for its departure for Alexandria. He did not seem to be very interested and was totally inefficient. This aroused heretical thoughts in Zameret's mind. Perhaps, in spite of everything, the fate of the "Darien" had not been finally determined? Maybe his colleagues in Palestine had changed their minds in light of the situation in Kladovo, the sailing conditions in the Mediterranean, and the fact that independent organizers were carrying on with their *aliyah* activity? (The "Libertad", a ship carrying an immigrant group organized by Dr. Confino, arrived in Palestine in July 1940.) Shemarya Zameret impatiently cabled Palestine on August 7, 1940:

> The ship has not yet been dispatched. The He-Atid company is doing nothing about it. Cable if the ship has been leased to He-Atid or to the Spitzer company. I have to know for future arrangements.

But his hopes were to be dashed. The reply was clear: "The contract with He-Atid is in force. Concerning Spitzer, we are trying to renew our contacts."[28]

Zameret, familiar with the shipping market, knew that without the "Darien" the chances of rescuing the Kladovo group were small. He repeated his arguments on August 11, 1940, and five days later he was instructed to send the "Darien"[29] as quickly as possible to Alexandria![30] Zameret carried out his instructions and in approximately another ten days[31] the "Darien" left the port of Piraeus.

Two months after the decision to stop all *aliyah* activity (June 1940), a new decision was taken in Palestine — to renew it. Apparently the motivating factor for this shift was the Kladovo group.[32] Lacking primary data regarding the session (or other forum) at which this new resolution was adopted, one may only assume that the reasons were both subjective — the loss of prestige in the eyes of world Jewry which viewed the Kladovo debacle as a failure of the Mossad and the Zionist movement, and objective — a sense of responsibility and an obligation to resolve the problem. The continuing activities of other *aliyah* groups also contributed to this decision.

Yehuda Braginsky, one of the most experienced Mossad operatives, who had not been involved previously in the Kladovo affair, was called to duty. The Mossad team had shrunk and Braginsky had to reorganize it, this time from Istanbul where, after Italy's entry into the war, the opening of the Western Front, and the uncertainty concerning the fate of Switzerland, it was more convenient to work. As far as *aliyah* was concerned, too, the departure from Rumanian or Bulgarian ports made Istanbul a most convenient site for organizational activities. Braginsky was told by Golomb that the Mossad was obligated to bring the Kladovo people to Palestine and that a ship was ready for this purpose. The ship was in Alexandria at the moment, but would shortly be in Istanbul. He, Golomb, would get the money for the voyage from the Zionists in the United States.[33]

233

The Final Stage of the Kladovo Rescue: Plans vs. Reality

At this point the attempts to rescue the Kladovo group entered a new phase. Braginsky thought that matters would now develop in a seemingly simple fashion and the group would surely be saved. However, as things turned out, several months later the "Darien" had yet to reach a spot where it could pick up the

Kladovo refugees! And when it finally did reach Sulina, in December 1940, the Kladovo group could not meet the ship. How and why did matters take such a turn?

It is a story of delays, mistrust and misconceptions concerning the urgency of the situation. The first delay concerned the foreign currency needed for the purchase of coal for the "Darien". The $14,000 needed was expected to come from Zionist Federations in the United States. But they thought that they had given the money for the "Darien" long ago (the purchase of the "Vatan"). Unable to follow the events in detail, they were unwilling to send money again unless Spitzer made a direct request for it. The Americans feared it might evaporate in the general Mossad budget, as had happened before, and the Kladovo people would remain behind.

Spitzer was asked by Braginsky to request the money, but he too was hesitant. He had been hit by the Mossad's retreat over transport during the summer and was struggling daily in order to provide sustenance for the refugees. How would a plea to finance the Mossad plan affect his resources? Spitzer did not know the exact story behind the disappearance of the "Darien". He was bitter in his criticism of the Mossad's handling of the situation. Golomb, knowing this, felt that a meeting between Braginsky and Spitzer would be of the utmost importance, and Braginsky was instructed to meet Spitzer shortly after arriving in Istanbul. However, the meeting failed to materialize because it was difficult for Spitzer to obtain a visa to Turkey and for Braginsky to get to Bulgaria. This failure to meet and discuss face-to-face the chances for the departure of the Kladovo group and the possible dangers, was to play a crucial role in the unfolding of events. Much of the mistrust could have been avoided had Spitzer and the Mossad people met early in the fall of 1940.

Finally, Spitzer appealed to the Zionist Organization in the United States to send the necessary funds, and expressed his readiness to deduct the money from the aid to be sent for the Kladovo refugees. The money arrived in Istanbul a month after the arrival of the "Darien" and Braginsky (late October). On November 2, the boat, loaded with coal, left for Constanza. It was now believed that two or three weeks would suffice to outfit her to carry the refugees. However, there was another delay while the "Darien" brought 160 legal immigrants from Constanza to Istanbul, where they changed for another ship to Palestine.[34]

Why was this trip made when time was running out for the Kladovo transport? There was only one month before the Danube was expected to freeze over as had happened the previous year. No more time was available for working on the safety precautions for the trip, so why were not all efforts directed solely towards finalizing the Kladovo affair? The sources fail to provide a satisfactory reason. Budgetary constraints, and political uncertainty regarding Germany's intervention in Greece made the trip attractive.[35] It also meant that the "Darien" was not in Constanza during the first week of November which the aliyah organizers felt to be risky.

Spitzer was taken by surprise by the Constanza — Istanbul voyage. He had made preparations for the group to leave at the beginning of November. They had split up into smaller groups, appointed group leaders and arranged their belongings. Twice, on November 9 and November 11, the group was told that they would leave in a few hours and would be in Sulina within six days. But twice the planned departure was delayed. Spitzer ordered a postponement after he learned of the delay in the Darien's preparations, which only served to confirm his doubts about the Mossad's reliability and the sincerity of its desire to solve the Kladovo problem.

Spitzer was not prepared to transport the refugees down the Danube unless there was a boat waiting for them in Sulina. He was not going to put them at risk by allowing their ultimate departure from or stay in Sulina to become a means of pressure on the Mossad. Messages regarding the obstacles and delays to the departure of the "Darien" from Constanza were reaching him, and he waited for information that the ship was waiting in Sulina harbor.[36]

Spitzer's attitude was based on past experience, but it resulted in the failure of the Kladovo group to be in Sulina when the "Darien" did arrive there at the beginning of December. (It could have been the last few days of November — the exact dates are hard to trace.) Nor were the refugees on board on December 29 when the "Darien" returned to Constanza after waiting in Sulina almost a month. How did this happen?

In a report to the JDC and to Naḥum Goldmann,[37] Spitzer listed the events of December until the moment he decided against sending the group. In brief, the report explained that a chain of faulty planning, on the part of both Spitzer and the Mossad agents, led to the repeated postponement of the refugees' trip down the river. The months of November and December were very difficult from the point of view of illegal immigration. Two major disasters had occurred. One, on November 25, was the sinking of the "Patria" in Haifa harbor. The boat was packed with Jewish refugees whom the British planned to expel to Mauritius. This tragedy took the lives of more than 200 people. The second disaster occurred shortly after (December 11), when the "Salvador" sank in the Sea of Marmara with more than 300 refugees abroad. This boatload had been organized by the veteran private illegal immigration activist, Baruch Confino, of Bulgaria.

These incidents further weakened Spitzer's confidence in the illegal immigration system. The conclusion he reached in December 1940 was that the refugees were better off in Yugoslavia than on board the "Darien", as long as their final entry into Palestine was still in doubt.[38]

What was the faulty planning referred to by Spitzer? The refugees were scheduled to leave for Sulina on December 2, 1940,[39] in two Yugoslav riverboats. They had already begun to board the boats when the shipping company demanded an enormous financial bond because of the hazards of the journey along the 100 km. Bulgarian frontier, and the danger of the river freezing over. The company also demanded government guarantees which were not

235

forthcoming. On December 5, 1940,[40] the company cancelled its contract and the refugees were compelled to disembark and return to the Sabac camp. An alternative plan was then worked out. The people would travel by train to Prahavo on the Yugoslav-Bulgarian border, and from there continue on a tugboat ("Remorcor") along the river to Sulina. The tugboat would be in Prahavo on December 12, Spitzer was told, and he should lease a train to transport the refugees there. Spitzer found that he could have the use of a train on December 13. On Friday, December 13, the members of the group Sabac packed their belongings again and prepared to board the train. The journey seemed imminent. In the evening, a 24-hour delay was reported in the "Remorcor"'s arrival in Sulina; that day too the first word of the "Salvador" and "Patria" disasters reached Spitzer. His hesitations and fears increased. The winter grew colder, the dangers became more numerous, and the tugboat postponed its arrival at Prahavo by another 24 hours, and then again.

Finally, on December 16, word arrived that the tug was waiting at Pravaho. On December 17, the food and refugee–laden coaches were instructed to set out at four the following morning. The December 18 newspapers carried stories of the freezing of the Danube. Again Spitzer hesitated — should he send the people on or not? He decided to summon a session of the Jewish community leaders to take a collective decision. The meeting was set for the following day. But that morning Alexander Shapira (the Mossad's contact in Rumania) sent word that the captain of the tug had been instructed to return to Rumania because of the condition of the river. The tug had waited for its passengers in Prahavo from midday on December 16, until the morning of the 19th. Since the refugees had not arrived, it turned about and returned safely to Rumania. On December 20, Spitzer travelled from Belgrade to Sabac to inform the people of the cancellation of the trip.

Thus, at the last moment, once again, the group's voyage fell through, after the "Darien" had waited for the refugees over twenty days. This time it was the judgment of those in Yugoslavia that resulted in the cancellation of the journey. This is what Spitzer wrote in his report to the JDC:

> ... We must consider thoroughly if, after the last attempt, and in view of the unambiguous decision of the British authorities to deport the people, there still is justification for such trips. To travel just for the sake of travelling, to use Jewish money just to get to Mauritius, or to any other colony in the Indian Ocean — this cannot be the purpose of our efforts. Thus it is better for the people to wait here until the opportunity arises to reunite them with their relatives. Naturally, we shall see how things develop in the spring.[41]

In this report, Spitzer does not mention that he wrote to Ruth Klüger–Aliav that Shapira had informed him on December 20, 1940, of *another tugboat* ready to transfer the people, urging that they be sent immediately. But Spitzer reasoned that there was no way the people could arrive on time. Moreover, the tug flew the Greek flag, and Spitzer doubted that the Rumanian authorities would permit it to enter the Sulina harbor. And, if the immigrants were to board the tugboat, the Yugoslav government would not permit their return if problems arose.

The "Darien" waited for the Kladovo refugees until December 29, when it received instructions to leave for Constanza and pick up other immigrants. The Kladovo refugees' despair was profound; they sought aid from Storfer and the heads of the Jewish community,[42] but in vain. Nor did the Mossad renew its activity on their behalf. The people remained in Yugoslavia, awaiting the spring. Perhaps then they would be rescued. However, the Nazi invasion of Yugoslavia on April 6, 1941, preceded the coming of spring. The Kladovo refugees served as hostages, and were the first group of Jews in Yugoslavia to be murdered by the Germans, in September 1941, in retaliation for an act of sabotage perpetrated in the area.[43] The tragic end of this affair would become, to some community leaders, symbolic of the failures of the Mossad in its program of illegal immigration.

Renewed Dispute over the "Darien"

The complications of the "Darien" affair did not come to an end with the conclusion of the story of Kladovo. While the "Darien" was anxiously waiting for the arrival of the Kladovo refugees at Sulina, throughout the month of December 1940, the question of the ownership of the vessel cropped up once again. Were the Mossad operatives actually entitled to use the ship for the purposes of illegal immigration? In mid-December, Yehuda Arazi and David Hacohen demanded that the ship be returned to them. Hacohen and Arazi needed the ship again for sabotage operations on the Danube. Some of the plans that had been mentioned in the summer of that year were being revived.

Both Arazi and Hacohen claimed that they had a concrete task for the ship and that its execution was extremely important for the overall chances of cooperation with the British. But again they referred to more than one plan.[44] Both were very uneasy about the long period during which the boat was under the Mossad control, and were most impatient to get it back right away. The boat belonged to the British, they claimed, who had consented to lend it to the Mossad since it could serve both their need to camouflage the "Darien" and immigration; but now the boat was needed and should be returned instantly. The fact that the "Darien" was waiting for the Kladovo people could not change the situation. They were willing to think of an alternative solution for the refugees, or help in getting another boat, but the "Darien" had to be returned.

Arazi and Hacohen came to the Mossad with their unacceptable demands during the most dramatic moments of the Kladovo affair. Every other day the chances of getting the group out either seemed successful or fell through. The legal argument about the ownership of the vessel seemed irrelevant. Hacohen and Arazi, angry and aggressive, appealed to the central leadership in Palestine for help. At that point, the conflict of interest between the Haganah leadership and the

237

Mossad, who served within the two frameworks of immigration and cooperation, became crucial. Eliahu Golomb knew of the struggle to rescue the Kladovo people, and the obstacles in the way of "cooperation" because of the hesitation, for political reasons, of the British. He could not maneuver any longer between both sides, but had to decide clearly to support one or the other.

Golomb did not adhere to the guideline laid down by Katzenelson the previous summer, which stated that in case of conflict priority should always be given to immigration. On December 27, 1940 he called Braginsky in Istanbul and informed him that the "Darien" should be returned to Arazi.[45] The conflict shifted back to the people operating directly in the field. Braginsky would not agree, and he answered accordingly.[46] But others who were involved directly in both operations, like Ruth Klüger–Aliav, faced a more difficult dilemma. They were authorized by the Haganah to act on both fronts, and were obligated formally and morally to obey the instructions of the proper leadership. Could they have opposed a clear and direct order from Golomb to hand the ship over? They had neither the knowledge nor the right to evaluate the relative feasibility or importance of one course of action as against another. They could plead the Kladovo cause and claim that their moral responsibility towards the Kladovo people and other refugees awaiting rescue was supreme. But in the end they would have to accept Golomb's decision and act on it. It was very difficult to put Katzenelson's guideline into practice.

Arazi and Hacohen pressed vehemently. Many months of effort and planning for cooperation with the British were involved, and personal ambitions were at stake. Could all this be set aside because of the stubbornness of some immigration fanatics? Under the prevailing circumstances, no large-scale immigration could take place; but in the long run, should cooperation be achieved, the chances for Zionism and for immigration were enormous. Must these be sacrificed because of the shortsightedness of a few extremists? It was a bitter struggle. Meetings were arranged at which the arguments flew back and forth. Envoys from Palestine were sent to try to resolve the dilemma through consensus.

The "Darien" left Sulina on December 29 without the Kladovo group. On board were 160 refugees from Rumania, and in Constanza others who had learned that the boat was not full were waiting. Braginsky was fully determined not to hand the ship over to Arazi and Hacohen regardless of the Kladovo failure. The 160 refugees on board had no other place to go but Palestine, and their lives were his responsibility. Ruth Klüger–Aliav, Z. Schind and S. Zameret, perplexed and frustrated, were moving from one position to the other. The drama heightened when the "Darien", on its way from Sulina to Constanza, ran aground and was in danger of sinking. Feverish rescue efforts to save the refugees and to prevent the ship from being lost were successful, but the "Darien" was badly damaged and needed repairs.

At this unfortunate moment, David Hacohen summoned the entire Mossad team to a dramatic meeting and read cables which he had received from Moshe

Sharett and Chaim Weizmann[47] casting doubt on the chances of cooperation with the British if the "Darien" affair failed. Hacohen appealed to the Mossad operatives to stop the "Darien" voyage, take off the 160 immigrants, and hand the ship over to him. David Hacohen won his struggle at this session.

On January 5, 1941, Yehuda Arazi sent a cable to Palestine[48] stating that the problem had been resolved and that he would be acquiring the "Darien" shortly. However, Arazi could relax for only a short time. Not one of the Mossad operatives in Istanbul, regardless of his position at the above meeting, was prepared to put the decision into practice and call on the refugees to leave the boat. Braginsky relates:

> Three days later Ruth phoned and asked to see me. She asked what the future had in store. I asked her if she was willing to continue the *aliyah* project together with me, on condition that she did not back down but go along with me to the bitter end . . .[49]

Ruth agreed and preparations for the trip continued. The "Darien" was repaired in Constanza, and 500 additional refugees were readied for the voyage. On January 31, 1941, Braginsky sent this wire:

> The management has decided to carry on business without interruption. At the same time you are requested to try to come to an agreement with Yehuda [Arazi — D.O.]. If there are difficulties or delays, Kadmon will join you soon. It is imperative to carry on.[50]

The following two weeks until the "Darien" left Constanza on February 19, were characterized by feverish preparations. The additional immigrants boarded, provisions were stored, etc. Meanwhile, Schind went to Sofia to organize another group of 300 immigrants there and to make the necessary arrangements to ensure the voyage. He also arranged to chain an engineless hulk, the "Struma", to the "Darien", which would enable another 350 refugees to be transported. Schind

Illegal immigrants under British guard in Haifa port

239

almost succeeded in these negotiations, but the German invasion of Bulgaria obliged the "Darien" to depart hastily, without the "Struma". The ship finally left Varna on February 27, 1941, and arrived at Istanbul on March 3, anchoring there for seven days. Forty survivors of the "Salvador" and a number of refugees from Poland and Czechoslovakia boarded the ship there.

All this time David Hacohen was still trying to find a solution for the several hundred refugees on board the "Darien" in order to release it for his own purposes. In his letter to Jerusalem[51] he mentions alternatives such as disembarking in Egypt, in Benghazi, in the Greek islands, in Athens, or even in other places. But once again stark necessity was decisive, and on March 10, 1941, the "Darien" put out to sea on its way to Palestine. On March 19 it was captured by the British and confiscated — essentially returning it to its legal owners [the British].

The illegal immigrants were placed in a detention camp at Athlit (near Haifa) for a year and a half. This, then, was the end of the tragic odyssey of the "Darien" — filled with failures, and one single success — rescuing 786 refugees from Rumania, Poland and Bulgaria.

Conclusion

The Kladovo–"Darien" affair came to an end. The boat failed to achieve its original goal, to carry the Kladovo refugees to safety — but it did take others to Palestine. The Kladovo group was left behind to wait for another opportunity, another boat, but this did not transpire.

At each stage of the affair we see how close the refugees were to being rescued and how in fact they were not. The line dividing success from failure and life from death was very fine. It was woven by human actions and decisions, through deliberate calculation and manipulation of reality. In historical perspective we can regard some of these decisions as human errors. At least three times during the history of the voyage the people were close to final rescue. Had they reached the Black Sea in the winter of 1939 they would have joined the three thousand people stranded during those months on other boats (the "Sakariya" and the "Hilda") and would probably have reached Palestine during the first months of 1940. In June 1940 and again in December, they were very close to completing the voyage, but on both occasions considerations either of safety or of relatively less danger guided the decisions that prevented the voyage from being concluded. In June and July 1940, the Mossad's decision to halt immigration and to sell the "Darien" were major obstacles to the rescue of the refugees. In September and October 1940, after preparations to move the Kladovo group were resumed, the "Darien" was still not completely relieved of other responsibilities. Twice the Mossad people failed to realize the urgency of bringing the voyage to an end as quickly as possible as the war situation in the Mediterranean and Southern Europe became more unstable.

240

The loss of time in the summer of 1940 and again in October, when the "Darien" made an extra trip with legal immigrants to Istanbul, deeply injured the credibility of the Mossad. Spitzer understood the delay in October as representing a non-committal attitude on the part of the Mossad people. This interpretation, together with the tragic fate of illegal immigrants in Haifa harbor in November 1940, were responsible for the extra-cautious behavior of Spitzer that prevented the departure of the refugees for Sulina where the "Darien" was waiting throughout most of December 1940. Was this simply shortsightedness on Spitzer's behalf?

The ambivalence of Zionist policy towards illegal immigration was demonstrated in the clash between Arazi and Hacohen, and the Mossad, during December 1940 and January 1941. The orders from Tel Aviv were in conflict with the goals as understood by Braginsky when he was sent to resume illegal immigration. They collided also with the moral commitment to rescue. Although the Kladovo group did not reach the "Darien", the boat was still needed for illegal operations, for many refugees in Bulgaria and Rumania were desperately waiting for transport. In reality, it was very difficult to cooperate with Great Britain in the war effort, and to act against it in illegal immigration.

The conflict had far-reaching effects on Mossad work in the following months. The people in Istanbul acted against a direct order from the central leadership; this raised the question of discipline and obedience to the legitimate authority. One could dispute a policy decided upon by the authorities, but one could not disregard it — not even the dedicated Mossad operatives. Most activists in Istanbul agreed with this concept, but alas, they acted differently. Although the "Darien" did complete an immigration voyage, the dispute over the boat shook the Istanbul group to such an extent that they did not continue with illegal immigration operations thereafter. The Mossad did not resume serious work in Istanbul until two years later.

The misgivings and hesitations over illegal immigration during the war grew stronger as a result of the Kladovo failure and the "Darien" conflict. The possible connection between illegal immigration and the rescue of European Jewry had to wait for a period of close to two years before it could take form.

Translated by Yoel Lerner and the author.

---

1   The details of the Kladovo refugee affair are known from a number of major sources:
a) Letters sent by members of the group recounting their experiences, in the CAHJP (Central Archives for the History of the Jewish People), the Vienna Archives, AW/2515; Storfer's material (Storfer was a Jew whom the Germans had put in charge of immigrants from the Reich in 1939), in CAHJP; CZA L22 (Geneva files); Yad Vashem Archives, Jerusalem; JDC Archives, New York City.
b) Reports sent by the leaders of the Yugoslav Jewish community pertaining to the group, mainly to the JDC and the Agency to request funds. They are to be found in the JDC Archives L6–43, and in the CZA, L-15, L-22.

c) Storfer's correspondence with the JDC concerning the group, in the Vienna Archives (CAHJP).

d) Ehud Avriel, *Open the Gates* (Hebrew), (Tel Aviv, 1979), oral testimony, the Institute of Contemporary Jewry; interview with Avriel in the fall of 1979; Avriel's letter to Storfer referring to financial difficulties following the departure of the group (December 28, 1939), in the Vienna Archives.

e) Agami's testimony, Haganah Archive (HHA) 14/3033.

f) The Yeḥieli report, HHA 14/153.

The primary sources do not reconstruct the story. Only Ehud Avriel tries to do so in his book and his testimony. He refers only to the first stage of the affair, the group's departure from Vienna until its arrival at Kladovo. The responsibility for the reconstruction of the experiences of the group is the author's alone, and the possibility of minor errors cannot be overlooked.

2   The boat which was assigned to take the group from the Black Sea to Palestine was known by the name of the "Dreamer". It was offered to the Mossad agent after difficulties in regaining another ship, the "Dora", that the Mossad had leased. The "Dreamer" was offered by the Greek Vernikos family who owned a small shipping company and worked with Mossad people in 1939.

3   The deportation of German Jews to Lublin was part of a large-scale German plan to concentrate and isolate the Jews in a Jewish enclave in the Nisko-Lublin area. This was to lead to the eventual extermination of the Jews. Their disappearance would be a "natural" result of their lack of a "healthy body" which caused the Jews to exist as parasites throughout Europe. The first groups of Jews sent to Lublin came from Vienna and Prague. The people arrived at a site lacking minimal living conditions and basic provisions for human habitation in the future. Viennese and Prague community leaders who visited Lublin returned wholly stunned by what they had seen, and did everything in their power to prevent a continuation of the deportations there. One group left the "Protektorat" on October 18, with 1,000 people. Two groups left Vienna, one of 912 people on October 20, and the other, of 672 people, on October 26. The Germans stopped this project at the end of October because of organizational difficulties, and not because of the intervention or opposition of Jewish community leaders.

4   At that time some 3,000 refugees were concentrated in Rumania. More than 2,000 were organized by the Revisionist immigration center and would emigrate on the "Sakariya" in February 1940. Another 700 were organized by the Mossad and would leave for Palestine on the "Hilda" in January 1940.

5   For a wider discussion of this topic, see Dalia Ofer, *Illegal Immigration to Palestine during the Second World War 1939–1942* (Hebrew, unpublished dissertation, The Hebrew University, Jerusalem, 1981), chapter 1.

6   This was declared in a very important speech of Berl Katzenelson's in the last session of the Zionist Congress in August 1939. (B. Katzenelson, *Writings*, 9 (Hebrew) (Tel Aviv, 1948), pp. 61–82.

7   In September 1939 the British captured the "Tiger Hill", "Parita" and "Naomi Julia", confiscated the ships and jailed the crews. Such action deterred people from concluding deals with immigration agents. For further discussion on British policy, see Ofer (above, n. 5), part 3, chap. 1.

8   Dr Baruch Confino, an optometrist, a member of the Zionist movement in Bulgaria, organized Aliyah Bet from Bulgaria as a private individual.

9   The most detailed source for a description of progress of the "Vatan" deal is the Yeḥieli report, HHA 14/153, which was written about six months after the actual events and is, generally speaking, extremely reliable. Another source is a group of letters, *ibid.*, Shamir file 4195 I, asking the Zionist organizations in the United States for help in financing the deals. These letters from October 1939 to April 1940 are an important though fragmentary source for the "Vatan" affair as well. References to the "Vatan" are to be found in the Storfer material in CAHJP, AW 2515, especially where he is apologetic regarding himself, yet on the offensive regarding the Mossad — mainly in his correspondence with the JDC. A comparative analysis of the sources proves their reliability and clarifies the story. The "Vatan" affair is also referred to in Ruth Klüger–Aliav's book, *The Last Escape*, (Tel Aviv, 1974), but this is later evidence

which has undergone reworking. I refer *infra* to the above first three sources without mentioning this for each detail.

10 From Storfer's correspondence, CAHJP AW 2515, in a letter dated March 31, 1940, it is clear that negotiations for the "Vatan" were initiated by a Jewish organization engaged in illegal immigration. The negotiations were carried out with the Slovakian Danube Company "Cedock", and involved a Jewish agent named Ḥayyimovitzi who was somehow connected with He-Ḥalutz in Prague. Storfer calls the man a cheat and a pig, saying that at the last moment the Turkish goverment forbade the sale of the "Vatan" because of the confiscation of the "Sakariya" in Palestine. From British documentation as well, we know that the Turkish Foreign Office demanded that the British return the "Sakariya", promising to warn Turkish ship-owners to refrain from renting their ships for illegal immigration. In his report, the British Consul in Istanbul, Morgan, quotes the Turkish government regulation of March, concerning the supervision of Turkish ships in times of emergency, PRO CO733/429, April 4, 1940.

11 Storfer himself categorically denies that his actions in any way affected the failure of the "Vatan" deal. He views this as a rude accusation levelled at him by the Mossad agents who opposed him and tried to persuade the Joint not to support him. At the same time the delays in transferring the funds resulting from Storfer's various demands for supervising the ship, the sale, etc., certainly delayed execution of the deal. Such a delay, under the unstable conditions of the time, could easily lead to cancellation. On Storfer and Mossad relations see Dalia Ofer, "The Rescue of European Jewry and Illegal Immigration: Possibility and Reality," (Hebrew), *Yahadut Zemanenu* 1 (1983):179–199; (English), *Modern Judasim* (1984):159–181. See Storfer report, April 7, 1940, CAHJP AW 2514.

12 HHA, the Yeḥieli Report 14/153.

13 *Ibid.*, and CAHJP AW 2515, Mitteilung 48, April 7, 1940 where it is clear from Storfer's comment that the people already on board the Danube boats on their way to the Black Sea were compelled to turn back: "Das turkische Schiff scheint nicht zu sein. Die Kladover Leute waren bereits der Donau ausgefahren und mussten zurückkehren. Man kann sich vorstellen welche Depression dadurch enstanden ist." From this one sees how certain the Mossad agents were of the "Vatan" deal — so certain that they were willing to set a departure date for the Black Sea and a rendezvous with the ship. This strengthens Yeḥieli's statement that the cancellation was a completely unexpected surprise for them.

14 HHA, Agami Oral Testimony 3033 and CAHJP AW 2515, and Mitteilung 50, April 15, 1940 and letters quoted by Storfer May 5, 1940 and May 19, 1940.

15 HHA, Shamir file 4195 I, Yeḥieli and Lichtheim to New York, June 9, 1940; cables from Moshe to Mereminsky, May 22 and May 30, 1940.

16 The transfer of funds from the JDC to the Mossad was required at the same time that Storfer demanded large sums to purchase the three ships. The JDC pressured to solve the travel problem of the Kladovo group with the help of Storfer. Storfer may have been ready to do this, but his hands were tied by the Nazis who wanted people to leave the Reich itself and not only adjacent countries.

17 HHA 14/153, Shamir files 4195 I.

18 A precise reconstruction of dates in this matter is very difficult. The material at our disposal consists of cables, sometimes with the date not marked, or unintelligible. A comparative analysis of cables to Palestine and to the United States led to the afore-mentioned reconstruction, and a comparison of this with the Yeḥieli report strengthened my case. At the same time, the report — composed approximately two months later — may err by a day or two. From two letters cited in Storfer's report, the acquisition of the "Darien" seems to have been at the end of May (CAHJP AW 2515, May 29, 1940). If the dates of the letters Storfer mentions are correct — May 19, 1940 — then the events we mentioned must have taken place a week to ten days earlier. In any case, these points do not lead to substantial changes in the details or in the development of the story.

19 HHA, Shamir files 4195 I.

20 *Ibid.*, and Yeḥieli report 14/153, and Agami oral testimony 3033.

21 *Ibid.*, and interview with Ruth Aliav, Tel Aviv, 1976.

22 HHA, Schind oral testimony 3031.

243

23 HHA, Arazi oral testimony, and David Hacohen, *My Time (Time to Tell)* (Hebrew), (Tel Aviv, 1974).

24 This conclusion was reached after careful examination of conflicting accounts regarding the "Darien"'s tasks. The two different versions appear in two separate testimonies of Arazi's in 1949 and 1954, and in Hacohen (above, n. 23). HHA contains a great deal of material, mainly cables sent by the participants in the affair.

25 Oral History Department, Institute of Contemporary Jewry, The Hebrew University, Jerusalem; Yeḥieli testimony; HHA, Schind testimony 3031.

26 This was achieved after Sima Spitzer promised the government in Yugoslavia that the refugees would be receiving immigration certificates through the Jewish Agency. CZA L15/324, Barlas to Spitzer.

27 Letters from the family and friends of the Kladovo people in Vienna and Palestine are the main sources for the reconstruction of life in Kladovo and Sabac. The letters are scattered throughout CZA, HHA, CAHJP. One of the most important collections comprises 40 letters in the Yad Vashem archives. Many letters were left with families and some of them are of great interest to the historian.

28 HHA, Shamir file 4195 I, Zameret to Ovdim (Arazi), August 3, 1940.

29 *Ibid.*

30 *Ibid.*, August 8.

31 There is no mention of the exact date of the boat's departure, but from the contents of the cables, it can definitely be concluded that the "Darien" left between August 24 and 28. David Hacohen's denial that the "Darien" was ever sent to Alexandria cannot be accepted.

32 See HHA, Shamir file 4195 I, Braginsky to Saharov, October 16, 1940. In this letter Braginsky refers to the decision to resume work in the following sentence: "Many things encouraged us to resume activities, as you surely understand, but one was the prestige of Zionism in America . . ." The letter reflects the hesitations, the debate and the decision relating to a resumption of activity. An attempt to establish the date of the decision shows that it is connected with the announcement of the date of Yehuda Braginsky's trip to help Zameret, i.e. mid-August, as Schind says in his letter, HHA 14/209. In a series of telegrams on this subject during the summer of 1940 and through mid-September, mention is made of a ship called "Darlington" costing £20,000.

33 Braginsky, *A Nation Seeking a Haven* (Hebrew), (Tel Aviv, 1979), p. 260; also his letter to Saharov, October 16, 1940; HHA, Shlomo Shamir file, 4195 I.

34 This event is missing from all oral testimonies and recollections of Mossad activists in Istanbul. However, it is confirmed by two independent sources: a list of boats leaving Rumania between November 1940 and December 1944 (CZA S25/2493), and the German Consul in Istanbul, Yad Vashem Archives JM/3141, November 7, 1940.

35 JDC Archives, Turkey 15–32, Ruth Klüger–Aliav to Spitzer, February 13, 1941.

36 CZA L22/14, Spitzer to Ruth Klüger–Aliav, December 12, 1940.

37 *Ibid.*, January 9. 1941. A shorter version of the report in English translation, JDC Archives 15–32.

38 *Ibid.*, Spitzer to Ruth Klüger–Aliav, December 23, 1940.

39 *Ibid.*, also CAHJP AW 2515, two letters from a Kladovo refugee, December 3 and 8, 1940.

40 CZA L22/14, Spitzer to Ruth Klüger–Aliav, December 23, 1940. Also PRO FO371/12114, Campbell (British Embassy in Belgrade) to Foreign Office, December 20, 1940.

41 JDC Archives 15–32, January 9, 1941.

42 CAHJP AW 2515, letters from Sabac, December 3 and 8, 1940.

43 The fate of the Kladovo group in Sabac is described in depth in a forthcoming paper by H. Wiener.

44 HHA, Arazi testimonies, Hacohen (above, n. 23), p. 162.

45 *Ibid.*, 14/209, Golomb to Braginsky.

46 *Ibid.*, December 29, 1940, Braginsky to Golomb.

47 Braginsky (above, n. 33), p. 282.

48 HHA 14/209.

49 Braginsky (above, n. 33), p. 282.

50 HHA 14/209.

51 ZA S25/3124, to Reuven, signed D., undated. The letter expresses disappointment at the failure of the "Darien" affair, but regards this with resignation. The people cannot be taken off the ship. The agent of British Intelligence (Major Taylor of S02) is not in Istanbul to help David Hacohen: "I wrote you in my last letter that I wanted to find a solution together with the tailor, i.e. with his assistance, to remove the goods from the ship immediately after it left the straits, and to do this with the help of the British diplomatic and naval authorities. I wanted to suggest they be put off in Palestine, or maybe Egypt or Benghazi but if not, then in Greece or on the islands. Nothing came of all this because of his [the tailor's — D.O.] absence from here and because of the order from Cairo not to involve HMG. With his help I could have hoped to be able to ignore this decree, but since my arrival he has not been here; on the contrary, he should be in your area."

David Hacohen revealed that he travelled to Istanbul knowing there was no chance of changing the situation, but nonetheless hoping. What was left was as follows: "At any rate, we are obliged to do everything to resume activities and present the tailor with a fait accompli and search for ways *at least to save face and the future of our work*. [My emphasis — D.O.] From the letter, we see that Hacohen was, without a doubt, very worried about the "Darien" affair, and truly feared that this act might rule out further cooperation with the British. His personal disappointment was profound.

PALESTINIAN JEWRY AND THE JEWISH AGENCY: PUBLIC RESPONSE TO THE HOLOCAUST

DINA PORAT

*H*istorical research on the behavior of the free world in the face of the Holocaust has dealt quite extensively with the relationship between humane activity and political realism, often pointing to the preeminence of the latter. Similar conclusions have been reached in the case of certain Jewish organizations in the thirties and forties.

The Palestine situation posed a particular dilemma: How did the Zionist leaders of varying viewpoints incorporate the yishuv's deep personal solidarity with the Jews of Europe into their political designs vis-à-vis the British? D. Porat raises this issue and elucidates the leadership's concern to avoid confrontation with the Mandatory Power.

The Jewish community in Palestine received information about the situation of the Jews in Nazi-occupied territories from the beginning of the second World War. But it was only in the autumn of 1942 that the significance of this information became clear — planned mass extermination. The Jewish Agency Executive, the leading political framework of the Palestinian Jewish community (the *yishuv*) convened on November 22, 1942, with David Ben-Gurion at its head, to evaluate the situation and examine possibilities for action.

One of the subjects raised at that meeting was how to give public expression to the deep shock of the *yishuv*. Moshe Shapira, the executive member on behalf of Mizrachi (religious party), proposed a day of mourning with fasting and prayer in the synagogues, accompanied by a general strike and organized public meetings "like that held in connection with the White Paper." This spontaneous proposal combined a traditional religious response, to which no one took exception, with actions that had political implications and to which most of the members present objected. Eliahu Dobkin (Labor Party), Isaac Gruenbaum (General Zionist

Party), Dr. Werner D. Senator (non-Zionists), and especially Eliezer Kaplan and Dr. Bernard Joseph (both Labor Party) argued that such a strike would hurt the war effort against Germany. Joseph even proposed that, instead of striking, the usual work-day should be lengthened by two hours in order to further the war effort. The opponents of Shapira's proposal carried the day, and the Executive decided that Joseph and the "Committee of Four" — Shapira, Gruenbaum, Dobkin, and Dr. Emil Schmorak, who since 1939 had been charged with providing help to the Jews in Nazi-occupied Poland — should seek more appropriate ways of expressing public grief.[1]

Apparently, Shapira's proposal for a reply like that expressed in connection with the White Paper provoked the greatest opposition, for the stormy demonstrations against Britain's closing the doors of immigration had signaled both the deterioration of relations between the *yishuv* and the British, and the acrimonious controversy between activists and moderates within the *yishuv*. Thus the proposal of a general strike again raised a key political question and confronted the Jewish Agency Executive with the necessity to give practical expression to the slogan Ben-Gurion had coined at the start of the war: "We must aid the army as if there were no White Paper and fight the White Paper as if there were no war."[2]

The Jewish Agency had to decide how to express forcefully the horror of the *yishuv* at the news of the Holocaust and, in light of the news, to pressure the British to permit Jewish immigration into Palestine and to concentrate effort and resources upon the rescue of European Jewry — all without impairing the British war effort. Conversely, it had to determine how to continue its support of the British without neglecting the urgent need to rescue European Jewry.

It must be remembered that the Agency session was held less than one month after the turning point in the British war effort at el Alamein. During the months when there had been the real danger of a German conquest of Egypt and Palestine, there was a rapprochement between the British and the local Jewish community, expressed in recruitment policies and military cooperation. Now the fear arose (which later proved justified) that Britain's military success would change its attitude to the *yishuv*. The Jewish Agency Executive had to consider whether this was the right moment to permit relations with the British to deteriorate.[3]

These questions were not discussed in depth. This was the first meeting of the Jewish Agency Executive entirely devoted to a discussion of the plight of European Jewry and the members had not yet asked themselves whether and how their position had changed vis-à-vis the Mandatory Government and the White Paper. Therefore, they maintained the stance they had taken since the outbreak of the war, and the outstanding moderates in the Executive opted against demonstrations or any other forceful response which might cause friction between the *yishuv* and the British.

The Three Days of Mourning

The Committee of Four, with the addition of Joseph, had to operate in conjunction with the General Council of the Jewish community in Palestine *(Va'ad Le'umi)* headed by Izḥak Ben-Zvi. The General Council was responsible for internal affairs of the *yishuv*, including national conferences and statements on its behalf. In a joint meeting it turned out that most of the members of the Executive of the General Council, especially Yosef Sprinzak, one of the most outspoken moderates, supported the decision of the Agency Executive not to strike or demonstrate. A resolution was passed calling for a "day of assembly" on which the Elected Assembly would convene. During the afternoon, economic sectors nonessential to the war effort would strike and the municipalities would hold public meetings. The subject was again referred to a joint committee of the Executives of the Jewish Agency and the General Council to further define the content of the "day of assembly", so that the organized response would encompass the entire Jewish community.[4]

On November 23, 1942, the newspapers carried the Agency Executive announcement of the systematic extermination of European Jewry, and a few days later the Executive of the General Council, with the consent of the Jewish Agency Executive, resolved to proclaim three days, November 30 to December 2, 1942, as days of "alarm, protest, and a call to action."[5] What brought about the extension of public expression to a three-day period? The answer is to be found in the press, which vividly revealed the indignation and rage among Palestinian

Day of mourning for Jewish victims of the Nazis; a prayer service on the Mt. of Olives

Jewry upon reading the Agency Executive's announcement which turned doubts, rumors and bits of information into a clear and frightful reality.

These feelings were understandable, for most of the *yishuv* consisted of persons who had left Europe a few years before the war, and feared for the safety of the families, friends, and communities they had left behind. The press was full of letters and articles demanding that every effort be made to stop the murder immediately and avenge these war crimes. "*Al domi!* The *yishuv* must not remain silent!" "Every hand in Israel will avenge!" "Protest! Rescue! Revenge!" These slogans, which appeared in banner headlines in the press almost daily in late November and early December 1942, were evidence of the agitation that gripped the *yishuv*.[6] The national institutions could not ignore these reactions and thus decided to broaden the scope of the response.

On the first day of national mourning, a special session of the Elected Assembly was convened. Members of the Jewish Agency Executive, the chief rabbis, representatives of the settlements and municipalities, and members of the consular corps were present. After a number of speeches and the prayer "*El Malei Rahamim*," a petition in the name of the entire *yishuv* was read out calling upon the Allies and world Jewry to rescue and avenge the victims of the Nazis. The session concluded with the vow not to remain silent nor to permit the world to remain silent. The following day public meetings sponsored by the municipalities were held throughout Palestine. The third day was one of fasting and prayer, with transportation stopped and strikes called from noon to midnight in sectors nonessential to the war effort. Needless to say, all festivities and various forms of entertainment were cancelled.[7]

A study of the events of those three days shows that the joint committee of the Jewish Agency and the General Council did not permit the agitation within the *yishuv* to turn into protest demonstrations against the British, who showed no intention of repealing their ban on Jewish immigration despite the news of the Holocaust. On the contrary, the Agency and the General Council directed the *yishuv* to find more moderate forms of expression. While the Jewish national institutions broadened the scope of the response, they did not deviate from their political principles.

The three days of mourning were a special event in the history of the *yishuv*. They were a spontaneous demonstration of unity, with every faction and party participating. "The large square near HaBima [the main theatre in Tel Aviv] and the side streets around it were filled with crowds . . . silent and overwhelmed with emotion . . . sorrow deeply etched on every face . . . and out of the silence rose the vow of the *yishuv*."[8] Grief and anxiety over the survival of the Jewish people united the *yishuv*. The Agency's announcement of the extermination of European Jewry and the three days of mourning mark the dividing line in the *yishuv*'s consciousness between the first three years of the war, when it did not grasp the implications of what was happening in Europe, and the following three years.

Attempts to Coordinate World Jewish Reaction

"What happened here a week ago was something tremendous," Ben-Gurion said, summarizing the days of mourning, and proposing that this kind of action be continued.[9] To be sure, this was the question facing the Jewish Agency Executive: how to achieve more tangible rescue results than the *yishuv's* expression of unity and its emotional response — though this in itself was an achievement in a community composed of so many factions and parties. Two main spheres of action were indicated: a) setting up a rescue fund; b) coordination of expressions of grief with Jewry throughout the free world, especially England and the United States, in order to influence non-Jews in the democratic nations where public opinion and pressure carried some weight. Through demonstrations, conferences, and a sympathtic press it might be possible to exert pressure on various governments to aid rescue efforts, and open Palestine to Jewish refugees.[10]

Since communications in wartime did not enable full coordination with these Jewish communities, the Jewish Agency Executive proposed to send a delegation from the *yishuv* to the United States and, if possible, to England and South Africa as well. Armed with appropriate materials, the delegation would call press conferences, be received by public figures and ministers, and work with the help of local Jewish communities. Ben-Gurion opposed the idea because he thought that a broad delegation of Jews from the free world should come to a Zionist Conference in Palestine that would deal with the danger to European Jewry and, as a consequence, with the Zionist enterprise as well. Despite Ben-Gurion's opposition, a joint committee of the Jewish Agency Executive and the General Council was appointed to determine the composition of the delegation that would leave for abroad. At the same time, it was agreed that subsequently they would also consider how to implement Ben-Gurion's proposal.[11]

The committee could not reach a decision because of the disputes which arose. The Labor Party Central Committee and the Histadrut suggested that Berl Katzenelson or Golda Myerson, "one of our own", be included in the delegation. Mizrachi members wanted to send Rabbi Meir Berlin. The General Council was concerned that despatching envoys without prior coordination with members of the Zionist Organization of America "would result in insult and failure,"[12] as this act would likely be interpreted as an imposition of the will of the Zionist leadership in Palestine upon its American colleagues. The Executive of the General Council and the Committee of Four feared that a united delegation in the name of the *yishuv* was an impossible dream, and they reached the very conclusion of the Jewish Agency Executive, namely, to despatch Gruenbaum alone.[13] The proposal for a united delegation was dropped as a result of the various factions' inability to reach an agreement. Now every party or organization could send its own representative abroad, independent of the Jewish Agency Executive. Meanwhile, time was passing and no one left Palestine on behalf of the national institutions — not even Gruenbaum. As Moshe Shertok admitted in May 1943, for months the idea remained "just a proposal of the Executive."[14]

A parallel process was in operation in the United States. An American delegation which was supposed to come to Palestine at the request of the Jewish Agency Executive, never left because of endless arguments over its composition.[15] Therefore the *yishuv* continued to organize its public response alone, but with a sharper sense of isolation from the rest of the Jewish people. They felt as if they bore the entire burden of response. Ben-Gurion expressed this feeling: "We are in a terrible state because of the lack of communication . . . among members of the [General Zionist] Executive scattered all over the world."[16]

The Month of Mourning

Meanwhile the news of the extermination of European Jewry had also roused public opinion in Washington and London. Jewish public figures and institutions, Christian religious leaders, and humanitarian and professional organizations pressured the British and American governments to take a stand and embark upon rescue operations. On December 17, 1942, Anthony Eden, the British Foreign Minister, read a statement in Parliament on behalf of the eleven Allied governments and the French National Committee. He reported that the attention of the Allies had been directed to the news that the German regime intended to exterminate the Jewish people, and that the Allied governments denounced this barbaric policy and promised to take active measures to punish the criminals. The Members of Parliament stood at attention for a moment of silence to demonstrate their sympathy. The same day, the statement was published in the newspapers and read on all the radio stations of the Allied Powers.[17]

Eden's statement was received in Palestine as an indication of the success of mourning. A joint statement published by the Jewish Agency Executive and the General Council expressed a feeling shared by many: "The cry of the *yishuv* during the three days of mourning breached the wall of silence around this terrible massacre . . . and the leaders of mankind in the free world have been aroused."[18] At the same time, it did not escape the national institutions' attention that this sympathetic statement made no mention of rescuing the Jews or of opening Palestine to Jewish immigration, and they did not fail to express their bitterness at this fact in their joint statement.[19]

Together with Eden's statement, information arrived that Himmler had ordered the extermination by January 1, 1943 of the survivors of Polish Jewry who were concentrated in 53 ghettos and of the Jews remaining in the Reich (Austria, Germany, and Czechoslovakia).[20] It was obvious that not only was time short but that, in fact, it had already run out, for only a few days remained until that date. Rage again welled up in the *yishuv*, and the same day on which the Allies' statement was received, the General Council proclaimed thirty days of mourning — from December 18, 1942 to January 16, 1943. The members of the national

251

institutions assumed that the three days of mourning had helped bring about the statement of the Allies. (In fact, the main factors behind that statement were the pressure of organized Jewry in Britain, the Polish government-in-exile, and local public opinion.) They therefore hoped that the month of mourning would move the Allies at least to declare their willingness to extend tangible aid to the survivors. Thus, the *yishuv* would serve as an example to the Jewry of the free world.

"The whole way of life of the *yishuv* must be an expression of mourning, rage, and demands upon ourselves and others to rescue whatever can be rescued," stated the General Council's declaration of the month of mourning. The *yishuv* was required to restrict its festivities, the press and teachers were requested to give prominent treatment to the subject, and special prayers were recited in the synagogues.[21]

In Britain, the Allies' statement aroused a wave of harsh public criticism of the government for confining itself to a mere expression of sympathy instead of adopting active measures. The editors of the most influential newspapers, prominent religious leaders, heads of trade unions, and Members of Parliament wrote articles, made speeches, and submitted questions to Parliament.[22] Foreign Minister Anthony Eden declared the government's intention to do everything in its power, but "tremendous difficulties" stood in the way. Nonetheless, under pressure of public opinion, the British government would consider several practical proposals.[23]

Gruenbaum proposed that the Jewish Agency Executive publish a reply to Eden's statements and declare the readiness of the *yishuv* and the Jewish people to absorb into Palestine all the Jews who would hopefully be rescued. This would solve one of the major difficulties, namely, finding a haven for the refugees and the means to support them. Ben-Gurion, Joseph, and Dobkin objected to this proposal on the grounds that the Allies' statement was significant enough and that yet another statement would only diminish the effect of the first. Statements were only idle talk. Moreover, the Zionist Executive in London had already published a demand for concrete rescue work and had expressed the wish that the government let "half a million Jews in Palestine do their duty and fulfill their mission" with regard to their brothers. The Jewish Agency Executive decided that it would be sufficient to issue another statement in the name of the General Council, and this was done.[24]

It is possible that the Agency Executive lost a valuable opportunity to exert pressure on the British government precisely at the moment when that government had taken a defensive, apologetic stance under the fire of a unified public opinion regarding its failures. Perhaps a more forceful response on the part of the *yishuv*, such as a mass demonstration or general strike, might have seemed justified to British public opinion and the Mandatory government might not have been able to clash with the *yishuv* at that moment. It would be hasty, however, to state categorically that the British government would have felt constrained by the combined pressure at home and in Palestine to make significant concessions regarding rescue actions and Jewish immigration into Palestine. This key question will be dealt with again, later on.

The Internal Debate about the Nature of the Mourning

The emphatically religious character of the three days and the month of mourning led to controversies within the *yishuv*. In leftist circles, distaste was expressed for the despised "Diaspora" custom of fasting and lamentations, and parading through the streets with the chief rabbis, bearing scrolls of the Law, leading the community. This custom, they felt, was not befitting the renewed life of the people in its own land. Fasting, they claimed, was in fact "an expression of weakness . . . a very nice messianic affair," but nothing more.[25]

On the other hand, some secular Jews felt that it was precisely traditional religious custom which united all parts of the people; in time of trouble, the differences between the Jews in Palestine and in the Diaspora, and between religious and secular Jews within the *yishuv*, should not be emphasized.[26] This view was expressed by Isaac Tabenkin and Berl Katzenelson, the two prominent ideological leaders of the Labor Party. Tabenkin saw genuine grief in the weeping of Jews, religious as well as secular, and their tears, he felt, were in no way inferior to other forms of response. Berl fasted because he felt that in this way he was expressing his participation in the plight of the Jews, a tragedy that was above all party disputes and questions regarding a way-of-life; he was deeply grieved that not all the youth in Palestine completely shared this feeling.[27]

Ben-Gurion, however, feared that organized mourning was merely an easy, uncommitted outlet for sadness and bitterness, and might be a substitute for a sober view of the situation. He felt that the days of mourning lacked "a sufficiently Zionist character," that is, not enough emphasis on Erez-Israel as the center of the people and of action.[28] The minutes of the Jewish Agency Executive meetings contain no explicit resolution, but it seems that at that stage, namely the first months of 1943, the Executive decided to entrust the religious expression of grief to the Chief Rabbinate and the General Council, and to search for more efficient and influential rescue activities.

During the month of mourning, the feeling grew within the public and the national institutions that this was a decree that had been imposed upon them and that the public could not endure. Those who made their living in the entertainment industry complained that their livelihood was being jeopardized and that some means should be found to ensure that the burden of public response would weigh equally on all sectors of the economy. It must be remembered that during the months following the German retreat from North Africa, thousands of soldiers from the Allied armies passed through Palestine, all of them starved for entertainment and diversion. The General Council Executive decided to permit the performance of plays and screening of films, but prohibited dancing and orchestras "which are in marked contrast to the mood of the *yishuv*." This very general definition made it possible to evade the prohibition.[29]

There were some, however, who supported the idea of mourning and tried to pressure the institutions to proclaim a continuing collective expression of mourning even after the month had elapsed. Among the most prominent of these was *Al Domi* (do not be silent), a group of intellectuals who attempted to rouse the *yishuv* and its institutions to view the rescue of European Jewry as the supreme task of the hour.[30] Others, however, thought that the month of mourning was artificial, a form of lip service expressed in public weeping and hysteria that was difficult to continue, and that the *yishuv* must express its strength in the face of the calamity. Someone coined the slogan "Not *al domi* (do not be silent), but *al dema* (do not cry)."[31]

Berl Katzenelson, who was an adherent of the other ideas of *Al Domi*, opposed the idea of a "regime of mourning" and was not "willing to demand that sadness be written on every face or that they give up things which make them happy." It had to be a spontaneous expression, not imposed and organized.[32] Ben-Zvi was of an even more extreme opinion, and consistently stated that he did not see the good of a public response. Gruenbaum did not want to bring daily life in the *yishuv* to a standstill because, in his view, it represented the only ray of hope in that terrible period. Gruenbaum's statements drew withering criticism, for being chairman of the Rescue Committee (an enlargement of the Committee of Four), and expressing himself generally in a provocative manner, he had been the target of bitterness and frustration over the Holocaust and rescue work.[33]

The End of the Month of Mourning and its Political Aftermath

The month of mourning apparently failed. Despite the efforts of the General Council, there were only "negligible signs of mourning." Public feeling had cooled and the *yishuv* had quickly gone back to its "merrymaking". Even private individuals complained that daily life had returned to normal, and condemned this. Yet it was probably difficult to continue to make ritual gestures that would never influence any government to change its policy or save European Jewry. Nor did the scepticism of the chairman of the General Council Executive (Ben-Zvi), and the chairman of the Rescue Committee (Gruenbaum), contribute to the success of the month of mourning.[34]

As the month drew to a close, the question arose as to which public occasion should mark its conclusion. In the Rescue Committee and the General Council, the well-worn ideas were again raised: a special session of the Elected Assembly, a fast, a strike, etc.[35] Meanwhile, however, representatives of the opposition parties, the Revisionists and Agudat Yisrael, had joined the Rescue Committee and rejected these earlier actions out of hand. They felt that concrete actions, not just statements, should be demanded of the Allies, by combining a forceful, even dramatic, response on the part of the *yishuv* together with a similar one by British

254

and American Jewry, and by reinforcing the pressure of British and American public opinion on His Majesty's Government. The Aguda and Revisionist representatives on the Rescue Committee, headed by Yosef Klarman, repeatedly proposed mass rallies, a strike even of work essential to the British Army, a journey by every man, woman, and child in the *yishuv* to Jerusalem to sit in front of Government House and the High Commissioner's office until their demands were met.[36]

In the Executive Committee of the Histadrut (the General Labor Unions organization), Hillel Frumkin and Aharon Ziesling demanded "a public expression which would attract the Diaspora to join it." They felt that the Jewish community in Palestine wished to continue to express its demands for rescue, but in a more forceful way than the month of mourning. "We differ from America in several respects, especially when it comes to demonstrations," said David Remez, chairman of the Histadrut Executive Committee, in reference to the fact that American Jews had several times postponed a mass rally which was to have been held in New York.[37] The Histadrut Executive tried to win support for their proposal in various bodies. Avraham Haft, the Histadrut representative on the Rescue Committee, favored the general strike demanded by the Revisionists and proposed, in the name of the Histadrut, that if not the entire population, at least 500 representatives from all parts of the country travel to Jerusalem and fast for three days in front of the High Commissioner's residence.[38]

In response to Joseph and Senator who from time to time reiterated their proposal to work overtime in order to emphasize that the rescue of the Jews would be accomplished only with the victory of the Allies, Remez proposed, in the name of the Histadrut, that the workers should work additional hours during the days following the strike.[39] Haft also tried to convince the Labor Party to support the Histadrut's initiative but his complaints that the Jewish Agency Executive had no interest in the subject and that the General Council's proposal of two minutes of daily silence was a mockery, did not even evoke discussion, much less a resolution.

In a joint meeting of the Jewish Agency Executive and the representatives of the Histadrut, Remez demanded that the Agency issue "another political alarm." The Agency's reply was that it could not work under pressure from Agudat Yisrael and the Revisionists, but only in keeping with its own views.[40] Some members of the General Council Executive, too, were not satisfied with the action taken thus far. One of these was Shlomo-Zalman Shragai, who was also a member of *Al Domi* and who had resigned from the Rescue Committee in protest over the Jewish Agency's unwillingness to organize an appropriate public response.[41]

255

It seems that the tragic events in Europe made possible a rare combination of forces, as representatives of the Histadrut, the Revisionists, and Agudat Yisrael all supported the same ideas in opposition to the national institutions, because of their desire to put teeth into the *yishuv*'s response. Nonetheless, they were unable to outweigh the views of the Jewish Agency Executive and the majority of the

General Council Executive who repeatedly rejected proposals that ran counter to the accepted political line. They mustered the official arguments: the Rescue Committee could not accept a resolution before the proposal had been submitted for discussion by the various bodies represented thereon; it was impossible to appoint a committee because important members were absent. There were also more substantive, though ironic, arguments: the fast proposed by the Histadrut, that bastion of secular Socialist Zionism, was too redolent of the spirit of the Exile.[42]

But the main arguments, of course, were political. First was the fear that mass demonstrations would provoke clashes with Arabs in the cities with mixed populations, especially Jerusalem. Pro-Nazi sentiments had increased in the Arab world, particularly in 1941–1942 when the British had been in grave trouble on the various fronts. The Jewish Agency Executive, which was responsible for the security of the *yishuv*, did not want to give the Arab population a pretext to renew the disturbances of 1936–1939.

The second political argument was that mass demonstrations and strikes affecting the war industry would cause an open rift with the British at precisely the time when, some two months after the start of the German retreat in the Western desert, weapons searches, arrests, and British harassment of the recruiting offices had begun. The British no longer needed Palestine Jewry's military strength. Rather, they feared its increase. The *yishuv*'s resentment against these British measures grew and the Jewish Agency Executive feared that a harsh public reply to the British policy regarding Jewish immigration and rescue work would ignite a conflagration whose flames the Revisionists would fan. Such a situation would give the Mandatory government the pretext for harshly oppressing the *yishuv*, and the outcome might cause severe damage to Zionist achievements and political aspirations. For all these reasons, the Jewish Agency Executive felt that it was its duty "to beware of harmful activities" and to weigh carefully "the extent of the responsibility" that it was assuming by engaging in overly-rigorous activities.[43]

The Revisionists wanted to force the Jewish Agency Executive to reconsider its policy on this matter of principle, and their representatives on the Rescue Committee proposed that the subject of public response be decided by the Executive of the General Zionist Council, the supreme authority of the Zionist Organization. At that time the Revisionists were not members of the Zionist Organization and thus could not air their demands in the Council Executive,[44] but apparently they made this proposal anticipating that public opinion during the debates would demand forceful action.

The following meeting of the Zionist Council Executive (January 18, 1943) was the first since the start of the war that discussed the news from Europe; among the issues raised in disorder and an atmosphere of pain was the question of the *yishuv*'s reply to the events in Europe. Those who related to this issue spoke in general terms, insisting on a great outcry in order to shake up the Jews and the free world, without taking into account the possible consequences. Gruenbaum claimed that the proponents of loud public expressions were deluded if they thought that either the Allies or the Germans would be impressed by the cries and protests of the *yishuv*.

As the Revisionists had expected, the debaters expressed their feeling that the public was pressuring them: "Jews are crying out . . . they are besieging this very building and demanding action" and "now people are saying, at last, even in the Zionist Council Executive they're talking about the Diaspora . . . some say that our institutions aren't doing anything, while in the meantime the Revisionist circles and Agudat Yisrael try to exploit the situation." Despite these unequivocal statements, not one of the discussants made any practical proposals nor was any resolution on the issue passed during this meeting.[45] Hence the Jewish Agency Executive's policy remained in effect and the month of mourning came to an end without being marked by any public event.

Public Reaction during February and March 1943

During January and February 1943 it became increasingly clear that the deportations from various countries to the extermination camps in Eastern Europe were continuing rapidly and systematically. In Palestine there was a growing sense of depression, for in the meantime the *yishuv*'s rescue attempts had come to naught and the Allies had done nothing beyond issuing their statement at the end of December. On February 22, 1943, a session of the Elected Assembly was convened "to demonstrate solidarity with the victims whose numbers mount daily, and to express disappointment before the whole world over the inactivity of the democratic states." Statements on behalf of the Chief Rabbinate and Agudat Yisrael were issued; Ben-Gurion and Gruenbaum made speeches; during the conference there was a two-hour curfew, and that night all forms of amusement and entertainment were cancelled. During the curfew there was a general strike, even by workers in the army camps. The statement which the Elected Assembly published reflected the *yishuv*'s feelings of despair and impotence in the face of the so-called enlightened world's indifference to the plight of the Jewish people. The only threat they could utter against the Allies was that "Jewish blood spilled in vain will give you no peace."[46]

The agenda of the Elected Assembly was similar to those of previous meetings which had marked the beginning of the three days of mourning and the month of mourning, but here despair and weariness were more clearly felt. The session lasted only two hours, but even then — as the members of the General Council Executive complained — it was necessary to mediate among at least nine different bodies. When Ben-Gurion spoke, Gruenbaum demanded equal time, and if the Chief Ashkenazic Rabbi addressed the delegates, the Chief Sephardic Rabbi must do likewise; if there was a statement on behalf of Agudat Yisrael, the Revisionists felt slighted; then the women demanded representation, and so it went, endlessly.[47] This weariness was felt to an even greater degree in the next session of the Elected

257

Assembly, which convened on March 24, 1943. The session was devoted to defense mobilization and financial affairs; only at the opening was the plight of European Jewry discussed. Gruenbaum analyzed the news which had been received by the Rescue Committee and the session issued a proclamation, even more desperate than the first, against the indifference of the Allies.[48]

During the four months that had elapsed since the Jewish Agency's statement regarding the annihilation of European Jewry, four public events had been organized in Palestine in response to the news of the Holocaust — all with much the same format. The public and the national institutions had the feeling that a fixed form of response had developed and become routine, and that repetition had detracted from its effectiveness. "The same curfew, the same fasting," more speeches by the Chief Rabbis, the same old statements. "We're tired of conferences, and have said everything that could be said. Meetings — they are all a farce." The members of the institutions which debated the form of the *yishuv*'s response had already adopted their positions, so that even in those discussions there was nothing new.[49] It almost seemed as if the public response of the *yishuv* had become an issue which was slowly being forgotten, until two events reawakened the debate: the Bermuda Conference and the Warsaw Ghetto uprising, both of which occurred on April 19, 1943.

The Shaping of Agency Executive Policy

Debate over organization of a public event to be held on the eve of the Bermuda Conference (an Anglo-American conference on refugees) began in early March. Once again, Yosef Klarman and Avraham Haft, speaking at the Rescue Committee meeting, proposed a mass demonstration in Jerusalem. This time, Agudat Yisrael, HaShomer HaZair, and the Left Poalei Zion supported the idea, stating unequivocally that they could not accept the Jewish Agency's contention that any mass political activity might endanger the *yishuv*. On the contrary, Ya'acov Zerubavel, leader of Poalei Zion, wanted "any friction between the government and the Jewish population resulting from a demonstration against the tragedy in the Diaspora" to be made public abroad. The representatives of the immigrant organizations in the Immigrants Council which had been set up alongside the Rescue Committee demanded a mass assembly, at least in Tel Aviv if not in Jerusalem; and at a meeting of the representatives of the settlements and municipalities, there was unanimous support of the mass assembly. "If something is not planned that will involve many people, there will be demonstrations," Ben-Zvi warned the General Council Executive, referring to spontaneous expressions beyond the control of the national institutions.[50]

Gruenbaum and Shapira tried to communicate to their colleagues on the Jewish Agency Executive their sense that the pressures within the Rescue Committee and the population at large for forceful public action were growing as the Bermuda

Receipts for contributions to the special fundraising campaign for the survivors of the Holocaust

Conference approached: "In various quarters people are demanding... a new reply: a general strike, a demonstration of tens of thousands in Jerusalem ... until now we have rejected these demands, but it seems ... that it is becoming ever more difficult to go on rejecting them, especially since the English, despite the terrible catastrophe, had not eased the restrictive immigration laws one whit." He reminded his listeners that there were complaints that the Jewish Agency Executive was not doing anything to shake up the public in the free world; that terrible news continued to arrive from Europe, and that Bermuda might be the last chance to rescue European Jewry. Therefore, one of the members of the Jewish Agency Executive should be in the United States in order to rouse public opinion during the Conference. Another of his arguments was that the Jewish Agency Executive had thus far rejected every proposal made by the Rescue Committee; the time had come to reconsider them.[51]

Some Labor Party members expressed their opposition to the Jewish Agency's position in writing and in person, within the Labor Party, in the Zionist Council Executive, and in the Histadrut Executive: "Our leaders are making a serious mistake in taking a stand against a popular movement which they consider unnecessary."[52] Nonetheless, the same members of the Labor Party feared demonstrations as much as did the Agency Executive, and sought a more moderate response.

259

The Jewish Agency Executive rejected all these pressures and arguments. Demonstrations, they felt, were as ineffective as more moderate actions; they could not exert pressure on the British and the Americans in Bermuda. All they could do was provide some sense of relief to the *yishuv*, while they cause problems and even hurt it. The members also objected to Moshe Shertok, head of the Jewish Agency's Political Department, staying in the United States until the opening of the Bermuda Conference. The Agency Executive was willing to approve another conference of the *yishuv* to be organized by the General Council, and a petition in the name of the *yishuv* to be sent to Bermuda, but no more.[53]

It may be that because the Jewish Agency Executive was preoccupied with practical matters it paid no attention to the divergence between its own views and public sentiment for a response to the Allies' indifference to the fate of the Jewish people. Even if the Agency's arguments were logical and compelling in view of the political situation, the Jewish community in Palestine did not wish to hear them; and it was difficult for people to understand why the Jewish Agency Executive restrained their desire to protest. Because of the dimensions of the carnage, the magnitude of the disaster, and family and Zionist movement ties between the Jews in Palestine and the Jews in Europe, it was inevitable that the reaction of the *yishuv* to the Holocaust would be first and foremost an emotional one: "Our Zionism is an outcry; We can not remain silent; Jewish history will never forgive us; our brother's blood cries out to us." Bitter experience had shown that there was nothing to be gained from any of the various forms of response, ". . . but it is simply not in accordance with human respect for the living and the dead that tens of thousands of Jews were cut down like grass, with no outcry, no echo worthy of the name." These utterances and others like them were repeated many times.[54]

Apparently, as long as there was still some hope, however faint, that the response of the *yishuv* would affect Allied policy, the Jewish Agency Executive was willing to join in organizing days of mourning and public gatherings. However, when this hope proved false, the Executive came to the conclusion that there was no point in continuing to deal with the subject. Its decision not to have Moshe Shertok remain in the United States for the Bermuda Conference is evidence that, even before it began, the Executive thought that the conference would be of no real value, and that the *yishuv*'s response would not change the outcome or Allied policy.

Such a response merely had a domestic value, helping to unify the *yishuv* and salve its conscience, but it was of no use in rescuing the victims of Nazism, and its organization could thus be entrusted to the General Council Executive. There would thus be a division of labor: the General Council would deal with the religious expressions of mourning such as had already been organized, and with the *yishuv*'s response in general — public meetings, petitions, statements in the Elected Assembly, etc., while the Jewish Agency Executive would deal with practical and political problems of rescue.

The General Council hoped that this division would extend its influence upon the *yishuv*, especially since it had an advantage over the Rescue Committee whose proposals to make the *yishuv*'s response more severe had been rejected by the Jewish Agency Executive. In the words of the members of the General Council Executive, the Elected Assembly had become "the only institution which informs the world," an institution whose purpose is to give the *yishuv* no rest; "and this is an inner psychological necessity."[55]

The Executive of the General Council thus began its preparations for another *yishuv*-wide assembly on the eve of the Bermuda Conference, as had been decided by the Jewish Agency Executive. But the members of the Histadrut Executive Committee, especially David Remez and Golda Myerson, had not yet given up. To the General Council they recommended an activity which would be different from the *yishuv* gatherings and mass demonstrations that had already become abhorrent to them, namely, to get the entire *yishuv* to sign a petition which the Elected Assembly would publish. It would be a mass project that would be carried out in the streets with the participation of the leaders and prominent public figures of the *yishuv*. For two days the institutions would cease all activities and devote themselves to this campaign which would achieve several ends. The petition would encompass the entire *yishuv* and imbue it with a sense of involvement, instead of the prevailing depression. The public would see that its leaders sensed their pain; "Our children and young people will remember that there were two days during which their parents showed a different spirit," said Remez. Golda Myerson hoped that it would also be possible to carry out such a campaign in the United States, England, and South Africa, among Jews and non-Jews, and that the expression of the opinion of two to three million persons would exert real pressure.[56]

Most of the members of the Jewish Agency Executive and some of the General Council Executive were against the signature campaign (the "petition" as they called it), arguing that it was nothing but a vain hope and a waste of time and energy. Ben-Zvi correctly doubted that it would be possible to agree on a text that everyone would sign and that it would be possible to carry out such a complicated project. Only after pressure on the part of David Remez, and extensive discussions, was it decided to appoint a sub-committee to consider the possibility of implementing the suggestion.[57]

The Bermuda Conference and its Aftermath

Meanwhile, the Bermuda Conference had begun on April 19, 1943, without being marked by any public event in Palestine. The protocols of the conference were not published, but it was known that every proposal submitted by the Jewish Agency Executive and the Rescue Committee had been rejected. The conference was described abroad as a maneuver to pacify the criticism of public opinion in the free world. The Elected Assembly was convened on May 3, 1943 to express the *yishuv*'s profound disappointment at the outcome of the conference which many had considered the last chance to rescue European Jewry, and to issue another

261

call "to everyone who has a human conscience, not to preclude the possible rescue of the few survivors because of political considerations."[58] It was obvious that this call was no more than the despairing rhetorical gesture of an isolated group. But "what can we expect of the Gentiles," asked Golda Myerson, "when the Jewish *yishuv* itself did not raise a cry to the very heavens?"[59]

At the meeting of the Zionist Council Executive held two weeks later, bitterness was expressed that no fitting public response had been organized in Palestine either before or after the Bermuda Conference. Explicit accusations were hurled against the Jewish Agency Executive for rejecting practically every proposal for fear of the consequences and lack of faith in the power of the *yishuv* to carry out any project, and for not having permitted a public response, as in the case of the *Patria*, for example. The Agency Executive was accused of not having considered public sentiment and not realizing the value of a public response for reinforcing sympathetic public opinion which had once more been aroused after the paltry results of the Bermuda Conference were made known in England and the United States. Gruenbaum, Shertok, and Sprinzak tried to calm the atmosphere, to minimize the value of any response on the *yishuv*'s part, and to postpone voting on a resolution.[60]

The next day, May 19, the British government, under pressure from its critics, scheduled a debate in Parliament on the results of the Bermuda Conference and the government's policy on the refugees.[61] Most of the Zionist Council Executive wanted the *yishuv*'s criticism and disappointment to be expressed alongside that of public opinion in the West. A resolution was accepted in principle on "the need for a mass public response to the lack of rescue efforts," especially if the debate in Parliament should prove fruitless.[62] This was the resolution which the Revisionists had sought four months earlier — a resolution formulated by the Executive of the supreme Zionist institution as a result of a strong public reaction against the policy of the Jewish Agency Executive and the General Council — but it came too late. The debate in Parliament produced no results, nor did the Jewish Agency Executive change its policy against public demonstrations. On the contrary, by mid-1943 it had additional arguments in its favor.

In early 1943, many in Palestine thought that public response by the *yishuv* would serve as an example and a motivating force for comparable action on the part of Jews in the United States and England.[63] However, after the Bermuda Conference, the Jews of Palestine concluded that in New York, London, and other centers of Jewish population the shock had worn off and life had returned to normal, to the usual internal dissension and dissipation of energies. The *yishuv* felt itself more isolated, even from the Jewish people in the free world.[64] Most of the members of the Jewish Agency Executive felt that no action taken by the *yishuv* had impelled Jewry to do anything up to then, nor would it do so after Bermuda, for the Jewish communities in the Diaspora lived under different conditions and their own internal problems determined their response to the Holocaust: their fear of growing anti-Semitism, of losing positions achieved with tremendous effort, their relationship with the government, and problems within the communities. Therefore, one should not be provoked by those who insist that the *yishuv*'s actions are important and can influence Jews and non-Jews; the time had come to face the fact that any strike or demonstration in Palestine received no more than two or three lines of coverage in foreign newspapers.[65]

Following the Bermuda Conference, the activities of the Irgun Zevai Leumi delegation in the United States were intensified. At the beginning of 1943, this delegation had set up an "Emergency Committee for the Rescue of European Jewry" headed by Hillel Kook (also known as Peter Bergson). The committee attempted to attract the attention of the American public by employing professional publicity methods such as taking full-page advertisements in the leading newspapers, organizing mass rallies, and staging a pageant in the large metropolitan centers, that was seen by Eleanor Roosevelt, U.S. Senators, and leading public figures who supported the committee. The Jewish establishment, the Zionists in particular, considered this activity irresponsible and dissipating of energies, and they categorically opposed it. At the same time, the Jewish leadership realized that the Revisionists were exploiting the vacuum created in the wake of their own lack of effective response to a public yearning for action.[66] The Jewish Agency Executive did not want a similar, and to their mind, undesirable, state of affairs to prevail in Palestine as well, namely, a situation in which a vociferous minority would raise basic questions in opposition to the official leadership. Ben-Gurion condemned the "gang . . . of lawless Irgun Zevai Leumi members who desecrate the name of the Jewish people among the Gentiles" for the sake of publicity.[67]

One must note that at this point the argument between Revisionists and the Zionist Executive, both in the United States and in Palestine, no longer concerned the specific question of a forceful response to the Allies' failings. That issue had become part of their acrimonious quarrel over the methods and style of Zionism in general. The Labor movement wanted to follow Weizmann's famous slogan, "One more goat, one more acre" or in this instance, "One more immigration permit, one more refugee" — silent, hard work which might bring solid results, as it did in the past, rather than what they considered high-flown rhetoric, grandiose declarations, and solemn ceremonies which they felt bore no resemblance to concrete action.

Reaction to the Warsaw Ghetto Uprising

On Passover eve, April 19, 1943, the Warsaw Ghetto uprising began and the whole Jewish world was stirred with profound pride as well as grief. The uprising may have been a factor in the change in the *yishuv*'s attitude to the position of the Jews in the Diaspora, and led to the growing feeling of solidarity with them. The public again pressured its representatives to let it express its desire to make sacrifices and to help. On May 6, the Histadrut held a special conference at which it declared seven days of fundraising "to encourage the ghetto defenders." At the Zionist Council Executive a proposal was made to organize community-wide fundraising. The representatives of the settlements, the cities, and the Executive Committee of the Histadrut met with the General Council Executive; as a result of their pressure it was decided to hold, if not a demonstration, at least a strike which would include the workers in the defense industry and the army camps, mass meetings, and the signing of a petition by the entire *yishuv* as had been proposed before the Bermuda Conference. The strike would be called "Warsaw Day" and would be unique, different from its predecessors, for "there has never been a day like Warsaw Day." The Agency Executive, as before, objected to the signing of a petition but was forced to relent since it had put the General Council in charge of this matter, and was obligated to abide by its decisions.[68]

The general strike and the petition were supposed to reflect the united stand of the *yishuv*, but Agudat Yisrael and the Revisionists did not agree to them because no one had consulted their representatives on the Rescue Committee, and because a strike and petition were, in their view, an inadequate response to so momentous an event as the Warsaw uprising. These two parties announced that they would not support the action of the National Council, nor would they participate in the petition which the public would be exhorted to sign, although they would not obstruct these activities.[69]

The public in Palestine paid no heed to the disputes between the parties, and the signing of the petition was a success. On June 15, 1943, over 250,000 adults and some 60,000 children from every settlement signed "the petition of the *yishuv*" which demanded that the Allies immediately undertake rescue and aid operations for European Jewry. A delegation on behalf of the General Council delivered the text of the petition and the signatures, along with a memorandum detailing recommended rescue measures, to the British High Commissioner and to all the consuls and representatives of the Allies and the neutral states in Palestine and in London. However, the question remained, would this enterprise have any effect upon the rescue measures? "What can I, you, and His Majesty's Government do? After all, everything depends upon Germany," Harold MacMichael told Ben-Ẓvi, in an attempt to defend his government.[70]

Last Debates

In the latter half of 1943, relations deteriorated between the *yishuv* and the Mandatory government, and also between the organized *yishuv* and the Revisionists. It was clear that any demonstration might turn violent, as a protest not only against the British failure to carry out rescue operations, but also against the British prosecution of Jews caught with weapons, and against the weapons searches, closure of the recruiting offices, and the refusal to establish the Jewish Brigade. The Agency Executive feared that "the provocative elements," "the lawbreakers among us" (that is to say, the Revisionists), might gain the support of the masses where bitterness against the British was increasing; then the Jewish Agency Executive would lose control of the situation and the public. The key members of the Labor Party who sat in the Jewish Agency Executive and the General Council, were determined not to let things develop that far. The Revisionists' insistence on a violent response — in December 1943, Dr. Aryeh Altmann, the leader of the Revisionists in Palestine proposed a demonstration that would be intentionally violent — was seen not only as a sincere and pained outcry against the tragedy of the Jewish people, but also as a political tactic: "The Revisionists are trying to make political hay out of the Jewish calamity, and it is our duty to warn these people not to play with Jewish lives. Of course, we must do everything we can, but we must not be led on by empty shouting," warned Kaplan.[71]

Gruenbaum cautioned the Zionist Council Executive against the delusion inherent in the Revisionists' proposals for, in his opinion, all the Jewish blood that had been shed in Europe had not moved the Allies to action and rescue. Shertok noted that the British had suffered many casualties and wounded of their own, and queried whether the death of a handful of people in clashes with the Mandatory police in Palestine, if such should occur, would trouble them.[72] Dr. Altmann's proposal also stirred up debate in the homes of the Chief Rabbis, Rabbi Yiẓhak Isaac HaLevi Herzog and Rabbi Ben-Zion Meir Chai Uziel, between members of *Al Domi*, several members of Agudat Yisrael, and "some of our comrades," as Gruenbaum later reported to the Jewish Agency Executive — all of whom had endorsed Altmann's proposal but strongly opposed deliberately provoked clashes with the British — and between Martin Buber and Shmuel Hugo Bergmann, who categorically rejected the proposal.[73] Apparently, then, at the close of 1943, the subject continued to stir up some portions of the public.

But this was practically the last debate on the subject; from the beginning of 1944, there was a change in the position of the supporters of a forceful response on the part of the *yishuv*, except for the Revisionists. A move towards the position of the Jewish Agency Executive was apparent, particularly among the members of the Histadrut's Executive Committee. First of all, it was becoming obvious that the Allies had no intention of sacrificing, in Gruenbaum's words, "even the tiniest fraction of their own interests" in order to save Jews.[74] Second, in the liberated countries there were possibilities to aid the survivors; and the satellite states of Rumania, Bulgaria, and Hungary were beginning to detach themselves from their alliance with Germany. These countries had a population of over one million Jews whose lives could be saved as a result. Therefore concern over the tragedy of European Jewry on the part of sympathetic non-Jewish circles had waned, and more people in the Western world thought that an Allied victory would bring about Jewish deliverance. No one heeded the *yishuv*'s protests that when victory came there would be no one left to save.

The *yishuv*'s envoys in Istanbul and Geneva who administered the practical work of rescuing Jews, had insisted from the very beginning that publicity and public statements would only hurt their endeavors. From mid-1943, they became even more insistent on this point, for they felt that there was now a possibility of carrying on direct negotiations with the satellite states and any publicity would bring the matter to the Germans' attention, thereby causing irreparable damage.[75]

For these reasons, the argument ceased within the Jewish Agency Executive and other *yishuv* institutions over the need for a public response. The public gatherings that were held in 1944 were devoted mainly to raising rescue funds. Then the German invasion of Hungary in March 1944 raised the subject all over again. At a meeting of the Histadrut Executive Committee, held a month after the invasion, at the height of the preparations for deporting Hungarian Jews to Auschwitz, members demanded that the General Council immediately declare a "Hungarian Jewry Day" to warn the world, which already knew very well the results of such preparations. Otherwise the *yishuv* would have to declare another day of mourning after the Jews' annihilation. However, these members doubted whether there would be any practical results from a day of this kind. A month later, at a meeting of the Jewish Agency Executive, Gruenbaum made a similar proposal; Ben-Gurion's reply was that the matter "is not the domain of the Jewish Agency Executive, but of the *yishuv*" (meaning the General Council).[76]

Shortly thereafter, this discussion became pointless. In a period of a few weeks, beginning in mid-May, 430,000 Hungarian Jews were deported to Auschwitz. The *yishuv* stood by powerless, stunned by the deportation, the efficiency of the death

Jerusalem, V-E Day (May 9, 1945); demonstration urging immediate Jewish immigration to Palestine

machine, and the vast number of victims. On June 5, 1944, a day of strikes, fasting, and public meetings, "a day of outcry for the rescue of the few remaining survivors," was proclaimed. A stern warning was issued to the governments of Rumania and Hungary, where there still were Jews, that the day of judgment was approaching, and the demand was made that the Allies enable rescue and immigration.[77]

Early in December 1944, the Elected Assembly called upon the Allies to save the few survivors, and upon the undergrounds, the churches, and the welfare organizations to aid in returning the Jewish children who were in hiding with Christians. In the second week of March 1945, as the war drew to a close and the full extent of the Holocaust became known, a week of mourning was proclaimed in Palestine, followed by a fast day and a curfew, and another demand was made to save the few survivors.[78]

This sequence of events and its analysis raises a number of questions that require an answer.

First, there is the question of the lack of cooperation between the *yishuv* and the Jewish communities in the free world, who failed to join in a common effort to rouse Western public opinion through unconventional means. It would seem that the answer lies beyond the technical difficulties of communication during time of war. The small *yishuv* — 450,000 people, mostly young newcomers to Palestine — was viewed by the Jewish communities abroad as an experiment whose value and future existence still remained to be proved. It did not possess the power to focus and activate the potential of the entire Jewish world — especially when most of this world was not Zionist, and was suspicious of the Zionist movement. The *yishuv*, and the Jewish Agency Executive, were not the leaders of the Jewish world that they wished to be.

The second question concerns the basic disbelief of the Jewish Agency Executive that the *yishuv* would be able to rouse Western public opinion to pressure the governments of the free world to engage in concrete rescue operations. In retrospect one must admit that this disbelief was an accurate expression of bitter Jewish realism. The extermination and suffering of millions of Jews did not move the British or American governments to act beyond verbal declarations; public opinion in the West was more concerned about its own casualties, especially in Britain. When public opinion did speak out for rescue operations, the voices were mainly those of religious circles, women's charitable organizations, intellectuals, and opposition political parties. But these circles did not possess real power, and the Western governments silenced their accusations and demands by making promises they never intended to keep.

267

The third question is whether the Jewish Agency Executive was correct in regarding mass rallies and anti-British demonstrations as potentially dangerous to the *yishuv*. The answer must be in the positive. The *yishuv* and its main military force, the Haganah, were still in an embryonic stage of development, and the British government which resented their growth could easily have suppressed them. The Jewish Agency Executive keenly felt its responsibility for the existence and development of the *yishuv*, and its potential ability to serve as a shelter for the survivors of the war. The Revisionists and Agudat Yisrael, who were in opposition to the national institutions, did not bear such responsibility; neither did the intellectuals such as the supporters of *Al-Domi*, nor the Labor Party members on the General Council Executive, nor the Histadrut. None of these represented the *yishuv* in matters of policy and security, and none of them was in direct contact with the British government. The control the Agency Executive exerted over the Jewish community in Palestine undoubtedly protected it from severe repercussions.

The gap that existed between the Executive members, particularly Ben-Gurion, Shertok and Kaplan, and public opinion in the *yishuv* was a manifestation of a difference between a leadership assuming strategic responsibility for the welfare of the community at large, and the impelling emotional needs of the public.

Translated by Carol Kutscher.

Abbreviations used in footnotes

CF–Committee of Four
CZA–Central Zionist Archives
EA–Elected Assembly *(Asefat HaNivharim)*
GCE–General Council Executive *(Va'ad Leumi* Executive)
HA–Histadrut Archive
HEC–Histadrut Executive Committee
HES–Histadrut Executive Secretariat
JAE–Jewish Agency Executive
LPA–Labor Party Archive
LPC–Labor Party Center
LPS–Labor Party Secretariat
RC–Rescue Committee
TUA–Teachers' Union Archive
ZCE–Zionist Council Executive *(HaVa'ad HaPo'el HaZioni* Executive)

1 Meeting of the Jewish Agency Executive (hereafter referred to as JAE), Nov. 22, 1942; Ben-Gurion was absent from the meeting. For the views of Dobkin and Gruenbaum, see also the meeting of the General Council Executive (hereafter, GCE), Nov. 23, 1942, J1/7255, and the meeting of the Committee of Four (hereafter, CF), Nov. 23, 1942, S26/1237, all in the Central Zionist Archives (hereafter, CZA).

2 Ben-Gurion's comments at the Labor Party Center (LPC), Sept. 12, 1939, 23/29 in the Labor Party Archive (hereafter, LPA); these appeared in Hebrew, with slight changes, as "We must help the English in their war...", *BaMa'arakha* 3 (Tel Aviv, 1950):18.

3 On relations with the British during the summer of 1942, see Yehuda Bauer, *From Diplomacy to Resistance — A History of Jewish Palestine, 1939–1945* (Philadelphia, 1970), ch. 5; Christopher Sykes, *Crossroads to Israel* (London, 1965), pp. 275–278.

4 GCE, Nov. 23, 1942, CZA J1/7255; CF, Nov. 23, 1942, CZA S26/1237.

5   GCE, Nov. 27, 1942, CZA J1/7255. For the text of the announcement see *Sefer HaTe'udot ...1918–1948*, ed. M. Atiash (Jerusalem, 1963), p. 332.

6   *Davar*, for example, published a news item (Nov. 24, 1942) about soldiers who came to the recruiting offices to demand the formation of "companies of ghetto destroyers" to be dispatched immediately to Europe; see also letters from two Palestinian soldiers in the Royal Engineer Corps to the GCE Nov. 30, 1942, in which they demanded the "strengthening of Jewish force" so that it could share in "the destruction of the ghettos and the rescue of the handful of survivors," CZA S44/471.

7   This was the eleventh session of the Third Elected Assembly (hereafter, EA). The principal speakers were Henrietta Szold and David Ben-Gurion. The resolutions of the GCE do not specify that there was no intention to call a general strike, as is evident in the demand made by Yosef Klarman, Revisionist representative on the Rescue Committee (RC) that *all* sectors be affected in the next strike. See the meeting of the RC, Jan. 15, 1943, CZA S26/1239.

8   M. Bar-Yehezkel, *BaMa'agal HaSatum* (Hebrew) (Tel Aviv, 1973), p. 49; E. Reiss, "Aid and Rescue Operations" (Hebrew), *Dapim LeHeker HaShoa VehaMered* 2 (1952), p. 24, and similar descriptions in the press of that week. Many vividly remember the three days of mourning, but have no recollection of other similar events.

9   From his remarks at a conference of Labor Party activists in Tel Aviv, Dec. 8, 1942, LPA Box 3/6; see also meeting of JAE, Dec. 6, 1942, CZA.

10 Meetings of the JAE, Nov. 22, 1942 and Dec. 6, 1942, CZA; Rabbi Y.L. Fishman and Moshe Shapira proposed a day of mourning in England and the United States; see also GCE, Jan. 11 and 17, 1943, CZA J1/7255.

11 JAE, Dec. 6, 1942, CZA. *Davar*, Dec. 14, 1942, published Joseph's statement to representatives of the press: "We want a delegation of Jews from America to come to Palestine because it is important for them to become familiar with what is happening here at first hand."

12 LPC, Nov. 30, 1942, LPA 4a/3; GCE, Dec. 14, 1942, CZA J1/7255; remarks by Ben-Gurion and Kaplan, JAE, Jan. 4, 1943, CZA.

13 CF, Dec. 10, 1942, CZA S26/1237. According to the GCE minutes, Dec. 14, 1942, CZA J1/7255. This resolution was not passed wholeheartedly because Gruenbaum was not considered to be representative of the entire *yishuv*.

14 The proposal was again raised at a meeting of the Labor Party Secretariat (LPS), Feb. 10, 1943, LPA 4/4a; at the JAE, April 22, 1943, CZA J1/7255; and at a meeting of the Zionist Council Executive (ZCE), May 18, 1943, CZA S25/297. Several months before, on Jan. 1, 1943, Rabbi Meir Berlin had gone to the United States on behalf of Mizrahi. Before his departure he met with several members of the Jewish Agency Executive and representatives of Polish Jewry, and was armed with relevant material. In the United States he worked with Leib Yaffe, one of the Keren HaYesod administrators, in an effort to rouse American Jewry to save the Jews of Europe. He returned to Palestine at the beginning of 1944 and reported on his trip to the JAE, Jan. 17, 1944, CZA J1/7256.

15 JAE, Jan. 4, 1943, CZA; on the inability to form a delegation, see Dr. Nahum Goldmann's letter to Kaplan, Jan. 11, 1943, CZA S25/1504.

16 JAE, Jan. 4, 1943 and Feb. 28, 1943, CZA.

17 Details on public pressure in Britain and the Allies' statement appeared in the daily press in Palestine, for example, *Davar*, Dec. 5–9, 1942; also see B. Wasserstein, *Britain and the Jews of Europe, 1939–1945* (London, 1979), pp. 170–175.

18 Ben-Gurion at JAE, Dec. 20, 1942; Dobkin at ZCE, Jan. 18, 1943, S25/29; Klarman at RC, Jan. 31, 1943, S26/1239; Remez at GCE, Feb. 15, 1943, J1/7255 (all CZA).

19 For the text of the announcement, see *Sefer HaTe'udot* (above, n. 5), pp. 334–335.

20 *Davar*, Nov. 22, 1942, printed Himmler's announcement that not one Jew would be left in Germany, and on Dec. 12, 1942, reported Himmler's statement that by the end of 1942 the extermination of half of all Polish Jews must be completed. It was obvious that the discrepancies between the reports were the result of the difficulties of getting reliable information and did not detract from the seriousness of the situation. The reference is to Himmler's order of July 19, 1942 to complete "the total purging" *(totale Bereinigung)* of Jews from the *General-Gouvernement* by Dec. 31, 1942. For the text of this order, see *Documents on the Holocaust*, eds. Y. Arad, I. Guttmann, and A. Margaliot (Jerusalem, 1981), Doc. 115.

21 *Sefer HaTe'udot* (above, n. 5), p. 335; CF, Dec. 10, 1942, CZA S26/1237; press of Dec. 17–18, 1942.

22 The press in Palestine reported on this at length from mid-December 1942 to February 1943; a banner headline in *Davar*, Dec. 19, 1942: "British Public Opinion Demands Immediate Action to Save Jews"; *HaZofe*, Jan. 5, 1943 cited the lead article in the *Manchester Guardian* supporting concrete action; see also Wasserstein (above, n. 17), pp. 173–178. Many thought that public opinion in Britain was more aware than American public opinion of the plight of European Jewry; Gruenbaum at RC, Mar. 14, 1943, CZA S26/1237; Shertok at ZCE, May 18, 1943, CZA S25/297. This was also H. Feingold's conclusion, *The Politics of Rescue; the Roosevelt Administration and the Holocaust* (New Jersey, 1970), p. 177.

23 See the daily press in Palestine, e.g. *Davar*, Dec. 19, 1942; for more on Eden's remarks see Wasserstein (above, n. 17), pp. 172–178. Lord Selbourne, Secretary for Economic Warfare, Herbert Morrison, Home Secretary, and Lord Cranborne, Colonial Secretary, were forced to reply to frequent questions regarding the Government's intention to undertake concrete action: *Davar*, Dec. 10, 13, 17, 1942.

24 JAE, Dec. 20, 1942, CZA; for the text of the GC's declaration, see *Sefer HaTe'udot* (above, n. 5), pp. 335–336; for the announcement of the Zionist Executive in London, see *ibid.*, p. 335 and the daily Palestine press of Dec. 19, 1942.

25 Ya'acov Zerubabel, at ZCE, May 18, 1943, CZA S25/297; Eliezer Pirei, *HaShomer HaZair*, Dec. 9, 1942; the quotation is from Sprinzak's remarks at the GCE, Feb. 15, 1943, CZA J1/7255; see also A. Katzenelson at GCE.

26 *HaPo'el HaZair*, Dec. 10, 1942; *HaArez* editorial, June 5, 1944; *BaMa'agal HaSatum* (above, n. 8), p. 49, etc.

27 Y. Tabenkin's remarks at the Kibbutz HaMe'uhad council, Ramat HaKovesh, Jan. 2, 1943, appeared in *Zeror Mikhtavim* 131 (Jan. 22, 1943); Berl Katzenelson, *Writings* 12 (Hebrew) (Tel Aviv, 1950), p. 222, includes remarks made at a Mapai young leadership seminar, June 6, 1944. Regarding his feelings on the matter, see Anita Shapira, *Berl* (Hebrew) (Tel Aviv, 1980), pp. 668–671.

28 JAE, Dec. 6, 1942, CZA. For an analysis of the negative effect of the formal, organized mourning on the capacity for action during the period of the Holocaust, see Fischel Schneersohn, *The Historical Psychology of Holocaust and Rebirth* (Hebrew) (Tel Aviv, 1968). These articles were published in the daily press, principally *Davar* and *HaZofe* during 1943–1945, and Schneersohn routinely sent copies of them to Ben-Gurion. See Ben-Gurion's letter to him dated Oct. 28, 1943, *Al Domi* folders in the Teachers' Union Archive, Tel Aviv (hereafter, TUA). Interestingly enough, despite the fact that they agreed in theory that the days of mourning had a negative effect, they arrived at opposite practical conclusions; Ben-Gurion opposing organized mourning, Schneersohn favoring it.

29 GCE, Dec. 14, 1942, CZA J1/7255; *Davar*, Dec. 16, 1942; RC, Jan. 31, 1943, CZA S26/1239: "They attacked us for prejudicing their livelihood." At the GCE, July 12, 1943, it was resolved that before each day of mourning the movie theater owners should be consulted, CZA J1/7256.

30 On this group, see Dina Porat, "*Al Domi*, Intellectuals in Palestine in the face of the Holocaust, 1943–1945" (Hebrew), *Zionut* 8 (1983):245–275. It included the author Rabbi Binyamin; professors Fischel Schneersohn, Martin Buber, Ben-Zion Dinur, and Yosef Klausner; Yizhak Yaziv of *Davar*, and others. The idea of a regime of mourning won adherents primarily among writers and intellectuals; see Yehuda Kaufman, *Moznaim* 18 (1944):341; Chaim Greenberg, *Davar*, July 30, 1943; S.H. Bergman's letter dated April 7, 1943 to *Al Domi*, TUA.

31 "Al Dema," *HaArez*, Jan. 8, 1943, in the "Against the Current" column and in recurring letters to the editor until the end of January.

32 B. Katzenelson, *Writings* (above, n. 27), p. 217.

33 Ben-Zvi expressed his objections and doubts about a public response at nearly every meeting of the GCE, RC, and JAE, and on other occasions, yet he was never criticized, whereas Gruenbaum's statement at the ZCE, May 18, 1943, created a stir, CZA S26/297; for example, A. Haft at the LPC, Feb. 10, 1943, LPA 3/4a; Yaziv in *BaMa'agal HaSatum* (above, n. 8), p. 93.

34 Ben-Zvi and Elmaleh's remarks at GCE, Jan. 17 and 31, 1943, J1/7255. At the ZCE, Jan. 18,

1943, S25/295, Dobkin voiced his doubts as to the possibility of perpetuating such an activity; his words were omitted from the text of his speech when it was published in a leaflet of the Jewish Agency's Office of Information on Jan. 21, 1943, S26/1240; A. Katzenelson said, "The people want active, not passive demonstrations," GCE, Feb. 15, 1943, J1/7255 (all CZA). See also letters of Ben-Ẕvi and S.Z. Shragai to the *Al Domi* group dated April 28, 1943 in the *Al Domi* folders, TUA: "We tried but did not succeed." The press also reflected this. The original plan was that each Thursday of the month of mourning would be a day of fasting, prayer, study, etc., but this was carried out only once. The press of June 13, 1943 carried a request by the GCE (apparently on the basis of prior experience) that the public demonstrate rather than use the day to tour the country. See also *BaMa'agal HaSatum* (above, n. 8), pp. 88–106, and Ben-Ẕion Dinur, "Remember" (Hebrew), *Devarim 'al HaShoa VeLekaḥa* (Jerusalem, 1958), pp. 14–34.

35 Meetings of GCE, Jan. 11, 1943, J1/7255; RC, Jan. 10, 1943, S26/1237, and Jan. 15, 1943, S26/1239 (all CZA).

36 Meetings of RC, Jan. 15, 1943, S26/1239; Jan. 28, 1943, S26/1237; Jan. 31, 1943, S26/1239; Feb. 7, 1943, S26/1239; Feb. 22, 1943, S26/1237; March 4, 1943, S26/1237 (all CZA).

37 See meetings of the Histadrut Executive Committee (HEC), Jan. 27–28, 1943, vol. 67m, Histadrut Archive (hereafter, HA); see also Gruenbaum's statements, RC, Jan. 15, 1943, S26/1239, expressing amazement at the delays in organizing the rally in New York, and Dr. Goldmann's letter of explanation to Gruenbaum dated April 5, 1943, S26/1234, (both CZA).

38 RC, Jan. 15, 1943, S26/1239; and GCE, Feb. 15, 1943, J1/7255 (both CZA).

39 GCE, Feb. 17, 1943, *ibid.*

40 LPC, Feb. 10, 1943, LPA 4a/3; JAE, Feb. 14, 1943, CZA.

41 S.Z. Shragai, in a conversation with the author, Feb. 6, 1981, Jerusalem. He was replaced on the Rescue Committee by Binyamin Mintz of Agudat Yisrael. Shragai also resigned from the joint subcommittee of the Jewish Agency Executive and the General Council Executive which had been appointed to organize the *yishuv*'s response. He felt that the public meetings and days of mourning were organized without complete faith in their effectiveness.

42 At a meeting of the GCE, Feb. 15, 1943, opinions were expressed against the fast, CZA J1/7255.

43 Ben-Ẕvi spoke about fear of the Arabs at the RC, Jan. 31, 1943, S26/1239, and at the GCE, June 1, 1943, J1/7256. The quotations are from Dr. Werner Senator, JAE, April 4, 1943, and from Gruenbaum, RC, Jan. 31, 1943, S26/1239. See also E. Reis, RC, March 8, 1943, S26/1237, and discussion, GCE, June 1, 1943, J1/7256 (all CZA).

44 The proposal was made by Klarman, RC, Jan. 15, 1943, CZA S26/1239.

45 ZCE, Jan. 18, 1943, where Y. Ḥazan, E. Reiss, and D. Zukhoviẕki (Zakay) demanded "a great outcry," CZA S25/295. The quotations are from remarks by Y. Sprinẕak and Dr. Rufeisen at that meeting. For remarks by Ben-Ẕvi regarding public pressure, and his warning that if the institutions did not coordinate the activity the communities would act on their own, see GCE, Dec. 14, 1942, CZA J1/7255.

46 For a summary of the news items see Gruenbaum's speech, EA, Feb. 22, 1943; the press of that date, and S26/1240. On the declaration of the Elected Assembly, see *Sefer HaTe'udot* (above, n. 5), pp. 339–340 (this was the twelfth session of the Third Elected Assembly); a discussion prior to the Assembly, at the GCE meeting Feb. 17, 1943, J1/7255, and after it, at the RC meeting, Feb. 22, 1943, S26/1237 (all CZA).

47 Statements by S.Z. Shragai and Sprinẕak, GCE, Feb. 17, 1943, CZA J1/7255.

48 *Sefer HaTe'udot* (above, n. 5), pp. 341–342. This was the thirteenth session of the Third Elected Assembly.

49 Gruenbaum, JAE, April 4, 1943; Rabbi I.M. Levin, RC, April 16, 1943, S26/1237; M. Kolodny (Kol) and Y. Zerubavel, ZCE, May 18, 1943, S25/297; the quotation is from statements by Moshe Erem, GCE, June 1, 1943, J1/7256 (all CZA). In Feingold's opinion, a "pattern for a regular protest ritual" developed in the United States as well, *The Politics of Rescue* (above, n. 22), p. 175.

50 Klarman and Haft's proposal, RC, March 8, 1943, S26/1237, and March 23, 1943, S26/1239 (both CZA); Po'alei Zion: Y. Lev, "The Yishuv Leadership and the Rescue of the Jews of Europe" (Hebrew), *Kol HaPo'el* (March 1943), given first as a lecture at the Central

Committee, Feb. 27, 1943, LPA 407/IV/278. For statements by Y. Zerubavel and M. Erem, see minutes of the Hiṣtadrut Executive Committee, March 31–April 1/2, 1943, HA vol. 67/m. For the demand of the representatives of Polish immigrants at the Rescue Committee, March 8, 1943, CZA S26/1237, see remarks by Dr. Menaḥem Landau; Y. Ben-Ẓvi's remarks, GCE, April 27, 1943, CZA, J1/7256.

51 JAE, April 4 and 11, 1943, CZA.

52 Reiss, ZCE, Jan. 18, 1943, S25/295, and May 18, 1943, S25/297 (both CZA); Hillel Frumkin, LPC, Feb. 10, 1943, LPA 3/4a, quoted from Leib Yaffe's letter to Dr. Goldmann, dated July 22, 1943; Leib Yaffe, *Writings, Letters and Diaries* (Hebrew), ed. B. Yaffe (Jerusalem, 1964), p. 205; see also HEC, Mar. 31–April 1/2, 1943, HA 67m.

53 JAE, April 4 and 11, 1943, CZA.

54 The quotations, in order of appearance, are: David Zukhovizki (later Zakay), ZCE, Jan. 18, 1943, CZA; Yaffe (above, n. 52), p. 201, from his letter to Dr. Stephen Wise dated June 2, 1943; letter sent to Gruenbaum and also published in the daily press on Dec. 6, 1944 by Schneersohn, Yaẓiv, and Rabbi Binyamin in protest against Shertok having opened the session of the Elected Assembly the preceding day with the announcement of the death marches of the Jews of Budapest, and immediately thereafter turning, with his colleagues, to a discussion of current *yishuv* concerns.

55 Sprinzak and A. Katzenelson, GCE, April 5 and 27, 1943, CZA J1/7256.

56 GCE, April 12, 15 and 27, 1943, J1/7256, CZA; HEC, March 31–April 1/2, 1943, 67m, and Hiṣtadrut Executive Secretariat (hereafter, HES), April 4, 1943, 14/43 (both HA).

57 JAE, April 11, 1943, and GCE, April 12, 1943, CZA J1/7256; D. Remez, S.Z. Shragai, and M. Ichilov were appointed members of the subcommittee. They had also volunteered to organize the event itself. See also HES, April 13, 1943, HA.

58 *Sefer HaTe'udot* (above, n. 5), p. 342.

59 See her remarks HES, April 29, 1943, HA.

60 ZCE, May 18, 1943, CZA S25/297. The critics were Y. Zerubavel, E. Reiss, M. Kolodny (Kol), and P. Rosenblüth (Rozen); the debate was carried over to the GCE meetings on May 31, June 1 and 3, 1943, CZA J1/7256. Sprinzak, A. Katzenelson, A. Elmaleh, and Y. Ben-Ẓvi opposed demonstrations because of their fear of the Arabs and the Revisionists, whereas Rabbi M. Ostrovsky, Y. Suprasky, and Z. Shazar demanded action and criticized the Political Department of the Jewish Agency for its fears. Their criticisms were directed largely at Joseph's stand against demonstrations and strikes.

61 Wasserstein (above, n. 17), pp. 204–205.

62 ZCE, May 18, 1943, CZA S25/297.

63 Yaffe (above, n. 52), pp. 199, 201, 202: "The Jews of Palestine are making a tremendous fuss . . . it was two Jews from Palestine who, with their outcries and protests, helped bring about the passing of the resolution on the mass demonstration." This is a reference to Rabbi Meir Berlin and to Yaffe himself who attempted to shake up the Jews of the United States, and to the mass demonstration held on March 2, 1943 in Madison Square Garden. See also GCE, Jan. 11 and 17, 1943, J1/7255; Klarman, RC, Jan. 31, 1943, S26/1239; *Sefer HaTe'udot* (above, n. 5), pp. 334, 340; E. Reiss, ZCE, May 18, 1943, S25/297; Shapira, JAE, April 4, 1943; Dr. Goldmann's letter to Gruenbaum dated April 5, 1943, S26/1234 (all CZA).

64 See discussions, JAE, Feb. 14 and 28, 1943, CZA; LPC, Feb. 10, 1943, LPA 3/4a; and Chaim Greenberg's famous article in *Davar*, July 30, 1943, "Bankrupt!".

65 Gruenbaum, RC, Mar. 23, 1943, S26/1239; Ben-Gurion, JAE, April 4, 1943; Shertok, ZCE, May 18, 1943, S25/297 (all CZA).

66 See Yonatan Kaplan, "Rescue Action by the Irgun Ẓevai Leumi Delegation in the United States during the Holocaust Period" (Hebrew), *Yalkut Moreshet* 30 (Nov. 1981):115–138, and 31 (April 1982):75–96; see also Yaffe (above, n. 52), p. 205; Rabbi Binyamin's articles in *Be'ayot* (April 1944) and in *BaMishor* (Feb. 10, 1944). Rabbi Binyamin called the "Emergency Committee for the Rescue of the Jews of Europe" formed in the United States "a sort of *Al Domi* group in Erez Israel."

67 JAE, June 4, 1944, CZA.

68 On the Hiṣtadrut conference of May 5–7, 1943, see HA, 68/m, and *Davar*, May 7, 1943; also Y. Zerubavel, ZCE, May 18, 1943, CZA S26/297. Opposition to the signing of the petition was

voiced at the JAE, June 6, 1943. Kaplan and Gruenbaum insisted that the resolutions of the GCE were binding.

69 RC, June 11, 1943, S26/1239, and GCE, June 21, 1943, J1/7256 (both CZA). See the debate on the authority of the General Council as against that of the Rescue Committee, and the attempts to pacify the representatives of Agudat Yisrael and the Revisionists with the contention that the oversight had been a mere "formal error." Gruenbaum formulated another public announcement which was submitted for the approval of the Jewish Agency Executive. The announcement stressed that ". . . the leaders of the self-defense and heroism in Warsaw and other Polish cities came from the Zionist movements," June 14, 1943, CZA S26/1240. This announcement was apparently not approved for publication, since it does not appear in *Sefer HaTe'udot* or in the press.

70 The petition which the public signed was formulated by the Histadrut Subcommittee on the Strike and the Petition, headed by Z. Shazar, and composed of M. Erem, M. Ya'ari, G. Myerson and A. Ziesling; the petition was then approved by Gruenbaum and Joseph. See meeting of HES, June 6, 1943, HA; for the text of the petition see *Sefer HaTe'udot*, pp. 343–344, and press of June 14, 1943; on the GCE delegation to the High Commissioner, see GCE, June 21, 28, and July 2, 1943, CZA J1/7256. Agudat Yisrael representatives agreed to join the delegation. A letter addressed by Ben-Zvi to Jews in occupied Europe and sent by courier stressed that the *yishuv*'s petition was an expression of its tremendous anxiety over their plight and of its solidarity with them; *Sefer HaTe'udot*, pp. 347–348.

71 GCE, May 31, June 1 and 3, 1943, J1/7256; Kaplan's remarks were made at JAE, Dec. 20, 1943 (both CZA).

72 Gruenbaum, ZCE, Jan 3, 1944, S25/118; Shertok, ZCE, May 18, 1943, S25/297 (both CZA).

73 On the meeting and the debate at the home of Chief Rabbi Herzog, Dec. 16, 1943, see Idov Cohen's letter to Dobkin dated that same day, S25/1235; also, that day's meeting of RC, S26/1237, and JAE, Dec. 19 and 20, 1943 (all CZA).

74 See press reports of the discussions in the Elected Assembly, Jan. 12, 1944.

75 See Dobkin's remarks on the evaluation of the envoys, JAE, Dec. 20, 1943; ZCE, Jan 3, 1944, CZA S25/118.

76 See remarks by M. Neustadt and J. Aharonovitz, HES, April 25, 1944, HA; JAE, May 21, 1944, CZA.

77 *Sefer HaTe'udot* (above, n. 5), pp. 355–356, and the daily press.

78 *Ibid.*, p. 366, and the press of December 1944 and March 1945.

PARTNERS AND ADVERSARIES:
JEWISH SURVIVORS OF WORLD WAR II,
THE JEWISH AGENCY, AND BRITAIN

YOAV GELBER

*J*ewish survivors of World War II, especially from Eastern Europe, constituted a 'hard core' component of the general displaced person problem, due to the complicated political situation in the communist countries and to anti-Semitic outbursts. For these Jews, Palestine loomed as the Promised Land and the answer to the 'Jewish problem' after the Holocaust. However, immigration to Palestine was severely curtailed by the British White Paper. Y. Gelber analyzes the impact of the survivors' situation on the formulation of Zionist policy at the end of the war, discusses the opposing tendencies within Zionist leadership, and shows how the plight of the survivors led David Ben-Gurion to the decision to wage an all-out battle against the White Paper. Gelber also traces the moral pressure exerted on the British through various channels, most notably the American government, to abandon that policy.

The 'survivors' or 'surviving remnant' was the term given to the European Jews who emerged alive from the Holocaust. Their actual survival was a matter of many vicissitudes and accidents of fate. Some Jews managed to endure the hell of the ghettos, the concentration camps, the death camps and the death marches. Some managed to hide in their home-towns, change their identity or find refuge with non-Jewish individuals or institutions, while others managed to escape in time to areas that were not conquered by the Germans, to neutral countries or to the U.S.S.R. The number of Jews left in Europe (not including the U.S.S.R. and Britain) after the war has been estimated at 1,153,000.[1]

The problem of returning people to their homes was one of the most difficult and complex which confronted the Allies at the end of the war. During the war years millions of people had been uprooted from their homes. These included refugees who fled the war, slave-laborers sent primarily to Germany, prisoners-of-war in camps and labor-detachments, ethnic Germans who were transferred from their occupied countries of residence to Germany, and collaborators of all nations, who retreated with the German forces. During the final stages of the war the Allied armies dealt with hundreds of thousands of displaced persons who were assembled in camps. Some of them were even returned to their homes, but the full extent of the problem was revealed only after victory had been achieved.

In March 1945 the number of displaced persons under the control of the Allies in Western Europe was estimated at 350,000, and on the eve of V-Day more than three million displaced persons were counted in the area of Germany that was conquered by the Western powers.[2] By September 1945 the figure had risen to 6,800,000 in Germany, Austria and Czechoslovakia, with another 6,870,000 displaced persons in the areas conquered by the Red Army. There were another 100,000 D.P.s in Italy, 250,000 in Denmark, and 140,000 in Norway. Approximately half the D.P.s were citizens of the U.S.S.R.[3]

All these masses of people had to be located and identified in order to separate refugees from collaborators. They were scattered in thousands of groups throughout the towns, farms and factories of Germany. It was necessary to assemble them, find them temporary accommodation and feed them. Then they had to be returned to their homes. Eleven million people were waiting to be repatriated, the vast majority of them located within the former German Reich.

As long as the fighting continued it was impossible to undertake the task of repatriation on a large scale. The seas were mined and infested with submarines, while the roads were destroyed. The continuing war prevented the allocation of logistic resources for the transportation of the millions of displaced persons. Apart from evacuating the refugees from the battlefront and sending them to assembly centers in the rear, the Allies limited themselves to dealing with the D.P.s wherever they were. In the summer of 1945, however, Europe experienced a mass population shift of millions of people, who made their way home across the continent by every possible means of transport. During the first month after victory almost three million people, including one and a quarter million Frenchmen and more than a million Russians, were returned to their homes from the areas conquered by the Western powers.[4] Part of this movement was self-motivated, while part was organized by the Allied military headquarters and the refugee organizations, chief among them UNRRA. They tried to introduce some semblance of order by concentrating the refugees in assembly centers, registering, identifying and classifying them, and determining the order of priorities for despatching them by the means of transportation available.[5]

With the passage of time this order of priorities was affected by political considerations stemming from the tension between the Russians and the Western Allies. The Russians insisted on mutuality and equality in the exchanges of refugees and released prisoners-of-war from Western countries who were in the area under their control, and Soviet citizens and prisoners-of-war who were in areas under Allied control. Many of the latter attempted to evade repatriation, and the Russians exerted pressure on Allied headquarters to force the return of Russian, Ukrainian and Baltic refugees, by delaying the transfer of British and American citizens and prisoners-of-war who had been liberated by them.[6] The Supreme Allied Command opted for the return of British and American citizens from the Russian areas, and consequently operated air-ferries which transferred thousands of people in both directions every day. By mid-July two million Russians had been sent East, and less than half a million were left in the area under Western control. At the same time the repatriation of citizens of Western European countries was completed.[7]

Border shifts between the West and the Soviet-controlled areas were another factor affecting the order of priorities. The highest priority was accorded to refugees from Western Europe located in areas that were destined to come under Russian control, as well as to Polish prisoners-of-war who refused to return to Communist Poland. In addition to these basic issues involving relations with the Russians, the Repatriation Committees which were set up in the various Commands to coordinate activities had to deal with many small groups with special characteristics and needs.[8]

Within the overall problem of 14 million displaced persons and 11 million people awaiting repatriation, the Jewish survivors were initially only a marginal element. In Western Germany there were at first only 25,000 Jewish (stateless) refugees out of a total of seven million displaced persons. The rest identified themselves or were identified in terms of their countries of origin, and were included with the large numbers of non-Jews of various nationalities in the camps and assembly centers. Most of the 25,000 stateless persons were from Central and Eastern Europe and had fled as refugees to other countries prior to the war, losing their previous citizenship without being given a new one.

During the first few months after victory the problem of the Jewish refugees was concentrated primarily in Eastern Europe and the U.S.S.R., and there are no reliable figures regarding its extent. It seems, however, that during the final months of the war thousands of Jews made their way from their places of refuge to their homes in liberated Eastern Europe, and when they realized that there was no one and no place to return to, they continued their wandering. The surviving members of the Zionist youth movements sought to reach Palestine, making initially for countries and ports from which they hoped to embark. Some people sought to be united with relatives in non-European countries and in order to do so had to leave the U.S.S.R., from which it would be impossible to emigrate. Others travelled in search of family members who had disappeared during the war, or in an attempt to regain possession of property they had left behind them in their flight. Within the general confusion of mass migration after the Germans' capitulation, the movement of the Jews was not particularly apparent. After a few months, however, when millions of displaced persons had returned to and been absorbed in their countries of origin the Jews remained one of the three 'hard core' components of the D.P. problem. Together with soldiers of the Polish army and their families who refused to return to Communist

276

Poland, and the Ukrainians who declined to go back to the U.S.S.R., the Jews — most of them from Eastern Europe — constituted the bulk of the occupants of the D.P. camps set up in Germany, Austria and Italy.

Alternatives Facing the Survivors

During the first few years after World War II the Jews of Europe considered their future. The process of deliberation was simpler in the countries of Western Europe, such as France, the Netherlands, Scandinavia and Italy, because Jewish citizens of those countries could find a place within the national, social, and economic life. In fact, the over-riding majority of the Jews, including many survivors from Central and Eastern Europe who had found refuge in these countries before the war, chose to remain there.

Thus, in the countries of Western Europe, the Jewish problems which had to be dealt with in the post-war years were — absorbing those returning from concentration camps and from neutral countries, reorganizing the Jewish communities, coordinating local and overseas aid efforts, providing employment and economic rehabilitation, returning apartments and property which had been transferred to others during the war, and locating Jewish children who had been 'farmed out' during the war, in order to restore them to Judaism and to their families. The Zionist solution to the question of Jewish existence, insofar as this concerned individual fulfillment through migration to Palestine, attracted only a minority of the Jews of those countries. Small groups, like that of the French resistance fighters (Armée Juive), constituted exceptions which proved the rule.

Matters were different in Eastern Europe, where the Jewish survivors faced a complex choice among several alternatives. Even before the war, various possible solutions to the question of their existence had been considered by the large Jewish communities of those countries. These ranged from maintaining the traditional framework of Jewish existence, through a national-Zionist or national-socialist solution, to assimilation within the pre-war environment, or within the framework of a re-ordered society. In the post-war world some of these options vanished as a result of the Communist regime instituted in the countries of Eastern Europe after their liberation by the Red Army. Traditional Jewish life seemed untenable within the framework of a Communist regime, in view of what had happened in the U.S.S.R. in the period between the wars. A socialist solution such as that advocated by the Bund in Poland was also impossible. The erstwhile members of the Bund had been dispersed, some being absorbed by the Communist Party, some by the Zionist movement, while yet others escaped from the dilemma and from the necessity of admitting the failure of their ideas by emigrating to the U.S.A. or Australia. The Bund ceased to be a factor in Jewish public life in Poland.

The Communist parties constituted a focal point of attraction for the Jews of Eastern Europe after the liberation. This was due primarily to the halo surrounding the Red Army as a liberating force. The Jews were attracted to

Communism for opportunistic reasons too, though it can be said that the attraction was mutual. The Communist regimes in Eastern Europe rested on a very narrow basis of popular support. The Jews were regarded as being among the elements that were most loyal to the regime, and consequently it was easy for them to obtain public positions. In turn, people whose world had crumbled about them during the war years saw this as an enticing opportunity to turn a new leaf and find personal rehabilitation.[9] On the other hand, the Communist regime, and particularly its accompanying economic structure, repelled many Jews who feared they would be unable to adapt and earn a living within that framework. The Communist regimes themselves, however, realized very quickly — even though the Jews sometimes preceded them in this — that the fact that they were being identified with the Jews made it more difficult for them to be accepted by the non-Jewish population. Consequently, the process of the Soviet regime's entrenchment in the countries of Eastern Europe during the post-war years was accompanied by the trend to free itself of the Jews and remove them from influential government positions.

Nor did liberation wipe out grass-roots anti-Semitism in Eastern Europe. The activities of the Banderovci in the Ukraine and Eastern Galicia, the robbing and murder of Jews in Polish towns, the distribution of anti-Semitic leaflets, the difficulties encountered by survivors who returned to their homes in obtaining their former apartments and other property, and finally a wave of pogroms culminating in Kielce in May 1946, were examples of the obstacles confronting the Jews who wished to rehabilitate themselves in their countries of origin. These led them to search for a different, safer, future — which could not be found in Eastern Europe. As a result, Jews who had realized the pointlessness of remaining in Poland, and later on also in Hungary, Rumania, Bulgaria, Yugoslavia and finally Czechoslovakia, decided to move to the West, to a place from which they could continue to any further destination they might decide on. In this way, the wave of 'escapees' shifted from being a small group of people trying to reach Palestine, to an extensive popular movement seeking to get out of the Communist countries of Eastern Europe — Poland, first and foremost.

In the D.P. camps in Germany, Austria and Italy, however, which housed these 'escapees', the goal of the 'Bericha' (escape) movement shifted from the exodus from Eastern Europe to immigration to Palestine. From the moment these camps were liberated they contained a Zionist nucleus which, after experiencing the Holocaust, saw Palestine, and Palestine alone, as the answer to the Jewish problem. This nucleus expanded when the survivors of the Zionist youth movements reached the displaced persons' camps from the East, and with the vigorous encouragement of emissaries from Palestine — first the Jewish Brigade soldiers and then, from early 1946, members of the welfare units — it gained a growing hold on the survivors in the camps. The secret hopes of many of these people may still have been inclined towards America, but their collective, politically significant, demand was directed unequivocally at Palestine and at the Power which ruled it.

Formulation of Zionist Policy Towards the End of the War

When the war ended the Zionist leadership had been engaged for more than a year in formulating its political program and demands for the Peace Conference. In June 1944, after the invasion of Normandy, Ben-Gurion was convinced that "we are approaching the end of the war. This means that we are approaching a decision regarding our affairs. I think that our political program is inadequate because it is not sufficiently concrete." The formula for the Jewish state within the Biltmore Plan and the 'Jerusalem Program' which had been approved by the Zionist Action Committee in October 1942, was now broken up by Ben-Gurion into three claims, which he presented to his colleagues on the Zionist Executive: a. To bring one million Jews to Palestine *immediately* after the conclusion of the war; b. To establish Jewish control over immigration; c. "To establish a Jewish state in Palestine, within a brief period of a few months." He also sought a loan of one billion dollars and "a claim of financial restitution for the Jewish people from Germany, to be used for Eretz Israel; not for individuals, not for those who suffered injury, but for the entire Jewish people, and in an appropriate amount." Ben-Gurion felt that the hundreds of thousands of Jews left in Europe would be "the first candidates for America's soup-kitchens. I say: we should establish soup-kitchens for them in Palestine, bring them here and feed them here." He felt the figure of a million Jews could be reached by drawing on the Jews of Islamic countries.

Ben-Gurion's audacious demand aroused the apprehensions and reservations of his colleagues on the Jewish Agency who were afraid to absorb so many immigrants in such a short time. They pointed to the difficulties which had been encountered in housing and absorbing the few immigrants who had begun arriving in early 1944. Rabbi Y.L. Fishman feared mass emigration in the wake of mass immigration, and Eliezer Kaplan warned of unemployment and rejected the idea of 'soup-kitchens.' I. Gruenbaum agreed with Ben-Gurion in principle, but did not believe that achieving a Jewish majority in Palestine in this way would solve the problem of Arab opposition to a Jewish state. M. Shapira stressed the political significance of absorbing the survivors: "A great many of them will not last, some may even die, but most of them will remain in Palestine, and together with us they will constitute the majority we need so badly." Ben-Gurion's frustration was apparent in his summation of the discussion: "I regard the implementation of the Biltmore Plan as having two basic roles: to prepare the Jews and to prepare the Gentiles. I find that preparing the Jews is more difficult than preparing the Gentiles."[10]

During the months that followed the Normandy invasion, it transpired that the war would not end as quickly as had been expected. The leadership of the Zionist movement and of Palestinian Jewry was involved with such issues as saving the Jews of Hungary, the problems created by the activities of the underground organizations, Irgun Zevai Leumi (IZL) and Lohamei Herut Israel (LHI), and negotiations to establish the Jewish Brigade. Development of a post-

Jewish Agency Executive, Jerusalem, 1944. From left: M. Shapiro, Dr. E. Shmorak, W. Senator, M. Shertok, E. Kaplan, Rabbi Y.L. Fishman, C. Weizmann, D. Ben-Gurion

war political program was not given high priority. Ben-Gurion's ideas were not generally accepted, even in Palestine, and against the background of the tension between Chaim Weizmann (the President of the World Zionist Organization) and Ben-Gurion, Moshe Shertok head of the Jewish Agency's Political Department found it difficult to obtain support for them in London. For many weeks arguments raged in Jewish Agency circles in London as to whether it was at all appropriate for the Agency to present demands to the British Government at this stage, and if so how they should be formulated. Finally, in October 1944, Weizmann submitted a flowery memorandum to the Colonial Secretary in which the Zionist demands were stated gently, with the emphasis laid on Britain's historical commitment to Zionism, the situation of the Jewish people as a result of the war, and Zionist opposition to the partition of Palestine, a solution about which rumors had been rife for approximately a year. Three weeks later, Weizmann met with Prime Minister Churchill and Herbert Morrison, the chairman of the Cabinet Committee on Palestine. Weizmann's object was to present the Jewish Agency's opposition to partition, but he does not appear to have impressed this upon them. Churchill made it clear that nothing would happen until Germany had been defeated, and that he himself was in close contact with America on the Palestine question. Weizmann refrained from making the demands which had been formulated in Jerusalem, explaining to Churchill that he was thinking in terms of the immigration of one hundred thousand persons per year for fifteen years.[11] Weizmann left the meeting feeling that Morrison "hated the idea of partition," and that the Zionists had to focus their efforts on changing the minds of the Conservative members of Parliament, who constituted the major obstacle in Churchill's path. He was convinced that with the support of the United States, the Jews could obtain all of Western

Palestine. He was also certain that he could persuade the President of the United States to support this view.[12]

The assassination of the British Resident Minister in the Middle East, Lord Moyne, on November 6, 1944 upset the political calculations. It destroyed the delicate balance between the supporters and opponents of partition on the British side, where Moyne was of particular importance because he was the Minister 'in the field'. His successor, Edward Grigg, rejected the idea of partition, believing that both Arabs and Jews would oppose it and would prevent the British from using it to bypass the problem of immigration.[13] He supported the idea of a Trusteeship in Palestine which would obtain international approval and would assure imperial interests in the region.[14] Shertok noted, after meeting him, that "we saw in the Minister a tendency to hide behind Russia's back with regard to the political issue."[15] Grigg on his part blocked Weizmann's attempts to obtain a recommendation from Churchill, which would enable him to meet Stalin or appear before the leaders of the three Powers at their conference in Yalta.[16]

Immigration and its Role in Zionist Policy at the End of the War

The suspension of the Partition Plan, the approaching end of the war, the liberation of the Jews in several European countries and primarily, the rapidly advancing termination of the immigration quota fixed in the White Paper, placed the question of immigration at the forefront of the Zionist political effort. Since it was obvious that matters of principle would not be decided in the Middle East, there was a growing demand in the Jewish Agency Executive to transfer the focus of political activity to London and the United States:

> We are approaching the end of the war, and we are all sitting here with the President [Weizmann] and the Chairman of the Executive [Ben-Gurion], while the main theatre of action at present is London and Washington. The moment of decision is approaching and we are here, 'peaceful in Zion.' This is no longer the time to argue about a few extra immigration certificates. We must fight for the principle... Dr. Weizmann's place now is in the United States, and Mr. Ben-Gurion should be there too...[17]

In the Mapai secretariat Sprinzak maintained that "Ben-Gurion should not concern himself with party matters... he should concentrate on Zionist and Jewish Agency affairs. Moshe [Shertok] must find someone else to deal with the Brigade affairs... and he himself should be involved in what is happening in London and Washington..." The differences of opinion between Ben-Gurion and Weizmann made it difficult to embark on a new political initiative. Ben-Gurion opposed the idea of Weizmann going to the United States alone, and insisted on a delegation consisting of Weizmann, Rabbi Fishman and himself. In a party forum he was more explicit on this matter. On the one hand, he analyzed the difficulties of the Jewish people and the Zionist movement in preparing a great immigration enterprise:

281

> ...Till now we have known that we face one great obstacle... the White Paper. It is becoming clear that... there is a red paper... And if one can get in [to Palestine] without permission under certain conditions... one can't get out [of Europe] without permission quite so easily. We can get a few Jews across the border illegally, but we cannot go to war over this. Most of the Jews of Europe are not prepared for war... They want to go to Palestine, but they will not fight if someone opposes this...

On the other hand he saw danger in the possibility that the Zionist political struggle would be conducted by Weizmann alone, or with Naḥum Goldmann's help:

> ...I am full of anxiety regarding this trip of Weizmann's to America because he does not understand his situation, and the situation of the Jewish people in the world... I am very apprehensive about Goldmann... because he is more involved in the affairs of the [World] Jewish Congress than with the fate of the Jewish people... He is not the man who can guide the [Zionist] Movement...[18]

The confrontation between Weizmann and Ben-Gurion took place at the meeting of the Jewish Agency Executive on February 11, 1945 and centered primarily on what Weizmann defined as the hostile attitude of the Palestinian Jewish community to Britain, and his claim that Ben-Gurion's program for the immediate immigration of one million Jews at the end of the war was unrealistic.[19] Although the Executive did not reach a decision in the argument between the two leaders, it accepted the principle that Weizmann's representation of Zionist affairs in his contacts with the governments of Britain and America had to be kept under scrutiny. It was agreed that public opinion in America, and primarily the Zionist movement and the Jews of the United States, should be activated to put pressure on the administration regarding an overall solution to the problem of Palestine, while at the same time a campaign would be conducted in London for the continuation and expansion of immigration to Palestine.[20] It was principally for this purpose that Ben-Gurion went to London at the end of March, and as V-Day approached, the center of Zionist political activity shifted to that city.[21]

News About the Survivors and its Influence on the Political Program

282

News about surviving Jews in Europe, which was revealed during the last few months of the war, was a principal factor in changing the emphasis of the Zionist struggle from the political solution to the question of immigration. The first Jewish parachutists dropped in Rumania returned to Palestine in the autumn of 1944 and brought news of the Jews who had survived there. At the end of that year information filtered through of Jewish survivors in other countries. Ruzka Korzcak reached Palestine from Vilna in December, bringing the information that there were 2,000 Jews living in Vilna at that time, but that the authorities were not able to guarantee their welfare and continued existence.[22]

At the same time news began to trickle through about the situation of the Jews who had been liberated in Western Europe. Rabbi Isaac Levi, the chaplain of the Second British Army, wrote from Belgium that "The youngsters of Brussels... are excellent material for re-education." He drew attention to the problem of children who had been left in the care of Christians, particularly in Holland, who were being treated well but would undoubtedly suffer from the influence exerted upon them. Levi wrote about hundreds of Jews who had escaped by virtue of false papers, and were now gathering in the liberated part of Holland and searching for something useful to do. He suggested that the children from the Christian foster-families should be assembled there so that Jews could look after them, but added that the resistance movement objected to this, maintaining that they should wait until the whole country was liberated.[23] When these and other items of news reached Palestine they brought to the forefront the question of the immigration of the survivors. In Jewish Agency and political party discussions, demands were made for "one hundred thousand immigration certificates, including thirty to forty thousand for children."[24] The continued restrictions of the White Paper and its limited allocation of immigration certificates gave rise to demands at the beginning of 1945 to embark on a public struggle within the *yishuv,* even at the price of worsening relations with the authorities. Ben-Gurion rejected this approach, maintaining that first the Zionist leadership abroad had to be made aware of the importance of immigration. He also claimed that the *yishuv* (the Jewish community in Palestine) was not yet ready for a struggle of this kind until it presented its case to the British government and the Zionist Office in London. "The one thing that is really dependent only on Palestine," he said, "is immigration, which does not depend upon the government. For this we need money and ships, but this has to be done, not talked about."[25] Just prior to Ben-Gurion's departure for London, in March 1945, Shaul Meirov complained that "Immigration is dying — choking or being strangled," and urged Ben-Gurion to try and find a way to the hearts of the Russians in order to solve the problem of embarkation from areas under their control.[26] Three days later Ben-Gurion bade farewell to his colleagues in the Labor Party, explaining the objectives of his journey and his evaluation of the situation of the Jewish people, Zionism and the *yishuv* at the end of the war:

> ...A Zionist solution to the Palestine question cannot be achieved without mobilizing the Jewish people and enlisting the help of public opinion and world leaders. However... there is only one force that can prevent an anti-Zionist solution, and that is the *yishuv*... At the same time we must maintain close contact with the Jews of Europe. And this is not so easy now... We have experience from countries which one cannot get into and we will have to find new ways of getting there. Our contact with the surviving Jews of Europe may be one of the crucial factors in determining the solution of the Palestine question... This obliges us not only to

283

undertake political activity. It obliges us... to open paths to Palestine from the East and the West by ourselves, and to increase awareness among the large Jewish communities that can help us...[27]

After Ben-Gurion had left for London the situation of the Jews in the countries which had been liberated from the Nazis became clearer. Ehud Avriel, the representative of the 'Mossad l'Aliyah' in Istanbul, reached Palestine from Constantinople in March 1945, and gave a detailed report of the situation in each country, as it was known to the members of the delegation there. He described the continuing anti-Semitism in Hungary and Poland, where the question of immigration was not ideological or political but derived from the fact that "the Jews cannot and do not wish to remain." On the other hand, he said:

> They are so wretched and depressed, have been through so much persecution and suffering, that they do not have the strength to withstand the immense forces seeking to conquer their hearts in Hungary and elsewhere... Anyone who cannot migrate to Palestine must live, must conform... and the soul of our Movement is in grave danger if we do not manage to get a great many Jews out of there within a short space of time.

He assessed that there were chances for immigration from only two countries, Rumania and Bulgaria, but even here, he felt, there would be many political and practical difficulties to be overcome.[28]

In effect, Zionist political activity had been frozen in Britain because of Weizmann's illness and an accident in which Ben-Gurion had been involved. This caused concern in Palestine regarding the push for immigration, particularly after Avriel's admonitions. Technical, bureaucratic, and political difficulties delayed even the utilization of the few thousand immigration certificates which had been allocated to the Jewish Agency by the British at the end of 1944. Information about the movement of Jews from the East to the liberated areas of Poland, the difficulties encountered in getting Jews out of Bulgaria, and the delays in the departure of certificate-holders from Rumania, aroused concern about the Russian attitude regarding the departure of Jews from the European countries under their control. Meirov cautioned, basing himself on the reports of emissaries, that

Shipment of clothing
and medicines from
the *yishuv* to liberated
Polish Jewry, 1945

> the news reaching us from the various diasporas is unprecedentedly grave.
> In the present condition of Europe's Jews... each day that passes without
> immigration is terrible... They have neither the time, the strength, nor the
> nerves to wait. The initial desire of the Jews to immigrate to Palestine will
> be lost in these circumstances.

In view of the lack of enthusiasm for illegal immigration in Italy and the
difficulties in leaving the Balkans, he warned against depending on the arrival of
illegal immigrants.

Eliahu Dobkin proposed that the demand for one hundred thousand
immigration certificates be placed at the center of Zionist political efforts, and
that an official demand be made to the British government. Meirov maintained
that making immigration dependent on an overall political solution could delay
it for an unlimited period of time, with all the dangers this involved:

> ...We know what kind of 'just world' is being prepared for us out there.
> And in this situation, if we do not demonstrate that Jews either come to
> Palestine or break into it (by other means), what little desire Jews have to
> immigrate dissolves. What will happen? Who will pay attention to us? In
> such a situation the entire question of the Jewish state will have no basis.

Meirov feared Weizmann's unwillingness to invest efforts in the matter of
immigration, and asked Shertok to focus his activities in London on it.[29]

What was clear in Jerusalem was not yet apparent in London. There the
debate focused on determining priorities between the efforts to reach a political
decision about the fate of Palestine, and solving the urgent immigration
problems, and the tactics this required vis-à-vis the British government.[30] At the
conclusion of a series of discussions, an official Jewish Agency memorandum
was drawn up and sent to Churchill by Weizmann on May 22, 1945. The
memorandum listed the first Zionist demand as a request for an immediate
decision regarding the establishment of a Jewish state in Palestine, followed by a
decision to grant the Jewish Agency the necessary authority to transfer as many
Jews as possible to Palestine, to grant an international loan to finance the
transfer and absorption of these Jews, to give the Jews preference in obtaining
restitution from Germany — and first and foremost to sequester German
property in Palestine on their behalf, and to ease the departure and transfer of
Jews to Palestine.[31]

News About the Concentration Camp Survivors, and its Influence

Meanwhile the first items of information about the situation of the survivors of
the camps in Germany, and the survivors of the Holocaust in general, became
known. With the conclusion of the war travel arrangements and the crossing of
borders in Western Europe were easier. Ben-Gurion made a short visit to
France, where he met French Jews and J.D.C. officials, heard about the
situation of the Jews in Belgium and Holland and received an initial report on

the state of affairs in Dachau.[32] Adroit journalists managed to visit the concentration camps individually and sent telegraphed reports about the situation there, or reported on it after their return to Britain.[33] At the end of May an urgent call seeking aid, primarily medical, for the camp survivors was sent by Dr. Greenberg, a leader of the survivors in Southern Germany, to the World Jewish Congress in Switzerland.[34]

David Shealtiel and Ruth Klüger, both emissaries of the Jewish Agency, reported from Paris about the pressure exerted on the Jews in the camps by the repatriation committees to return to their countries of origin, and on the difficulties encountered in absorbing a large group of children from Buchenwald who had been transferred to France. Most of them were given into the care of the OSE organization. In addition, approximately one hundred children who were supposed to immigrate to Palestine were regarded by the French authorities as being under their supervision, and only after lengthy discussions were they allowed to be placed under Jewish supervision in institutions near Paris. All these were alarming indications of what would happen to the other survivors in the camps. The emissaries in France noted that "Germany is the largest reservoir of migration to Palestine today, and the human material is of the most desirable type." They suggested opening a Palestine Bureau at the earliest opportunity and reinforcing the Zionist representation in Paris, from where it would be possible to influence activities among the Jewish survivors in all the countries of Western and Central Europe.[35]

The news from Europe did indeed begin to arouse Jewish public opinion in the West. Jewish organizations in England, such as the World Jewish Congress and the Board of Deputies, began to press the government to allow them to send delegations to examine the situation of the Jews in the camps, and to appoint permanent Jewish representatives alongside the occupation authorities in the British area of Germany.[36] Selig Brodetsky, the President of the Board of Deputies, who was also a member of the Zionist Executive, tried to convince his colleagues in London to join this initiative. Ben-Gurion had reservations about cooperating in the philanthropic efforts of the Jewish organizations, claiming that the problem was not that of the Jewish Agency's cooperation but the fate of the survivors themselves. There was a tendency to transfer the Jewish children from Germany to France, but France was not the new Palestine, and it would be better if the children were to remain in Germany. The attitude of the survivors in Europe to Palestine would be a crucial factor, and this attitude was dependent to a great extent on whether the Zionist movement could establish contact with them. The Jewish Agency in London had to be a center for all Europe, establishing contact with the occupation authorities and initiating projects rather than following the lead of other Jewish organizations.[37]

In Palestine, the news about the plight of the survivors accelerated the decision to demand a larger allocation of certificates.[38] In London, however, the members of the Zionist Executive were more preoccupied with matters of high policy than with the problems of the survivors. They were too impatient to wait for Churchill's delayed reply to their memorandum of May 22, and began to plan their next steps. In the process, fresh disagreements arose between Ben-Gurion and Weizmann over whether it was time to put an end to quiet diplomacy and come out with an open campaign against the British government, which was still adhering to the White Paper. Churchill's reply of June 9, which stated that the Palestine question would have to wait until the Peace Conference, depressed the members of the Zionist Executive and exacerbated the internal differences regarding what the response to it should be. Ben-Gurion demanded that the response should be tangible and forceful, maintaining that if it were not, the situation in Palestine would deteriorate. He claimed that the Prime Minister's letter was "the most serious blow we have received, and our people in London and America are living in a fool's paradise." The issue was not a Jewish state or partition, as was thought in the United States, but the continuation of the White Paper; and Zionist inactivity would be interpreted as acceptance of the White Paper. It was necessary to stop corresponding with the British government, he said, and begin acting in America and Palestine.[39] Weizmann, who felt his own position to be untenable, hinted that he intended to resign, and wrote as much to John Martin, Churchill's private secretary, so that it would reach the Prime Minister.[40] Ben-Gurion decided to go to the United States in order to direct Zionist activity vis-à-vis both the Administration and American public opinion.

Jewish and non-Jewish public opinion, and the press in America and Britain, had meanwhile begun to wake up to the situation of the survivors, particularly the former inmates of the camps in Germany and Austria.[41] Both public opinion and Jewish organizations criticized the pressures exerted on the Jews to return to their former countries, and the fact that they were being kept in camps on the basis of nationality, where they were at the mercy of a non-Jewish and often anti-Semitic majority of Poles, Lithuanians, Hungarians, etc. The lower echelons of the occupying armies and even of UNRRA, who were sorely overworked in the first few months after the liberation, often failed to display sensitivity and understanding of the special situation of the Jews, tending to incorporate them within more general categories. The British put pressure on the Americans not to grant the Jews a separate status from that of the non-Jews in the camps, basing their claims on the UNRRA constitution. The international organization did not oppose the operation of Jewish relief units under its auspices, provided this relief was not restricted solely to Jews.[42] The Jewish Agency negotiated with the heads of UNRRA in Europe regarding the operation of relief units from Palestine in the camps, and the possibility of these units functioning in separate Jewish camps, should these be established.[43]

Harrison's Mission and its Results

Meanwhile, the pressure of public opinion in the United States began to bear fruit. At the initiative of Henry Morgenthau, the Secretary of the Treasury, the State Department instructed Earl Harrison, the American representative at the

Inter-Governmental Committee for Refugees, to go to Europe and investigate the special situation of displaced persons who were unable to return to their countries of origin, primarily Jews. The Allied Supreme Command (S.H.A.E.F.) agreed to this mission, and President Truman gave it his blessing.[44] A senior member of the J.D.C. staff, Joseph Schwartz, was, at Harrison's request, attached by the State Department to the delegation.[45] The leaders of the Zionist Emergency Committee in New York had already established contact with Harrison and briefed him,[46] and Weizmann pressured them from London to hasten his departure.[47] The mission itself hinted at the Administration's inclinations in view of the pressure of public opinion, and the Supreme Command began to adapt to them.

On July 9, 1945 guidelines were issued to the commanders of the army-groups in Germany to concentrate the Jews in special assembly centers and permit the J.D.C. teams to take care of them.[48] Considerable time elapsed before the units in the field began to implement this order, and meanwhile Harrison had cabled Washington giving his impressions of the situation of the Jewish refugees and expressing sharp criticism of the attitude of the military. He advocated confiscating houses belonging to the German population and accommodating the Jews there, instead of housing them in difficult conditions in temporary camps, for due to the impossibility of repatriation they would probably remain in Germany for a long time, until their problem was resolved. Harrison also recommended transferring the supervision of these camps from the army to UNRRA, with the army continuing to help UNRRA so that it could discharge its functions efficiently.[49] The cable was circulated through the various departments of the administration in Washington, and the Pentagon requested urgent clarifications and explanations from Eisenhower.[50] Stephen S. Wise, who was in London for the discussions of the World Zionist Conference, asked via the American Embassy in London that the Commander-in-Chief immediately appoint a Jewish liaison officer in his headquarters, to coordinate the activities connected with the Jewish refugees.[51] The American High Command rejected this proposal vehemently, claiming that the members of the J.D.C. who were functioning within the framework of UNRRA and dealing with the Jewish refugees were quite sufficient.[52] In Washington, Henry Stimson, the Secretary of Defense, did not wait for Eisenhower's response, but cabled him again, stating that people in the capital were worried by the implications of Harrison's expected report, stressing the importance attached to this problem, and demanding that everything be done to improve the situation. In his reply to Stimson Eisenhower complained that Harrison had given him an impression very different from the one he had sent to Washington. He retreated from his initial violent opposition to Wise's request, stating that he would agree to the appointment of a Jewish advisor, but tried to explain the complexity of the Jewish problem within that of the general D.P. question.[53]

Harrison also voiced his reservations concerning the plight of the Jewish refugees in Germany at the meeting of the Inter-Governmental Committee for

Refugees and at the UNRRA Conference, which were both held in London at the beginning of August 1945. The British flatly opposed his recommendations. They believed that any person who was uprooted from his home as a result of the war should be regarded in principle as someone who could be sent back to his own country. The discussion of the D.P. problem should not be made public lest the people involved be encouraged to refuse to return to their countries, thereby increasing the numbers of people who had to be resettled.[54] Behind this stand lay considerations connected with Britain's Palestine policy, and it rested upon the position taken by the Commander-in-Chief in Germany.[55]

Until then the American and British military authorities in Germany and Austria had adopted a similar policy regarding the D.P.s. While the British continued to adhere to their policy, that of the American army began to change as a result of the pressure from Washington instigated by Harrison's reports. At the beginning of August Harrison sent his full report from London to President Truman. The report ended with a recommendation to enable any displaced person who so wished to immigrate to Palestine. At the end of the month, after Harrison had returned to the United States and met the President, the report was sent to Eisenhower with a covering letter from Truman. The President wrote to the Commander-in-Chief that while his policy was correct it was not being implemented by his subordinates as, for example, giving priority in housing to D.P.s who were victims of Nazism, over the German population. Truman wrote, "We must intensify our efforts to get these people out of camps and into decent houses, until they can be repatriated or evacuated. These houses should be requisitioned from the German civilian population." He demanded better supervision over the implementation of orders in the field, and asked that reports be sent to him at the earliest possible opportunity regarding the steps taken to correct the faults described in Harrison's report. Truman also announced that he was contacting the British government directly, and asking it to make an effort to open the gates of Palestine to those displaced persons who wished to migrate there.[56]

As a result of Truman's guidelines, American Headquarters in Germany ordered its units to treat the Jews exactly as they did Allied citizens, without consideration of their previous citizenship. In this way the Jews were no longer classified as nationals of their countries of origin. Although those who wished to return to their countries of origin would be treated as citizens of that country,

Jewish Brigade soldier teaching Jewish children Hebrew in D.P. camp in Bari, Italy

all those without citizenship, or who were Soviet citizens and did not wish to return home, would be defined as stateless and non-repatriable. They would be segregated from the other displaced persons, gathered in separate camps and housed in good quality accommodation which, when necessary, would be confiscated from the Germans. Special UNRRA teams would assume responsibility for these camps.[57] A few weeks later, Eisenhower reported to the President that most of the faults pointed out by Harrison had already been corrected.[58]

Harrison's report, and Truman's ensuing intervention, began a new era for the Jewish D.P.s in Central Europe. The President's appeal to Attlee to allow Jewish D.P.s to migrate to Palestine established a new dimension of international activity regarding the Palestine question. This appeal was made soon after the Jewish Agency issued a public demand for one hundred thousand immigration certificates, together with the rejection of the quota of 3,000 certificates set by the British government. Henceforth the demand for one hundred thousand certificates would be identified with the President's intervention and, because of the problem of the displaced persons, the United States would play a more important role in the political issue of Palestine.

Crystallization of the Labor Government's Palestine Policy

Ever since the assassination of Lord Moyne at the beginning of November 1944, the British Cabinet's discussions of the partition of Palestine had been held in abeyance, at Churchill's instructions. Nevertheless, the Partition Plan remained the only guideline for everything connected with the fate of Palestine, underlying British planning for the Middle East in the post-war period. As the planning teams continued their work they reached the conclusion that the implementation of partition would impose an unbearable burden on the British government and army, on the assumption that both sides — Arabs and Jews — would oppose this solution by force, and even if it were imposed upon them would wait for the appropriate moment to change it for their own benefit.[59] The Chiefs-of-Staff accepted these conclusions, recommending that the Cabinet defer announcing and implementing its new policy in Palestine at least until the end of the war against Germany and Japan, since the forces which would have to be brought in to keep order in the Middle East would be at the expense of the fighting fronts in Europe or the Far East.[60] Although Churchill disagreed with the generals, maintaining that the British should not be the policemen of the Middle East, he refrained from opposing them and expressing his view openly. He confined himself to explaining his views to his Military Secretary, General Ismay, instructing him to keep them to himself.[61]

Just as the British feared the day they would have to publish and implement the Partition Plan, they also feared the day the quota of immigration certificates fixed in the White Paper would be filled, and the British government would have no political program for resolving the Palestine question. Consequently, the bureaucratic echelon, followed by the ministers, began to press for the renewal of the government's discussions of the Palestine question.[62] The purpose of this pressure was not to speed up implementation of the Partition Plan. Quite the contrary, it was to bring about its annulment and engender an improvised, short-term policy that would provide an alternative to a permanent solution of the problem. Foremost among those demanding a retreat from partition and its replacement by another solution was Edward Grigg, the new Resident Minister in the Middle East.[63] His proposals, which required study and analysis by the Cabinet, delayed the resumption of the discussions.[64] His object was to ensure continued British presence in a united Palestine, which he regarded as the keystone of British military deployment in the Middle East. It was with this in mind that he developed the idea of an international trustee government over Palestine, with Britain as its administrator.[65]

Churchill realized that in view of the mood of the Cabinet and army chiefs it would not be possible to reach a positive decision on the implementation of the Partition Plan.[66] As a result, he attempted to persuade his colleagues to absolve the British government completely of the need to decide on the fate of Palestine, transferring this burden to the Americans.[67] The Chiefs-of-Staff rejected this idea vehemently. They claimed that the Middle East continued to be of supreme strategic importance to Britain, and British strategic interests should not be dependent upon American policy in Palestine, the results of which would be borne by Britain without its having any control over it.[68]

At the Potsdam Conference, on July 24, 1945, Truman asked Churchill directly to annul the restrictions on immigration to Palestine.[69] Churchill, who was to fall from office two days later, had no time to reply to this appeal, which was handed on to his successor, Attlee. The Colonial Secretary and the Foreign Minister advised him to equivocate and say that the new government needed time to study the issue, which was being discussed in its various departments.[70]

After June 1945 the government departments did in fact discuss future policy in Palestine, managing to keep the deliberations secret for several weeks and prevent leaks. Five alternatives were presented: a) partition on the basis of the recommendations of the Cabinet Committee appointed in July 1943; b) an international trusteeship government, in accordance with Edward Grigg's recommendations; c) continuation of the policy of the White Paper; d) seeking the consent of the Arabs for continued Jewish immigration at the current rate (1,500 per month); e) continuation of immigration at that rate without being dependent on Arab agreement.[71] The discussion was cut short because of the elections and the change of government in July 1945, but the preparations toward a decision continued at the bureaucratic and ministerial levels. On August 22 the new Labour Government appointed another Cabinet Committee to consider the various alternatives, and this was headed by Herbert Morrison, who had headed the previous Cabinet Committee. Hull, the new Colonial Minister, suggested that the Government decide to stick to the policy of the White Paper with regard to immigration during an interim period, until a long-

Refugees boarding ship in Marseille, and coming ashore in Haifa

term policy was formulated, and at the same time attempt to convince the Arabs to agree to continued immigration at the existing rate. After reaching an interim decision, he felt that the committee could begin to formulate a new policy. Hull wanted the short-term policy to be determined quickly and presented in a separate report, before the long-term policy was formulated.[72] At the same time he submitted to the members of the Committee a new solution that had been prepared by the Colonial Office, which involved dividing Palestine into autonomous regions on the basis of a Jewish or Arab demographic majority.[73]

Various recommendations were submitted from different departments of the British administration: the Foreign Office, the High Commissioner in Palestine, Lord Gort, and the Chiefs-of-Staff. Since the Foreign Office placed its major emphasis on the need for the continued "goodwill of the Arab peoples," it suggested rejecting the two long-term solutions, and the continuation of immigration without Arab consent. It recommended seeking Arab agreement for the immigration of 1,500 persons per month, and if this should be denied, the matter should be brought for the decision of the five world powers.[74]

In contrast to the position of the Foreign Office, the High Commissioner, Lord Gort, disapproved of seeking the Arabs' consent. He claimed that there was no chance of obtaining this, and that continued immigration after this request had been denied would only heighten their anger and hostility. Of all the alternatives Gort preferred the continuation of immigration within the existing framework while emphasizing its temporary nature, which derived from the continued war against Japan, the situation in Europe and the agreed position of world public opinion.[75]

The military assessment of the situation which the Chiefs-of-Staff had been asked to prepare in June had the greatest influence on the Committee's conclusions. It was based on a document produced by the intelligence sub-committee in which all branches of the armed forces participated, which analyzed the expected reactions to each of the five alternatives by the Jews, the Arabs of Palestine, the Arab states, and the Muslims in India.[76] The Chiefs-of-Staff made it clear that Britain did not have sufficient forces in the Middle East to guarantee its internal security, no matter which of the five alternatives was chosen. At that time the British army had only one division in Palestine for purposes of internal security. Any new policy would require reinforcements. The Chiefs-of-Staff explained that only at the end of 1945 would they be able to transfer to the Middle East the troops required to continue enforcing the White Paper, and only in the spring of 1946 would there be sufficient troops in the area to ensure quiet if partition was to be implemented, or even if only immigration was continued. They stressed that any decision which would arouse the Arabs' ire would not only complicate internal security, but would also hamper the functioning of the Middle Eastern base, particularly in Egypt. Any decision except the one involving the continuation of the White Paper policy could also make it necessary, in their opinion, to reinforce the British army in India.[77]

The time frameworks delineated by the Chiefs-of-Staff in their assessment were not practical in view of the political pressures exerted upon the government, and consequently they reduced them as the discussion in the Cabinet Committee approached.[78] Thus, they recommended that the Minister of Defense support Hull's proposal, but requested that the new policy not be made public before the end of October 1945, to enable them to transfer to the Middle East the minimum reinforcements necessary to maintain internal security in view of the anticipated reactions to this pronouncement from the Jews.[79]

The Cabinet Committee considered the various recommendations, its main concern being their effect on Britain's position in the Middle East. It reached the conclusion that an interim solution was preferable to the continuation of the White Paper policy. Morrison wrote in his report to the Cabinet:

> We have in effect to choose between the possibility of localised trouble with the Jews in Palestine and the virtual certainty of widespread disturbance among the Arabs throughout the Middle East and possibly among the Muslims in India. In terms of force the latter represents a military commitment twice or three times as great as does the former.

In regard to the relations with the United States, the Committee maintained, Britain would be exposed to criticism if there were disturbances of any kind, whether made by the Arabs or the Jews. In the long run the Committee envisaged a possibility of international trusteeship on the basis of the principles of Lord Altrincham's (Edward Grigg) plan.

After making a token statement about the sufferings of the Jews of Europe and the success of the Jewish enterprise in Palestine, the committee recommended:

a.   That the immigration arrangements should be continued in accordance with the White Paper, making an effort to obtain Arab agreement for immigration at the current rate even after the quota was filled;

b.   That before applying to the Arabs, the United States should be apprised of the situation, and of the fact that a long-term policy was being prepared and would be submitted to the United Nations Organization when the time came;

c.   That the Middle East be reinforced with the troops necessary for implementing this policy.[80]

Even before rumors began to circulate about Britain's newly-formulated policy, however, the internal security situation in Palestine began to deteriorate with the renewed activities of the Jewish underground groups, IZL and LHI. The Colonial Secretary hastened to inform the government of this, warning that there was a possibility that the mainstream Jewish underground forces, the Palmach and the Haganah, would join in a general uprising, which would intensify still more with the release of Palestinian soldiers serving in the British army. His principal demand was to hasten the despatch of military reinforcements to Palestine.[81] The Chiefs-of-Staff made it clear that Palestine would absorb the only two reserve divisions available to the British throughout the world. They insisted that no announcement be made concerning Palestine until the necessary reinforcements had reached the Middle East.[82]

In preparation for the discussions in the Cabinet Committee and the government plenum about British policy in Palestine, the British representatives in the Middle East met in London for a series of discussions with senior officials of the Foreign Office and the Colonial Office, and then with the Chiefs-of-Staff. In these deliberations the considerations and orientations prevalent in London were presented to them, and they were asked to give their views about the considerations entering into short-term policy decisions — such as the manner and timing of an approach to the Arabs on the question of continued immigration — as well as on the various long-term political solutions.

Two plans were outlined to the assembled representatives. The first was Bevin's plan for a three-part federation comprising a Jewish area of Palestine, an Arab area of Palestine, and Transjordan. Bevin wished to place Emir Abdullah at the head of the federation. This plan was received with reservations by many present. The High Commissioner, Lord Gort, claimed that this was in effect partition under another name, while the ambassadors to the Arab countries pointed out that those countries would fiercely oppose the strengthening of Abdullah. At the next session of the forum Bevin agreed that his plan was not practical. At the same meeting the plan of Colonial Secretary Hull to grant autonomy to a Jewish and an Arab region in Palestine was discussed. This plan was also received with reservations, particularly by Lord Gort, who claimed again that this was tantamount to partition, which everyone had agreed was the worst possible solution as far as Britain was concerned. Some of the ambassadors claimed that continued adherence to the White Paper had a great advantage in that at least one of the sides had agreed to accept it as a solution. Bevin replied that the influence of America made a solution of this kind unacceptable. In his opinion it would be necessary to delay the decision about the long-term policy as far as possible, on the assumption that the pressure to allow Jewish immigration would weaken with the passage of time.[83]

At a Cabinet discussion on September 11, 1945 Morrison presented the Committee's recommendations, which were accepted unanimously, and emphasized the need to keep them, as well as the very existence of a Cabinet Committee on Palestine, secret. During the discussion it was noted that the importance of the Arabs should not be exaggerated. Recommendation was made to attempt to draw the United States into joint action, since public opinion there criticized Britain passionately, but the administration did not share responsibility or help resolve the complex situation. Other considerations included whether it would not be better to announce straightaway that it was Britain's intention to transfer the Palestine question to the United Nations Organization, whether there was any point in deferring a declaration about future policy, and whether it was not preferable to inform the Jewish Agency in advance of Britain's intentions in Palestine. Hull replied that he was in contact with the Jewish Agency, but it had adopted an uncompromising line and insisted that the White Paper "was dead." At the conclusion of the discussion it was decided to re-examine the military implications of the situation, leaving the determination of when the new policy was to be proclaimed to Prime Minister Attlee and those ministers directly involved.[84]

The next day the Chiefs-of-Staff met the senior officials of the Foreign and Colonial Offices, the High Commissioner and the ambassadors to the Middle East, and explained to them the problems arising from the need to send reinforcements to the Middle East.[85] The ministers recommended determining the timing of the declaration on the basis of military considerations alone, thereby rejecting the Foreign Office's request to delay it until the end of the period of pilgrimage to Mecca.[86] Paget, the Commander-in-Chief in the Middle East, asked that no declaration be made until October 31, when additional forces would have reached the Middle East to reinforce the division already operating in Palestine.[87] The Colonial Office, on the other hand, pressed for as early a pronouncement as possible, requesting that the government meet to determine the timing.[88]

A few days after the Cabinet meeting there was a significant change in the situation. Till then the discussion had been conducted by the British, on the basis of regional considerations in which the attitude of the United States and the question of the Jewish D.P.s in Europe were only of minor importance. In the second week of September, however, the American administration entered the picture dramatically. As a result of Harrison's report, President Truman communicated with Attlee, told him about Harrison, his mission and his conclusions, and drew his attention particularly to the recommendation to grant one hundred thousand immigration certificates to Jews who had survived the Holocaust. The President made it clear that he concurred with Harrison's view, reminded Attlee of his appeal to Churchill at the Potsdam Conference, and concluded:

> The main solution appears to lie in the quick evacuation of as many as possible of the non-repatriable Jews, who wish it, to Palestine. If it is to be effective, such action should not be long delayed.[89]

Truman's letter was handed to Attlee after a delay; the President grew angry and on September 14 informed the British government, through Byrnes, his Secretary of State, that he would issue a public declaration that evening in which he would mention Harrison's report. Now the British were alarmed. Bevin informed Byrnes that a declaration of that nature coming from the President, without waiting for a British reply, would harm the relations between the two countries.[90] Attlee hastened to cable the President the same day, explaining that the letter had reached him only after a delay and that was the reason he had not answered it; Attlee informed him of the Jewish Agency's refusal to accept the existing quota of immigration certificates. Byrnes recommended to the President that he postpone his statement for the moment.[91]

Two days later Attlee sent a detailed reply to the President's letter. In it he opposed the segregation of Jews from non-Jews in the camps, explaining that the British occupation authorities were doing their utmost to ease the conditions of all the displaced persons. More could be done, he wrote, if refugees from Europe were transferred to UNRRA refugee camps in North Africa. With regard to Palestine, Attlee reminded the President that the British had to consider the Arabs as well as the Jews, noting that Truman had committed himself to consulting them before making a decision about the future of Palestine. He firmly rejected Harrison's recommendation concerning the immigration certificates, and noted that the British government was formulating a long-term policy for Palestine which it intended to submit to the United Nations in the near future. Meanwhile, he explained, the British were formulating their immigration policy for the interim period, and this would be brought to the President's attention as soon as possible.[92] Truman agreed with him that the British were up against difficulties in Palestine, but noted that it also made problems for the Americans. After consulting with Byrnes, the President promised not to take any action until the Secretary of State returned to Washington.[93]

When the Palestine question was discussed again in the full Cabinet, on October 4, 1945, Attlee had to note at the beginning of the debate that the background to the political decision regarding Palestine had changed

296

significantly since the previous discussion. At the meeting a cable from Halifax, the British Ambassador in Washington, was read, analyzing the mood of public opinion in the United States, and the resultant possibilities open to the British.[94] It appeared that as soon as Parliament met, pressure would be exerted on the government to publish an announcement about its Palestine policy and hold a debate on the subject, making it difficult to delay the discussion, as the General Staff demanded. In the discussion it was made clear that it would no longer be possible to ignore the link between the question of the Jewish D.P.s in Europe and the Palestinian problem. Some ministers claimed that the absorption of one hundred thousand refugees in Palestine would cause the Middle East to explode, but would not solve the problem in Europe. It was also maintained that the impression that the Jews of Europe were living in unbearable conditions would have to be set right. However, the participants agreed that a policy announcement made by His Majesty's Government could not ignore the situation in Europe. In this connection a proposal was made to send a committee to Europe "...to establish the facts with regard to the present plight of the Jews." The Home Secretary reported on the pressures to allow Jews who did not wish to remain in Germany into Britain, and warned that additional pressure could be expected in the future. In such an atmosphere, several of the participants in the discussion claimed, any declaration of a new policy had to emphasize the fact that the White Paper of 1939 was no longer relevant.

In view of the new considerations raised in the discussion, Bevin asked for time to examine the possibility of a new approach to the problem, and the submission of new proposals to the government. While a long-term solution would be transferred to the United Nations Organization, he would meanwhile work for the immediate formation of a joint Anglo-American Committee which would examine a) what could be done forthwith to improve the situation of the Jews in Europe; b) what rate of immigration to Palestine could be permitted in the near future; c) the possibility of easing the situation in Europe by immigration to other countries, including the United States and the Dominions.[95]

Palestine and the Survivors in the Camps

The British now began arguing with the Americans about Harrison's conclusions and recommendations. In a cable to the President, the day after the discussion in the Cabinet plenum, Attlee claimed that the question of the Jewish refugees in Europe and the Palestine problem were two separate problems, and that each one of them was difficult to solve.[96] By so doing he was hinting at British opposition to the American attempt to link the two together. The acceptance of Harrison's recommendations meant admitting that there was no future for the Jews in Europe, the Foreign Office officials wrote to their counterparts abroad. This was a counsel of despair which should not be accepted in view of the continent's chaotic condition, and appeared to constitute an admission of the validity of the Nazis' claim that the Jews had no place in Europe. In addition, it would have an effect on the desire of other refugees, not necessarily Jews, to return to their homes.[97]

At the same time Bevin and Hull prepared an amended version of the proposals to the Cabinet's Palestine Committee, in accordance with Bevin's explanations at the October 4 meeting. One of the innovations was a paragraph that would be added to the declaration of the new policy, stating that the government would take steps for immigration to continue at its present rate during the period when the Joint Committee was at work, and would also prepare a proposal for a permanent solution which would be submitted to the U.N.O. Together with the publication of this declaration, the United States would be invited to participate in preparing the proposal.[98] The Cabinet Committee also decided to incorporate another paragraph in the declaration, mentioning the possibility of a change in the immigration quota as a result of British initiative or of an interim recommendation of the Anglo-American Committee. Although the advantages of joint action with the United States, particularly regarding the European aspect of the problem, were recognized, apprehensions were expressed concerning Arab reaction to direct American involvement in the Palestinian problem, especially after Truman's appeal for the immigration of one hundred thousand refugees had become public knowledge. The Committee left the decision on this matter to the government.[99]

The next day, October 11, the Palestine question came up once again for discussion in the cabinet. Bevin stressed the need to find a solution to the problem as part of overall British policy in the Middle East, and to soothe the uproar in American public opinion which was poisoning relations between the United States and Britain in other spheres as well. He attacked Harrison's report, and urged that the two countries jointly undertake further investigation of the situation of the Jews in Europe. He stated that it was important for the United States to contribute to resolving the problem through its own absorption of European Jews. Various reservations were expressed about the proposed committee's method of work and jurisdiction, and at the end Bevin was empowered to contact the Americans.[100]

Until a reply was received from Washington, the discussion between Britain and the United States focused on Harrison's report and the extent to which it was correct. An open debate was held on the subject in the American press, and Halifax provided current reports on it to London.[101] The Americans rejected the British claim that the Jewish policy in their areas of occupation was contrary to the joint principles drawn up at the UNRRA Conference held in London in August 1945.[102] Public figures reiterated Truman's appeal to Attlee, adding arguments of their own.[103] Although the Zionist leaders in America attempted to put pressure on the President to avoid postponing a solution to the problem by means of another committee,[104] Truman had already decided to accept the British invitation, despite the differences of opinion on the question of immigration. Now it was the Americans who asked the British to delay the pronouncement of the new policy and the establishment of the joint committee, at least until after the elections in New York, which were due to be held on November 6. Despite the ire of the British, Truman refused to change his mind, and was angered by Attlee's intention to mention the American commitment to the Arabs, which the President had denied, in his announcement of the new policy. Nevertheless, Halifax reported that after the elections in New York it would be possible to reach an agreement with the Americans.[105] The arguments continued even after the elections, however.[106] In the middle of November Bevin informed the British Cabinet of the American response and the continued differences of opinion stemming from Truman's statement that he continued to support the immediate immigration of one hundred thousand refugees. That same day Bevin made an announcement in Parliament regarding British policy in Palestine, and the establishment of the Anglo-American Committee.[107]

Zionist Policy in Preparation for the Struggle Against the British Policy

The Zionist leadership and the *yishuv* in Palestine were prepared for a change in British policy. The ascent of the Labour government in the wake of the British elections of July 1945 had aroused great expectations, in view of that party's traditionally pro-Zionist stand, and especially because of the resolutions passed at its conference held at the end of 1944. Against the background of these expectations, the World Zionist Conference met in London at the beginning of August 1945. On his way to the conference by ship from the United States, Ben-Gurion drew up the balance-sheet of the Jewish people after the war, recording the demographic changes in the Jewish world. He noted the dangers threatening Jewish existence under Communist regimes in Eastern Europe on the one hand, and the inequality between sovereign Arab states and the Jewish community in Palestine under the Mandate on the other.

He came to the following conclusions: The Zionist movement, based on the *yishuv* and supported by American Jewry, must work for the immediate migration of all the Jews in Muslim countries, most of the Jews in Western Europe, as many Jews as possible from Eastern Europe, and pioneers from the Anglo-Saxon and Latin American countries. In order to do so, the Jews should insist on the immediate establishment of a Jewish government in Palestine. In Ben-Gurion's opinion, a Jewish state was the only alternative to an unavoidable process of gradual extinction of the Jewish people that would reduce Judaism solely to a religion.[108]

The conference in London disappointed its participants. No new inspiration for the Jewish people or the Zionist movement came out of it, and it dealt primarily with arguments and disagreements, focusing mainly on the renewed dispute between Ben-Gurion and Weizmann. The only new elements at this conference which had some bearing on the Holocaust and the ensuing vicissitudes of the Jewish people were the representatives from the Jewish Brigade and a delegation of Zionist youth from the survivors in Poland. In effect, it was difficult to issue a clear political demand from this conference, because of internal differences and, primarily, because of the change of government in Britain and the fact that everyone was waiting for a new and favorable Palestine policy which, it was hoped, would be adopted by the Labour government.[109]

While the anticipation of the British opening move extended into the ensuing weeks, Truman raised the demand for one hundred thousand certificates — not as a result of Zionist pressure, but in the wake of Harrison's report.[110] At the same time details of what was happening in the British government's debates, the attitudes of the various departments and the army, began to leak out in London.[111]

However, the information which had been leaked to the Zionist leaders in London was not accurate, and may even have been intended to mislead them deliberately. On the one hand, Weizmann, Ben-Gurion and Shertok feared a secret British conspiracy; on the other, semi-official delegates had approached them and brought them encouraging news. Ben-Gurion was not convinced by them, but for Weizmann these were a straw to catch hold of. From one of Bevin's messengers he heard hints of plans for a trusteeship government, which were then being discussed in the Cabinet's Palestine Committee, and without being apprised of the details he was told that they would not disappoint the Zionists. Rumors about the expected continuation of the White Paper, immigration at the rate of 1,500 persons per month, and the submission of the entire Palestine question to the United Nations Organization appeared in the press.[112] The members of the Zionist Office in London received confirmation of this from members of the British government and Labour Party leaders.

Weizmann still wanted to try and maneuver between the British and the Americans, and to meet Bevin. However Ben-Gurion wished to sever all contact with the British government until it took the initiative and summoned the Jewish Agency for discussions. He also wished to explain the reasons for this severing of relations in a pronouncement to the Jewish people, which would be accompanied by Weizmann's resignation from the Jewish Agency. At the same time, the *yishuv* and the Jews of America would have to strengthen the Haganah, intensify illegal immigration activities, and mount an extensive campaign to gain the support of public opinion in America, Britain and the Dominions. Weizmann feared Ben-Gurion's more extreme proposals, and as a result of his pressure it was decided to wait until an appeal was made to Prime Minister Attlee.[113]

In Palestine, however, patience was running out. The IZL and LHI had long since increased their activities against the British, and every rumor or item of news from London caused an uproar. Towards the end of September, when the existence of the British Cabinet's Palestine Committee became known, various rumors spread about its negative line, and Ben-Gurion announced that they were not far off the truth. The Zionist Executive debated what should be done and how to react. Should a "calming" line be adopted and information from unchecked and unofficial sources be ignored, or should they wait for official information and meanwhile "enable rumor-mongers to take control of the public." Moshe Sneh's proposal to organize large demonstrations was rejected for the moment, and it was decided instead to hold a closed meeting of the members of the Zionist Executive and the editors of the Jewish press in Palestine, whose object would be solely informative. The differences of opinion between Weizmann and Ben-Gurion in London, echoes of which had reached Palestine, did not make it any easier to reach decisions.[114] The realization that the Labour Party's accession to power would not, after all, fulfill Zionist expectations was difficult to accept.[115] Now everyone was waiting for the opening of the British Parliament, on the assumption that this would be marked by a government pronouncement concerning its policy in Palestine.[116]

Weizmann attempted a last-minute appeal to the Prime Minister, warning him of the expected confrontation between the Jews and Britain. He deprecated the fact that the government had not seen fit to make the Jewish Agency a party to its discussions about the future of Palestine. Attlee replied that the government was aware of the Jewish Agency's views: "If we thought that further consultation were required at this stage or that it would serve any useful purposes, we should certainly arrange it; but at the present juncture that is not so."[117]

Meanwhile, in London, Ben-Gurion had formulated his assessment of the situation. In his view there was nothing left to do in Britain and no further value in the discussions being held in London. Consequently, the London Office should be closed and the movement be conducted from Palestine, where the future depended on the *yishuv*. However, considerable aid would now be required from America to support the *yishuv*.

In effect, Ben-Gurion had already decided that the time had come to embark upon an all-out struggle against the White Paper, which would continue even though this might not be officially announced. In preparation for the struggle he asked Goldmann to make sure that American journalists come to Palestine to 'cover' it, and that the American Zionists concentrate on organizing help for the *yishuv*. He intended returning to Palestine in order to examine his battle-plan before revealing it publicly, but decided first to visit the survivors' camps in Germany in order to see their situation for himself, to make them part of the struggle and explain to them why the Jewish Agency had decided to reject the quota of immigration certificates it had been allotted. This decision was personal and not institutional, and Ben-Gurion asked Goldmann to transfer the special fund for financing the initial steps in the struggle, amounting to a quarter of a million dollars, to an account in his name in an American bank — an unusual and unprecedented request.[118]

A few days later Ben-Gurion changed his mind and decided to give instructions for the immediate opening of the struggle in Palestine, even before his return. Once again this was his own personal decision, reached without consulting his colleagues in London with whom he had spent the last few

301

months. Ben-Gurion informed Palestine that he would not return until he had completed crucial preparations in Europe for an "armed immigration" able to protect itself both at sea and on shore. He also advised that activities in Europe, purchasing arms, training, funding wireless communications, the mobilization and transfer of immigrants, required the establishment of a central headquarters in France.

There was no reason to delay the Zionist reponse as long as the White Paper continued in effect, and the response in Palestine should not be restricted to immigration and settlement. Ben-Gurion urged undertaking 'x' (a code letter for 'special action') and 'reprisal'; not individual terrorism, but retaliation for every Jew killed by the White Paper authorities. The entire 'x' enterprise must be weighty and impressive. "We must avoid the loss of life as far as possible." Toward that end he held that the two rival factions (IZL and LHI) must be invited to cooperate fully, providing there was one unified command and absolute discipline. A continual effort was required to ensure unity within the *yishuv*, and primarily among the fighting men.

Ben-Gurion urged that the Zionist response be audacious and calculated, and recognized that it would have to extend over a considerable period. He did not anticipate a quick and easy victory.

Finally, he stressed that world public opinion was "almost as important as the [Zionist] response itself," and urged setting up wireless transmitting stations in Palestine, Europe and, if possible, in America.[119]

Two days later Ben-Gurion left for a short visit to France, where he met officers from the Jewish Brigade and emissaries from Palestine, and also gave various instructions regarding organization for the struggle and large scale illegal immigration. On his return to London he found replies and expressions of support from Palestine.[120]

While Ben-Gurion was dealing on his own with preparations for the struggle against the British, Weizmann and the other members of the Executive were waiting in London for the desired meeting with the Foreign Minister, which had been postponed several times. The meeting was finally held on October 8, and Weizmann returned from it with the impression that "Bevin wants to do something, but he does not know in which direction to go." From Bevin's words he concluded that the government did not intend to make a new policy pronouncement. Jewish Agency officials in London continued to wonder who was worth meeting. Shertok proposed writing to the British government that the Jewish Agency regarded the lack of policy as negative and as a continuation of the White Paper, and could no longer restrain the *yishuv* and prevent turmoil in Palestine. Ben-Gurion repeated his demand to sever all contact with the British government, to begin a propaganda campaign against it, and to express violent opposition in Palestine. Weizmann maintained that Ben-Gurion's proposals were a last resort, while the latter replied that the time had now come to implement them. The discussion ended inconclusively, but with the clear feeling that there were differences of opinion between Ben-Gurion and the other participants: Weizmann, Shertok, Remez, Shmorak, Locker, Namier and Mrs. Dugdale.[121] Ben-Gurion hastened to inform the Jewish Agency Executive in Palestine of his views, listing his arguments against what was being done in London.[122] Weizmann's readiness to accept another invitation to a meeting with Bevin led Ben-Gurion to write to the President of the World Zionist Organization, threatening to resign from the Executive and demanding to convene the Executive and the Action Committee in Jerusalem for reformulation of policy and election of a new Executive.[123]

Echoes of the disagreements in London quickly reached Palestine where the Haganah's initial activities against the British had begun, outstanding among them being the assault on the illegal immigrants' detention camp at Atlith. Tension increased even more as a result of the clash with the frontier force at Kfar-Giladi, and of various searches and curfews conducted by the British as part of their activities against the IZL and LHI. The Jewish institutions in Palestine prepared themselves to expand the struggle, making it a public campaign in which the entire *yishuv* would participate through strikes and demonstrations, alongside the operations undertaken by the joint opposition movement in which the Haganah, IZL and LHI participated. The expected pronouncement in Parliament about the British policy in Palestine was to be the sign to begin action.

Meanwhile, however, differences of opinion had been revealed regarding the struggle itself and who had the authority to conduct it. Once again Ben-Gurion was called back home, but at this stage he preferred to prepare the European side of the struggle, and concentrate on the survivors, "because these Jews currently fulfill a crucial role in the Zionist fate." [124] Instead of returning to Palestine, he went to France to examine the preparations being made there, and continued on to his first tour of the D.P. camps in Germany. From his meetings with the activists in the camps and with the members of the Brigade, he reached the conclusion that the goal should be to gather all the survivors together within a geographic enclave, where it would be easier to influence and direct them. In discussions with the American commanders — Eisenhower and Bedell-Smith — he asked for help in absorbing the torrent of Jews escaping from Eastern Europe, recognition of them as refugees with all that this implied as regards housing and feeding them, and enabling emissaries from Palestine to work among them. The idea of concentrating the Jews in one area was not implemented, but Ben-Gurion helped to alter the attitude of the American occupation authorities to the refugees in the camps, and to those who crossed borders to join them. He also made it possible for orderly and systematic contact to be established during the next few months between the emissaries from Palestine and the refugees.

Ben-Gurion was almost the only member of the Zionist leadership to grasp the essential role of the surviving remnant in the struggle for a Jewish state in Palestine. He contended that only the pressure of the survivors, and the consequent reactions of public opinion and its influence on the American administration, could bring about that goal. One cannot exaggerate the importance of the survivors in his conception of the Zionist campaign; as early as the summer of 1944 he told a group of soldiers of the Jewish Brigade about to leave for Europe:

> ...There is a second mission [the first was the military one] assigned to you by the providence of Jewish history. Hitler not only annihilated one-third of the Jewish people, but also gave the most fatal blow to its hope in his country... The enemies of Zionism now have a new argument. The problem of Jewish refugees and Jewish immigration has lost its acuteness and urgency — only few Jews have remained in Europe, and these would get along in their countries... and this is the crucial question: Where are they heading?... More than anything else, the fate of our campaign [for a Jewish state] depends on the will and stand of the Jews in Europe.[125]

The developments on the European continent, in Great Britain, and in the United States in the summer of 1945 seemed to strengthen Ben-Gurion's conviction. In the following autumn and winter he felt that the most important sector of the Zionist front was not the anti-British armed operations in Palestine, but the D.P. camps and the clandestine migration routes in Europe. It was this sector that demanded his personal presence, influence and leadership.

Translated by Dorothea Shefer-Vanson.

1   M. Proudfoot, *European Refugees* (London, 1957), pp. 318-323.
2   Appendix No. 1 to Murphy's letter to the Secretary of State of 22.6.1945, NA800.4016 DP/6-2245.
3   The data are taken from Proudfoot (above, n. 1), pp. 158-161.
4   Appendix No. 2 to Murphy's letter (above, n. 2).
5   See, for example, the order regarding evacuation arrangements for displaced persons issued by the headquarters of the 30th British Corps in Germany, 3.6.1945, P.R.O., W.O. 171/4086.
6   Proudfoot (above, n. 1), pp. 207-220.
7   Report to the Cabinet Committee on Refugee Affairs, end of July 1945, P.R.O., CAB 88/71.
8   See, for example, the minutes of the S.H.A.E.F. Repatriation Committee held on 16.6.1945, P.R.O., W.O. 204/3464, and the order regarding the repatriation of displaced persons from Yugoslavia 4.8.1945, P.R.O., W.O. 171/4086.
9   See Y. Bauer, *Flight and Rescue* (New York, 1970), p. 19.
10   Minutes of the meeting of the Jewish Agency Executive, 20.6.1944, CZA.
11   The Jewish Agency's Memorandum, submitted by Weizmann to Colonial Secretary Sir Oliver Stanley, 16.10.1944, CZA S-25/7677.
12   Weizmann's report to the Jewish Agency Political Committee in London about his meetings with Churchill and Morrison, 6.11.1944, CZA Z4/10389I. In contrast to what Weizmann reported about his meeting with Morrison, see Morrison's letter to Churchill, 3.11.1944, PREM 4/52/3. See also Weizmann's report on the meetings to the Jewish Agency Executive in Jerusalem, 19.11.1944.
13   Grigg to Churchill, 27.1.1945, PREM *ibid.*
14   Grigg to Foreign Secretary Eden, 29.1.1945, *ibid.*
15   Shertok's summary of Grigg's meeting with him and Ben-Gurion, Minutes of the Jewish Agency Executive, 14.1.1945, pp. 1-4.
16   See Weizmann to Grigg, 25.1.1945, and Grigg's letter (above, n. 14).

17 Rabbi Fishman, at the meeting of the Jewish Agency Executive, 22.1.1945, p. 2, and also Ben-Gurion's proposals, pp. 4-5.
18 Minutes of the meeting of Mapai's Secretariat as a political committee, 15.1.1945, LPA 26/45.
19 Minutes of the Jewish Agency Executive, 11.2.1945 (speeches made by Weizmann and Ben-Gurion).
20 Minutes of the Jewish Agency Executive, 18.2.1945.
21 Shertok's report to the Jewish Agency Executive, 15.3.1945; minutes of the political committee of Mapai, 12.2.1945 (speeches by Ben-Gurion, Shertok and Meirov), LPA 26/45; minutes of the Secretariat of Mapai, 12.3.1945 LPA 24/45.
22 Report by Ruzka Korczak, 11.12.1944, CZA S25/3879. See also the detailed report by I. Trachtenberg to the Mapai Central Committee, 17.1.1945, LPA, 25/45. For additional information which reached Palestine at the beginning of 1945 about the situation of the Jews in Poland, Rumania and Hungary, see letters and reports in HA 14/160.
23 Rabbi Levi to Moshe Yuval, 12.12.1944, CZA, S25/4899. For the problem of the Jewish children in Holland in general see, J.S. Fishman, "Jewish War Orphans in the Netherlands — The Guardianship Issue 1945-1950," *The Wiener Library Bulletin* 27 (1973-74):1-6.
24 Eliahu Dobkin (head of the Jewish Agency Immigration Department) at the meeting of the Political Committee of Mapai, 15.1.1945, LPA 26/45, pp. 8-9.
25 Ben-Gurion at the meeting of the Political Committee of Mapai, 12.2.1945, *ibid.* pp. 6-7.
26 Minutes of the meeting of the Mapai Secretariat, 12.3.1945, LPA 24/45, pp. 8-10.
27 Minutes of the meeting of the Mapai Central Committee, 15.3.1945, LPA 23/45.
28 E. Avriel's report to the Mapai Bureau, 21.3.1945, LPA 25/45.
29 Minutes of the Mapai Central Committee, 29.4.1945, LPA 26/45.
30 Minutes of the Zionist Political Committee in London, 1.5.1945, CZA Z4/10379I.
31 The Jewish Agency's Memorandum to the British government, 22.5.1945, CZA S25/7677.
32 The Diaries of Ben-Gurion, 10-15.5.1945, Ben-Gurion Archives (BGA) 1385.
33 Radio broadcast from Prague by David Grahamm, 16.5.1945, and report by the J.T.A. correspondent, S. Goldschmidt, on the situation of the Jewish survivors in Dachau, 17.5.1945, Archives of the World Jewish Congress, London.
34 Dr. Greenberg to the representatives of the World Jewish Congress in Geneva, 31.5.1945, JDC Archives.
35 Ruth (Klüger) and David (Shealtiel) to the Political and Immigration Departments of the Jewish Agency, 11.6.1945, CZA S25/5241.
36 The correspondence concerning this is found in P.R.O., F.O. 371/51120.
37 Minutes of the Political Committee in London, 5.6.1945, CZA Z4/10379 I.
38 Shertok to the High Commissioner, 18.6.1945, CZA S25/7679.
39 Minutes of the Political Committee in London, 8-14.6.1945, CZA Z4/10379 I. Churchill's letter of 9.6.1945, in BGA 1385.
40 Weizmann to Martin, written on 16.5.1945 and delivered on 14.6.1945, PREM 4/52/3.
41 See, for example, "Plight of Jews in Germany," *Times*, 21.7.1945.
42 Wynant to the Secretary of State, 25.7.1945, *Foreign Relations of the United States* 1945 (hereafter, FRUS), 2, pp. 1178-1179.
43 Dobkin to Rattigan (Deputy Director of UNRRA in Germany), 28.8.1945, CZA S53/1596.
44 Grew to Truman, 21.6.1945; appended to it is a draft of Harrison's letter of appointment for Truman's signature, NA 800.4016, DP/6-2145. Meir Weisgal was behind Morgenthau's initiative. See his letter to Morgenthau of 14.6.1945, and also notes made by G. Agronsky about a discussion with Frankfurter and Morgenthau on 19.6.1945, CZA Z5/991.
45 Byrnes to Wynant, 5.7.1945, NA *ibid.*, DP/7-645. The idea of giving Harrison an aide who was conversant with Jewish matters also came from Weisgal; see his above letter to Morgenthau.
46 Weisgal to Harrison, 25.6.1945, and his cable of the same day to Weizmann, CZA Z5/991. For previous connections with Harrison see Weisgal's cable to Linton, 6.4.1945, *ibid.*
47 Weizmann to Weisgal, 28.6.1945, *ibid.*
48 Murphy to the Secretary of State, 10.7.1945, NA 800.4016, DP/7-1045.
49 Harrison to Morgenthau, 28.7.1945, and Morgenthau to Grew, 1.8.1945, *ibid.*, DP/8-145.
50 Stimson to Eisenhower, 3.8.1945, copy in the JDC Archives.
51 Stephen Wise to Eisenhower, 7.8.1945, *ibid.*

52 Eisenhower to the U.S. Embassy in London, *ibid.*

53 Exchange of cables between Eisenhower and Stimson, 10.8.1945, *ibid.*

54 Wynant to the Secretary of State, 10.8.1945, NA 800.4016, DP/8-1045.

55 General Dewing (Chief-of-Staff of the British Control Commission in Germany) to the Under-Secretary of State for War, 18.8.1945, P.R.O., F.O.371/51122, WR-2093.

56 Copies of Harrison's report and Truman's letter to Eisenhower of 31.8.1945, P.R.O., F.O.371/51125. Truman's letter was released for publication on 29.9.1945.

57 Colonel Newman's instructions, in Eisenhower's name, 22.8.1945, copy in F.O. 371/51123; and also Eisenhower's order to the American commanders in Germany, 20.9.1945, FRUS 1945, 2, pp. 1201-1202.

58 Eisenhower to Truman, 5.11.1945, NA 800.4016, DP/11-545.

59 Memorandum of the Joint Planning Staff about "Defense Requirements in the Levant," 12.1.1945, P.R.O., CAB 119/147, J.P.(44)285.

60 Memorandum of the Chiefs-of-Staff about "Internal Security in the Middle East," 23.1.1945, P.R.O., PREM 3/296/9, C.O.S.(45)63(0).

61 Churchill to Ismay, 28.1.1945, *ibid.*

62 Morrison to Churchill, 26.2.1945, P.R.O., CAB 127/270.

63 E. Grigg to Eden and Stanley, 11.3.1945, P.R.O., CAB 119/147.

64 E. Bridges (the Secretary of the Cabinet) to Churchill, 11.4.1945, P.R.O., CAB 127/270.

65 Two memoranda by Grigg about "The Security of the Empire in the Middle East". The memoranda were prepared in June 1945 and, after being approved by Churchill, were distributed on 2.7.1945, as C.P.(45)55, 56; copies in P.R.O. PREM 3/296/10.

66 Churchill to Leopold Amery (Minister for India), 29.4.1945, P.R.O., CAB 127/270.

67 Churchill to the Secretary of State for the Colonies and the Chiefs-of-Staff Committee, 6.7.1945, *ibid.*

68 Ismay to Churchill, 12.7.1945, P.R.O., CAB 120/659.

69 Truman to Churchill, 24.7.1945, P.R.O., PREM 8/627.

70 Memorandum submitted by the Colonial Office to the Prime Minister, 27.7.1945, and Bevin to Attlee, 30.7.1945, *ibid.*

71 Foreign Office memorandum to the Cabinet, 11.6.1945, P.R.O., F.O. 371/45087, E-3975.

72 Memorandum submitted by the Colonial Secretary to the Palestine Committee, 1.9.1945, P.R.O., CAB 95/14.

73 "A New Policy for Palestine," memorandum submitted by the Colonial Secretary to the Palestine Committee, 1.9.1945, *ibid.*

74 Foreign Office memorandum to the Palestine Committee, 1.9.1945, *ibid.*

75 High Commissioner to the Colonial Secretary, 23.6.1945, *ibid.*

76 Memorandum (final amended version) of the Intelligence Sub-Committee on "A Middle-Eastern Policy", 31.7.1945, P.R.O., CAB 119/148.

77 Memorandum of the Chiefs-of-Staff about "A Middle-Eastern Policy", 30.8.1945, C.O.S.(45)555(0), *ibid.*

78 Summary of the meeting of the Chiefs-of-Staff Committee, 4.9.1945, *ibid.*

79 Brief prepared by the Army Council Secretariat for the Secretary of State for War, 6.9.1945, P.R.O., W.O.32/10260.

80 Report of the Palestine Committee to the Cabinet, 8.9.1945, P.R.O., CAB 129/2, C.P.(45)156.

81 "Security Conditions in Palestine," memorandum by Hull, 10.9.1945, *ibid.*, C.P.(45)165.

82 Brief submitted by the Army Council Secretariat to the Secretary of State for War, 11.9.1945, P.R.O., W.O. 32/10260.

83 Minutes of the discussions of senior officials and representatives in the Middle East, led by Bevin, 6-10.9.1945, copies in P.R.O., F.O. 226/277.

84 Secret appendix to the minutes of the Cabinet meeting, 11.9.1945, P.R.O., CAB 128/3.

85 Minutes of a discussion on defense arrangements in the Middle East, 12.9.1945, P.R.O., CAB 119/148.

86 Memorandum submitted by the Colonial Secretary to the Cabinet, 28.9.1945, C.P.(45)196, P.R.O., CAB 129/2. For the attitude of the Chiefs-of-Staff, see their memorandum and the accompanying letter from Brigadier Hollis to the Prime Minister, 21.9.1945, P.R.O. PREM 8/627.

87 Memorandum submitted by the Chiefs-of-Staff to the Cabinet, 1.10.1945, C.P.(45)200, P.R.O., CAB 129/2.

88 Hull to Attlee, 19.9.1945, P.R.O., PREM 8/627.

89 Truman to Attlee, 31.8.1945, P.R.O., PREM 8/89.

90 Henderson to Rowan, 14.9.1945, *ibid.*

91 Attlee to Truman, 14.9.1945, P.R.O., CAB 120/660.

92 Attlee to Truman, 16.9.1945, *ibid.*

93 Truman to Attlee, 17.9.1945, *ibid.* The short-circuit in communications between London and Washington continued, nevertheless, and at the end of the month declarations were made in the American capital to the effect that Attlee had not yet replied to the President's appeal. These pronouncements led Attlee to send a telegram of protest to Truman, mentioning his reply of September 16 and adding that the question of immigration was still being discussed, and no solution had been found (Attlee to Truman, 1.10.1945, *ibid.*).

94 Halifax's cable of 3.10.1945, P.R.O. PREM 8/627.

95 Minutes of the cabinet meeting, 4.10.1945, P.R.O., CAB 128/1. Field Marshal Smuts put the idea of a joint Anglo-American action to Churchill as early as April 1945, and hence his name was mentioned as a candidate to chair the committee.

96 Attlee to Truman, 5.10.1945, P.R.O. CAB 120/660.

97 Foreign Office to the Embassy in Washington, 5.10.1945, P.R.O., F.O. 371/51124, WR-2947. Memorandum of the British Embassy to the State Department and the letter sent by the Minister (Meakins) to the head of the European Affairs Desk (Mathews), 6.10.1945, *FRUS 1945*, 2, pp. 1192-1196.

98 Memorandum of Bevin and Hull to the Palestine Committee, 9.10.1945, P.R.O., CAB 95/14.

99 Report by the chairman of the Committee, Morrison, to the Cabinet, 10.10.1945, P.R.O., CAB 129/3, C.P.(45)216.

100 Minutes of the cabinet meeting, 11.10.1945, P.R.O., CAB 128/1. Halifax submitted the invitation to the State Department on October 19, see *FRUS* 1945, 2, pp. 771-774.

101 The British Embassy in Washington to the Foreign Office, 19.10.1945, P.R.O., F.O. 371/51125, WR-3132; Halifax to the Foreign Office, 3.11.1945, P.R.O., F.O. 371/51126, WR-3266.

102 Byrnes to Wynant, 26.10.1945, and memorandum of the State Department to the British Embassy, 27.10.1945, *FRUS 1945*, 2, pp. 1198-1200, and also Halifax's cable to the Foreign Office, 4.11.1945, P.R.O., F.O. 371/51126, WR-3268.

103 See, for example, Morgenthau's speech at the B'nai Brith convention on 7.11.1945, attached to his letter to Dean Acheson, NA 800.4016, DP/11-845.

104 Wise and Silver to President Truman, 30.10.1945, CZA S25/5214.

105 Halifax to the Foreign Office, 27, 29.10.1945, P.R.O., PREM 8/627.

106 Halifax to the Foreign Office, 7.11.1945, *ibid.*

107 Minutes of the cabinet meeting of 13.11.1945, P.R.O. CAB 128/2; the text of Bevin's announcement in Parliament that same day, CZA S25/7679.

108 Ben-Gurion's Diary, 30.7.1945, BGA 1385.

109 See CZA, S25-1905-6 and S25/1912. For the behind-the-scenes activity, see also Zaslani's letter to Kollek, 11.8.1945, CZA S25/816, and Joseph's report to the Mapai Secretariat, 28.8.1945, LPA 24/45.

110 Goldmann to Shertok, 13.9.1945, CZA Z5/387. A. Ilan, *America, Britain and Palestine*, [Hebrew] [Jerusalem, 1979], p. 191, attributes Harrison's recommendation to Zionist influence, but provides no evidence of this. Elsewhere in his book (p. 193), he himself states that "at that stage Truman was only interested in solving the problem of the Jewish displaced persons, and not in Zionism."

111 Ben-Gurion's Diary, 13.9.1945, BGA 1385.

112 See Shmorak's review of the situation in London, Minutes of the Jewish Agency Executive in Jerusalem, 21.10.1945, pp. 1-3, CZA.

113 Minutes of the Jewish Agency Executive in London, 20, 25.9.1945, CZA S25/1720.

114 Minutes of the Jewish Agency Executive in Jerusalem, 23.9.1945, pp. 1-4, and also the discussion of the situation in London at Mapai's Political Committee, 25.9.1945, LPA 24/45, pp. 1-24.

115 Kaplan's report to the Central Committee of Mapai, 27.9.1945, LPA 23/45, pp. 5-11.

116 Minutes of the Jewish Agency Executive in Jerusalem, 30.9.1945, pp. 2-6.
117 Weizmann to Attlee, 21.9.1945, and the draft of Attlee's reply, PREM 8/88.
118 Ben-Gurion to Goldmann, 27.9.1945, BGA 95.
119 Letter from 'Avi-Amos' [Ben-Gurion] in London, 1.10.1945, BGA, 600.
120 Ben-Gurion's Diary, 3-4.10.1945, and 6-7.10.1945, BGA, 1385.
121 Minutes of the Jewish Agency Executive in London, 8.10.1945, CZA S25/1720.
122 Ben-Gurion to the Jerusalem Executive, 8.10.1945, BGA 95.
123 Ben-Gurion's Diary, 10.10.1945, BGA, 1385. The letter was sent to Weizmann on 12.10.1945.
     On further criticism of Weizmann's negotiations, see Joseph's report at the meeting of Mapai's
     Secretariat, 11.10.1945, LPA 24/25; minutes of the Jewish Agency Executive, 14.10.1945.
124 Ben-Gurion's Diary, 29.10.1945, BGA 1385.
125 Ben-Gurion's speech to the soldiers of the Jewish Brigade Group, Haifa, September 25, 1944,
     Israel Defense Forces Archives.

ABBREVIATIONS

AB	Analecta Bollandiana
BHG	Bibliotheca hagiographica graeca
BIJS	Bulletin of the Institute of Jewish Studies, London
BZ	Byzantische Zeitschrift
CAB	British Cabinet Papers
CAHJP	Central Archives for the History of the Jewish People, Jerusalem
CHJ	Cambridge Historical Journal
DBFP	Documents on British Foreign Policy 1919-1939, 1st series
DHL	Das Heilige Land — Organ des Vereines vom h. Grabe
EB	Encyclopaedia Britannica
EHR	English Historical Review
EI	Encyclopaedia of Islam
F.O.	Foreign Office (papers), London
FRUS	Foreign Relations of the United States
HUCA	Hebrew Union College Annual
JESHO	Journal of the Economic and Social History of the Orient
JJLG	Jahrbüch der jüdisch-literarischen Gesellschaft
JJS	Journal of Jewish Studies
JMH	Journal of Modern History
JNUL	Jewish National and University Library, Jerusalem
JPOS	Journal of the Palestine Oriental Society
JQR	Jewish Quarterly Review
JSS	Jewish Social Studies
J.T.A.	Jewish Telegraphic Agency
KS	Kiryat Sefer
MEJ	Middle East Journal
MES	Middle Eastern Studies
MGH	Monumenta Germaniae Historica
MGWJ	Monatsschrift für Geschichte u. Wissenschaft des Judentums
NA	National Archives, Washington, D.C.
PAAJR	Proceedings of the American Academy for Jewish Research
PEQ	Palestine Exploration Quarterly
PL	Patrologiae Latinae
PREM	Prime Minister Private Office (papers), London
PRO	Public Record Office, London
QDAP	Quarterly of the Department of Antiquities in Palestine
REJ	Revue des Etudes Juives
TUGAL	Texte und Untersuchungen zur Geschichte der altchristlichen Literatur
TZ	Theologische Zeitschrift
WO	War Office (papers), London
WP	Weizmann Papers, Rehovot
Yediot	Yediot haḤevra leḤaqirat Ereẓ-Yisrael veAtiqoteha
ZDPV	Zeitschrift des Deutschen Palästinavereins

309

PICTURE CREDITS

D. Bahat, *Jerusalem: Selected Plans of Historical Sites and Monumental Buildings* (Jerusalem, 1980)   6, 9 bottom

Y. Barnai, *The Jews in Eretz-Israel in the Eighteenth Century* (Jerusalem, 1982) 173

M. Berger, *Magbit haHitgaysut v'haHazala* (Jerusalem, 1970)   223, 259

Cathedra   24, 25, 27, 32, 35, 143, 145, 147, 150, 157

Central Zionist Archives, Jerusalem   199, 223 top, 239, 248, 280, 284, 289, 292

J.R. Hacker   115, 126

M. Ish-Shalom, *Christian Travels in the Holy Land* (Tel Aviv, 1965)   113, 128

Israel Museum   49, 50, 54, 61, 117, 152, 183

Jerusalem City Museum   47, 48, 69

Jerusalem Municipal Archives   51, 62, 68

Qadmoniot   7, 9 top, 10

Yad Izhak Ben-Zvi Archives   194, 221, 225, 266

CONTRIBUTORS

ISRAEL BARTAL, Department of Jewish History, The Hebrew University of Jerusalem.

ALEX CARMEL, Department of Land of Israel Studies, and Middle Eastern History, University of Haifa.

RICHARD I. COHEN, Department of Jewish History, The Hebrew University of Jerusalem.

MENACHEM FRIEDMAN, Department of Sociology, Bar-Ilan University.

EVYATAR FRIESEL, Department of Jewish History, The Hebrew University of Jerusalem.

YOAV GELBER, Department of Land of Israel Studies, University of Haifa; Coordinator of Research, Yad Vashem, Jerusalem.

ABRAHAM GROSSMAN, Department of Jewish History, The Hebrew University of Jerusalem.

JOSEPH R. HACKER, Department of Jewish History, The Hebrew University of Jerusalem.

MOSHE IDEL, Department of Jewish Thought, The Hebrew University of Jerusalem.

JACOB KATZ, Professor Emeritus of Sociology and Jewish History, The Hebrew University of Jerusalem.

AMNON LINDER, Department of History, The Hebrew University of Jerusalem.

ARIE MORGENSTERN, Ph.D., The Hebrew University of Jerusalem.

DALIA OFER, Institute for Contemporary Jewry, and the School of Education, The Hebrew University of Jerusalem.

DINA PORAT, Department of Jewish History, and the Schapelski Chair of Holocaust Studies, The Rosenberg School of Jewish Studies, Tel-Aviv University.

RACHEL SIMON, Research Associate, The Shiloah Center for Middle Eastern and African Studies, Tel-Aviv University.

ISAIAH TISHBY, Professor Emeritus of Jewish Thought, The Hebrew University of Jerusalem.